Y0-BUN-985

CENTRAL AMERICA: FRAGILE TRANSITION

INSTITUTE OF LATIN AMERICAN STUDIES SERIES

General Editor: Victor Bulmer-Thomas, Professor of Economics and Director, Institute of Latin American Studies, University of London

The Institute of Latin American Studies, a member of the School of Advanced Study of the University of London, was founded in 1965. The Institute is dedicated to research on Latin America in the social sciences and humanities. The purpose of this series is to disseminate to a wide audience the new work based on the research programmes and projects organised by academic staff and Associate Fellows of the Institute of Latin American Studies.

Victor Bulmer-Thomas (*editor*)
THE NEW ECONOMIC MODEL IN LATIN AMERICA AND ITS
IMPACT ON INCOME DISTRIBUTION AND POVERTY

Victor Bulmer-Thomas, Nikki Craske and Mónica Serrano (*editors*)
MEXICO AND THE NORTH AMERICAN FREE TRADE
AGREEMENT: WHO WILL BENEFIT?

Walter Little and Eduardo Posada-Carbó (*editors*)
POLITICAL CORRUPTION IN EUROPE AND LATIN AMERICA

Eduardo Posada-Carbó (*editor*)
ELECTIONS BEFORE DEMOCRACY: THE HISTORY OF
ELECTIONS IN EUROPE AND LATIN AMERICA

Rachel Sieder (*editor*)
CENTRAL AMERICA: FRAGILE TRANSITION

John Weeks (*editor*)
STRUCTURAL ADJUSTMENT AND THE AGRICULTURAL
SECTOR IN LATIN AMERICA AND THE CARIBBEAN

Central America: Fragile Transition

Edited by

Rachel Sieder
Lecturer in Politics
Institute of Latin American Studies
University of London

JL
1416
.C45
1996
West

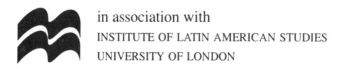

in association with
INSTITUTE OF LATIN AMERICAN STUDIES
UNIVERSITY OF LONDON

First published in Great Britain 1996 by
MACMILLAN PRESS LTD
Houndmills, Basingstoke, Hampshire RG21 6XS
and London
Companies and representatives
throughout the world

A catalogue record for this book is available
from the British Library.

ISBN 0–333–66311–X

First published in the United States of America 1996 by
ST. MARTIN'S PRESS, INC.,
Scholarly and Reference Division,
175 Fifth Avenue,
New York, N.Y. 10010

ISBN 0–312–16010–0

Library of Congress Cataloging-in-Publication Data
Central America : fragile transition / edited by Rachel Sieder.
p.   cm. — (Institute of Latin American Studies series)
Includes bibliographical references (p.   ) and index.
ISBN 0–312–16010–0 (cloth)
1. Central America—Politic and government—1979–   2. Democracy–
–Central America.   I. Sieder, Rachel.   II. Series.
JL1416.C45   1995
320.9728'09045—dc20   95–51281
                                                             CIP

© Institute of Latin American Studies 1996

All rights reserved. No reproduction, copy or transmission of
this publication may be made without written permission.

No paragraph of this publication may be reproduced, copied or
transmitted save with written permission or in accordance with
the provisions of the Copyright, Designs and Patents Act 1988,
or under the terms of any licence permitting limited copying
issued by the Copyright Licensing Agency, 90 Tottenham Court
Road, London W1P 9HE.

Any person who does any unauthorised act in relation to this
publication may be liable to criminal prosecution and civil
claims for damages.

10   9   8   7   6   5   4   3   2   1
05   04   03   02   01   00   99   98   97   96

Printed and bound in Great Britain by
Antony Rowe Ltd, Chippenham, Wiltshire

CONTENTS

v

PREFACE

This book arose from a study group which took place throughout 1994 at the Institute of Latin American Studies, University of London, which aimed to examine different aspects of the current transition in Central America, analysing the substantive shifts, reforms and realignments currently taking place throughout the region. For the purposes of this study group, Central America included Guatemala, El Salvador, Nicaragua, Honduras and Panama. The case of Costa Rica was omitted, given that the main focus was on aspects of post-conflict transition. Participants were from both the UK and Central America. All contributors to the volume were able to revise their chapters after group discussion of an initial draft during 1994.

The editor gratefully acknowledges the financial support of the European Commission for the study group. She also wishes to thank Victor Bulmer-Thomas, James Dunkerley and Tony Bell for their editorial input and Alison Loader de Rojo for preparing the script. A particular thank you to the Centro de Estudios para la Aplicación de Derecho (CESPAD) in San Salvador for the support they provided for the chapter on judicial reform.

LIST OF CONTRIBUTORS

Stephen Baranyi is currently visiting research scholar at the Department of International Relations at the London School of Economics, University of London, where he is engaged in research on the role of the United Nations in Guatemala. He is also policy analyst at the Central American Committees for Human Rights, London. His recent publications include 'Beyond Traditional Peacekeeping? Caveats from International Theory and from UN Experiences in Central America', *Estudios Internacionales* (1994) and ' Central America: A Firm and Lasting Peace?' in *SIPRI 1995 Yearbook: World Armaments and Disarmament* (Oxford: 1995).

Rodolfo Cerdas Cruz is a researcher at CIAPA, the Centro de Investigación y Adiestramiento Político-Administrativo, in San José, Costa Rica. He is author of 'Costa Rica since 1930', in Leslie Bethell (ed.), *The Cambridge History of Latin America*, Vol. VII (Cambridge, 1990); 'Colonial Heritage, External Domination and Political Systems in Central America', in Louis W. Goodman, William Leogrande and Johanna Mendelson Forman (eds.), *Political Parties and Democracy in Central America* (Boulder, San Francisco and Oxford, 1992); *El Desencanto Democrático: Crisis de Partidos y Transición Democrática en Centroamérica y Panamá* (San José, 1992) and *The Communist International in Central America, 1920-1936* (London, 1990).

Ricardo Córdova Macías is Executive Director of the Fundación Dr. Guillermo Manuel Ungo in San Salvador. He has published widely on Salvadorean and Central American politics. He is co-editor (with Raúl Benítez) of *La Paz en Centroamérica: Expediente de Documentos Fundamentales, 1979-1989* (México, 1989); co-author (with Mitchell Seligson) of *Perspectivas para una Democracia Estable en El Salvador* (San Salvador, 1992); and author of *Procesos Electorales y Sistema de Partidos en El Salvador (1982-1989)* (San Salvador, 1992).

Patrick Costello is a freelance writer and researcher specialising in human rights and Latin America. He is currently contributing regular issue papers on Latin American countries (including Haiti, Guatemala and Cuba) to the United Nations High Commission for Refugees and has been a member of

UN missions to Haiti and South Africa. For three years he coordinated the Guatemala work of the Central America Human Rights Committee in London. He is author (with David Archer) of *Literacy and Power: The Latin American Battleground* (London, 1989).

James Dunkerley is Professor in Politics at the Institute of Latin American Studies and Queen Mary and Westfield College, University of London. He is author of *Power in the Isthmus: A Political History of Central America* (London and New York, 1988); 'El Salvador since 1930', in Leslie Bethell (ed.), *The Cambridge History of Latin America*, Vol. VII (Cambridge, 1990); *Political Suicide in Latin America* (London and New York, 1992); 'Beyond Utopia: The State of the Left in Latin America' in *New Left Review* (July/August 1994); and *Pacification in Central America* (London and New York, 1994).

Diana Pritchard is visiting associate professor at Indiana University. In addition to her academic interests in environment and development topics, she has conducted research on refugee issues in Kenya, Britain, Tanzania and Central America. She is currently co-editing *North Korea in the New World Order* for Macmillan Press.

Rachel Sieder is Lecturer in Politics at the Institute of Latin American Studies, University of London. She was formerly research fellow at the Institute (1993-1994). She is currently engaged in research on 'good government' and post-war institutional reform and reconstruction in Central America. She is editor of *Impunity in Latin America* (London, 1995) and author of 'Honduras: The Politics of Exception and Military Reformism (1972-1978)', *Journal of Latin American Studies* (1995).

Laurence Whitehead is a Fellow of Nuffield College, University of Oxford. He has published widely on Mexican and Central American politics. He is co-editor (with Guiseppe Di Palma) of *The Central American Impasse* (London and Sydney, 1986) and (with Guillermo O'Donnell and Philipe Schmitter) of *Transitions from Authoritarian Rule* (Baltimore, 1986). He is author of 'The Imposition of Democracy' in Abraham Lowenthal (ed.), *Exporting Democracy: the United States and Latin America* (Baltimore, 1991); 'The Alternative to Liberal Democracy: A Latin American Perspective', *Political Studies* (1992).

LIST OF FIGURES

LIST OF TABLES

LIST OF ABBREVIATIONS & ACRONYMS

AID	United States Agency for International Development
AOJ	Administration of Justice
APO	Alianza Política de Oposición, Nicaragua
APROH	Asociación para el Progreso de Honduras
ARENA	Alianza Republicana Nacionalista, El Salvador
ASC	Asamblea de Sociedad Civil, Guatemala
ASIES	Asociación de Investigación y Estudios Sociales (Guatemala)
ATJ	Apoyo Técnico Judicial (El Salvador)
BIEN	Brigada de Investigaciones Especiales y Narcóticos, Guatemala
BIRI	Batallón de Infantería de Respuesta Inmediata, El Salvador
CACIF	Cámara de Agricultura, Comercio, Industria y Finanzas, Guatemala
CDHES	Comisión Nacional de Derechos Humanos de El Salvador
CEAR	Comisión Especial de Atención a los Repatriados, Guatemala
CEDEM	Centro para Estudios Democráticos
CEJIL	Center for Justice and International Law
CENIDH	Centro Nicaragüense de los Derechos Humanos
CEPAL	Comisión Económica para América Latina
CERJ	Consejo Etnico Runujel Junam
CES	Cuerpo Especial de Seguridad, Honduras
CESPAD	Centro de Estudios para la Aplicación de Derecho (El Salvador)
CIA	Central Intelligence Agency
CIAPA	Centro de Investigación y Adiestramiento Político-Administrativo (Costa Rica)
CIAV	Comisión Internacional de Verificación y Apoyo, UN/OAS
CIIR	Catholic Institute for International Relations
CIREFCA	Conferencia Internacional sobre Refugiados Centroamericanos
CIVS	Comisión Internacional de Verificación y Seguimiento
CNJ	Consejo Nacional de la Judicatura, El Salvador

CNR	Comisión Nacional de Reconciliación, Guatemala
CNR	Coordinadora Nacional de Repoblación, El Salvador
CO	Commanding Officer
COHEP	Consejo Hondureño de la Empresa Privada
COPAZ	Comisión para la Consolidación de la Paz, El Salvador
CONDECA	Consejo de Defensa Centroamericana
COPMAGUA	Coordinadora de las Organizaciones de Pueblos Mayas de Guatemala
CORELESAL	Comisión Revisora de la Legislación Salvadoreña
COSEP	Consejo Superior de la Empresa Privada, Nicaragua
COSUFFAA	Consejo Superior de las Fuerzas Armadas, Honduras
CPRs	Comunidades de la Población en Resistencia, Guatemala
CREALC	Centre de Recherche sur L'Amerique Latine et les Caraibes
CREM	Centro Regional de Entrenamiento Militar
CRIES	Coordinadora Regional de Investigaciónes Económicas y Sociales
CSJ	Corte Suprema de Justicia
DEA	Drugs Enforcement Agency
DIC	División de Investigaciones Criminales, Honduras
DN	Dirección Nacional, Nicaragua
DNI	Departamento Nacional de Inteligencia, El Salvador
DNI	Departamento Nacional de Investigaciones, Honduras
DNU	Dirección Nacional Unitaria, Honduras
EC	European Community
EMP	Estado Mayor Presidencial (Presidential Guard), Guatemala
EPS	Ejército Popular Sandinista
ERP	Expresión Renovadora del Pueblo, El Salvador
EU	European Union
EZLN	Ejército Zapatista de Liberación Nacional
FBI	Federal Bureau of Investigation
FDN	Frente Democrático Nacional, Nicaragua
FDP	Fuerzas de Defensa de Panamá
FMLH	Frente Morazanista de Liberación Nacional, Honduras
FMLN	Frente Farabundo Martí para la Liberación Nacional, El Salvador
FN-380	Northern Front -380, Nicaragua
FNT	Frente Nacional de Trabajadores, Nicaragua

FONAPAZ	Fondo Nacional para la Paz, Guatemala
FP	Fuerza Pública, Panamá
FPL	Fuerzas Populares Revolucionarias 'Lorenzo Zelaya', Honduras
FPM	Frente Patriótico Morazanista
FRENO	Frente Nacional Pro-Constituyente, Panamá
FSLN	Frente Sandinista de Liberación Nacional
FSP	Fuerzas de Seguridad Pública (Honduras)
FUSADES	Fundación Salvadoreña para el Desarrollo Económico y Social
FUSEP	Fuerzas de Seguridad Pública, Honduras
GAO	United States General Accounting Office
GN	Guardia Nacional
GSP	General System of Preferences
ICITAP	International Criminal Investigative Training Assistance Program
IEJES	Instituto de Estudios Jurídicos de El Salvador
IIDH	Instituto Interamericano de Derechos Humanos
IMF	International Monetary Fund
INC	Instancia Nacional de Consenso, Guatemala
INCEP	Instituto Centroamericano de Estudios Políticos
INTA	Instituto Nacional de Transformación Agraria, Guatemala
IPM	Instituto de Previsión Militar
IS	Internacional Socialista
MAS	Movimiento de Acción Social, Guatemala
MINUGUA	United Nations Verification Mission in Guatemala
MISURASATA	Miskito, Sumu and Rama Sandinistas *Asla Takanka*
MLN	Movimiento de Liberación Nacional, Guatemala
MPL	Movimiento Popular de Liberación ('Cinchoneros'), Honduras
MPS	Milicias Populares Sandinistas
MU	Movimiento Unificado (El Salvador)
NAFTA	North American Free Trade Agreement
NCOORD	National Coordinating Office on Refugees and Displaced of Guatemala
NGO	Non-Governmental Organisation
OAS	Organization of American States
OECD	Organisation for Economic Cooperation and Development

xv

OIE	Oficina de Inteligencia del Estado, El Salvador
ONUCA	United Nations Observer Group for Central America
ONUSAL	United Nations Observer Mission in El Salvador
ONUVEN	UN Observer Force for the Verification of the Nicaraguan Elections
ORP	Oficina de Responsibilidad Profesional, Honduras
PAC	Patrulla de Autodefensa Civil, Guatemala
PAN	Partido de Avanzada Nacional, Guatemala
PCH	Partido Comunista de Honduras
PCN	Partido de Conciliación Nacional, El Salvador
PDC	Partido Demócrata-Cristiano, El Salvador
PDCG	Partido Demócrata-Cristiano Guatemalteco
PDCH	Partido Demócrata-Cristiano de Honduras
PDD	Partnership for Democracy and Development in Central America
PDH	Procuraduría para la Defensa de los Derechos Humanos, El Salvador
PDHG	Procuraduría de Derechos Humanos de Guatemala
PH	Policía de Hacienda, El Salvador
PID	Partido Institucional Democrático, Guatemala
PINU	Partido de Innovación y Unidad, Honduras
PLC	Partido Liberal Constitucional, Nicaragua
PMLH	Partido Morazanista de Liberación de Honduras
PN	Policía Nacional
PNC	Policía Nacional Civil, El Salvador
PR	Partido Revolucionario, Guatemala
PRD	Partido Revolucionario Democrático, Panamá
PRH	Partido Revolucionario Hondureño
PRTC	Partido Revolucionario de los Trabajadores, Honduras
PS	Policía Sandinista
PTH	Partido para la Transformación de Honduras
PTJ	Policía Técnica Judicial, Panamá
PUD	Partido de Unificación Democrática, Honduras
RAAN	Región Autónoma Atlántica del Norte, Nicaragua
RAAS	Región Autónoma Atlántica del Sur, Nicaragua
RN	Resistencia Nacional, Nicaragua
ROL	Rule of Law
SAP	Structural Adjustment Programme
SIPROCI	Servicio de Protección Civil, Guatemala

SIU	Special Investigation Unit, El Salvador
SPI	Servicio de Protección Institucional, Panamá
TSE	Tribunal Supremo Electoral
UCA	Universidad Centroamericana
UCN	Unión del Centro Nacional, Guatemala
UEA	Unidad Ejecutiva Antinarcotráfico, El Salvador
UESAT	Unidad Especial Anti-Terorista (Panama)
UN	United Nations
UNHCR	United Nations High Commission for Refugees
UNO	Unión Nacional Opositora, Nicaragua
UNTAC	United Nations Task Force for Cambodia
URNG	Unidad Revolucionaria Nacional Guatemalteca
US	United States
USAID	United States Agency for International Development
WOLA	Washington Office on Latin America
YATAMA	Yapti Tasba Masrika Aslika

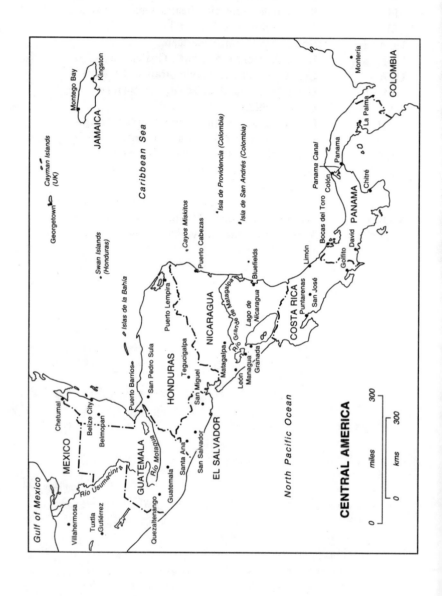

CENTRAL AMERICA

CHAPTER 1

INTRODUCTION

Rachel Sieder

In 1978, of the six Central American Republics (Costa Rica, El Salvador, Guatemala, Honduras, Nicaragua and Panama), only Costa Rica was ruled by an elected civilian regime; by 1995, all countries in the region had elected civilian governments. In 1982, El Salvador, Guatemala and Nicaragua were racked by civil war; by 1995 the civil wars had ended everywhere except Guatemala, and even there the level of conflict was significantly less than that experienced in the early 1980s. A transition of some kind has evidently occurred in Central America in recent years. This chapter aims first to signal the nature and distinct features of that transition, and secondly to indicate a set of criteria for judging current progress towards a more democratic order in the region.

The Central American Transition

Compared to the Southern Cone countries of Argentina, Brazil, Chile and Uruguay, the nature of both authoritarianism and the transition to procedural democracy were quite distinct in Central America. In the Southern Cone, the authoritarian regimes of the late 1960s and 1970s were perhaps best described as 'national security states' – instances of institutionalised military rule which suppressed or transformed the preexisting features of liberal democratic politics. Political parties were either outlawed (Chile) or reconstituted and restrained (Brazil), the weight of the executive was greatly increased, elections either ceased or became highly controlled affairs and free association was radically and violently curtailed. More inclusive authoritarian regimes, such as that of Velasco Alvarado in Peru (1968-1975), attempted a major restructuring of preexisting forms of politics, marginalising political parties and instituting more corporatist forms of representation.

In Central America, however, the nature of authoritarianism was altogether more complex. Here, as James Dunkerley and I argue in chapter three, open military dictatorships were the exception rather than the rule.

1

The region was instead characterised by the phenomenon of 'mixed regimes', where the division between civilian politics and military intromission was all but indistinguishable in practice. Prior to the 1980s, the Central American militaries were comparatively small in number, but their weight in local politics was considerable. This was generally bolstered by foreign (principally US) influence over domestic developments, traditionally far in excess of anything experienced in the Southern Cone. Military rulers relied on fraudulent elections and quasi-constitutional forms in order to legitimate their rule, as in the phenomenon of *zancudismo* in Nicaragua or the use of military parties in El Salvador.[1] In turn, the region's weak civilian elites depended on the military to maintain them in office. Elections, competitions within a highly restricted spectrum of parties which invariably excluded the radical left, were used to legitimate those already in power.

The literature examining the transition from authoritarian rule in the Southern Cone is extensive. Most authors agree that the impetus for transition emerged from divisions within the authoritarian regimes themselves. Splits between so-called 'hardliners' and 'softliners' in the military, and between business elites and the military over economic issues were much analysed features, as were the elite pacts or elite convergence which paved the way to a return to democratic rule.[2] The transition in Central America was, however, distinctive in many respects. More than a transition from authoritarian to democratic rule, it was fundamentally a transition from war to peace. In contrast to the transition in the Southern Cone, the mass opposition played an important role in Central America. The emergence of armed insurgent movements in Nicaragua, El Salvador and Guatemala at the end of 1970s was a response to the lack of legitimacy and representativeness of existing regimes. Through civil war, opposition movements forced a negotiated shift in the political *status quo*, even though they ultimately failed to overthrow the incumbents by force (except in the case of Nicaragua in 1979). In addition, given traditionally greater levels of penetration by extra-regional actors in domestic affairs and the highly internationalised nature of the regional conflict in the 1980s, the Central American transition was also much more international in character than those which occurred in the Southern Cone. In this context, features such as internal political convergence and elite pacts were not so central: the national and international dimensions of the transition from war to peace were always more important.

Multiple Transitions

The literature on the process of democratisation in Central America reflects three distinct but overlapping phases: first, the shift to electoral democracy during the 1980s; secondly, the move towards regional peace after 1987; and lastly, the current phase of post-conflict reconstruction, each of which will briefly be outlined here.

The Shift to Electoral Democracy

Since the early 1980s, elections have taken place throughout the region. In Honduras in 1980 (constituent assembly) and in 1981, 1985, 1989 and 1993 (presidential and parliamentary); in El Salvador in 1982 (constituent assembly), 1984, 1989 and 1994 (presidential), and 1985, 1988, 1991 and 1994 (parliamentary); in Guatemala in 1984 (constituent assembly), 1985 and 1990 (presidential and parliamentary), and 1994 (parliamentary); and in Nicaragua in 1984 and 1990 (presidential and parliamentary) and 1987 and 1994 (regional assemblies).

Throughout the 1980s much of the debate, particularly with regard to El Salvador and Guatemala, centred on whether these elections expressed an authentic process of democratisation, or whether they were merely façade or 'demonstration' elections designed primarily to please US domestic and congressional opinion and prop up illegitimate authoritarian regimes in the midst of civil war.[3] Many maintained that the shift to elections signalled little more than the success of the Reagan administration's doctrine of low intensity conflict, a strategy which aimed to promote a particular model of democracy – one in which the radical left was excluded from power – through a mixture of military and political means.[4] Conversely, the holding of elections in 1984 by the Sandinistas may be interpreted as a response to external pressure, the FSLN (Frente Sandinista de Liberación Nacional) moving away from a purely participatory model of democracy towards a mixture of participatory and parliamentary forms in an attempt in part to marshall international support in the face of US aggression.

In contrast to the blatant electoral manipulation of previous periods, the elections of the 1980s were relatively well-ordered, but the range of opinion which took part in them was considerably restricted. Except in Nicaragua, radical left currents were either directly prohibited from competing, or practised a form of 'self-exclusion', usually related to the excessively high levels of repression visited upon their representatives. In Nicaragua, it was the right which practised self-exclusion, responding to considerable pressure exerted by the Reagan administration for a boycott of the 1984 poll. Whilst in Guatemala, El Salvador and Honduras the party of government did change throughout the 1980s, the introduction of electoral mechanisms did not signify a definitive rupture with the authoritarian past. Nor were elections the outcome of a process of pact formation or elite convergence associated with the transitions in the Southern Cone. In El Salvador, the far-right ARENA (Alianza Republicana Nacionalista) party never accepted the legitimacy of the Christian Democrats and their US-backed reformist project, whilst the armed forces tolerated the election of José Napoleón Duarte (1984-1989) because of their need for continued US funds. In Honduras, President Suazo Córdova's attempt in 1985 to subvert the constitutional order illustrated the fragility of the democratic order. Even amongst the elites, then, divisions remained acute during the 1980s. In this sense, it is difficult to single out any one of the electoral processes of this period as 'foundational' or 'transitional' elections. Politics was still seen essentially as an exclusive, zero-sum game – a form of war by other means. Although the introduction of elections was an important component of the transition, it remains highly questionable whether this alone would have led to peace and the democratisation of the respective national polities.

The Move Towards Peace

In the second half of the 1980s, the governments of Central America edged slowly towards a regional peace settlement. The plan put forward by Costa Rican President Oscar Arias in 1986 was eventually adopted (with minor modifications) by the other governments of Central America – including that of Nicaragua – much to the displeasure of the Reagan administration, which continued in its efforts to isolate and undermine the Sandinista regime through political, economic and military means. With the signing of the Esquipulas II regional peace accords in 1987, debate focused on the impact that changing domestic and international factors and the advent of peace would have on the prospects for democratisation in the region.[5] The Esquipulas Accords aimed to provide the means for a negotiated settlement to the conflicts, but also contained important clauses whereby each signatory country committed itself to progressive democratisation. Democracy was understood to mean liberal, pluralist and participatory regimes elected by means of free and fair elections. The signing of the accords by the Sandinista government signified the defeat of the Sandinista model of democracy, with its stress on direct participatory forms and socio-economic redistribution, and a victory for a more procedural model of classical liberal democracy. The features of Esquipulas II, which served as the basis for subsequent national peace processes, included the initiation of dialogue with domestic opposition groups; the decree of amnesties; a commitment to cease-fire negotiations; the establishment of national reconciliation committees to verify the process of cease-fire, amnesty and democratisation; freedom of expression and association; the holding of free and fair elections; and the repatriation and resettlement of refugees and displaced persons.[6]

In the years subsequent to the signing of the accord, this model of democratisation came to be seen by both domestic and international actors as a way to bring an end to the civil wars. It was concluded that only peace would open the way to reconciliation, facilitate the reintegration of insurgents, promote demilitarisation, lend credibility and legitimacy to political systems distinctly lacking in both and provide the stability essential for economic reactivation. The revolutionary left in particular began to reevaluate the value of 'bourgeois democracy' and adopt a more gradualist strategy favouring negotiation. This tendency was greatly strengthened in the wake of the collapse of the Soviet bloc in 1989, the US invasion of Panama in December of the same year, and the electoral defeat of the Sandinistas in February 1990, all of which signalled (directly or indirectly) the continuation and indeed strengthening of US hegemony over the Central American region. Ultimately, war had forced both sides in the civil wars significantly to reduce their maximalist positions. However, Carlos Vilas has noted that, whilst all sides gradually came to accept the existing model of electoral democracy as a viable proposition, the legitimacy of Central America's electoral regimes was more the result of exhaustion and weariness after a decade of war and crisis than of any affirmative mandate – a variant of what has been referred to as 'democracy by default'.[7]

The terms of peace were subsequently reached in Nicaragua, involving a cease-fire (albeit subsequently broken by both sides in the run-up to the 1990 poll); reform of the electoral law; acceptance of the electoral result; the negotiation of the transition accords signed between the FSLN and the government-elect of Violeta Chamorro in the wake of the Sandinistas' electoral defeat; and the subsequent demobilisation of the contra rebels (the last element a factor that depended more on decisions in Washington than in Managua). Honduras, which had not suffered civil war itself, was subsequently cleared of the contra rebels, and in 1990 the government of Rafael Leonardo Callejas (1990-1994) passed a broad amnesty to encourage reintegration of the few hundred individuals who had taken up arms or gone into exile during the early 1980s. In El Salvador, a peace accord between the FMLN (Frente Farabundo Martí para la Liberación Nacional) and the government of Alfredo Cristiani (1989-1994) was finally signed at

Chapultepec in Mexico in December 1991, and gradually (although not completely) implemented over the following three years. In Panama, where democracy was forcibly and directly imposed by the US invasion of 1989, the government of Guillermo Endara (1989-1994) faced a somewhat different set of concerns with regard to post-conflict reconstruction. By 1995, only Guatemala had a final peace accord yet to be signed and even in this most intractable of the Central American conflicts, considerable progress has been made since the signing of the Esquipulas Accords.

When transitions are as distended and complex as has been the case in Central America, where the different national transitions have by no means been simultaneous, it is difficult to distinguish between the phases of transition and consolidation. However, it is argued here that Central America has now entered a third phase of post-conflict democratic consolidation.

Post-Conflict Reconstruction

Rather than analysing the causes and initial phases of transition in Central America, it is on this third stage of reconstruction and consolidation that the present volume concentrates. Those features of this phase explored in the subsequent chapters include the implementation of the respective peace accords; the negotiations and conflicts involved in renegotiating institutional responsibilities and restructuring the state; and the progress towards increased participation in and legitimation of the respective national political systems. Certain key questions are addressed: how secure are recent advances? What has been the impact of the transition (firstly to electoral democracy and latterly to peace) on actors and institutions in the region? How has the balance between domestic and international forces changed and what have the implications been for the democratic transition? Can universal notions of citizenship and democratic practices be consolidated in the prevailing economic and political climate?

The book is divided into three sections:

– *Actors*, with chapters on political parties and party systems (Rodolfo Cerdas Cruz), the military (James Dunkerley and Rachel Sieder) and returning refugees (Diana Pritchard);

– *Institutions*, with chapters examining executive-congressional relations (Ricardo Córdova Macías) and the judicial system (Rachel Sieder and Patrick Costello);

- *The International Context*, with chapters analysing the overall shifts affecting the region in recent years (Laurence Whitehead) and the impact of the United Nations on the Central American peace process (Stephen Baranyi).

The following chapters place emphasis on the detail of current developments in the region on the understanding that in a period characterised by the highly fluid and rapidly changing nature of events, it is only by means of close examination that significant shifts can be traced. Each chapter draws on the experience of at least three of the Central American countries. However, all the contributors stress the importance of basing analysis on a thorough understanding of discrete national differences. Whilst common trends and 'demonstration effects' are in evidence throughout the region, no regional 'transition prototype' exists. The countries examined in this volume include Nicaragua, Guatemala, El Salvador, Honduras and Panama. Costa Rica is excluded on the basis that, although the regional conflict of the 1980s undoubtedly affected that nation's political system, a liberal democratic system of government was consolidated in Costa Rica long before the crisis of the 1980s, in contrast to elsewhere in the region, where the advent of democracy is comparatively recent.

Analysing Consolidation

Evidently, the outcome of any process of transition involves the modification of laws, institutions and the behaviour of political actors.[8] As Stephen Baranyi and Laurence Whitehead both note in their respective chapters, in Central America this process has been highly dependent on changes in the international environment. The chapters in this volume chart the substantive shifts of recent years in Central America rather than provide any ideological definition of democracy against which to measure national developments. Democracy is understood here as a process rather than a given set of preconditions and institutional arrangements – a variable rather than an absolute.[9] Political systems can therefore become more or less democratic – in one sense, democratic consolidation is an ongoing process in all democracies. However, what concerns us here is the particularly formative stage in what Manuel Alcántara has called 'countries in the process of democratic consolidation'.[10] Consolidation is understood as an increase in the permanence and stability of the democratic system. There is no guarantee that democratic transition will necessarily unfold into 'full' or consolidated democracy. However, a number of features are posited here as essential to democratic consolidation:

The Existence of Universal Rights and Obligations

The construction of a democratic system involves the guarantee of universal rights and obligations for all citizens. Whilst these should include universal and equal political rights – a democratic regime is inclusive not exclusive – they are not reducible to this electoral dimension alone. Especially important in the Central American context is respect for basic human rights, such as the right to life and liberty, as is respect for the rights of minorities. Strengthening the rule of law and achieving generalised acceptance of the constitutional order are essential for democratic consolidation. Limits on power, be it the power of the executive or the military, are essential; no absolute power can be democratic. In Central America, where there is little democratic tradition and scant faith in institutions of state or political parties, institutional reconstruction and reform of key political actors is a necessary component of democratic consolidation, a point stressed in the chapters on political parties, the military, executive-congressional relations and the judiciary.

A Responsive and Representative Political System

Any democratic system should be characterised by its efficacy, legitimacy and accountability. This involves the construction and strengthening of effective channels for consultation and consensus-building between civil society and government to ensure that the latter responds to the demands of the former. It also involves the strengthening of the power of contestation of civil society, an area examined by Diana Pritchard in her chapter on refugees and reintegration. By this it is meant that civil society should be structured and have real autonomy *vis-à-vis* the state. As Alain Touraine has pointed out, if the state exerts total domination, political participation can be conformist or revolutionary, but not democratic.[11] Democracy is not merely about electoral participation, but rather about effective participation for all sectors and governance that is seen as legitimate by all citizens. However, both Ricardo Córdova Macías and Rodolfo Cerdas Cruz, writing about parliament and political parties respectively, note the considerable lack of accountability and legitimacy of both parties and state institutions in Central America today. Mechanisms for effective participation are significantly absent throughout the region. As Rodolfo Cerdas points out in his chapter, the fact that most parties in Central America lack a strong link with their electorate is a legacy both of the authoritarian past and the weak power of the parties *vis-à-vis* the military. The party system, and to a lesser extent the institutions of state, are currently both in formation and in crisis and appear unable to respond effectively to the demands of civil society, in particular of previously marginalised groups such as women, indigenous peoples and peasants. The effective reform of both the party system and state institutions, involving the extension of effective participation, representation and accountability, is therefore critical to the phase of democratic consolidation.

Eradication of Military Dominance

Although the tradition of 'mixed regimes' referred to above resulted in the preponderance of the military in Central America's political systems, the region's armies were transformed and their power increased to an unprecedented degree by the crisis and subsequent US intervention of the 1980s. The need for a new democratic role for the military is stressed in the following chapters on political parties, the military and the judiciary. The chapter by James Dunkerley and Rachel Sieder focuses on the institutional dimensions of the process of demobilisation and demilitarisation, highlighting the fact that the former does not automatically guarantee the latter. One of the central problems identified in the chapter on the judiciary is that of impunity. Democratic consolidation must involve making the armed forces subject to the rule of law: no absolute power can be democratic – the military must be subject to checks and controls. However, whilst appreciable variation exists throughout the region, the autonomous power and impunity of the military remains considerable.

The Existence of a Minimum Level of Consensus on the Democratic Rules of the Game

A consolidated democracy must involve a commitment by all sectors and participants to uphold the democratic system, even if the outcome of elections or congressional decision-making does not go in their favour. Elections in a democratic system must offer voters the possibility of changing the government or what Adam Przeworski has famously referred to as 'the institutionalisation of uncertainty'.[12] The corollary to this is that none of the players should adopt any alternative to democratic procedures as a means to attain power, and none should have the power of veto over democratically elected governments. This involves an end to the tradition of coercive, arbitrary and authoritarian politics so predominant in the region and a shift to mechanisms of consensus, necessarily a slow and gradual process of construction of a democratic political culture.

Legitimacy of the System

The legitimacy of any democratic system ultimately depends on its capacity to deliver results to its citizens. This naturally entails meeting the minimum conditions set out above, but it must also involve a socio-economic dimension. Although the existence of socio-economic inequality does not *ipso facto* preclude the existence of democracy – considered here as a process rather than an outcome – the *consolidation* of democracy, contingent as it is on the increased legitimacy of government, may ultimately be inhibited by extremes of socio-economic injustice. Such extremes have historically characterised Central America and continue to characterise the region. Whilst the traditional, exclusive, agro-export model was decisively weakened during the last decade, it remains unclear whether or not it will be superseded by a more inclusive model of development.[13] In a context of increasing internationalisation of production and of shrinkage of the state, the capacity of national governments to exercise effective control over their economies is increasingly being called into question, a point made by Rodolfo Cerdas Cruz in his contribution to this volume. Such lack of control is particularly acute in such an impoverished and highly penetrated region as Central America. It may yet prove that the transition to democracy fails to provide a means for economic development and greater socio-economic justice. The implications of this for the legitimacy and permanence of the democratic system have yet to be seen.

Notes

1. *Zancudismo* refers to the relations of the Somoza dynasty with bourgeois political parties in Nicaragua after 1950; the Somozas exercised their power through the offices of the Partido Liberal Nicaragüense (PLN) which consistently won less than fair elections, while the opposition parties – including the official Conservatives (*'Zancudos'*) colluded in Somocista control in exchange for minority representation in congress.
2. See O'Donnell, Schmitter and Whitehead (1986); Diamond, Linz and Lipset (1989); Higley and Gunther (1992); Baloyra (1987) and Malloy and Seligson (1987).
3. For a useful discussion see Booth and Seligson (1989); see also Blachman and Sharpe (1992), pp. 33-52.
4. See Lowenthal (1991), especially chapter four; Gils, Rocamora and Wilson (1993), especially the chapter by Richard Wilson. For a less than convincing defence of the Reagan administration's role in promoting democracy in Central America see Zarate (1994).
5. See Moreno (1994) and Dunkerley (1994).

6. For the full text of the Esquipulas Accords see Moreno (1994), pp. 191-8.
7. Vilas (1993), p. 10.
8. For a useful discussion of the transition literature see Diane Ethier's chapter in her edited volume (Ethier, 1990).
9. The idea of democracy as a process is taken from Booth (1989), pp. 40-59.
10. [Editor's translation]. The phrase used by Alcántara is 'países en vías de consolidación democrática'; see Alcántara (1992), pp. 123-46.
11. Touraine (1992), p. 68.
12. Przeworski (1986), p. 58.
13. For a discussion see Bulmer-Thomas (1991).

I: ACTORS

CHAPTER 2

POLITICAL PARTIES AND PARTY SYSTEMS

Rodolfo Cerdas Cruz

This chapter sets out to analyse political parties in Central America within the context of the multiple, rapid and as yet inconclusive transitions affecting the region in the 1990s.[1] Due emphasis is placed on the particularities and differences which have characterised the development of each country (historical, cultural, political and economic) as well as their external relations. By recognising these differences, the significant continuities and similarities between the party systems in each country can be identified. Lastly, a critical comparison of the current state of political parties in Central America is provided.

The formation of political and party systems in Central America must be analysed by examining the behaviour of key actors, both internal and external to these systems. Firstly, the armed forces – a determinant factor in the nature of the region's party systems, having long occupied a role which transcends the strictly military. Secondly, the insurrectional groups, who have challenged the established order and – initially by means of armed struggle and subsequently via negotiation – forced previously closed systems to become more open, although these systems themselves are still in a process of formation and definition. The participation of the armed forces within the configuration of a new democratic political framework is clearly essential, and the incorporation of insurrectional groups into the system, transformed into duly legalised political parties, is critical for the future of the transition and the formation of a truly representative party system. In addition to these broad characteristics, a number of more specific but no less significant factors must also be examined: for example, the nature of the region's political elites and their current restructuring; the successive adjustments and readjustments of different political forces and their respective political parties; and the impact of this fluidity, expressed both in the composition of political parties, and in the overall structure and functioning of the party systems themselves.

Particular attention is devoted here to the crisis currently affecting the political parties. Given its implications not only for the future of the democratic transition, but also for the question of governability, this crisis

15

merits detailed analysis and reflection. The lack of prestige, the inefficiency and the permanence of the political parties is linked to the problem
of the institutional spaces required for their efficient functioning. These
spaces do not always exist, or if they do exist, they are often insufficient
to incorporate new parties or to provide legitimacy for the overall system.
In this respect, the origins of party formations (internal to, external to, or
against the system); their relationship to the armed forces; and the role of
ideological currents and doctrinal definition play a significant role and also
deserve consideration. In addition, the broader institutional context directly
linked to the parties and electoral questions is also examined, given that
popular perceptions are not only of the political parties themselves but also
of Congress and electoral bodies responsible for the organisation,
administration and oversight of electoral processes.

Transition in the Transition

The most important characteristic of the party process in Central America
is that it is taking place within the context of an unfinished democratic
transition. This substantially affects the party system, not only in terms of
the dominant political context but also to the extent that this political
transition to democracy coincides with other transitions which affect both
society and the overall political system:

– Structural adjustment of the economy, involving policies of
privatisation and commercial liberalisation, which seeks to
abandon state protectionism and any remnants of populist policies
from the Alliance for Progress period still present in the region.

– The transition which has taken place since the inevitable
fragmentation of local economies which followed the decline of
the model of the Central American Common Market of the 1960s,
towards a new kind of regional integration, still taking shape in the
1990s.

– The multiple changes which have occurred at the level of state
structure, with the adoption of policies which seek to reduce the
size of the state and to adapt it to the postulates of neo-liberal
doctrine currently in vogue.

– At a more general level, the global transition processes which have affected the region following the end of the Cold War, the break up of the Soviet Union and the emergence of new blocs and actors with significant influence in the isthmus, such as the recently formed NAFTA (North American Free Trade Agreement), the EU (European Union), Japan and the 'Asian Tigers'. In terms of the effort they must make to become competitive and integrated into the new world market in an advantageous manner, these developments have implications for every country in Central America.

These transitions, complex and difficult to assess, have had various effects on the political parties which must be considered in order to grasp the current state of play in Central America. These multiple and simultaneous processes of transition combine with other conditions affecting the formation and development of the political parties and their corresponding party systems.

Historical and Political Determinants

In the first instance, the distinct conditions and characteristics of the political and party systems in each country of the region make it imperative that national specificities are taken into account. This evidently limits the applicability and significance of analogies and generalisations. Many analysts, influenced by Central America's physical smallness and overestimating previous attempts at regional unity (which ultimately failed to prevent the adoption of different paths of development and national systems) have referred to the Central American isthmus as a single entity, employing highly questionable concepts such as 'the divided nation' or 'the nation of lost unity'.[2] By contrast, it is maintained here that perhaps the notion of 'truncated unity' is more appropriate and useful for referring to the process of nation-formation in Central America as a whole. In signalling the inconclusive or truncated nature of the formation of a single nation in the isthmus (a feature evident in other Latin American subregions), local and regional problems of 'backwardness' and the difficulty of forming a single nation in the area are recognised. In addition, such an approach opens up the possibility of less rhetorical and more plausible attempts at regional integration, providing a new conceptual basis for a more realistic form of political, economic, party, social and cultural regional integration. This would be built not on the basis of an abstract unifying ethic (as weak as it is useless), or on the basis of ignoring or under-estimating the profound national differences which have impeded previous attempts at union, but rather on the basis of a realistic appraisal of those national differences and specificities within a systematic framework of socio-economic comparison, of effective political and institutional collaboration and of a meaningful and effective encounter between states and peoples.

In these terms, an analysis of the political systems of each of the countries considered here is sufficient to demonstrate the substantial differences which characterise them. In El Salvador and Nicaragua, the uneven end to the civil wars has involved a series of setbacks, stalemates and advances. The reconstitution and extension of the internal party systems in both countries has occurred in highly distinct political contexts, including that relating to the changing role of the decisive actor, the armed forces. In Guatemala, the armed conflict continues, political confrontations between the military, civilians and the guerrilla have been transferred to a negotiating table currently in deadlock; and the elite is divided and undergoing a difficult process of reconstitution in the context of a conflict between the different branches of the state. The final outcome in Guatemala is, at best, unpredictable. If to this we add problems of leadership, formation and *modus operandi* of the political parties, and the difficulties of effectively integrating actors into the political system, it is clear that the Guatemalan peace process is not only *sui generis* but also that it is still in the initial stages. In Honduras, by contrast, a predominantly bipartisan political system remains in place. Two smaller parties, the Partido de Innovación y Unidad (PINU) and the Christian Democratic Party (PDCH), have participated in elections for a number of years, although largely in a symbolic capacity. Much more recently, a new left-wing party has appeared, although this will not become truly incorporated into the politico-electoral system until the next presidential elections in 1998. The Panamanian case, although displaying certain historical continuities in terms of political parties, presents significantly different problems of democratic transition and electoral and political reconstruction to those encountered in the rest of Central America.

Although similar features are present in many of these countries, care should be taken when evaluating their true significance. For example, the presence of the armed forces in the political life of the nation is highly significant in all the countries and plays a decisive role in their political systems. But whilst the tutelage of the transition and of the political parties is evident in the case of Guatemala, and to a lesser and more primitive extent in the case of Honduras, this is nothing like the situation prevailing in El Salvador, Nicaragua or Panama.[3]

In the case of Panama, the process of incorporation into the electoral process – both of long-established political parties such as the Partido Revolucionario Democrático (PRD) and newer movements such as Papa Egoró – has been highly successful. In the case of the Frente Farabundo Martí para la Liberación Nacional (FMLN), the formation and operationalisation of a new legal party structure, the formation of alliances and even electoral participation has been more difficult and complicated. In Nicaragua, this process has been highly contradictory and corrosive, as much for the old anti-Sandinista opposition – which came together under the banner of UNO (Unión Nacional Opositora) during the 1990 elections – as for the Sandinistas themselves, who have entered into a process of open dispute and division following their exit from government.

New Parties, Ex-Guerrillas and Military Power

Given that the democratic transition in Central America has been, above all else, a transition from civil war to peace, it is essential to analyse the position of two key actors – the armed forces and the guerrilla – within the new democratic political context. It should be noted that the role of the military in each country has been quite distinct: in Guatemala, the army was the real force promoting the transition[4] and has assumed a supervisory position, playing a decisive role at the critical moment of Jorge Serrano's attempted *autogolpe* in 1993. In El Salvador, the military has shifted to a less protagonistic, although no less important role. At international level, this has been limited by the terms of the Chapultepec Peace Accords signed in December 1991 between the government of El Salvador and the FMLN and the intervention of ONUSAL (United Nations Observer Mission in El Salvador), charged with monitoring compliance with the peace settlement. Internally, limitations have been set by a civilian business sector which has appropriated political space and power; the support of the hegemonic regional power; and of a dynamic and relatively well-structured popular movement. In Honduras, the army appears to have extended well beyond its previous limits and entered into the private business sphere, considerably enlarging its economic, financial, social and political influence in a direct challenge to other business and trade union sectors. This also contradicts the new US policy orientation towards the region, especially as regards the size, functions and budget levels of the armed forces. In Nicaragua, although the creation of the Instituto de Previsión Militar (IPM) echoes the Honduran experience, the armed forces fulfil the function of guaranteeing the political and physical survival of the Sandinista Front. At the same time, the armed forces are seeking an acceptable form of institutionalisation which will overcome their former status as a partisan armed group. In Panama tutelage is external, to the extent that the possibility of another US intervention – in the event of civil disturbances or political loss of control – is an omnipresent Sword of Damocles in the minds of local politicians. Given the absence of well-structured and reliable national armed forces, local fears are focused rather on the proliferation of the non-regulated private security agencies which currently exceed in number the official forces of the Panamanian state (see chapter three). Evidently, despite the fact that the armed forces have a predominant and often decisive role in every country in the region, the significance and concrete effects of this role vary substantially in each system and have different quantitative and qualitative implications according to specific national contexts.

The process of legalisation and integration of certain actors until very recently excluded from the political and electoral systems of these countries has been different in each country – be they guerrilla movements such as the URNG (Unidad Revolucionaria Nacional Guatemalteca) in Guatemala, the FMLN in El Salvador, the contra in Nicaragua and the Cinchoneros or the Morazanista Front in Honduras; or defeated governing movements, such as the Sandinistas in Nicaragua and the coalition formed around the PRD (Partido Revolucionario Democrático) during the regime of General Noriega in Panama. In Guatemala, the peace negotiations are still unconcluded and whilst the crisis within institutions and amongst the political elite is becoming increasingly acute, one of the actors called upon to participate in the party system (the URNG) remains excluded; meanwhile the rest of the political parties display the symptoms of a crisis as generalised as it is profound. In Guatemala, acute institutional and political upheaval, resulting in a turnover of incumbents within all branches of the state, is occurring simultaneously with very worrying levels of abstention and indifference, despite the ongoing discussions about the essential components of political democracy. The referendum of 30 January 1994 is evidence of this phenomenon (see Figure 2.1). Given this party crisis and the electoral attitude of the population, it is pertinent to ask what role certain entities, such as the so-called Civic Committees, will play in the future and what their significance will be in a crisis of political representation such as that currently observable in Guatemala.

By contrast, in El Salvador the Peace Accords guaranteed the entry of the guerrilla to the politico-electoral system as a political party. However, the problems involved in transforming an alliance of different guerrilla groups into an effective political party capable of participating in an

Figure 2.1
Guatemala: Results of 30 January 1994 Referendum

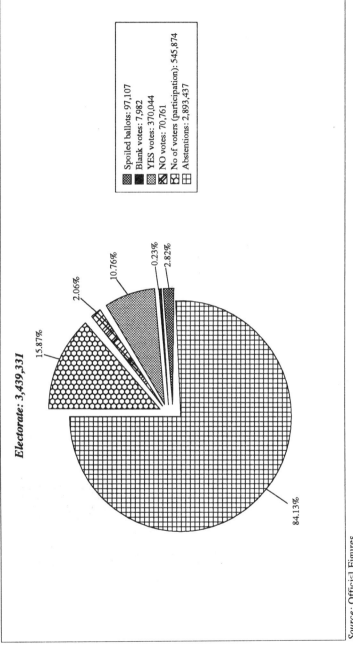

Electorate: 3,439,331

15.87%

2.06%

10.76%

0.23%

2.82%

84.13%

Spoiled ballots: 97,107
Blank votes: 7,982
YES votes: 370,044
NO votes: 70,761
No of voters (participation): 545,874
Abstentions: 2,893,437

Source: Official Figures.

Figure 2.2
El Salvador: Results of 1994 Presidential Elections (1st round)

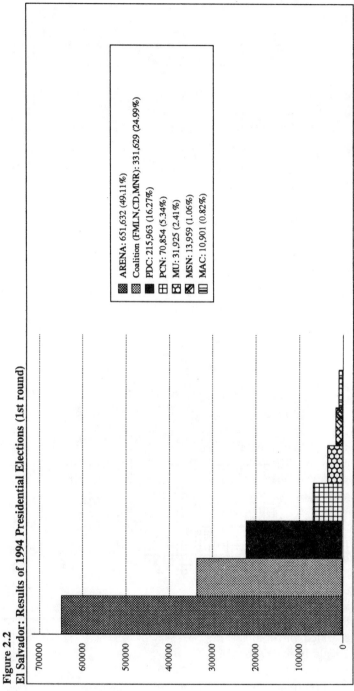

ARENA: 651,632 (49.11%)
Coalition (FMLN,CD,MNR): 331,629 (24.99%)
PDC: 215,963 (16.27%)
PCN: 70,854 (5.34%)
MU: 31,925 (2.41%)
MSN: 13,959 (1.06%)
MAC: 10,901 (0.82%)

Source: Tribunal Supremo Electoral de El Salvador, *Escrutinio Final: Reporte de Votación para Presidente y Vicepresidente por Departamento de la Eleccion del 20 de Marzo de 1994.*

electoral coalition with the opposition Democratic Convergence have been considerable. Not only was the process of converting the guerrilla into a party fraught with tensions and highly time-consuming, it was also accompanied by extremist actions by the far-right which sought to destabilise the peace process and block the implementation of the Peace Accords. The conduct of the guerrilla leadership, some of whom appear to have markedly divergent strategies and objectives from others, has not helped to reduce the cost of the incorporation of the FMLN into the Salvadorean party system, the latter itself barely entering a phase of consolidation. The emergence of contradictions in the first session of the new legislature (1994-1998) about who had or had not reached agreements with the ruling ARENA (Alianza Republicana Nacionalista) party was only the beginning of a process which appears to be heading inexorably towards the liquidation of the FMLN as a common political front for dissimilar groups, as was publicly called for by Joaquín Villalobos, one of the historical leaders of the movement.

The electoral results of 20 March 1994 are shown in Figure 2.2, giving the votes polled by each party or coalition for the first round of the presidential elections; Figure 2.3 shows the subsequent electoral distribution produced in the second round on 24 April 1994. This demonstrates the processes of separation (political divisions within electoral coalitions) and regrouping of the different political forces (agreements and electoral rejection) beyond the original party sympathies. Figure 2.4 shows the pattern of voting in the election for congressional deputies with the results party by party, given that the party identification lost in the coalitions formed for the presidential poll was reestablished (albeit partially) in the competition for congressional deputies, establishing the basis for the subsequent development of the political system.

In Honduras, although the guerrilla movements opted to dissolve themselves and no significant negotiations of any type took place, the system chose to open up, admitting a fifth member to the select club of four which, until the last election, comprised the Honduran party system.[5] This would seem to be more the result of a self-saving operation by a closed electoral system undergoing an acute crisis of credibility than of organised party pressures. Electoral abstentionism, which reached 35.03 per cent in the presidential elections of November 1993, combined with the rigidity of the system – demonstrated by voting patterns in the congressional elections, which mirror almost exactly the results in the presidential poll – are particularly acute symptoms of the exhaustion and dysfunctionality of the overall political system in Honduras as much as of the parties themselves. Figure 2.5 gives the votes polled by each party in the presid-

Figure 2.3
El Salvador: Results of 1994 Presidential Elections (2nd round)

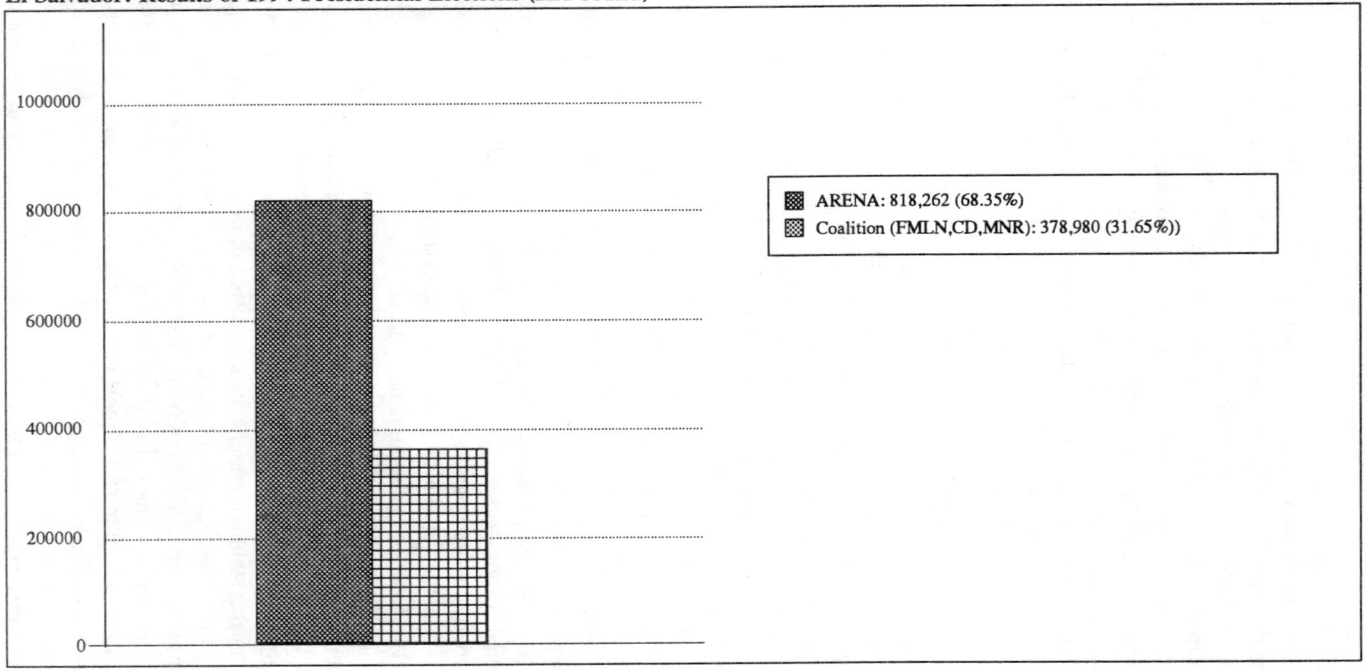

ARENA: 818,262 (68.35%)
Coalition (FMLN,CD,MNR): 378,980 (31.65%))

Figure 2.4
El Salvador: Results of 1994 Congressional Elections (2nd round)

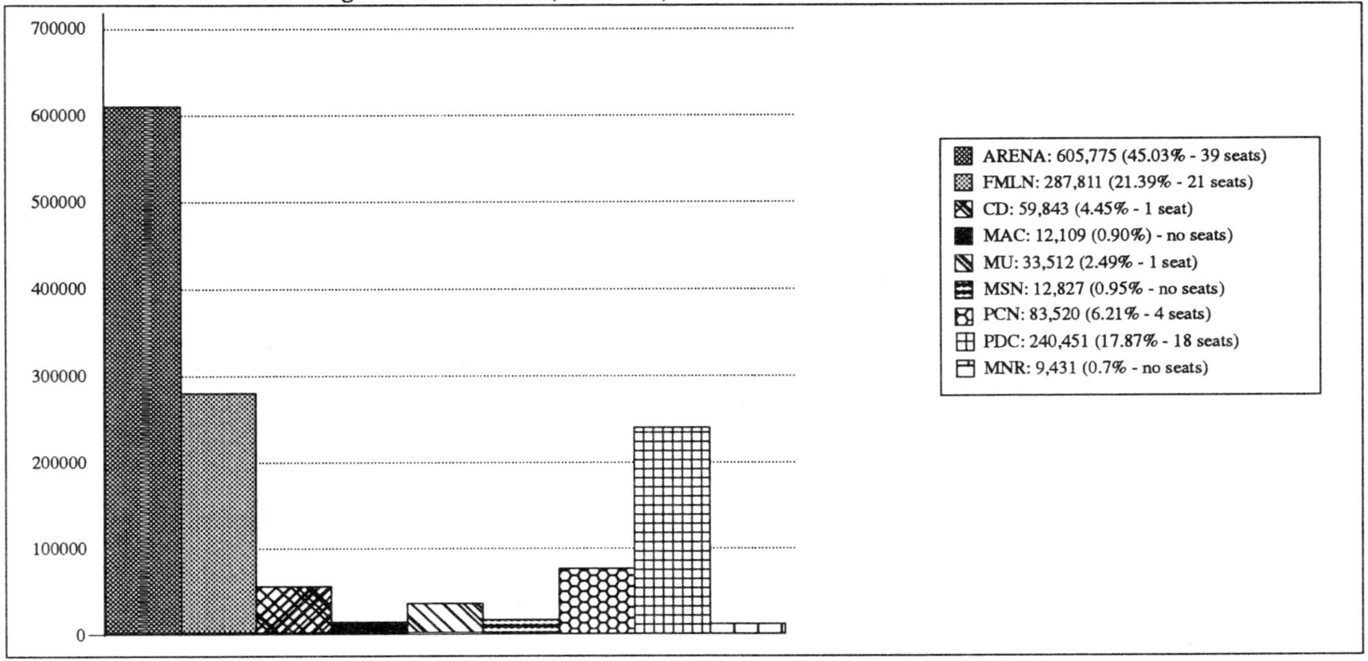
700000
600000
500000
400000
300000
200000
100000
0
ARENA: 605,775 (45.03% - 39 seats)
FMLN: 287,811 (21.39% - 21 seats)
CD: 59,843 (4.45% - 1 seat)
MAC: 12,109 (0.90%) - no seats)
MU: 33,512 (2.49% - 1 seat)
MSN: 12,827 (0.95% - no seats)
PCN: 83,520 (6.21% - 4 seats)
PDC: 240,451 (17.87% - 18 seats)
MNR: 9,431 (0.7% - no seats)

Source: Tribunal Supremo Electoral de El Salvador, *Escrutinio Final: Reporte de Votación para Diputados de la Elección del 20 de Marzo de 1994.*

Figure 2.5
Honduras: Results of 1993 Presidential Elections

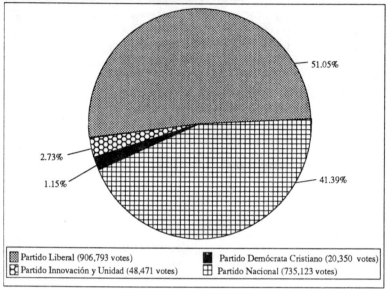

Partido Liberal (906,793 votes)
Partido Innovación y Unidad (48,471 votes)
Partido Demócrata Cristiano (20,350 votes)
Partido Nacional (735,123 votes)

Figure 2.6
Honduras: Results of 1993 Congressional Elections

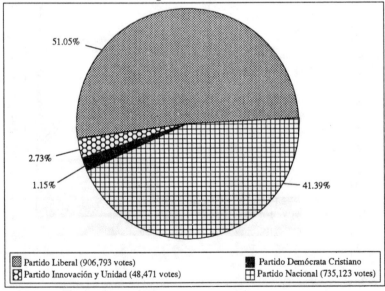

Partido Liberal (906,793 votes)
Partido Innovación y Unidad (48,471 votes)
Partido Demócrata Cristiano
Partido Nacional (735,123 votes)

ential poll; and Figure 2.6 shows the results by party for the election of deputies. The acutely bipartisan character of the system, its rigidity and the concurrence of voting patterns should not obscure the grave problems of credibility and legitimacy facing parties and state institutions in Honduras. The aforementioned admission of a left-wing party to the next electoral contest would not appear to be a sufficient response to such a complex problem, which has its origins in the unstable and subordinate relation of civil to military power, the insufficient integration of national territory and population, and the high degree of external dependence which, despite rhetoric to the contrary, continues to characterise the country's political system.

In Nicaragua, the displacement of the FSLN from government has not been followed by the ascendance of a coherent political group capable of responding to popular aspirations. The UNO coalition began to unravel the moment it assumed the presidency and the political life of the country has come to be characterised by division.[6] The persistence of armed groups – contras, *recompas*, *revueltos* etc. – indicates not only the problems involved in incorporating different armed sectors into civilian life, but also the serious difficulties the political system faces in effectively opening up to include the different groups that comprise the Nicaraguan political scenario.[7] The resurgence of certain sectors which present themselves as non-ideological technocrats, despite their roots in political parties strongly linked to the authoritarian *Somocista* past, is a predominant trend. The Atlantic Coast elections, the only electoral process to have taken place since the 1990 presidential poll, could be taken as indicative of a tendency in this direction (see Figure 2.7 for the Northern region; Figure 2.8 for the Southern region results).

In the case of Nicaragua, the existence of formal and non-formal alliances, and the successive, contradictory and often highly opportunistic participation of various actors in such transactions, tends to indicate both the still precarious character of the political system and the embryonic condition of the party system. It also illustrates the objective difficulties faced by political forces in constituting clearly differentiated political parties, distinct from the institutions within which they operate and capable of reaching working agreements with their opponents which would allow for the functioning of the system. This has become a serious and worrying characteristic, even inside the political parties, division and lack of cohesion are the defining characteristics, as is indicated by the process of division within the FSLN between a moderate sector (led by Sergio Ramírez Mercado), which has been systematically expelled from the structures and leadership of the party, and a radical sector which has conc-

Figure 2.7
Nicaragua: Results of 1994 Elections for the Northern Atlantic Region

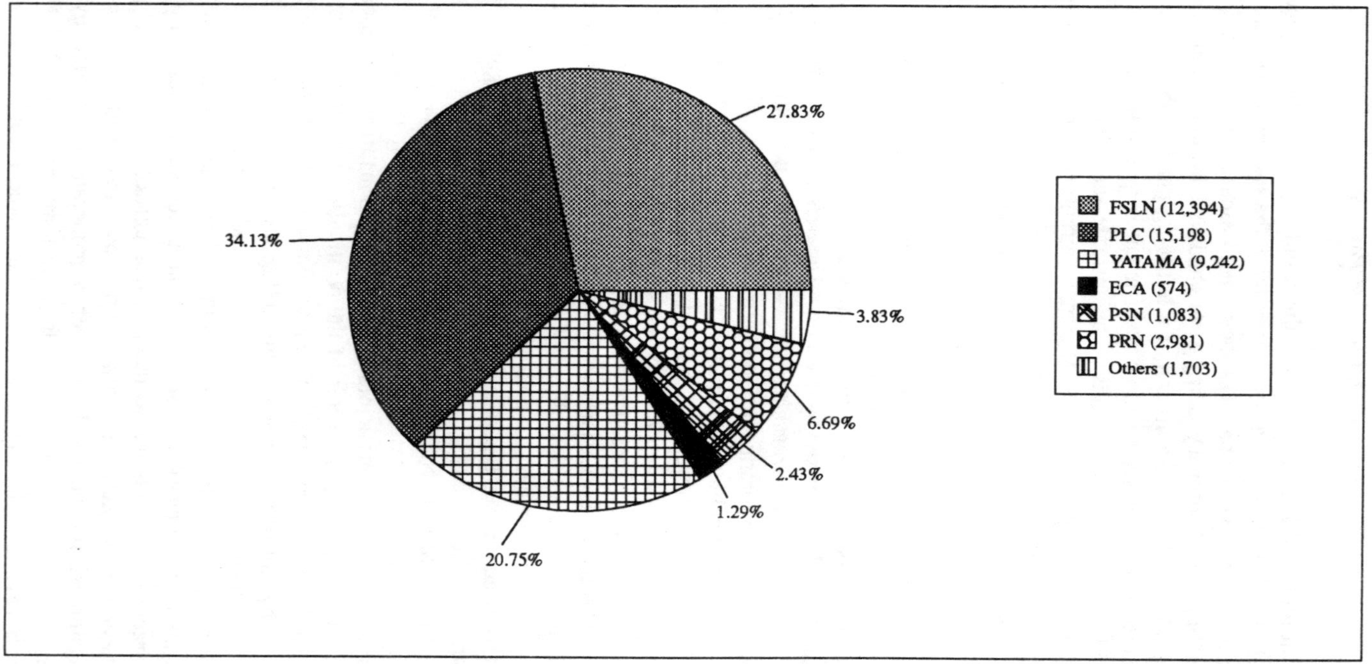

Legend:
- FSLN (12,394)
- PLC (15,198)
- YATAMA (9,242)
- ECA (574)
- PSN (1,083)
- PRN (2,981)
- Others (1,703)

Pie chart values: 34.13%, 27.83%, 20.75%, 6.69%, 3.83%, 2.43%, 1.29%

Figure 2.8
Nicaragua: Results of 1994 Elections for the Southern Atlantic Region

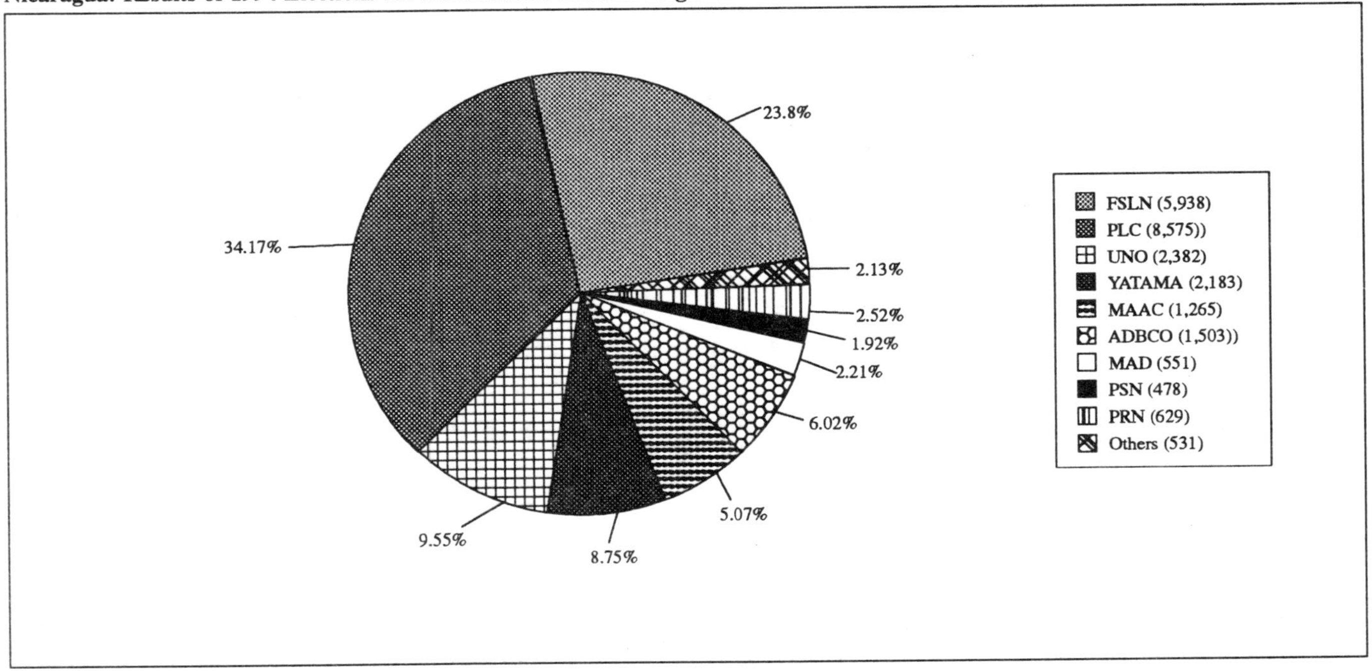

FSLN (5,938)
PLC (8,575)
UNO (2,382)
YATAMA (2,183)
MAAC (1,265)
ADBCO (1,503)
MAD (551)
PSN (478)
PRN (629)
Others (531)

23.8%
2.13%
2.52%
1.92%
2.21%
6.02%
5.07%
8.75%
9.55%
34.17%

entrated power in a highly authoritarian fashion in the hands of an increasingly intransigent and dogmatic elite (led by Daniel Ortega and Tomás Borge). The historical tendency for every political group in Nicaragua to have its own armed force continues today, whether that be the national army, constitutionalist army, National Guard, Sandinista army, contra etc.[8] In addition, the tendency for important political sectors to treat political parties as a means by which to divide up post-electoral spoils also persists. Although the development of sectors favouring negotiation and modernisation of the political system within the UNO, FSLN and the government constitutes a significant political advance, it also reveals the aforementioned embryonic nature of the party system and the slow pace of institutional development.

In Panama, by contrast, the overthrow of General Noriega by armed US invasion in 1989 opened up a process of democratic transition which has permitted not only a significant level of electoral organisation by the parties, but also the rapid recovery of the PRD and its participation, from an early stage, in the contest for parliamentary representation and decision-making power. Thus, according to numerous opinion polls, the PRD has managed to maintain its party profile since the elections held at the start of the 1990s, through the referendum of 15 November 1992 and the elections of 8 May 1994, as have the other parties of the anti-Noriega opposition coalition (which fell apart upon taking power in 1990). In addition, the proliferation of new electoral contenders has been a notable feature: the number of participants in the 1994 elections reached eighteen at one point, although in the end only fourteen took part in the poll. In all these cases, whether based around groups (such as the Solidarity party) or around well-known personalities (for example, the case of the popular singer Rubén Blades), the parties have been devised primarily to meet the legal requirements for registration. This is not to say that the previous political formations were much more than formal affairs; personalism and transitory electoral formations have long been a characteristic of Panamanian politics. One exception to this was the PRD and, to a certain extent, the Christian Democrats, both of whom managed to build a consolidated national structure which went beyond the historical *caudillismo* of a given leader or group of people, although the Christian Democrats are currently in such a state of crisis that they are threatened with political and organisational collapse.[9] In any case, this proliferation of electoral groups of a purely personalistic, sectarian or conjunctural character reached unprecedented levels in the elections of May 1994. This in turn has necessitated the formation of alliances and coalitions, giving the Panamanian political system a unique character, both in terms of the actors which make it up and of the problems of governability which it faces. In addition, it must be remembered that, uniquely within the region, Panama is subject to explicit North American tutelage which reserves the right of direct military intervention at the point when certain relatively ill-defined limits are overstepped by any given actor within the political system.

External Factors

In general terms the international context is highly favourable for democratic development, although not necessarily for that of party systems. The presence within the region of entities promoting the modernisation not only of institutions but also of political parties – such as the Internationals, German foundations, North American bipartisan organisations, sister parties or governmental organisations charged with promoting democratic consolidation – have, irrespective of their ideological orientation, strengthened the organisation of political parties in the region.[10] However, in many cases these efforts suffer from a desire to duplicate models which are rooted in quite distinct socio-political conditions. In addition, they often ignore critical problems related to the acute crisis of political representation in general, and political parties and parliaments in particular, which must be addressed as a matter of urgency. The political impact of the globalisation of news about corruption scandals and the crisis of political systems previously held up as examples, such as Italian Christian Democracy, French Socialism, the Communist leaderships in the ex-Soviet Union and Eastern Europe, or sister parties in Venezuela, Mexico and Brazil, has profoundly and irreversibly undermined old partisan beliefs and traditional political loyalties.

The international context has also influenced the development of other politico-electoral phenomena. Firstly, the negative effect on the electoral prospects of certain candidates or parties who are thought or known to be subject to veto by the international actors who control access to international credit. Examples of this are the FSLN in Nicaragua and the PRD in Panama. Behind the efforts of certain candidates and leaders to distance themselves from the existing party structures – whether this be Ernesto Pérez Balladares, current President of Panama, or Sergio Ramírez Mercado, the leader of the new party Movimiento de Renovación Sandinista, a split from the FSLN – is a political realism which recognises that the sectarian political model of the previous decade is no longer viable. However, also present in the region are nationalist tendencies which reject direct or indirect foreign intromission, are highly critical of the political parties and advance certain policies which do not necessarily favour the democratic process.

There are two other distinctive elements which directly influence the party question. The first has to do with the fact that weak institutionalisation throughout the region and the lack of credibility of existing institutions are opening up spaces for actors previously absent from the electoral sphere, most particularly for the Catholic Church. The latter not only enjoys a high degree of popular credibility and a significant profile in the defence of human rights, but also, in the case of Panama, has assumed a much broader role in electoral politics, oriented towards the conformation of parties which function within a modern, democratic politico-electoral system.[11] The wider significance of this contribution by the Church is inevitably open to interpretation. However, it is a development which undoubtedly opens up a new space for the management of political parties which, nonetheless, must confront their own specific problems.

The second aspect, expanded on below, is that external conditionality, together with the respective national processes of social and political recomposition of power blocks, is tending towards a programmatic homogenisation of the parties and the dilution or even disappearance of their ideological and doctrinal differences. Under the tutelage of international organisations and in the light of sectoral interests linked to trade liberalisation and non-traditional exports, the ideological and programmatic approximation of parties previously identified as Liberal, Social-Christian or Social-Democrat has advanced to the stage that there is now little to differentiate them. Looking at current developments in Honduras, Costa Rica, Panama and Guatemala, it would be fair to say that in practical terms political parties are separated by the struggle for power but – in that they no longer administer certain areas of the economy – are united by the Structural Adjustment Programmes (SAPs) of the World Bank and other international organisations.

These similarities go far beyond the promotion of a market economy and the acceptance of political democracy; rather they constitute a tightly delineated form of common conduct which means the parties echo each other in terms of discourse, what they try to do when in government and what they ultimately manage to achieve. Objectively, this phenomenon has the effect of transforming the traditional parties, characterised until recently by their ideological position or their links with certain social sectors, into an under-developed type of catch-all party, lacking programmes, prepared to make all kinds of offers and to accommodate all sorts of demands (at least during the electoral campaign). By separating campaign promises from policy, and the behaviour of the candidate from that of elected representative, this phenomena aggravates the crisis of credibility affecting all the parties and traditional leaderships in the region, and poses a number of questions for the future of political representation.

The Problem of Political Elites

Evidently, the return of the military to the barracks and the redefinition of their functions and location within the national political system supposes the existence of a civilian political elite with shared language and methods and a minimum level of coherence in their political action, together with party mechanisms capable of acting as political channels for various social demands. The problem is that this civilian political elite, for example in Guatemala, has been almost destroyed by the autocratic regimes and violence which have affected the region. Only recently has an adequate climate for elite reconstitution developed, and the resulting disjuncture has negative consequences for the process of democratic transition. In this respect, it is important not to confuse other power structures – such as economic power structures – with those specifically related to political power. Although it is far from easy, a social actor can shift from one sphere to the other, combining or taking over political and economic power, as did Somoza García in Nicaragua and as it would appear the Honduran military leadership is currently trying to do.[12] A professional political elite is not recruited overnight from the business sector.[13]

In other cases, the closed political system systematically excluded other, subordinated social sectors and forced them to seek participation via armed struggle. The development of this phenomena combined with external factors profoundly divided countries such as Nicaragua and El Salvador and delayed the development of an alternative, nationally acceptable civilian leadership capable of participating constructively in the political system and negotiating with the legitimate representatives of other political forces from within that system without trying to destroy it. In addition, as in the case of El Salvador after 1932, leading social sectors chose to abdicate the direct exercise of political power to the military, who subsequently ended up expropriating it for themselves. As this model ceased to be functional, these elites have had to regain control over government in a politically and socially legitimate fashion while at the same time preventing the rebel forces from gaining political control. The development and political and electoral successes of parties such as ARENA in El Salvador, MAS (Movimiento de Acción Social) and PAN (Partido de Avanzada Nacional) in Guatemala, or figures such as Alfredo

Cristiani, Alvaro Arzú or Rafael Leonardo Callejas can be seen in this light.

In some countries in the region, for example in Honduras, no one actor exercises hegemony within the political system, opening up the space for the armed forces to claim firstly the role of arbiter and latterly permanent political power, substituting their own hegemony for the organic weakness of the other actors in the political system. In this respect the civilian elites must shoulder much of the responsibility; it is they who time and time again have sought military influence for their own advantage. Their condition as actors within the political system has been restricted by the military who, without having to exert much effort, have secured a privileged position within that system largely because of the attitudes prevalent within the civilian sector. This has been reinforced by constitutional arrangements in Honduras which, despite certain pretences and claims to the contrary, afford the armed forces a key role in political and institutional affairs. Article 1 of the Law of the Armed Forces, which defines their competences and functions on the basis of constitutional norms, defines the military as 'an institution of a permanent nature, essentially professional, instituted to defend the territorial integrity and sovereignty of the Republic, *to maintain peace, public order and the dominion of the Constitution, ensuring that the principles of free suffrage and alternation in the office of the Presidency of the Republic are not violated* and with responsibility for the external defence *and internal security* of the nation'.[14]

In other cases, such as Panama, conflicts within the oligarchy have been dictated by external hegemony – an oligarchy which was always externally oriented and closed to other sectors. After the coup of 1968 the social system opened up, even though the political system remained closed. The latter did not begin to follow suit until some ten years later, above all as a result of pressure exerted by international Social Democracy, in an attempt to complement the social opening promoted by *torrijismo* with a political opening. The establishment of a blatantly corrupt and dictatorial regime under General Manuel Antonio Noriega only served to frustrate the entire process of modernisation of the system. This subsequently degenerated into a totally discredited political and party system which generated the conditions for its own liquidation by external military intervention. The overthrow of the Noriega regime by the US invasion was interpreted by some members of the old oligarchy as the best opportunity to attempt a return to the oligarchic system which had preceded Torrijos. They wanted a relatively open political system with periodic elections, but one where social mobility would continue to be tightly circumscribed. In practical terms, this has involved a dual problem: firstly, a delay in the emergence of an alternative national leadership to *torrijismo* without Torrijos able to transcend sectoral and commercial interests and promote national integration; and secondly, chronic delay and weaknesses in the development of the political and institutional mechanisms required to solve the critical problem of nation-formation and nationality. This continues to be one of the main problems afflicting the institutional and political life of Panama. It directly affects the formation of the parties, aggravating their endemic tendency to division and perpetuating their inability to adopt policies which would allow them to overcome their own self-destructive tendencies and establish the normal functioning of the system.

In all these cases it is evident that the withdrawal of the military from the direct exercise of political power and their return to the barracks is a necessary but insufficient condition for democratisation. What is required is, in the first instance, a favourable context for the development of modern political leaderships, today only in the embryonic stage; and secondly, party political mechanisms capable not only of organising electoral participation but also of channelling the social demands of the population into the overall political system. At present the political system itself is in an elementary stage, restricted solely to electoral processes.

Continuity and Change in the Party System

To a certain degree, it is possible to signal the simultaneous existence of rupture and continuity when referring to the political parties and party systems. Some new political formations without clear antecedents in the recent past have recently appeared, whilst other parties with their roots in the distant past have prolonged their existence in the present. In some cases, a change in name has failed to disguise the persistence of political groupings which have exhausted their previous programmes and organisational models. Some of the older parties have kept their original name and undergone substantial modifications, but this has failed to transform them into new politico-electoral entities. Thus both continuity and discontinuity exist; the most relevant factor is the overall political context within which such party formations operate and which gives them their new purpose, function and character.

In effect, apart from those parties which have achieved some degree of permanence and continuity, party formations and political coalitions throughout the region tend to be characterised by their fluid and transitory nature. The constant appearance of new political groups, the formation of alliances and their subsequent disappearance only to be superseded by yet more groups, is part of a process which is only at the most preliminary stage of constituting a real party system. This is not just a question of appearance and disappearance of parties, as signalled by La Palombara and Weiner;[15] it is rather a problem more specific to the character and origins of both party systems and politicians in Central America. The projected and provisional transition to democracy has a direct impact on the definition of party actors. This involves a complex process in which a wide range of social sectors attempt to participate in the redefinition of new spheres of power currently taking place. Many of these parties are little more than transitory groupings through which certain social sectors attempt to guarantee themselves a place at the negotiating table where the key questions are being discussed. These can range from questions relating directly to political affairs, such as the constitutional reform in Nicaragua, to questions more related to economic and trade matters, such as the eventual use and destiny of the returned Canal Zone in Panama once the Torrijos-Carter accords reach completion.

In this respect, both the proliferation of parties and the concentration of the electorate around only a few of them forms part of the contradictory dynamic which characterises the process of formation of a new party system. An additional dimension of this phenomenon is the projection the parties have within the system, or rather the transitory and fluid nature in which parties and coalitions appear and disappear. The system itself is beginning to show the ill effects of the acute instability and lack of definition which characterises its constituent units. However, to affirm that party systems today in Central America involve a plurality of parties of scant ideological differentiation and tend not to permit the formation of definitive and stable hegemonies is merely to describe the phenomena occurring within the region. A more fundamental problem has to do with the very nature of the parties, the functions they carry out and the structures which make them up. In this sense, differences are evident between El Salvador, where the Partido de Conciliación Nacional (PCN), ARENA, the FMLN and the Christian Democrats possess defined structures, albeit distinct in origin and character and certainly not immune from internal crisis and division; and the situation in Nicaragua, where apart from the FSLN (which has divided between a radical and a moderate wing, the latter leaving to form a new party) it is difficult to speak of any real party organisation. In Nicaragua, in addition to the transitory nature and constant division of the parties, new coalitions of a wholly transitory nature have frequently appeared. In Guatemala, party structures are in a state of backwardness. The effect of the disappearance or exclusion of the main political leaders, whether Jorge Serrano Elías of MAS, Jorge Carpio Nicolle of the Unión del Centro Nacional (UCN), or General Ríos Montt and his movement, has been devastating.[16] The decline and near-disappearance of other political formations, such as the Movimiento de Liberación Nacional (MLN) or the Partido Revolucionario (PR) and latterly the ascendance of the PAN of Alvaro Arzú, is testimony to both the continuity and rupture of the party system and to delays in the complex process whereby its constituent units are formed. Honduras, which in formal terms appears to be a competitive system dominated by the traditional parties, suffers not only from the tutelage of the armed forces but also from a significant degree of deterioration within the parties themselves, marked by divisions and split amongst their respective leaderships, which increases popular lack of confidence in the parties and reduces them to mere electoral structures.

In Panama, as noted previously, apart from the *caudillismo* of the disappeared leader Arnulfo Arias Madrid, only the PRD, and to a lesser extent the Christian Democrats – currently in a process of terminal decline – display truly operational organisational structures on a national scale. The proliferation of political parties and the formation of new coalitions, together with the continued survival and alliance of older ones, confirms both the dialectic of rupture and continuity of the party systems and their competitive and pluralistic character. However, in the case of Panama this proliferation has failed to resolve either the problem of the programmatic and ideological features which should define the different parties, or the fact that the main actor with decisive influence on the national political and party dynamic – the US government and, more specifically, its different constituent (and not always harmonious) agencies – is both legally and formally external to the system itself.[17]

Under such conditions, it may be concluded that both the party system and its constituent units are in a process of transition which, although it coincides in general terms with the wider process of democratic transition currently taking place in Central America, has its own characteristics and dynamic. In fact, the party system, with all its limitations and perhaps indeed because of these, maintains a dialectical and highly dynamic relationship with the overall political system. What happens in one sphere directly affects the other; the setbacks and oscillations which arise in the party system and its respective constituent parts have a direct impact on the processes of democratic consolidation.

The Current Crisis of the Political Parties

Despite the embryonic character of the parties and party systems, a number of common characteristics exist which represent an unfavourable combination for the democratic future of the region. These include defects associated with the recent origins of parties and party systems, and distortions characteristic of older party formations and systems. The specificities which characterise the current crisis of these parties and their projection into the corresponding party systems tend to weaken the system as a whole, even bringing into question its very essence, and to delay the process of democratic consolidation. This is the case throughout almost the entire region: in Guatemala, where parties have long existed within an authoritarian and military system of domination and control; in El Salvador, with parties like ARENA and the FMLN (new) or Conciliación Nacional and the Christian Democrats (traditional); in Honduras, with Liberals and Nationalists; in Nicaragua with liberals and conservatives (traditional) or Sandinistas (new); and in Panama, with the PRD, the Arnulfista Party and the Liberal Party in their different guises (traditional) or Papa Egoró and Solidaridad (new). In all these cases the tendency towards division and internal recomposition of parties, alliances and coalitions, together with difficulties and setbacks in the process of defining the parties themselves, marks not only the process of democratisation but also the provisionality characteristic of the current party system, that is if indeed under such conditions it is possible to talk of a system at all.

Some of the characteristics of the Central American party systems can be outlined in descriptive terms.[18] In the first instance, the process of *de-ideologisation* mentioned above: the end of the Cold War, external conditionality promoting structural adjustment programmes, the opening up of the market, promotion of free trade and the restructuring and reduction of the state have set acute limitations on the parties' room for manoeuvre. In consequence the main parties have moved closer together in terms of their programmes, and ideological debates have been indefinitely postponed. This does not refer to the familiar question of the 'end of ideology', nor to the loss of the social or political integrationist function performed by the parties. On the contrary, this process of de-ideologisation reveals another characteristic of the party elites: their *out-of-dateness*. In many cases, in contrast to what one might expect in a period of radical change such as that currently affecting the region and the rest of the world, the return of civilians to power has effectively brought back the old ruling elites previously displaced by authoritarian regimes. These have returned with their old practices and defects and have proved increasingly unable to respond to the rapid changes occurring in the transition. This has not only weakened their authority and their role *vis-à-vis* the military, but also compared to other more dynamic social groups directly linked to the processes of production for export or modernisation of the state and the financial sector.

These features of de-ideologisation and out-of-dateness have become mechanisms for *mimicry* amongst parties and leaderships. This constitutes another characteristic of the regional party phenomena, to the extent that in programmatic, political and ideological terms it makes little difference whether the electorate chooses one or the other sector. The limited room for manoeuvre of each party and their shared political conceptions combine negatively to generate a pragmatic opportunism which characterises leaderships and parties. As there exists little electoral choice, the voters tend either not to choose, that is to abstain (as in the case of Guatemala and Nicaragua); to make an improvised choice of a new arrival on the electoral scene, as occurred in Panama with Rubén Blades and previously in Guatemala with Jorge Serrano; or to give themselves over to authoritarian nostalgia, as tends to be the case in Guatemala with General Efraín Ríos Montt.

Under these conditions the control of the electoral mechanisms which allow one or other sector of the leadership to capture the presidential nomination becomes the central issue for those party formations most relevant to the system. This objective reflects another common characteristic of the parties in the region: *party infighting*. This refers to a focusing on internal party disputes in order to remove adversaries who attempt to take control of the party or to capture the main nominations. At its most acute, this accelerated infighting implies the political annihilation of one's adversary. Infighting gives rise to two highly significant consequences: firstly, the phenomena which could be referred to as *'political cannibalism'*, whereby structures and leaderships within each political party or movement are irreconcilably opposed. Eventually this may imply the disappearance of leaderships, the frustration of potential new elites, or the division of the party and the emergence of new proto-parties. This would be the case of the Honduran parties, the FMLN in El Salvador, and the UNO or the FSLN in Nicaragua. The second negative consequence of this party infighting is the *chronic loss of social permeability*, which prevents the parties from meeting, interpreting and channelling the most important social and political demands of the population. The divorce between leaderships and parties caught up in internecine struggles on the one hand and the demands of the mass of the population on the other is becoming increasingly acute and means that the parties are failing to fulfil their functions in a democratic system.

Limited by an unavoidable external conditionality; de-ideologised and out of date in a world of rapid change; bogged down in insoluble internecine battles and divorced from the fundamental concerns of the citizenry, the parties and their leaderships tend to concentrate their attention on the opportunist takeover of certain key institutions which they try to use for their own interests or those of certain clientelist constituencies. Such an approach, together with other diverse phenomena such as influence-peddling and particularly the deals which tend to accompany privatisation programmes, feeds the generalised phenomenon of political corruption.[19] This in turn has become another characteristic of the party system throughout the isthmus, added to the separation between campaign promises, the real intentions of the government and the record of the administrations. This is symbolically and most evidently represented by the huge gulf between the figure of the candidate and his or her behaviour once elected, be that as mayor, congressional representative or President.

Inevitably, this set of factors has had a direct effect on the entire system, producing a notorious separation between the parties and their leaderships, and between government and electorate. Each of these components has its own disintegrative logic which in turn prevents the consolidation of the system. Governments have tended to separate themselves from their parties in order to implement their non-declared policy programme in accordance with the demands and conditionalities facing them. The parties, in turn, resent this abandonment and try to distance themselves from those actions of the administration which are perceived as clearly unpopular and electorally damaging. Leadership corruption results in political scandals which permit internal feuding and demand that one faction distances itself from another, in this manner constituting a negative dynamic which tends to weaken traditional mechanisms of political representation.

This is clearly demonstrated in Figure 2.9, which illustrates the degree of popular satisfaction with political parties in Central America and Panama. The highest levels of approval, in Costa Rica and Honduras, do not exceed 25 per cent. In the case of Honduras it should be noted, in addition, that in the last presidential elections of November 1994 levels of abstentionism reached 35.03 per cent of registered voters and serious doubts were raised regarding the accuracy of the electoral register. According to calculations provided by Leticia Salamón based on the official electoral results, in 1985 abstentionism was of the order of 19.0 per cent; in 1989 this had grown to 25.9 per cent and by 1993 had reached

37.4 per cent, significantly larger than the 33.2 per cent and 29.4 per cent of the vote received by the winning and losing parties, respectively.[20] In any case, these figures should be viewed within the wider context where, according to regional opinion polls, political parties and parliaments throughout the region – including Costa Rica – score lowest in terms of citizen confidence in institutions. The first place is occupied by the Catholic Church.

Figure 2.9
Central America and Panama: Satisfaction with Political Parties

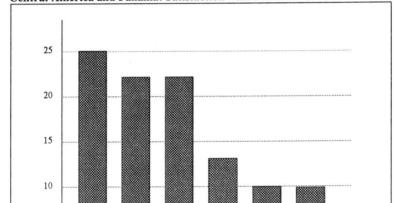

Source: UNIMER/IIDH, Encuesta de Opinión, Octubre-Noviembre 1993.

This phenomenon becomes even more complicated to the extent that new actors with decision-making power emerge within the system, marginalising others who, according to constitutional and legal norms, should perform these functions. The emergence of economic *czars*, either through the Central Banks, treasury or foreign trade ministries for example, centralises decision-making over key areas of economic policy, over which the parliaments end up having little or no say. In addition, discussion and negotiations regarding certain subjects over which parliament and the legislative branch should have a central decision-making role have been transferred to other fora, reducing the political relevance of the former within state structures. One can refer here to negotiations regarding economic restructuring, tariff reductions, the value of the currency, policies towards regional integration or towards the global market, in the field of economic policy; state restructuring, the decision to abandon certain functions of government and public service provision, and programmes for labour mobilisation, in the area of social policy; or the development of negotiations to sign peace accords and open up the party system to rebel groups, to mention specifically political subjects. All these examples signal the absence of significant participation by parliament, parliamentarians and political parties in the process of discussion, decision-making and solution of these questions.

Popular rejection of the perceived climate of generalised corruption combines with the inefficiency and dysfunctionality of the parties and congressional deputies, the lack of clout of parliamentary decision-making, and the strictly instrumental and electoral character of party formations in the hands of leaders who – ultimately – behave in an almost identical fashion. Therefore the majority of the population opts for the various alternative forms of political behaviour mentioned above: either abstention-ism, on the increase in Guatemala, Honduras and Nicaragua; or the search for new figures on the political scene or those who have deserted their own party structures and who appear to represent a viable protest against the system (the cases of Blades in Panama and, to a certain extent, Serrano Elías and also De León Carpio in Guatemala).[21] Certain tendencies have also emerged which hanker after a return to authoritarian government, hoping to overcome the inefficiency, corruption and sectarian interests which are presumed to characterise the behaviour of the political elites and their parties.[22] Under such conditions, when a political unknown can transform the established system, or where such figures could eventually set in motion an authoritarianism enjoying widespread electoral support, it is obvious that the region's party systems are of a highly precarious and qualified nature. Such fragility is linked not only to the weaknesses of the parties themselves but also to aspects of the overall political environment which condition their behaviour.

Institutional Spaces, Parties and Electoral Institutions

The development of political parties and corresponding party systems requires a series of institutional and legal factors which legitimise not only their formal existence, but also their effective participation in the country's electoral and political process. The legalisation, for example, of the FMLN in El Salvador or the National Resistance (RN-Contra) in Nicaragua, lacks any real significance if not accompanied by a series of guarantees for the eventual composition, development and effective functioning of the new parties, together with the concession of institutional and political spaces where they can participate in decision-making and the administration of public affairs.

In a similar sense, the organisation of the electoral process, with the corresponding drawing up of the electoral list, regulation and oversight of the electoral process and the transparency of the institutions charged with electoral administration – both during the campaign and during the ballot and final count – are vital factors in any consideration of the party system. From this perspective, the organic weakness of the electoral institutions has a direct effect on the behaviour of the political parties. The exclusion or inclusion of voters – related to the electoral conditionality which the Electoral Tribunals can set according to ephemeral political interests – and the subordination of electoral bodies to political parties, governments or the armed forces which weakens impartial administration of the process, both tend to strengthen perceptions which significantly impede the consolidation of the party system. A generalised lack of confidence in both electoral processes and in the institutions charged with overseeing the transparency of the vote is perceptible throughout the region.

Therefore, parallel to the process of formation of a new party system is the question of the adequate institutional development required for electoral and party-political tasks to be carried out. This involves the solution of the logistical and technical problems of organising efficient, transparent and legitimate electoral processes (in terms of both human and material resources). In addition, the electoral institution has to convince the parties and the electorate that it has both the institutional capacity and the impartiality necessary to administer the electoral process. This is not a minor detail: the development of political parties is in many cases linked to the extension of the vote and one of the mechanisms for structuring this has been the formation of local electoral committees. In regional terms, this phenomenon tends to be linked in one way or another to the problem of construction of citizenship. In this sense, the political parties perform a dual function: to integrate important sectors of the population to the social processes of economic transformation currently affecting these societies, and to draw into the political system diverse sectors which until recently were completely excluded. However, in both these areas the electoral institutions are acutely deficient. Technical and professional development is insufficient to facilitate adequate administration of electoral processes and the institutions responsible for such administration lack credibility. One has only to note the demands made for correction of the electoral registers in Honduras and El Salvador and compare the levels of popular confidence in the region's electoral tribunals. Although it is the case that they have succeeded to a certain extent in improving their image, particularly in the case of the Panamanian Electoral Tribunal, and to a lesser extent those of Nicaragua and Guatemala, the situation is far from consolidated or stable.

Figure 2.10
Central America and Panama: Satisfaction with Supreme Electoral Tribunals

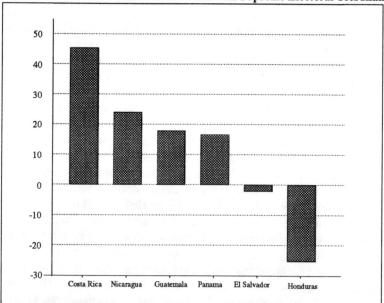

Source: UNIMER/IIDH, Encuesta de Opinión, Octubre-Noviembre 1993.

This is clearly demonstrated in Figure 2.10, which shows levels of popular satisfaction with the functioning of Electoral Tribunals throughout the region. Except in the case of Costa Rica, this is very low, although the Electoral Tribunals scored higher than other highly controversial or discredited institutions. In the case of the Panamanian Electoral Tribunal, the last election was particularly important and in a relatively short space of time the prestige of the Tribunal and popular confidence in the institution (now among the highest in the region) experienced a marked improvement. This demonstrates not only the need for but also the possibilities of democratic institutional development in the electoral arena, despite the well-known negative precedents throughout the region, of authoritarianism and rigged elections.

The tendency to form Electoral Tribunals from party representatives, as in the cases of El Salvador and Honduras, has been a negative factor which has tended greatly to weaken their prestige and credibility. There are also a number of additional problems which affect the very nature of the democratic process, such as those related to the exclusion of ethnic groups, via diverse forms of discrimination and literacy requirements. However, in another sense, all of this is evidence that institution-building and the fulfilment by the political parties of the functions of integration, socialisation and mobilisation are inextricably linked, each directly affecting the other. Together in turn they influence the strengthening or weakening of the political system overall. The opening up of spaces not only for the proselytising activities of the parties but also to facilitate their effective intervention in the centres of political power constitutes, then, a defining element of the character, structure and functioning of the political parties.

In historical terms, the holding of elections has been a consistent feature of authoritarian regimes in Central America. This phenomenon – represented by so-called *zancudismo* in Nicaragua, by military parties like Conciliación Nacional in El Salvador, and by the violent and repressive exercise of power in Guatemala – were usually accompanied by the holding of elections in which opponents of the preexisting structures of power were able to participate, while at the same time lacking any real political and institutional space. In this sense, the question raised by Héctor Rosada Granados for the case of Guatemala becomes increasingly relevant – perhaps what existed were 'parties within a system' rather than a system of parties as such.[23] Although it is impossible to generalise to this extent for the whole region, it is certainly true that over-optimism should not obscure the embryonic nature of Central America's parties and party systems.

Although the progressive changes of the recent period represent a positive improvement on the previous system within which the parties lacked an effective role, they have not achieved the consolidation either of a party system or of an adequate legal and institutional framework to regulate electoral conduct, such as is required for democratic consolidation. Certainly the advances which have been made are both broad and significant. However, it should be recognised that these are still the early stages and that changes are required in the long term, with regard both to the parties themselves and to the overall political system. In terms of the latter, the development of institutions and a democratic political culture are other essential elements. If these changes fail to materialise, Central America could be moving towards not so much a representative democracy – for which the adequate foundations will be lacking – but rather towards what Guillermo O'Donnell has referred to as a 'delegative democratic space'.[24]

The Origins and the Nature of the Parties

Apart from their pluralistic, competitive and relatively non-hegemonic character, political parties and party systems in Central America are directly affected by their different origins. Some of them have their origins not only outside the existing political system, but also one of their main ideological and programmatic planks was precisely their anti-systemic nature. This is the case for the Communist parties, the FSLN in Nicaragua, the FMLN in El Salvador, or the recently created Partido de Unificación Democrática (PUD) in Honduras. In each of these cases, the process of integration to the new system has been slow and complex. This is partly because of the difficulties faced by guerrillas and subversive movements when they try to become political parties capable of participating in elections, but also because of the need for other actors within the system to afford recognition to these new parties and cede the political and institutional spaces necessary for their representatives and nominees to act effectively.

In other cases, the origins of the parties are directly linked to the military, who used them as a means to legitimise their controlling role in government. Many variants of this pattern exist: while in Guatemala the military relied indiscriminately on a number of parties, in El Salvador this function was performed primarily by the PCN. In Panama, by way of contrast, the military government of General Torrijos was the point of departure for the creation of the PRD and the subsequent attempt to open up the political system to multi-party competition. In Nicaragua, General Somoza García used all the mechanisms at his disposal to control political power: apart from the National Guard, which he manipulated at whim, Somoza controlled the so-called Liberal party, stitched up various deals with the Conservative Party, and promoted the aforementioned *zancudismo*. In Honduras, in contrast to the other countries, the military have historically functioned independently of the parties, acting as arbiter in some cases and as supreme decision-maker in others. Here the Liberal and National parties originate within a system of which they have been an enduring feature since the beginning of this century. Something similar occurred in the case of Panama, with the various liberal parties and the *panameñista* party of ex-President Arnulfo Arias, today divided after the death of its historic leader. Some of the Guatemalan parties formed within the system also demonstrate a notable continuity, for example the Movimiento de Liberación Nacional or the Partido Revolucionario.

The nature of the Christian Democrat parties which held power in Guatemala and El Salvador and which – through one of the vice-Presidents – formed part of the government set up after the overthrow of General Noriega in Panama tended to be determined by the ideological definition of these movements, in turn restricting the social classes towards whom they were able to direct their message. In the case of El Salvador, the historic role of the Partido Demócrata-Cristiano (PDC) was, within a very short space of time, overtaken by national political events. The party now appears to have been displaced by other actors and to have entered a period of terminal decline. In Guatemala, the Christian Democrats raised high expectations but were seriously weakened not only by their inability to confront and resolve the main problems affecting Guatemalan society, but also by the serious and widespread accusations of corruption which were made against the administration of Vinicio Cerezo (1986-1990). In Panama, the Christian Democrats ended up in dispute with their own allies, marginalised from power and preaching to a dwindling percentage of the population. At the same time, the spectre of party division has become a reality in the cases of both El Salvador and Panama. In general, the Christian Democrat movements have tended to become increasingly conservative, accepting the ideological theses of neo-liberalism which, ultimately, have deprived them of both a political profile and electoral significance.

A second tendency of party development is linked to a complex process, mentioned above, whereby the Central American oligarchy have recovered political power in the face of the failure of the military and other political parties. When referring to this tendency, it is particularly important to bear in mind national specificities and great care should be taken when making generalisations. In some cases the phenomenon is very evident and, despite conflicts and setbacks, appears to be developing in a clearly defined manner; in others, this tendency is somewhat less than certain. Thus, the recovery of power by a civilian business sector which has decided to take part in national political life is particularly evident in the case in El Salvador, where the armed conflict exhausted the political possibilities both of the PCN and the Christian Democrats, and also demonstrated the dangers and limitations of complete control by the military. The formation of the ARENA party, initially an extremist reaction against the revolutionary process but later transformed into a party which brought together a diverse range of groups of the Salvadorean dominant class, was an important watershed to the extent that it represented a recovery of political power by a civilian sector from the military. It also implied the emergence of a modernising business sector which judged itself capable of achieving political control of state and society via the mechanisms of the free market and free electoral competition. This phenomenon could also be occurring in the case of Guatemala, with the PAN, and in the case of Honduras through the figure of ex-President Rafael Leonardo Callejas. The breadth and socio-political significance of this process is obviously subject to interpretation and debate. Much depends on the extent to which such developments involve an overall revision of civil-military relations in Central America and are directly linked to the evolution of the respective party systems and parties.

Conclusions

The development of political parties in Central America demonstrates particularities specific to a process of transition to democracy which involves instability, impermanence and change. A combination of old and new parties of diverse origins and political and social orientations currently exists. There are those which survived the rapid changes which have occurred in the region (the Liberal and National parties in Honduras; Liberal Constitucionalista and Conservative in Nicaragua; and, to a lesser extent, the various liberal parties in Panama and the MLN and PR in Guatemala). Then there are those which have developed out of the revolutionary struggle of the last decades (the FSLN in Nicaragua; the FMLN in El Salvador; various groups in Honduras), or from modernising processes which have occurred since the 1960s (as is the case of the PRD in Panama and the Christian Democrat parties in Guatemala and El Salvador).

The rupture of traditional political systems by means of both violence and negotiation, together with the subsequent readjustments of the various political and social forces in each country, has affected political parties and systems throughout the region. In addition, the current generalised crisis of the parties and their leaderships has facilitated a proliferation of parties and proto-parties of a highly dissimilar nature. The resulting phenomenon is a complex one: the crisis of the parties continues unabated, new parties have been unable to consolidate themselves, political unknowns sometimes achieve electoral victory, and older parties maintain a significant chunk of their former electoral support whilst failing to resolve their crises of credibility. This phenomenon has been accompanied by a widespread decline in the credibility of institutions including parliament, the judiciary and other organs of state, together with the parties and their leaderships. The deficiencies of which the parties stand accused are not merely technical or administrative, but rather political and ethical problems of credibility and respect.

Processes of de-ideologisation and mimicry between the parties and their leaderships aggravate the crisis, making the parties almost identical in their political campaigns and with little to distinguish them once they are in government. The institutional opportunism which subordinates public interest to the sectarian interests of the parties and their leaders, and the generalised corruption which has tended to characterise a wide range of administrations, is combined with the lack of social permeability of the parties and their leaderships with respect to the needs and demands of the population.

All these factors tend to widen the gulf between masses, parties, government and leadership. The phenomenon of inter-party cannibalism, which begins in the pre-electoral stage with accusations made against co-aspirants for the presidential nomination and continues and worsens throughout the electoral campaign when all manners of accusations and charges are made against the opponent, has the end result of destroying the prestige of all political leaders. In addition to the above, the gap between campaign promises and government policy, between the behaviour of the candidate and that of the elected representative, has combined with a generalised frustration amongst the population about a transition to democracy which it was hoped would bring improvements and which instead has been accompanied by drastic programmes of economic adjustment and state cut-backs, with the consequential worsening of services, labour mobility and high levels of unemployment and delin-quency. This indicates the reasons for and scale of what I have referred to as the 'democratic disenchantment' of the Central American transition. All these factors constitute a negative overall context which affects not only the parties, their functions and political significance, but also the very process of democratic transition.

The party systems, in turn, demonstrate the ill effects of the weak-nesses and insufficiencies of their constituent units. It is true that the diverse systems and subsystems all affect each other, and not only in a negative sense. However, this inter-connection might lead one to suppose that, within a complex and contradictory process of incomplete transition to democracy, the efforts of the main actors in the political system might respond to a coherent strategy of institutional and political development. However, in many cases, such a strategy appears to be more evident amongst the military than amongst the civilian elites themselves, making the process of transition and democratic consolidation even more difficult. The question of civil-military relations therefore assumes a particular importance for the transition to democracy and for the future of the party formations and their respective systems, and requires a realistic and imaginative approach which takes into account the particularities of national and regional development.

Finally, two kinds of limitations which appear to affect the Central American context should be noted. Firstly, despite the geographical smallness of the region and certain similarities between the respective countries within it, a series of national specificities continue to exist which cannot be underestimated or overlooked. On the contrary, it is only on the basis of these that generalisations can be made and an overall strategy for cooperation and development devised. This *caveat* also applies when analysing the significant influence of the international context on the political life of Central America. Local conditions either advance or block external initiatives and pressures advanced in the name of democracy, the free market, human rights and the environment. The failure to take into consideration the substantial differences in systems, political cultures and historical legacies of countries as different as Nicaragua, Guatemala, El Salvador and Honduras, and to an even greater extent Panama, could mean that well-intentioned initiatives will either fail or have negative consequences.

The transition to democracy and the consolidation of a democratic and open party system in each of the countries forms part of a transformation which is wider and more far-reaching than many analysts are prepared to admit. A process of readjustment has taken place not only within the traditional dominant groups, but also within the dominated classes, their organisations and representatives. This phenomenon also extends to the military establishment, which – independent of its previous ideological tendencies – has tended instinctively to seek its own protection, through the creation and development of the Institutes for Military Provision (IPMs), which have moved into the private sector, generating domestic and foreign alliances which are not yet clearly defined and which signal dangers for democratic and party systems.

Some questions are thus raised which could affect the democratic development of the region and relocate transitions and party organisations within a new socio-political context. Does the prospect exist of hegemonic military parties, or will the armed forces opt to guarantee their interests through the existing civilian leaderships? Will the existing parties manage to overcome their current crisis and widespread lack of prestige while avoiding authoritarian temptations? Or will they resort to anti-party reactions and a new type of *caudillista* experiment around the figure of the political maverick or unknown? (this seems to be an embryonic tendency throughout the region). Will a new generation of party leaders able to incorporate modernising, democratic sectors and more capable of achieving a viable and efficient governing consensus emerge? Or will the system be unable to avoid political rupture as a consequence of the failure of its constituent units to renew themselves?

Finally, it is pertinent to note that both the formation and the functioning of the parties and their respective systems, and indeed of the democratic order itself, are closely related to adequate and efficient institution-building. In the absence of this, the process cannot develop further than the initial stages. But this complex process, in all its different aspects and stages, also presupposes and demands prolonged, substantive and coherent efforts to resolve the difficult problem of the formation and development of a democratic political culture, in contrast to the traditional, authoritarian political culture which has characterised the majority of Central American political systems since the Colonial and post-Independence period. All these tasks currently form the nucleus of the current political and party debate in the Central American region and Panama.

Notes

1. The methodology employed here combines observation of the electoral processes which have taken place throughout the isthmus, interviews with the leaderships of the most significant political organisations in each country, together with public opinion surveys and analyses linked, above all, to the problem of institution-building of electoral tribunals throughout the region. In this respect, the author acknowledges the contribution of the Inter-American Institute of Human Rights and its Electoral Evaluation and Promotion Programme (IIDH/CAPEL). The opinions contained here are the sole responsibility of the author.

2. For example, Woodward (1976). A somewhat more nuanced approach is adopted by Alain Rouquié (ed.) in his introduction to *Les Forces Politiques en Amérique Centrale* (Rouquié, 1991).

3. Edelberto Torres Rivas, referring to Central America, talks about bourgeois or liberal democracy in the case of Costa Rica; 'supervised democracy' (*'democracia vigilada'*) in the case of Guatemala, El Salvador and Honduras; and 'difficult democracy' in the case of Nicaragua. He does not include Panama although this could correctly have been characterised as a 'controlled democracy' (Torres Rivas, 1994), p. 27.

4. A number of different opinions exist regarding the Guatemalan transition: for Marta Elena Casáus Arzú the process of 'political transition was carried out by one of the organic intellectuals, Fernando Andrade Díaz Durán, who – given his relations with the main fractions of the national and regional oligarchy, his good relations with a sector of the military and the support of certain US lobbyists – was able to begin the restructuring of the dominant class and, in 1984, promote the holding of elections for a Constituent Assembly and, a year later, general elections'; see Casáus Arzú (1992), pp. 60-61. It is probable that the role of Fernando Andrade was of great social and political importance. However, the critical decision was that taken by the armed forces to adopt a new doctrine which, substituting that of national security, oriented the process to facilitate a return of civilians to government under the strict supervision of the military. In this light, the electoral fate of Andrade Díaz Durán should come as no suprise; Casáus Arzú describes it in the following terms: 'The discredited nature of the political parties and his lack of a team or social base of support eventually obliged him to withdraw his bid for the presidential nomination', *ibid.* footnote 27, p. 61. Surely this is evidence that his role and influence, above all within the army, has been overestimated.

5. This refers to the Partido de Unificación Democrática (PUD). Four groups came together to form the PUD: the Partido de Renovación Patriótica (PRP), which was an alliance of former pro-Moscow communists, with its origins in the Honduran Communist Party (PCH); the Partido Morazanista de Liberación de Honduras (PMLH), formed out of the old Frente Morazanista de Liberación Nacional, linked to Cuba and Libya; the Partido Revolucionario Hondureño (PRH), a small Social Democratic grouping which had remained in clandestinity since the 1960s; and the Partido para la Transformación de Honduras (PTH), formerly the pro-Beijing Marxist-Leninist Communist Party of Honduras. The inscription of the new party isolates the two left wing terrorist groups formed in the 1980s who still reject participation in the formal political sphere. The oldest of these groups is the Movimiento Popular de Liberación 'Cinchonero' (MPL); formed in 1980, the MPL existed until 1986 as a unified organisation, but following the failure of a project to create guerrilla training camps in the Nombre de Dios mountain range in the north of the country, it split into two factions, one political and the other military. The latter continues to exist today, carrying out isolated terrorist and criminal acts in the areas of Tegucigalpa and San Pedro Sula. The other armed group, which also concentrates its few cadres in the capital and San Pedro Sula, is the Frente Patriótico Morazanista (FPM), set up in 1988 by dissidents from the PCH.

6. Even the former Resistencia Nicaraguense (RN-Contra) has registered as a political party under the terms of the 7 May 1993 accord of the Council of Political Parties; *La Nación*, San José, 8 May 1993.

7. *Recompas* refers to those soldiers of the Ejército Popular Sandinista demobilised after 1990 who subsequently took up arms; *revueltos* refers to armed groups comprised of both *recompas* and contras – former enemies who subsequently joined forces in pursuit of their collective demands.

8. However, the approval of the new Military Code by the Nicaraguan legislature in August 1994 and the subsequent decision by EPS (Ejército Popular Sandinista) Commander in Chief General Humberto Ortega to accede to President Chamorro's demands and stand down from his post contributed signficantly to the depoliticisation of the EPS.

9. It should be noted, however, that in May 1994 President-elect Pérez Balladares appointed former Christian Democrat Guillermo Chapman to his cabinet as Minister of the Economy; Christian Democrat José Antonio Sosa as Attorney General and asked José Chen Barria, also a Christian Democrat, to continue in his post as Comptroller General.

10. The Socialist International (IS), an international alliance of Social Democratic parties and others of a sympathetic persuasion, has been particularly active in Central America, as have German policy and research foundations such as the Friedrich Ebert and Friedrich Naumann Foundations, allied respectively with the German Social Democrat and Christian Democrat parties.

11. The inter-party agreement signed by all the Panamanian political parties in Santa María la Antigua not only established a Code of Ethics to regulate behaviour in the electoral campaign, but also designated the Church as the guarantor of the Code.

12. General Somoza García ruled Nicaragua between 1933 and 1956, establishing the economic power of the Somoza dynasty which ruled Nicaragua until 1979.

13. The example of Fernando Andrade in Guatemala mentioned by Marta Elena Casáus perhaps demonstrates something of this phenomena; see also Daalder (1990), p. 78.

14. *La Gaceta* (Tegucigalpa), 25 February 1975 [Editor's translation]. The italics (mine) indicate the political functions of the army and its role as the final arbiter of the Honduran political system. One commentator has noted, 'the two traditional parties, Liberal and National, compete for military favour...Of particular significance was the visit made in April 1991 by a group of Liberals led by the President of the Executive Council of the Liberal Party to the Head of the Armed Forces, General Luis Alonso Discua Elvir to '*discuss the problems of the country and the convenience of preserving social order*' and to request that he '*contribute to the timely conclusion of the rules concerning the forthcoming elections*' (*El Heraldo*, 19 April 1991); Salamón (1994a), pp. 71–7 (italics in original).

15. Joseph La Palombara and Myron Weiner state 'The creation of parties has been a continuous process. The historical graveyards are cluttered with parties which dominated the political scene but which subsequently failed to adapt to new

circumstances and therefore died, were absorbed by new more active movements, or withered into small marginal parties', cited in Daalder (1990), p. 25.

16. General Ríos Montt's *de facto* regime lasted from 1982 to 1983, during which time some of the worst highland massacres perpetrated by the army occurred in Guatemala's counter-insurgency war. The terms of the 1985 Constitution barred Ríos Montt from running for the Presidency in the 1990 elections (those who had previously occupied the Presidency by means of a *coup d'état* were prohibited from standing). At the time of writing, Ríos Montt was contesting the constitutional ban in the hope of competing for the Presidency in the 1995 elections.

17. These agencies include the local US Embassy, AID (Agency for International Development), the DEA (Drugs Enforcement Agency), the Pentagon and Southern Command in Panama, and the US Congress.

18. I have referred to these characteristics of the regional party crisis elsewhere (Cerdas, 1993, p. 157).

19. Recent accusations and counter-accusations of corruption made against ex-President Serrano Elías, the previous Congress and the Supreme Court of Justice in Guatemala; against the government of President Calderón Sol and his ARENA party in El Salvador (1994-); and against members of the current Liberal Party Honduran government of Carlos Roberto Reina (1994-), indicate that the phenomenon of corruption is not only a characteristic of the political situation in the isthmus, but also a corollary of the problem of narco-trafficking and the revenue this generates. The effect of these on politics and parties tends to be catastrophic.

20. Salamón (1994a), p. 141.

21. Ramíro de León Carpio, the former Human Rights Ombudsman, was catapulted to the Guatemalan Presidency in June 1994 when he was selected by congress to replace President Serrano Elías after the latter attempted to dismiss congress, the members of the Supreme Court and the Constitutional Court.

22. The case of General Ríos Montt in Guatemala has been mentioned above. One might also add that of General Díaz Herrera in Panama who so unnerved the government of President Endara and, to a certain extent, the case of Daniel and Humberto Ortega in Nicaragua.

23. Héctor Rosada Granados (1986), pp. 85-6.

24. O'Donnell (1994), p. 134.

CHAPTER 3

THE MILITARY: THE CHALLENGE OF TRANSITION

James Dunkerley and Rachel Sieder

The armed forces of Central America have been important and often decisive political actors over the last fifteen years. In three cases – El Salvador, Guatemala and Nicaragua – this importance derives immediately from the waging of civil war, where operational considerations came to determine much of public policy. However, in all the countries the military were influential in politics before the generalisation of the conflict in the mid-1970s. In Guatemala this dominance has a particularly long history and appears to transcend alterations in the ideological landscape at home and abroad. In other cases, such as Panama and Honduras, the influence of the soldiery emerged much later and proved to be ideologically more malleable, albeit highly resilient in strictly institutional terms. Nicaragua has manifested a persistent strain of partisan armies (Liberal and Constitutionalist until the 1920s; Guardia Nacional (GN) and Sandino's nationalist guerrillas; Ejército Popular Sandinista and the contras), each linked more or less directly to an ideological current since the 1850s. In the case of El Salvador, a most energetic and confident civilian political elite was displaced from administration of the central state by officers in the 1930s, and when they returned thanks to US pressure fifty years later even the most reactionary elements remained prey to the military lobby, which retained important powers of veto.

Whilst open military dictatorships of a type frequently encountered in South America were to be found in the isthmus before the wars of the 1980s, such regimes were not common outside of Honduras or Panama, where harsh repression was not visited upon the popular sectors. Instead, the pattern was of armies either establishing their own 'front parties' (Partido Institucional Democrático (PID) in Guatemala; Partido de Conciliación Nacional (PCN) in El Salvador; to some degree Partido Revolucionario Democrático (PRD) in Panama) or engaging in variable civilian alliances (Partido Nacional (PN) in Honduras; Movimiento de Liberación Nacional (MLN) in Guatemala) or providing the coercive wing of a more integrated/corporatist political system, as in the case of Nicaragua under both the Somozas (GN) and the Frente Sandinista de

Liberación Nacional (FSLN) (Ejército Popular Sandinista – EPS). It is worthy of note that during the 1980s, when military operations extended throughout the isthmus and fierce fighting took place in three of its states, it was only in Guatemala that open military dictatorship prevailed for any length of time (Ríos Montt and Mejía Victores, 1982-85).

This fact is frequently interpreted as a reflection of US influence – which is assuredly the case – but it should also be seen as reflecting a longer-term local pattern of 'mixed regime' in which the division of coercive, ideological and administrative labour differs not only from the classic prescriptions of liberal democracy, but also from the experience of the rest of Latin America (with some partial exceptions in the cases of Mexico and Paraguay). Such a local pattern prior to the 1980s might be explained by a combination of small military establishments – no army over 15,000 strong, no significant navy or (outside Honduras) air-force; the relatively narrow set of managerial controls required for plantation-based societies; the extreme difficulty of securing institutional anonymity (and even caste-like differentiation) in small nation-states. One important consequence of such a pattern – especially after the formidable expansion of the military in the 1980s – has been the renegotiation of the precise parameters of institutional responsibilities, it often requiring major conflict to achieve what appear from the outside to be distinctly minor alterations. However, because the exercise of the military *fuero* has generally been most decisive at the margins we will here address these matters of detail at greater length than some might consider justifiable. Equally, whilst the military may be monolithic in both its self-image and the eyes of its (many) victims and critics, one has to recognise the organisational (and sometimes ideological) stress caused in recent years which is conducive to internal differentiation.

During the 1980s the combination of severe social conflict, increased US influence and correspondingly enhanced international attention served either completely to destroy or to alter the internal balance of the region's regimes. This process, which effectively began in 1978 with the FSLN offensive in Nicaragua and a marked upturn in violence in El Salvador and Guatemala, sharpened recognition of the importance of regional strategy within Central American armies. However, neither Somoza's tardy pleas nor Washington's rather disorganised efforts to revive the regional defence system (CONDECA), which lacked a real operational core, served to produce a significant shift towards centralised military coordination. Such collaboration as was identifiable related to intelligence matters and *ad hoc* operations in border areas, such as the infamous Río Sumpul massacre of 1980 involving Salvadorean and Honduran troops. The cool relations between the Salvadoreans and Hondurans caused by the 1969 war were, though, never properly repaired by the 1980 treaty over the frontier; those between Honduras and Nicaragua lacked an historic or cultural animosity to complement ideological antagonism; right-wing Guatemalan nationalism overlapped sufficiently with radical *Sandinismo* to complicate support for Washington against the FSLN, whilst the Guatemalan officers were able to keep their distance from the noisily US-dominated operations in El Salvador, where most of the fighting was away from their shared border.

Although events since 1987 have made public much material and information on the armed forces, a great deal of military activity still has to be analysed outside normal scholarly procedures. This state of affairs naturally increases the premium on anecdotal and impressionistic sources as well as rooted assumptions/prejudices for which no countervailing evidence yet presents itself. As a result, this chapter echoes much civilian material on the military in addition to courting the risks of speculating about contemporary events at a time of change. There is, however, a very strong case for attempting to assess the specifically institutional features of civil-military relations in a period of political change, when short-term arrangements and matters of detail acquire enhanced importance. It is both for this reason and because it is still too early to hazard the construction of a serious model for relations between the state and civil society for the post-conflict era that the analysis here is on the military apparatuses themselves. Moreover, we have not here focused on the role of the USA which arguably provides much of the framework within which the shifting relations of power have been disputed. However, even if one must accept the importance of North American 'circumscription' of Central American affairs, there is no corresponding need to subscribe to those theories which ascribe a preordained logistical 'logic' to isthmian developments and which see the 'invisible hand' of Washington behind every major move in the region. The picture we paint is one of difference, detail and, often, fluidity. The enormous weight of US influence seems, by contrast, to have been directed in this period towards cajoling regional actors into negotiating in general rather than to determining the precise nature of the matters that are the concern of this chapter.

El Salvador

The military settlement in El Salvador is distinctive in a number of ways. First, it stemmed from a strategic impasse on the battlefield, and thus must be seen as involving two military institutions (the armed forces of the state and the rebel Frente Farabundo Martí para la Liberación Nacional – FMLN). Secondly, it resulted from sharp, direct and public pressure from Washington on San Salvador. But in threatening to withdraw its patronage the USA was no more able to enforce precise decisions than it had been over the previous decade, when it was almost unreservedly supporting the state against the guerrillas. Thirdly, the negotiation (1990-91) and implementation (1992-94) of the settlement depended heavily on the United Nations (UN), which in both New York and San Salvador (via the UN Observer Mission in El Salvador, ONUSAL) interpreted its notably broad brief in a dynamic and usually innovative manner. Finally, the terms for ending the twelve year civil war formally agreed at Chapultepec Castle, Mexico, in January 1992 themselves embodied substantial structural changes to the military institutions as well as laying out a procedural framework for demobilisation and transition.

These changes involved the total demobilisation and disarmament of the FMLN; the (constitutional) removal from the armed forces of all normal police functions; the dismantling of the five Rapid Response Infantry Battalions (BIRIs) created during the 1980s as the army's 'shock-troops'; a substantial (40-50 per cent) reduction of the military's overall enlistment; the abolition of the military intelligence service (Departamento Nacional de Inteligencia – DNI), to be replaced by a civilian body (Oficina de Inteligencia del Estado – OIE); the dismantling of the powerful paramilitary security forces – Guardia Nacional (GN) and Policía de Hacienda (PH) – and the quite extensive Civil Defence and territorial reserves; the establishment of a new National Civil Police (PNC), to include significant numbers of ex-FMLN fighters and personnel from the existing Policía Nacional (PN), itself originally scheduled to be phased out by October 1994 (and finally demobilised by the end of December 1994). At the same time, the Chapultepec agreement gave great weight to the establishment of two investigative commissions – the Ad Hoc Commission (composed of Salvadoreans) to investigate the human rights and profes-sional records of individual members of the army's officer corps, and the 'Truth Commission' (composed of non-Salvadoreans) to investigate and publicly identify human rights abuses by all parties since 1980, during which time some 75,000 people had been killed.[1]

It is worth noting that the Accords did not allow for the integration of the FMLN into a new military apparatus. Neither did they provide for a civilian defence minister, legislative oversight of the details of the military budget or promotions and postings. Equally, they did not address the issue of military control of a string of state bodies regulating infrastructure and communications.[2] Nonetheless, the implementation of the accords in 1992-

93, whilst uneven and hotly contested, was largely successful in the narrow military terms that concern us here. This achievement should not, however, be interpreted as corresponding to a broadly applicable model; it is derived, rather, from general policies and instruments for settling a conflict that was as violent as those in Guatemala and Nicaragua, but possessed its own particular character. This is perhaps best summarised as a developing stalemate between 1981 and 1989 between the Salvadorean armed forces, the FMLN and the USA in which the civilian interests/allies/components of each of these actors clashed with further pursuit of purely coercive activity for both internal and external reasons.

By 1990 there were very good military as well as political reasons for Washington to accept a cease-fire. The expenditure of $1,020 million in military aid to El Salvador since 1980 had produced some very poor results indeed. There had been modest progress towards realising the slogan of 'KSSSS' – 'Keep it simple, sustainable, small and Salvadorean' – and even before the FMLN offensive of November 1989 it was plain that the US Military Group had failed to achieve the three core aims it had set in 1981: i) that the Salvadorean officer corps subordinate itself to civilian authority; ii) that it respect human rights; and iii) that it 'rationalise its own internal methods of governance so that talent was nurtured, success was rewarded, incompetents were weeded out, and the officer corps became operationally effective'.[3] In November 1989 the indiscriminate aerial strafing of the capital's *tugurios* combined with the patently planned execution of the Jesuit priests was so similar to the methods employed almost nine years earlier – the massacre of El Mozote and the killing of the Maryknoll nuns – that it was difficult to credit that in the interim the military had been expanded sixfold (regular forces from 7,250 to 43,500; paramilitary forces from 5,000 to 12,600); that 1,000 had been trained in the USA and at least 60 US advisors had worked near (sometimes on) the 'front line' for eight years; or that its equipment had been comprehensively upgraded (to include 42 combat aircraft and 27 armed helicopters).[4] Whereas in the early 1980s the trading in Washington of military aid (wanted by the Reagan administration) for formal human rights 'conditionality' (required, then requested, by Congress) was a theatre that suited both parties – as the executive and Salvadorean military bluntly recognised – now this was neither diplomatically nor operationally viable. Moreover, the long-standing conviction amongst Salvadorean officers that Washington would continue to fund the war effort regardless because of its immovable anti-communism was no longer justified and was even provocative to the North Americans.[5]

The FMLN's interest in a settlement stemmed, of course, from the reasonable expectation that its offensive would guarantee a negotiated reward whereas the full capture of state power by force was no longer viable or – for some – desirable.[6] Equally, the rebels' relatively low reliance on external allies made the collapse of the Soviet Bloc, and then Sandinismo, an important but not decisive issue. In terms of their own military objectives the key issue was 'purification' of the state army – long seen as intrinsically necessary and a prerequisite for fusion with FMLN forces. This purge was not only necessary, in the eyes of the FMLN, because of the general levels of brutality exhibited by the state forces – over half of the 482 bodies found at El Mozote were of children – but also because whilst the rebels generally observed the Geneva Convention (the exceptions are individually identified), the government forces did not: not a single rebel prisoner of war was taken between January 1980 and July 1982 (during which time 34,000 people were killed).[7] However, in September 1990 the rebels suddenly proposed complete demilitarisation along Costa Rican lines. This was rejected and in November UN negotiator Alvaro de Soto made a confidential counter-proposal that called for the abolition of the two paramilitary forces and the military intelligence service together with investigation of human rights violations and removal of those responsible.[8] The UN proposal coincided almost exactly with the halving of US military aid by Congress because of inaction over the Jesuit killings, and it was immediately followed by a string of fierce FMLN attacks that badly mauled the military. The first part of de Soto's proposals was agreed in Mexico in April 1991, and in September of that year the FMLN finally accepted that it could not win both a purge of the armed forces and the inclusion of its own cadre within a reformed institution, settling instead for the purge and some representation in the Policía Nacional Civil (PNC).

The army itself resisted any negotiation until May 1990, but it was already prey to increased civilian pressure over the cost of the war – not least in terms of military corruption – amidst sharp economic recession. It also confronted the proven inability of first the large-scale 'hammer and anvil' and then the more mobile '*cazador*' strategies. Lastly, of course, it faced the tangible threat of a US pull-out, raising a spectre that had plenty of precedents for those more inclined to celebrate than denounce US intervention. Moreover, with the capture of the high command by the 1966 *Tandona* graduating class in late 1988 and the election of the ARENA government in March 1989, the most belligerent civil-military alliance was now in power and yet was palpably failing to secure a result. The seven-year excuse provided by the Christian Democrats had gone. For many in ARENA the purely political challenge posed by the FMLN would be slight whereas the military's veto on cease-fire talks restricted the rebels to a sphere where their destructive capacity was high.[9] De Soto's proposals and the 1991 agreements certainly posed a grave threat to many in the officer corps, but, as we have seen, they also fell short of a total dismantling of the institution. They effectively separated a partisan high command closely associated with death-squad activity, command of the paramilitary forces and direction of the massacres of the early 1980s from a now large – 2,300 – officer corps for which the reasonable prospect of institutional survival, peace, US support and more modest (but more solid) funding was evidently an acceptable exchange for selective expulsions without any intake of ex-guerrillas.

The arrangements for demobilisation proceeded with only two short delays – in June and November 1992 – caused by government efforts to evade the letter of the Accords on other matters. By 15 December the entire rebel force was disbanded, and the FMLN command reported to the UN that it had surrendered all its arsenal. However, an explosion in the Santa Rosa neighbourhood of Managua on 23 May 1993 revealed a hidden cache there, greatly embarrassing both the ex-guerrilla leadership and the UN, which subsequently collected weapons from another 128 sites in El Salvador, Nicaragua and Honduras that accounted for almost a third of the total rebel arsenal.[10] UN Secretary General Boutros-Ghali called this the 'gravest violation of the peace accords', and it confirmed a predictable response by the guerrillas to the risk of completely disbanding themselves whilst their erstwhile enemy was only reduced in size and thereby acquired – for the first time in fifteen years – a monopoly on armed force. The energy and interventionism of ONUSAL was aimed at alleviating this natural fear, which was, in fact, not without real foundation. Although the seventh ONUSAL report – for the first quarter of 1993 – identified only six politically-motivated killings and 32 resulting from robbery, by June the national human rights commission (CDHES) reported 308 illegal killings (against 225 in all 1992), and in the first week of November five senior FMLN figures were shot in an apparently concerted operation by at least one death squad.[11] This development was considered sufficiently serious to the precarious state of the law nearly a year after rebel demobilisation that Boutros-Ghali sent his envoy Marrack Goulding to San Salvador and ordered an ONUSAL investigation whilst Cristiani, claiming sovereignty for the judiciary, established a state investigation and called in bi-lateral foreign aid. However, the risks attached to repudiating the UN precisely at the moment when the transition it had brokered was in greatest danger were apparent to the most novice politician. ONUSAL was reincorporated into the process, and the issue of death-squad activity moved into the formal political arena (now agitated by an election campaign) where allegations of past ties became sharper with the publication of US documentation.[12]

Demobilisation of government forces produced a reduction of the total military from a claimed 63,175 (in reality probably 55,000) to some 31,000 personnel. A good proportion of this reduction came from the paramilitary security forces (GN and PH), which the government first attempted to retain simply by changing their names and legal status – provoking a halt in FMLN demobilisation and sharp ONUSAL intervention – but by the end of June 1992 they had been abolished, most non-conscripted troops entering a new Policía Militar. Similarly, the army's five 'elite' battalions (BIRIs) were dismantled, some troops being redeployed, others re-entering civil society. Perhaps more telling, the formal abolition of the controversial military intelligence agency (DNI, often seen as central to death-squad activity) in June 1992 produced not a single applicant for posts in its civilian successor, which likewise inherited no files.[13] In a similar vein, the leadership of the new civilian police (PNC) – which had to train and equip 5,700 new recruits in two years with slight and insecure funding – was altered from parity to favouring the PN (11 posts) at the expense of the FMLN (six) although the left accepted this under protest. Those veterans of both sides who were not incorporated into the police or reformed army were entitled to benefit from the distribution of land, which, as in Nicaragua, is evidently a necessary (if insufficient) resource for the disarming of large forces in a rural society. Yet this process too – whilst better administered and more advanced than in Nicaragua – proceeded very slowly: by September 1993 only 1,024 of the 22,000 veterans assigned rights had benefited, and landlords were denouncing invasions of property and direct action in a manner depressingly reminiscent of the 1970s.[14] Greater success was registered in the much less taxing tasks of amending the constitution to remove the military from responsibility for internal order, drafting a Basic Law of National Defence, and forming a new civil-military academic council responsible for the curriculum, staffing and intake of the military academy.[15] Similarly, the army's commitment to adjust its arsenal to the revised needs of a national defence was a necessarily far more extended and negotiable process than the surrender of powerful automatic weapons by the GN, PH and PN.

Undoubtedly, the most publicised, controversial and even dangerous aspect of the Salvadorean demilitarisation experience lay in the provisions for investigation of human rights violations and the purge of military personnel over which the FMLN had remained insistent when negotiating in 1991 and which were represented in the reports of the Ad Hoc Commission (delivered 23 September 1992) and the Truth Commission (published 15 March 1993). The Ad Hoc Commission only began work in mid-May 1992, and even though its work was extended for a month beyond the original schedule, it managed a detailed review of the records of only 232 senior members of the officer corps.[16] Of these its confidential report recommended the removal (or in a very few cases, reassignment) of 102 men, including all but two of the army's five generals and all its full colonels. This effectively purged the existing high command led by General René Emilio Ponce and thus created a political crisis, out of which Cristiani sought to escape by delaying the implementation and disguising the form of the officers' removal. It was only in June 1993 that the high command was replaced – by a group from the 38th *tanda* headed by the pugnacious Colonel Humberto Corado Figueroa – and even at the end of 1993 at least eight affected officers were still formally in post. All those identified by the Commission retained their residual rights upon retirement.

The report of the internationally staffed Truth Commission created even more bitterness because its detailed findings were made public. The Commission consulted 2,000 direct sources on 7,000 victims and indirect information on another 20,000 of the 75,000 people adjudged to have been killed since 1980. It paid particular attention to the massacres of 1980-83 and the internationally famous killings of priests, nuns and lay workers. In addition to finding state forces responsible for 85 per cent of the total death toll, the Commission, which had an observer on the Ad Hoc Commission, named 40 officers – all bar a handful in the high command – that it recommended removed from the armed forces. This step distinguished the Commission from that led by Judge Rettig in Chile, where direct assignation of responsibility had been scrupulously avoided despite the prior existence of an amnesty applicable to most of the crimes covered. No such amnesty had been introduced in El Salvador, but once the detail and directness of the Commission's report was apparent, the government moved immediately to introduce one although this also benefited fifteen FMLN commanders deemed responsible for the execution of eleven mayors (rebel forces being identified as causing 400 deaths and 200 disappearances).[17]

The amnesty caused widespread outcry – even the dismay of the US government – but its apparent restoration of impunity received some tacit support from the FMLN, most notably ERP (Expresión Renovadora del Pueblo) leader Joaquín Villalobos (one of the commanders named by the Truth Commission), who had vigorously defended the confidentiality of the Ad Hoc Commission's report and had earlier been identified as favouring an improved land deal for ex-guerrillas in return for allowing Cristiani to implement the purge in a graduated (and possibly partial) manner.[18] Here the logic of the ex-guerrilla command was less transparent than in the case of the arms caches since the question of human rights and a purge of the military had been at the heart of their demands from January 1980. The issue is still cloudy, and many sympathetic to the FMLN, such as those at the Universidad Centroamericana (UCA), found this position incoherent in its inconsistency. This may reflect the very specific divisions of the Salvadorean leadership or it might be an expression of a broader pattern of changing priorities as the position of erstwhile antagonists alters with the implementation of the peace settlements. (Some parallels with the activities of the Nicaraguan EPS during 1993 might well be drawn). In all events, the outcome was that the issue of war crimes and a military purge caused far less institutional crisis than public outcry during 1993. This, together with the continued high-profile of ONUSAL, surely fortified the transition in the short-term. Yet doubts must remain as to the medium-range consequences in a society where vigilante violence had become firmly rooted. However, in terms of demilitarisation and construction of a new post-war institutionality, the Salvadorean experience is both more advanced and more secure than that encountered in either Nicaragua or Guatemala.

Nicaragua

Since the electoral defeat of the Sandinistas in February 1990, Nicaragua has undergone a process of extensive demilitarisation – of both government and insurgent forces – quite without precedent in the region. However, while stability has been largely maintained throughout, the composition of the military and the extent of its functions continues to be highly contested both within and beyond Nicaragua's borders. The end of the Nicaraguan civil war (which had claimed some 50,000 lives since 1979) was a result of regional negotiations (Esquipulas), substantive changes in the position of the FSLN and – under the Bush administration – a shift in US policy from backing a military option to support for a political settlement, albeit one conditioned by the continued existence of the contra rebels. The contras themselves, who had proved manifestly incapable of winning the war and who remained exclusively dependent on the US for funding, had little say in the final outcome. Of equal importance in achieving a political settlement to the conflict was the considerable skill demonstrated by the FSLN in negotiating within the parameters laid down at Esquipulas. In the area which concerns us here, it is of fundamental relevance that no formal negotiated settlement between the Ejército Popular Sandinista and the contras ever took place. The extensive reduction of EPS forces which has occurred since 1990 rests largely on the Transition Accords reached between the executive of President Violeta Chamorro and the FSLN immediately after the February 1990 election.

Following the Sandinista victory in July 1979, the *Somocista* Guardia Nacional (GN) dissolved; ex-GN members, notorious for their abuse of human rights, took no part in the new revolutionary army, which was composed exclusively of guerrilla troops. From an estimated 5,000 at the time of the overthrow, the EPS expanded rapidly to approximately 18,000 in the first months after the revolutionary triumph.[19] Contra operations began by the end of 1981, after which the rebel force grew from approximately 500 combatants to some 15,000 at the height of the conflict in 1985-1986. The FSLN's response was vastly to increase the country's defensive capability: in 1983 (after the US invasion of Grenada) a national draft was introduced and regular EPS troops grew from 24,000 in 1981 to some 75,000 by 1986.[20]

Although the 1979-1990 regime became highly militarised in response to the external threat, the EPS remained subordinate to the ruling Sandinista *Dirección Nacional* and was directly controlled by the Ministry of Defence. The Policía Sandinista (PS) and the state security forces came under the purview of the Ministry of Interior, and the Sandinista Popular Militias (MPS) were controlled by both ministries acting in tandem.[21] Although the PS was a civilian force, there was no clear division between police and military functions, the security apparatus after 1979 performing not only peacetime functions of the maintenance of domestic order, but also guarding against counterrevolutionary activity from within and beyond Nicaragua's borders. However, in contrast to the state of affairs elsewhere in the region, police activities remained under the supreme control of the executive (*Dirección Nacional*), rather than operating as an autonomous *fuero* of the armed forces.

The Nicaraguan civil war was the most 'international' in character of those under consideration here; the insurgent forces funded by Washington and the conflict itself affecting the civil-military balance throughout the entire region. The peace settlement was also, by necessity, more dependent on external than domestic factors. The main thrust of the Esquipulas Accords signed by the Central American presidents on 7 August 1987 was to demobilise the contras.[22] By 1989, the contras looked like a spent force; support in the US Congress had eroded considerably since the Iran-Contra scandal became public in 1986 and in 1988 the blocking by Congress of

$36 million aid precipitated the first direct talks between the insurgent leadership and the FSLN at Sapoá in 1988.[23] In March 1989, US Secretary of State Baker brokered a bipartisan agreement on Central America, securing $49 million in 'humanitarian' aid for the contras but prohibiting further military assistance. This was recognition of the fact that Congress would no longer support the military option in Nicaragua, and the Baker team brought considerable behind-the-scenes pressure to bear on the rebel leadership to return to Nicaragua and take part in the forthcoming elections.[24]

External brokerage of the peace settlement in Nicaragua was only paralleled in the region by events in El Salvador. In the transition period responsibility for the contras' demobilisation was allocated to a joint Organisation of American States (OAS)-UN force, the International Commission for Support and Verification (CIAV); a UN force, ONUCA, was responsible for ensuring that rebel weapons were turned in and that sufficient guarantees of security were extended to those demobilised; in addition, ONUVEN (UN Observer Force for the Verification of the Nicaraguan Elections) was appointed to oversee the February 1990 poll.

The issue of the EPS moved centre-stage after the UNO's electoral victory. Chamorro herself consistently stressed the need for demilitarisation and advocated values of reconciliation and compromise (a broad political amnesty was passed on 25 April). Stability rested essentially on the consensus achieved between Chamorro, her Minister of the Presidency Antonio Lacayo, and the FSLN leadership. The Transition Accords, signed a week before the presidential inauguration, signalled both recognition by the new regime that some degree of continuity was necessary for the preservation of order and acceptance by the FSLN that reform of the military was vital to guaranteeing the post-election peace. Resisting calls by the UNO far-right for a wholesale purge, the agreement protected the existing privileges and rank of Sandinista officers serving in the EPS, guaranteed the integrity and professionalism of the armed forces and also reaffirmed Chamorro's constitutional role as Supreme Chief of the Armed Forces (a feature not without considerable symbolic importance at the time). In June 1990 it was announced that a 50 per cent reduction of the armed forces would take place within one year (from some 82,000 to 41,000), although these were to be principally drawn from the ranks of draftees and the popular militia, leaving the professional army largely intact.[25] The Sandinista leadership had already accepted the need for a reduction in the armed forces prior to their electoral defeat, mainly in response to the reduced contra threat and the economic crisis which gripped the country by 1988.[26] The EPS budget declined from $104 million in 1990, to $71 million in 1991, $42.9 million in 1992 and $36.5 million in 1993.[27]

The incoming administration had made it clear that Sandinista officers would not be replaced by ex-members of the GN or the contras, a move which would have been totally unacceptable to the EPS, the FSLN leadership and the vast majority of the Sandinista rank-and-file. A number of reforms were immediately implemented: the military draft, previously suspended in the run-up to the elections, was abolished and both the Ministry of the Interior and the Sandinista state security apparatus was disbanded. President Chamorro subsequently assumed the post of Defence Minister, but retained Sandinista General Humberto Ortega as Head of the Armed Forces, a move loudly denounced by the far-right of the UNO coalition, led by Vice-President Virgilio Godoy, the contra leaders (themselves excluded from a transition agreement which they saw as sanctioning continued Sandinista control over the military) and echoed in the US Senate by Jesse Helms.

The Godoy faction also made persistent calls for reform of the police. Following the elections, about half of the Policía Sandinista (PS) had left the force, a result of both ideological disenchantment and notoriously low levels of pay. The vacuum was subsequently filled principally by ex-contra members. Some limited reorganisation of the PS took place in 1990, such as the changing of the name to the less partisan Policía Nacional (PN). However, the existing command structure – as in the case of the EPS – was guaranteed by the Transition Protocols and continued to be staffed by Sandinista sympathisers. Controversy first surfaced in November 1991, when Interior Minister Carlos Hurtado declared a plan for creation of a municipal police force, envisaging a contingent of some 6,000 funded from local taxes and under the direct orders of mayors. Given that the most ultramontane elements of UNO – such as mayor of Managua Arnoldo Alemán – had their political stronghold in the municipalities and had long since demanded the transfer of police control to local government, the proposal increased FSLN fears of the creation of anti-Sandinista paramilitary forces. FSLN leader Daniel Ortega denounced the plan as unconstitutional and threatened to rearm the popular militias in response if the proposals were passed.[28] Hurtado was forced to resign in April 1992 as a result of differences with Lacayo and the proposed changes were never implemented. However, several members of the contra 'Commanders Council' were appointed to leadership positions within the PN, particularly in their traditional strongholds in the northern region.[29] Even this proved insufficient to meet Washington's demands for reform and in July 1992 $116 million in US aid was frozen in protest at the Chamorro government's failure to restructure the security forces and the EPS. Chamorro subsequently announced the 'departmentalisation' of the police, which effectively gave control to the mayors and removed it from the regional police headquarters (run by Sandinista officials). Plans for a new police academy were also announced.[30] Further insistence by US Secretary of State James Baker led to the removal in August 1992 of Sandinista police chief René Vivas, along with twelve other high ranking Sandinista police commanders, before the $116 million was finally unfrozen, demonstrating that, even without the contras, US influence remained considerable – a fact due in no small measure to the parlous state of the Nicaraguan economy. Vivas was subsequently replaced by Fernando Caldera Azmitia, also a Sandinista. However, the simultaneous creation of the post of Vice-Minister of Government with special responsibility for police affairs (filled by Antonio Avilés Iglesias, a cattle-rancher and former contra collaborator) effectively marked the placing of police affairs under civilian control, a measure which elicited considerably less enthusiasm on the part of the Nicaraguan left than amongst their Salvadorean or Honduran counter-parts, indicating the marked absence of any regional 'transition prototype' for establishing the formal division of powers.

Despite ongoing conflicts over political control of the EPS and PN, remarkable progress in demobilisation was achieved after February 1990. The EPS was cut to 28,000 by 1991 and stood at some 15,200 by early 1993, a reduction of approximately 75 per cent against 1985 levels.[31] Perhaps even more impressive was the largely successful reintegration of some 30,000 contra troops, particularly given the violence and bitterness of the civil war and the large numbers of civilian casualties it entailed.[32] However, a substantial sector of the population continued either to possess or retain direct access to automatic weapons, and demobilisation was accompanied by a general increase in violence and banditry.[33] From 1991 onwards, embittered elements of the contra took up arms in protest at the government's failure to deliver on promises to provide land and credit, particularly in the north of the country.[34] In a parallel move, since 1990 a limited number of demobilised EPS members ('recompas') also resorted to violence to press their demands for land, credit and severance payment. Recontra and recompa activity increased throughout 1993, and in the first six months of the year over 300 were killed in clashes between the EPS and the recontra.[35] In July 1993, recompa troops under the command of ex-EPS major, Victor Manuel Gallegos ('Pedrito el Hondureño') occupied the northern town of Estelí: the subsequent reimposition of order by force by the EPS, which included resort to aerial bombardment, elicited widespread condemnation from the Sandinista rank-and-file, but was significant in signalling the loyalty of the EPS to the Chamorro executive and consolidating their pretension to status as the *national* army of defence.[36] Between November and December of 1993 the EPS launched an offensive in the northern and central departments of Matagalpa, Jinotega, Estelí and Nueva Segovia to guarantee the coffee harvest and to wipe out remaining recontra bands. Following bloody exchanges in January, a peace deal was signed on 25 February 1994 between the government, the EPS and the recontra Northern Front 3-80 (FN-380), the last remaining rebel band, providing for demilitarisation of the northern region and the incorporation of demobilised FN 3-80 combatants into the ranks of the local police force.[37] Whilst sporadic fighting continues to pose a threat to public order in some areas, demobilisation of rebel forces has largely been secured throughout most of the country. Isolated skirmishes do not significantly threaten either the post-1990 peace or the institutions of state. In this sense at least, conflict in Nicaragua appears to have shifted decisively from the military to the political arena.[38]

The decision by Violeta Chamorro in September 1993 to remove General Humberto Ortega as chief of the EPS was largely in response to the tit-for-tat kidnappings of August 1993.[39] It was also the culmination of sustained pressure from the Godoy faction of UNO and the US far-right (led by Helms), the latter having successfully managed to withhold disbursement of $104 million in US economic aid since June 1992 in protest at the Chamorro government's tacit alliance with the FSLN.[40] It should be noted that after the Estelí uprising in July 1993, many Sandinista supporters were also calling for the removal of the General, who had previously outraged the rank-and-file by inviting the then Head of the Honduran Armed Forces, General Cantarero López, to Managua (August 1990) and presenting the Order of Camilo Ortega to US Embassy Defence Attaché, Lt.Colonel Dennis Quinn (February 1992).[41] General Ortega made it quite clear that he would only step down once a new armed forces law determined the length of his mandate, thus guaranteeing the institutional arrangements of the EPS. Amidst great controversy (including a boycott by hard-line UNO deputies), the new Military Code of Organisation, Jurisdiction and Pension was finally approved by the National Assembly on 23 August 1994, limiting the term of the armed forces chief to a single five year term. The law designated a military council responsible for nominating a candidate to succeed Ortega, and in December 1994 General Joaquín Cuadra Lacayo, Ortega's second-in-command, was unanimously proposed and appointed by the President.

The new statute aimed to regulate, professionalise and depoliticise the EPS, furthering their transition from revolutionary army to fully institutionalised army of national defence. Provisions included the prohibition of party affiliation amongst troops and officers, a reduction in the autonomy of military courts, and an explicit prohibition on the use of military intelligence for political purposes. Whilst the procedures for nominating the head of the armed forces were criticised by some on the grounds that they gave too much autonomy to the military, by far the most controversial aspects of the law were those relating to economic matters. Officers had no pension scheme during the 1980s and since 1990 had dealt with the problem in an *ad hoc* fashion by selling off Soviet tanks and helicopters on the international arms market.[42] The new statute permitted the military to own businesses for the purposes of operating a special pension fund through the Instituto de Previsión Militar. This was vehemently rejected by the far-right and the private sector, which – echoing charges laid against the Somoza dictatorship in the 1970s – alleged unfair competition and charged that the army had illicitly acquired most of its economic concerns during the 1990 transition period (the infamous *piñata*).[43] In the event of a victory for the far-right in the 1996 national elections initiatives to revise the military's institutional framework are in prospect, with predictably negative consequences for the country's political stability.

A major feature separating the EPS from other militaries in the region is its human rights record: systematic abuse of human rights was never a feature of the Nicaraguan military after 1979 and this continues to be the case, despite isolated cases of revenge killings by both government troops and recontra rebels. In this respect, reform of the armed forces in Nicaragua is a very different question from that in neighbouring states, where the heart of the peace settlement is concerned with issues of punishment for crimes against humanity and purging the armed forces and security apparatus of those responsible for the violation of human rights. The question of the internal political conditionality required for an effective peace settlement has in this sense been quite distinct in Nicaragua, economic rather than moral compensation constituting the critical variable.

Honduras

Civil war was absent in Honduras in the 1980s, the militarisation which occurred throughout the decade being more a consequence of the Reagan administration's covert war against Nicaragua than a response to the domestic insurgent challenge (which was negligible in both scale and impact). Given the weakness of the left, a negotiated settlement was neither a necessity nor a possibility. However, after an amnesty was decreed in 1990 the guerrilla renounced the armed struggle and most exiles have since returned.[44] With the end of the contra war, US aid to the Honduran military was massively reduced and the US embassy, along with international lending agencies and the greater part of the Honduran private sector, has been in the forefront of calls for a reduction in the size of the armed forces. The latter steadily resisted such demands but some shrinkage looks increasingly inevitable as aid returns diminish. Since 1990, as a result of both domestic and US pressure, some tentative advances were made towards reforming the security forces and ending the long-standing tradition of military impunity. However, it remains to be seen to what extent the domestic body politic is willing or indeed able to reduce the power of the military.

Institutionalisation of the Honduran armed forces took place after the Second World War. In 1954 the first Bilateral Military Assistance Treaty was signed with the USA and to date US influence has predominated. In 1956 the military, in their first foray into national politics, intervened to restore the Constitutional order after a particularly inept bid at *continuismo* by Vice-President Lozano Díaz. The Constitution passed the following year by the interim military *triunvirato* granted the armed forces effective autonomy from the executive, an autonomy which continues to the present day.[45] The consolidation of a central role for the armed forces in national political life was favoured by the historically weak and divided nature of Honduran civilian elites. Following an anti-communist coup in 1963, the first institutionalised military government (led by General López Arellano) was installed. After defeat in the 1969 war with El Salvador, a more reformist tendency within the army briefly gained the upper hand and the military administration which governed between 1972 and 1975 was characterised by a mixture of structural reforms (most notably land reform) and partially successful cooption of the popular movement. A transcendental change occurred in 1975, when decision-making within the armed forces changed from what had been essentially a form of personalised *caudillo* rule towards a more collegiate form embodied in COSUFFAA (Consejo Superior de las Fuerzas Armadas). However, military reformism in Honduras lacked both strategic vision and ideological coherence and by 1978 had reached an advanced state of decomposition, being largely characterised by selective repression of the popular movement and increased corruption within the officer corps. Formal power was handed back to civilian government in 1982, Liberal Party candidate Roberto Suazo Córdova assuming the presidency.

However, the transition to civilian rule in Honduras was followed by an unprecedented increase in the power of the armed forces, a consequence of the new strategy towards the region adopted by the Reagan administration which made Honduras a key element in Washington's war against the FSLN and the FMLN. Between 1978 and 1982 US military aid to Honduras increased almost twenty-fold, whilst the armed forces doubled in size to some 23,000 troops (from a 1980 figure of 11,000).[46] In 1982 Honduras became the second largest recipient of US aid in Latin America (after El Salvador), the $31.3 million disbursed in that year almost equalling the $32.5 million received between 1946 and 1981.[47] General Alvarez Martínez, Head of the Armed Forces between January 1982 and March 1984, and Suazo Córdova lent their full support to the covert war against the Sandinistas. The US base at Palmerola, Comayagua (built 1983) operated as the logistics centre for US army operations in the country and large-scale joint military manoeuvres involving thousands of US and Honduran troops continued to be held on a regular basis until 1991. After 1981, Honduras was also host to the contras, a force which at its height came near to equalling the size of the Honduran military itself.

By regional standards, human rights abuses in Honduras were relatively limited. However, the traumatic effect of the 'dirty war' of the early 1980s on the national psyche should not be underestimated. By 1980, an extensive counter-insurgency apparatus was already in place, including Battalion 3-16, a paramilitary group composed of operatives from the police force FUSEP (Fuerzas de Seguridad Pública), police intelligence section DNI (Departamento Nacional de Investigaciones), and the army. Selective assassinations of government opponents began in 1980 and after 1981 Battalion 3-16 orchestrated a campaign of disappearances and assassinations targeting both the Honduran and Salvadorean left. Coordination with Guatemalan and Salvadorean military intelligence was stepped up, often to devastating effect.[48]

The anti-communist zeal of Alvarez Martínez led him frequently to press for a full-scale military invasion of Nicaragua, a fact which created almost as much unease amongst his allies on Capitol Hill as it did amongst his fellow officers. Despite relatively successful attempts to cultivate support for the counter-insurgency amongst political and business sectors, Alvarez's belligerent line, combined with his increasingly wayward evangelical predilections and almost total marginalisation of COSUFFAA, eventually led to his removal in 1984 by officers led by air force commander, Colonel Walter López Reyes.[49] This internal coup was prompted by Alvarez's attempts to reduce COSUFFAA from 52 to 21 members and to restrict its mandate. Under López Reyes, COSUFFAA's former influence was restored and in 1985 COSUFFAA forced the closure of the controversial Regional Military Training Centre (CREM), which had played host to thousands of Salvadorean troops since its establishment under US auspices in 1983. Alvarez's autocratic, strong-man rule is perhaps best understood as a 'blip' in the trajectory of a military command structure largely characterised by traditions of *mando colectivo*, where a high degree of *esprit de corps* amongst the different graduating classes (*promociones militares*) has been a feature since the 1970s. López Reyes was subsequently forced to resign in 1987 by the hard-line General Humberto Regalado, whose alleged involvement in drug-trafficking later earned him the sanction of the USA. Discontent within COSUFFAA led to Regalado's replacement in late 1989 by his preferred successor, General Arnulfo Cantarero López who, lacking a base of support within the army, maintained a tenuous hold on power and was unceremoniously replaced in February 1991 by General Alonso Discua Elvir, one of the most powerful officers of the sixth promotion.

The Honduran armed forces comprises four branches: army, navy, air-force and police (FUSEP). The army is by far the largest branch and in 1994 numbered some 18,000 troops.[50] The air-force, equipped by the US with F-5 fighters in 1987, is the most powerful in Central America. The navy is very small (with less than a dozen patrol boats) but as drug-trafficking operations are extended in the region its importance is steadily increasing. The second most important branch of the armed forces, the FUSEP (currently numbering some 6,000 officers), has been controlled by the military since 1963, although it has its own organisational structure.[51] Until recently the FUSEP controlled a number of security bodies including the traffic police, treasury police, counter-insurgency battalion ('Cobras') and the intelligence and investigation unit, the DNI, formed in 1976.

Since the end of the contra war, the US have radically reduced support for the Honduran military, annual aid falling from $77.4 million in 1984 to $16.2 million in 1992.[52] In the face of the refusal of the high command to sanction a cut in troops, US ambassador Cresencio Arcos finally imposed a unilateral *fait accompli* by reducing military aid to a mere $2.7 million in 1993.[53] The historical weakness of the domestic political parties makes them singularly ill-placed to demand substantive concessions from the military. In October 1992 Congress failed to protest Discua Elvir's manoeuvres to extend his term and lent their seal of approval to an amendment to the armed forces law which permitted the General to remain in post for a second consecutive term. However, recent developments indicate a reduction of the political parties' traditional reliance on the armed forces. Pressure for a reduction in the size of the armed forces has been considerable, particularly given the extensive cuts imposed on other areas of national expenditure by the successive programmes of structural adjustment introduced since 1990. Initially the armed forces continued to play the anti-communist card, rejecting all entreaties to reduce their size; however, by 1994, following an announcement by President Reina of an across-the-board 10 per cent budget cut, the high command began to discuss which batallions would eventually be phased out.[54]

Nonetheless, whilst some reduction in the the size of the armed forces now appears inevitable, the significant increase in the military's economic power over the past decade is a factor militating against an overall reduction in their influence. The division between the public and private sphere is (as in Guatemala and El Salvador) considerably blurred, the armed forces maintaining responsibility for – *inter alia* – immigration, national cartographic activities and the postal service. The Instituto de Previsión Militar (IPM), established in 1973, is now one of the ten largest business concerns in the country, holding interests in banking, insurance, real estate, palm oil production, a radio station and a funeral parlour. The institution's profits in 1992 were estimated at some $40 million. The IPM's purchase in September 1991 of the newly privatised state cement company generated much displeasure within the increasingly belligerent national private sector association (COHEP), and the privatisation of the military-run state telecommunications monopoly, HONDUTEL, provoked considerable conflict throughout 1994 as local capital fought to prevent the IPM acquiring a majority share. Less institutionalised economic interests were also extended in recent years: drug-trafficking operations by the military were already considerable under the regime of Policarpo Paz García (1978-1980) but multiplied during the period of the contras' presence in Honduras, leading to internecine battles between military officers by the 1990s.[55]

Since 1991 a number of cases have focused both domestic and international attention on reducing the military's traditional immunity from prosecution for human rights abuse, constituting perhaps the most serious challenge to their power to date. Advances have been both gradual and cautious, but nonetheless significant. The May 1991 killing of five *campesinos* involved in a land dispute at El Astillero led to repeated calls for the alleged intellectual author of the massacre, Colonel Galindo, to stand trial in a civilian court. The following month, the failure of a military tribunal to sentence Colonel Erick Sánchez for shooting (and permanently paralysing) a civilian in a bar-room brawl in Tegucigalpa elicited widespread condemnation of the use of the *fuero militar* to protect members of the armed forces guilty of crimes against civilians. However, it was the rape, murder and mutilation of school student Riccy Mabel

Martínez in July 1991 and the sustained protest campaign this generated which finally provoked a change in traditional practice. In July 1993 the officers implicated, Colonel Angel Castillo Maradiaga and Sergeant Eusebio Llovares Fúnez, were sentenced to sixteen and ten years respectively. Intervention by the US embassy in the case was instrumental in securing the convictions: Ambassador Cresencio Arcos sent forensic samples to the USA for analysis by the FBI, signalling a growing impatience on the part of Washington with both the intransigence of the military and the manifest weakness of the local judiciary. Despite repeated calls from the media and the popular movement, it was not until the appointment of a new Supreme Court in 1994 that the issue of competing military and civil jurisdictions was formally resolved.

Steps towards substantive reform of the security forces were made in 1993, after a spate of drug-related assassinations by the San Pedro Sula DNI and rising public criticism prompted President Callejas to set up an Ad Hoc Commission with the specific remit of drawing up reforms to the security forces and judicial system. Allegations of the use of torture had long been levelled at the DNI and FUSEP by local human rights groups and since 1990 certain procedural measures to improve police practice had been instigated with US support.[56] However, the Ad Hoc Commission recommended the replacement of the scandal-ridden DNI by a civilian-controlled force, the DIC (División de Investigaciones Criminales) (see chapter six). The military themselves appeared only too happy to be rid of the DNI, which had long since become a distinct liability. Throughout 1994, pressure mounted for the FUSEP to be transferred to civilian control, a move strongly backed by the US and Honduran governments which the military were forced eventually to accept at least in principle. In May 1994, in the face of considerable opposition from the military high command, President Carlos Roberto Reina fulfilled his campaign promise to end mandatory military service, thus eliminating the highly unpopular practice of forced military recruitment. Importantly, the replacement of the draft with a voluntary and educational military service effectively transferred the power to set the size of the armed forces to the legislature. However, the implementation of the measure (subject to future ratification by a two-thirds congressional vote), proved less than smooth; military officers alleged the end of the draft inhibited their abilities to tackle the rising crime wave, whilst opposition leaders accused the military of manipulating the crime issue to force a reversal of the legislation and secure an increase in their budget.[57] In a concession to the military, President Reina in August 1994 approved a temporary military draft by means of a lottery. However, this proved insufficient to appease the military and in 1995, in an effort to secure congressional ratification for the reform, Reina suggested an increase in the defence budget 'to guarantee the existence of the institution, once Congress ratifies the elimination of forced military recruitment'.[58]

Another area where the military have recently come under considerable pressure is the question of human rights trials for the events of the early 1980s. Despite the absence of civil war in Honduras, the question of war crimes has considerable resonance, precisely because of the traumatic impact of events of the early 1980s on a society historically accustomed to comparatively low levels of overt violence. More recently, the 'demonstration effect' of the Salvadorean Truth Commission (published March 1993) should be noted. The long-standing call by local human rights organisations for a Truth Commission came to the fore when the disappeared became an issue in the 1993 election campaign. In an attempt to divert attention from what was proving to be a serious electoral disadvantage for PN presidential candidate Oswaldo Ramos Soto (signalled by human rights groups for his involvement in forced disappearances), President Callejas appointed Human Rights Ombudsman Leo Valladares to carry out an investigation. The final report, published on 29 December 1993 proved something of a bomb-shell, constituting the first official acknowledgement of the hundred-and-fifty-plus disappearances which occurred during the 1980s.[59] The Commission led by Valladares gained unprecedented access to confidential files in the US State Department, revealing evidence of a systematic campaign of human rights abuse by the armed forces and details of the involvement of US and Argentine officers in training both the Honduran military and the contra in kidnapping and torture techniques. Battalion 3-16 was found to be still active, despite claims by the high command in 1987 that it had been disbanded. The report named a number of high-ranking officers implicated in the disappearances, including Generals Regalado Hernández, Walter López Reyes and Discua Elvir, and recommended that they stand trial.[60]

Arguably, a limited number of punitive trials would not be looked on unfavourably by the USA, anxious to clip the wings of the recalcitrant Honduran whose involvement in drug-trafficking has led to considerable disquiet in Washington. More problematic would be securing the neutrality of the majority of the officer corps. In one sense, the collegiate style of the high command might lend itself to the eventual sacrifice of a handful of officers, at least in the form of a limited internal purge if not through the domestic courts. However, although the current conjuncture has the armed forces on the defensive, the leverage of the civilian authorities remains decidedly limited. Nonetheless, regional and international trends together with the steady and gradual pace of reform holds out the prospects of a lasting shift in the civil-military balance in Honduras.

Panama

The nature of the modern military – and therefore of the 'military question' –in Panama is quite different to that in the rest of the region. In fact, the military, known as the Panamanian Defence Force (FDP), was formally abolished on 12 February 1990 following the US invasion of 20 December 1989. However, this core element of a most insecure 'imposition of democracy' by force was not subsequently consolidated.[61] In the first place this was because the *de facto* abolition of the FDP only gave way to a profusion of not dissimilar police and paramilitary bodies. Perhaps more importantly, though, was the result of the referendum of 15 November 1992 on reforms to the 1983 Constitution, when 64 per cent of the voters rejected the proposal that, 'the Republic of Panama shall have no army' along with 57 other (less publicised and controversial) proposed amendments. It is undoubtedly the case that this result reflected the genuine unpopularity of the Endara regime. Nonetheless, the opposition Frente Nacional Pro-Constituyente (FRENO), led in this respect by the erstwhile pro-Noriega Partido Revolucionario Democrático (PRD), clearly exploited rising nationalist sentiment after the invasion and gave it an acutely practical application by questioning how it would be possible for Panama without a military force to assume its obligations to defend the Canal from the year 2000 under Article V of the 1977 Treaty.[62] Indeed it is a reflection not just of the political position after December 1989, but also of the anomaly at the heart of Panama's existence since 1903 that the PRD should attract significant support for its own anti-militarist formulation that included US forces: 'There shall be no army in the Republic of Panama'.[63]

The abolition of the FDP in 1990 was the second time that the USA had disbanded the armed forces of Panama, the first occasion being under the 1904 Taft Agreement when Washington backed the Conservative president Amador, killed off the development of a regular army and set up a notionally non-partisan police force. This service was institutionally weaker and more lacking in ideological foundation than the 'constabulary forces' established in Cuba, the Dominican Republic, Haiti and Nicaragua by Washington in the same period (although over time a comparable praetorianism did develop).[64] Between 1903 (Bunau-Varilla-Hay Accord) and 1936 (General Treaty of Friendship and Cooperation) US forces were deployed in Panamanian territory nine times, consonant with the

Republic's effective protectorate status and Washington's administrative disposition up to the 'Good Neighbour' policy. However, in addition to the presence of US troops in the Canal Zone – where Panamanian sovereignty was so theoretical as to exclude the flying of the national flag until 1959 – Washington's interference went as far as the confiscation of all the rifles held by the police in 1916 – a move that many held responsible for the ease with which Costa Rican forces were able to occupy and hold disputed territory in February 1921.[65] After the 1936 Treaty, which revoked Washington's formal right to intervene, the police was gradually expanded (to 2,000) and, during World War Two, again provided with some armament beyond hand-guns. A basic training school was established in 1948 under the command of Colonel José Antonio Remón; the Guardia Nacional (GN) was only established in 1953, after Remón had become president through a mix of populist rhetoric and aggressive exploitation of the spoils system (particularly around the Colón Free Trade Zone) that was later to be developed by Torrijos and Noriega.

The GN, like its namesake in Nicaragua, was not strictly an army, and most of its 6,000 (predominantly black and mestizo) members at the time of the 1968 coup were effectively police officers. On the other hand, by the end of the 1960s almost half of the GN's enlistment had received training at the US School of the Americas (where they accounted for one-ninth of all pupils up to the School's closure in October 1984), and the officer corps were sent to regular military academies abroad, including Mexico and Peru where there was an institutional ethos discernibly at variance with the Pentagon model. It is notable that the GN lacked the repressive trajectory of its Nicaraguan counterpart, had no need to engage in serious counter-insurgency operations (even after 1968), and was restricted to barracks during the 1964 riots over the Canal Zone when eighteen students were killed.

The coup of October 1968 – initially provoked by Arnulfo Arias's attempt upon entering office to remove the Presidential Guard from GN control – changed this position appreciably, not least by opening the country's first real experience of military government. Over the following decade the GN's enlistment rose to 15,000, its absolute budget rose tenfold, and under the fiercely corporatist 1972 Constitution (which continues to provide the basis for subsequent amendments) it became the country's leading political institution and acquired administrative functions which further expanded its management of patronage, contraband and a swathe of semi-licit enterprise. The fact that political parties were banned for a full decade (1968-78) and that the assemblies elected under the 1972 Constitution were explicitly limited to rubber-stamping decisions made by

Torrijos and the high command confirm the GN's authoritarian pedigree.[66] Equally – rather as in Honduras, but within the more consequential context of the Canal negotiations – it was pressure from the Carter administration which eventually secured a modicum of political competition and formal democratic administration. (This process was quite distended, lasting from the first set of constitutional amendments in 1978 to the 1984 elections, but Torrijos's death in 1981 played an important part in causing such a delay at a particularly charged moment in regional politics.) However, the GN's direct assumption of power during the 1970s was unusual in its form and rationale, and this only fell into line with local traditions of military-backed 'officialist' parties after 1984 (and even then the PRD, formed in 1978 on the eve of the Nicaraguan Revolution, is not usefully seen in the same light as the Guatemalan Partido Institucional Democrático or the Salvadorean Partido de Conciliación Nacional). Equally, proper recognition should be given to the scope for restricting and violating human rights: whilst the GN was indisputably authoritarian and systematically corrupt, it killed very few people, arresting, abusing and exiling numbers quite comparable on a scale with elected regimes elsewhere in Latin America. (Within Central America, its abuse of authority was closer to the levels witnessed in Costa Rica than Honduras, at least in the early 1980s.)

At the same time, the circumscription of democratic rights was matched by an expansion of some social liberties (the 1972 Labour Code), public expenditure and public employment (rising from 51,998 in 1971 to 107,000 in 1980, or from 13 to 25 per cent of the total labour force).[67] It is certainly the case that this high-spending and redistributionist trend was funded first (1971-82) by a markedly cavalier fiscal policy – Panama has one of the highest debts *per capita* in the world – and then (1983-89) by reliance upon taxing, laundering and occasionally directly generating cocaine revenues. Neither phase, then, possessed much greater 'substantive democracy' than that of a procedural character. Yet both assuredly militated to the benefit of sectors of the country's poor as well as giving the regime a critical quota of autonomy from the USA at a time when its political and military influence was directly focused on the isthmus.[68]

Although the democratising reforms to 150 of the Constitution's 275 articles were approved in April 1983, the GN was transformed into the Fuerzas de Defensa de Panamá (FDP) under a separate law hurriedly enacted in October of that year. It thereby acquired a much more traditional military aspect with a very small air-force and coastguard, the immunity of its commanding officer from presidential removal (a matter forgotten by President Delvalle when he tried to oust Noriega in February 1988), and, under Ley 20 designed to prepare it for defence of the Canal, direct responsibility for the country's ports and the (highly profitable) control of migration. It was at this juncture that Noriega (previously Chief of Intelligence and then Chief of Staff) took overall command. As a result, one should identify the quality of individual leadership as well as institutional expansion as a factor in an enhanced regional profile (sponsorship of Contadora; controversial ambivalence towards the Sandinistas); increased (and justified) civilian apprehension that the new FDP was seeking to deepen its political domination; and the increased role given to intelligence and specialist elites by the military.[69]

Noriega's early period of power was marked by the electoral fraud of 1984 and the infamous murder of radical oppositionist Hugo Spadafora (for which seven of the ten FDP members later charged were acquitted in September 1993). However, it was really only from 1987 that the FDP resorted to aggressively partisan intervention in politics, and this generated internal division with dangerous coup attempts in 1988 and 1989. Noriega's reliance upon populist mobilisation and anti-US rhetoric might be viewed as a renewal of the *torrijista* heritage – certainly sections of the PRD saw it thus – but there is a more convincing interpretation of the rabble-rousing and fixing of the 1989 poll in the antics of a desperate *caudillo* against whom neither the FDP's structures (which did not include the 'Dignity Battalions') nor US ineptitude nor the divisions of the domestic opposition provided short-term guarantees. By concentrating on the first of these the post-invasion management of civil-military relations has proved to be lop-sided, superficial and probably self-defeating in its evasion of the long and short-term dilemmas inherent in the nature of the Panamanian state.

The 1989 invasion was almost immediately successful, obviating the need even for formal surrender arrangements, let alone any negotiated political settlement. Aside from Noriega himself, who was removed to US jurisdiction on 4 January 1990, there were two broad prejudiced parties: the civilian and military supporters of the regime who were detained or persecuted by the invasion forces, and those citizens who were killed, injured or lost their property in the less than precise bombing and fire-control of the US troops. This latter group had the formal backing of the Endara regime for its compensation claim against the US government. This was eventually filed on behalf of 286 named victims at the end of 1993 even though the US Supreme Court had already rejected the Panamanian government's claim for some $400 million in reparations, largely for local enterprise.[70] On the other hand, the Endara government itself refused for over four years to concede an amnesty that might free around 60 Noriega supporters, allow 40 to return from exile, and drop charges against 800.[71]

The PRD predictably led the campaign for such a move, which was also backed by the organisations of those injured by the invasion, but the government no less predictably refused to issue an amnesty on the grounds that this would benefit many guilty of torture, fraud and murder, especially in the suppression of the 1988 and 1989 coup attempts.[72]

The difficulty with the government's position was that soon after the invasion it was re-employing hundreds of FDP personnel, including senior members of its anti-terrorist and intelligence branches – to serve in the new security apparatus. This burgeoning institutional network was founded on the Fuerza Pública (FP), which in three years came to number 11,650, including 11,000 in the Policía Nacional (PN), 300 in the National Maritime Service and 350 in the National Air Service.[73] Whilst the budget for these forces was under strict civilian control, and they possessed no proper military equipment or formal mission, their size approximated to that of the FDP, ex-members of which comprised at least 6,000 of the total enlistment. Subsequently, the government, asserting (controversially and without tangible evidence) that it was the target of several coup attempts, created three further forces: the investigative Policía Técnica Judicial (PTJ), under the authority of the Controlaría; the 500-strong Servicio de Protección Institucional (SPI) intelligence service, and the Tactical Weapons Unit, equipped with automatic weaponry and staffed by specially trained members of the PN, PTJ and SPI.[74] Indeed, Panama witnessed a veritable renaissance of paramilitary activity after 1990 with the creation of a Municipal Police in the capital and the existence of some 200 security firms employing 12,000 guards.[75] It can be argued that the frequently changing leaderships of some of these state forces (notably the PN and the PTJ) contributed to rather than curbed lawlessness, and only the FP was clearly subject to legislative oversight and authority.[76] Meanwhile, some 6,000 of the 9,000-strong US garrison in the Canal Zone were almost constantly engaged in a series of 'manoeuvres' known as 'Strong Roads' and largely dedicated to road-building and developing the new military installations at Veraguas. Their activities helped to sustain the campaign, led by Canal Zone workers, for renegotiation of the 1977 Treaties and a prolonged US military presence. Yet only once, in December 1990, did Endara rely directly on foreign troops to resolve a domestic crisis – when PN officers occupied their HQ in demand for improved conditions, and the president, claiming that this was a coup attempt, persuaded the SouthCom commander to surround the building with 500 soldiers and break up the protest.[77] It was this event that prompted Endara's creation of the new police forces, but his nationalist identity was already sufficiently tarnished that the matter failed to develop into a major crisis.

Very few of the developments noted above assisted the settlement of civil tension, so sharply evident in the high crime rates, or the political impasse expressed by the failure of Endara and the US to secure constitutional reform as well as by the impressive resilience of the PRD. Under no circumstances can they be argued to have reduced the level of the drug-trade, about which Washington continues to be seriously concerned. A sober appraisal of the post-invasion position could, then, stress the continuation of a paramilitary elite in a new institutional guise, the notable failure to reach a codified arrangement for the country's security forces, the absence of an amnesty or any formal negotiation with the quite numerous servants and supporters of the old regime, and the continued corrosive effects of *narcotráfico*. Against this, the maintenance of the electoral cycle, the evident capacity of Panamanian constitutions to withstand piecemeal reform, a still peaceable adaptability of the GN/ FDP/FP continuum, and the absence of any guerrilla conflict before or after the transition could all be interpreted as bolstering the redistributive aspects of a notably 'grey' service sector and reducing the threat of political violence. Neither scenario, however, involves a qualitative 'demilitarisation' of Panama, within the Canal Zone or without it.

Guatemala

At present, demilitarisation of Guatemalan society remains a distant prospect. During the past decade the counter-insurgency strategy developed after 1982 extended the influence of the armed forces into the lives of the rural population to an unprecedented extent, generating a profound transformation in the nature of military power. Partly in consequence, the division between civilian and military spheres in Guatemala – both substantive and perceived – is blurred to a degree without parallel in the rest of the region. Peace negotiations with the Unidad Revolucionaria Nacional Guatemalteca (URNG) insurgents have advanced intermittently since 1987, but the central issue of adequate human rights guarantees remains an insurmountable block. Developments since 1988 indicate a resurgence in popular organisation after the widespread and generalised repression of the early 1980s. However, it remains doubtful whether either developments in 'civil society' or the negotiations themselves will be able fundamentally to alter the balance of civil/military power within the foreseeable future.

The use of military force in Guatemala's civil war has been both more brutal in its impact and transformative in its effect than elsewhere in the region. Ample documentation exists of the legacy of systematic human rights abuse by the armed forces, which reached its peak during the 1978-1983 period. The campaign against the highland civilian population left over 100,000 killed or 'disappeared' and over 1 million displaced.[78] Following the scorched earth policies employed during the Lucas García regime (1978-1982), military strategy shifted to more sophisticated counter-insurgency policies aimed primarily at controlling the rural civilian population. Mechanisms included: mandatory participation in civil patrols (Patrullas de Autodefensa Civil, PACs); forced resettlement of the displaced rural population in camps or 'model villages', grouped together in army-controlled 'development poles'; and inter-institutional co-ordinating councils which centralised administration of all development projects at every level of government under military command. All these institutions were legalised in the Constitution of 1985.

It is generally agreed that the return to civilian rule in 1986 was part of a long-term military strategy begun under the regime of Mejía Victores (1983-1986), intended to improve the country's international image and facilitate greater aid flows. Following elections for a constituent assembly in 1984, presidential and congressional elections were held in 1985. However, although formal political power was returned to the civilian administration of Vinicio Cerezo in 1986, military control of the rural population has remained non-negotiable in the transition. The limits of Cerezo's room for manoeuvre were evident from the outset of his administration. Prior to leaving office, the Mejía Victores regime had passed an amnesty law (DL No. 8-86) covering the period March 1982 to January 1986 which Cerezo accepted in the hope of obtaining at least some measure of neutrality from the bulk of the officer corps.[79] As Cerezo himself stated: 'We are not going to be able to investigate the past. We would have to put the entire army in jail'.[80]

By 1990, human rights violations were again mounting in response to renewed guerrilla activity and urban mobilisations protesting the worsening economic crisis. A disgruntled sector of hard-line military officers (the '*Oficiales de la Montaña*') supported by elements in the private sector federation Cámara de Agricultura, Comercio, Industria y Finanza (CACIF) and the ultramontane Movimiento de Liberación Nacional (MLN) staged attempted coups in both 1988 and 1989, and only the firm support of Defence Minister General Gramajo maintained Cerezo's rule. However, for all his polished *civilista* discourse, Gramajo's primary concern lay with preserving military unity rather than shoring up the beleaguered civilian president. Following the subsequent accession of Serrano Elías to the presidency, a series of rapid changes occurred within the civilian political sphere (the abortive *autogolpe* in May 1993, the overthrow of Serrano and his eventual replacement by former human rights ombudsman, Ramiro de León Carpio). It is worthy of note that the high command did not decisively back either Serrano or his ill-fated Minister of Defence, General Samayoa, in their *autogolpista* pretensions, nor did they intervene against de León after his sudden accession to the presidency. To this extent, the 'back to barracks' tendency within the army has been significantly consolidated, even if in practice retreat from the exercise of power remains formal rather than substantive. The lack of a civilian political project, combined with the manifest weakness and corruption of Guatemala's political parties, has only served further to underline the centrality of the armed forces in national politics.

The distinction within the Guatemalan military between hard-liners, who favour a no-holds-barred military solution to the civil war, and those, currently in ascendance, who tend towards a negotiated solution, is often noted. However, such divisions are essentially fluid and their utility for analysing shifts within a military so steeped in a rigid and seemingly immutable culture of anti-communism remains debatable. Differences amongst the officer corps to date have essentially been about tactics rather than ideology. Nonetheless, limited advances should be recognised: there is now no military veto on the peace talks (as there was in 1987) and the possibility that a section of the officer corps is prepared to negotiate on substantive issues such as the abolition of the Patrullas de Autodefensa Civil should not be ruled out.

Despite considerable advancement since the first formal talks held between the URNG insurgents and the government of Vinicio Cerezo (1986-1991) in 1987, a negotiated end to the civil war in Guatemala remains far from imminent. Indeed, in the six years since the signing of the Esquipulas Accords, not even a partial cease-fire has been achieved. The Guatemalan military are notable both for their operational and ideological unity and for the almost total historical absence of a tradition of negotiation and compromise. In contrast to El Salvador and Nicaragua (where the armed forces were reduced by 80 per cent and 50 per cent respectively after the end of the civil wars), no troop demobilisation has occurred in Guatemala to date, indeed troop numbers increased after the signing of the Esquipulas Accords in 1987 (from 51,600 in 1985 to over 60,000 by 1991).[81] Guatemala is the only country in the region in which forced conscription into the army continues to occur and, in addition, some 500,000 or more individuals remain organised in the paramilitary PACs. The guerrilla challenge in Guatemala is far weaker than that of the FMLN in El Salvador and, unlike the contra in Nicaragua, has not relied significantly on any external sponsors capable of bringing pressure to bear in peace negotiations. Totalling between 1,000 and 2,000 armed combatants, the URNG's military activities in recent years singularly failed to shift the military balance sufficiently to affect substantially the terms of negotiations (as the 1989 FMLN offensive did in El Salvador). The Guatemalan military see themselves as the victors in the civil war and many officers are particularly opposed to the granting of concessions at the negotiating table to an opponent which has proved unable to extract the same on the battlefield.

The first meeting in October 1987 between the URNG and the Comisión Nacional de Reconciliación (CNR) – the latter set up within the framework of the Esquipulas Accords and headed by Bishop of Esquipulas, Monsignor Rodolfo Quezada – was vetoed by the army after the series of proposals presented by the URNG proved unacceptable to the high command. The most obvious demands were for the abolition of the apparatus of counter-insurgency – civil patrols, model villages and 'development poles'. However, it was the demands for establishment of a Truth Commission on past human rights abuses and the setting up of demilitarised zones which ultimately proved unacceptable to the officer corps.

A significant shift in external factors had occurred by the time of the second meeting in Oslo in March 1990. In the aftermath of the Cold War and the electoral defeat of the Sandinistas, the Bush administration began to push for a negotiated settlement in Guatemala. However, in contrast to El Salvador, US leverage against the Guatemalan military is minimal and progress in the negotiations is consequently dependant on internal factors to a far greater extent than in the other countries examined here. The Guatemalan army has long prided itself on its independence, and throughout the 1980s its nationalist disposition and operational autonomy were augmented by its ability to secure alternative sources of aid, notably from Taiwan and Israel. The amount of US military aid currently received by Guatemala is negligible.[82] However, mounting economic difficulties may yet mean that finding favour with the USA is more important to the Guatemalan elite than in the past. Certainly a powerful sector of the domestic business elite anxious to profit from regional economic integration is currently in favour of a negotiated settlement. Such calculations inevitably continue to affect civil/military relations. It should be remembered, however, that the Guatemalan armed forces have gained a degree of economic influence commensurate with their political power, long presiding over the most extensive economic interests of all the Central American militaries. The armed forces own the state electricity and telecommunications monopolies, along with the national airline, and extensive ranching, banking, insurance and real estate interests and at least one national television channel (*Canal 5*). Additional economic muscle is provided by involvement in drug-smuggling, this last a source of increasing concern to the USA. The US DEA estimated that in 1991 and 1992 150 tonnes of cocaine passed through Guatemala annually.[83] Unlike their Salvadorean counterparts, the military in Guatemala are economically reliant neither on the domestic bourgeoisie nor on US aid.

In contrast to the Reagan administration's failure to condemn human rights abuses during the 1980s, under Bush military aid was suspended in January 1991 in protest at the lack of action regarding the notorious June 1990 murder of US citizen Michael Devine by soldiers in the Petén, the abduction, rape and torture of Ursuline nun, Dianna Ortiz, and the December 1990 massacre of fifteen villagers in Santiago Atitlán. Washington's tougher stance encouraged a renewal of negotiations and the first official round of talks in April 1991 in Mexico City established an eleven point agenda for negotiation. The second round at Querétaro the following June achieved agreement on the first (and least controversial) point around the definition of 'democratisation'. However, three subsequent meetings in September and October 1991 and January 1992 failed to reach agreement on the issue of human rights. For over a year the URNG insisted on a set of demands wholly unacceptable to the government negotiating team.[84]

Issues surrounding a cease-fire, rebel demobilisation and re-incorporation into civilian life also proved a constant block to negotiations, given the rebels' understandable fear of reprisals and the tendency of a significant part of the officers corps to see talks merely as a negotiated surrender by the URNG. A new insurgent proposal in May 1992 postponed debate of demobilisation issues, instead focusing on refugee resettlement, constitutional reform, indigenous rights and economic change. In August 1992 agreement was reached to freeze recruitment into the PACs. However, the army only gave this undertaking on condition that recruitment could recommence in the event of an insurgent offensive. Since 1990 the URNG have met with a number of national social and economic groups, including the private enterprise confederation CACIF, and the cumulative effect of such contacts on future development should not be underestimated, even if the rebels' demands have yielded few tangible results to date.

Negotiations were at a virtual impasse throughout most of 1993, attention focused instead on the political crisis surrounding the May *autogolpe* and its immediate aftermath. Initial expectations that the de León administration might reach a rapid settlement with the URNG were soon disappointed when in October 1993 the hawkish Héctor Rosada (who replaced Bishop Quezada as mediator in the talks), presented a new peace plan to the URNG which attempted to separate technical negotiations for a ceasefire from talks on social and political reform and offered neither concrete guarantees for human rights nor the possibility of a Truth Commission. This was immediately rejected by the URNG. The January 1994 agreement to restart peace talks signal an appreciable advance after the previous months of deadlock, the URNG scoring a notable victory in the adoption of the 1991 Mexico Agenda as the basis for talks. This 11-point document includes substantive and operational aspects of a peace settlement, spanning the issues that gave rise to or have arisen from the war and aspects relating to bringing about the end to the armed conflict.[85] The role accorded to the UN as mediator in the negotiations (and in subsequent verification of any accord reached) must be seen as a positive step towards resolution of this most obdurate of the Central American conflicts.

The issue of human rights is at the heart of any future accord in Guatemala, which will almost inevitably be focused on securing certain basic guarantees for both ex-combatants and the civilian population rather than on significant troop demobilisation or restructuring of the armed forces, issues the high command has ruled off the negotiating agenda. However, although an agreement establishing formal guarantees for future observance of human rights has been reached, the refusal of the military to sanction an effective investigation of past war crimes (a point insisted on by local human rights organisations) is symptomatic both of the persistence of military power and a singular lack of interest on the part of civilian elites, and means that the immunity of senior officers remains absolute.[86]

Given the persistence of the civil war and the long-standing involvement of the police corps in counter-insurgency activities, it is perhaps unsurprising that little advance on the separation of military from police functions and the transfer of police control to civilian authorities has been made in Guatemala. Some attempts to reform the police occurred during the Cerezo administration. However, the central question of political control has never been addressed.[87] Under Serrano, joint police-military operations were stepped up in an attempt to improve lacklustre police performance, through such mechanisms as the creation of joint permanent patrolling operation, the 'Servicio de Protección Civil' (SIPROCI) which coordinated anti-narcotics operations with the US DEA. In May 1991 Interior Minister Hurtado Prem announced the creation of a Civil Guard to unify the Treasury and National Police (to be trained by Chilean

Carabineros). However, although the various police bodies are nominally under the jurisdiction of the Interior Ministry, they effectively remain under army control. In March 1992, SIPROCI was replaced by 'Hunapá', a joint force comprising army and Treasury Police members and commanded by a military officer, Col. Herman Grootewold.[88] After Hunapá troops were implicated in the killing of one student and the disappearance of at least 15 others in April 1992, they were replaced in November 1992 with an integrated task force, comprised of 2,200 agents from the Treasury Police, National Police and Military Ambulatory Police, and – like Hunapá – ultimately subject to military command. Since 1990, the extension of such 'anti-delinquency' bodies indicate an increase rather than a decrease in military control of the police. The recent decision to transfer police intelligence services to the office of the Presidency may signal a growing acceptance of certain 'professionalising reforms' by a sector of the military; however, the net effect of the recent transfer has yet to be seen and it should be noted that the military's own intelligence sector remains inviolate.

Despite the absence to date of a formal settlement in Guatemala, a number of developments since 1987 demonstrate important shifts within what might rightly be called 'civil society', indicating that certain calculations are being made against the possibility of an end to the civil war. These include: an increase in popular mobilisation and the emergence of indigenous organisations at national level; the return of refugees from Mexico; and growing resistance to the civil patrols. In the wake of the Serrano-*golpe*, the hegemony of the political parties all but collapsed and civil society is cautiously emerging as an autonomous political actor. The guarantees obtained to treat returning refugees as civilians and grant them three years exemption from military service or participation in the civil patrols constituted a significant concession by the armed forces. However, progress to date has been uneven; many refugees have returned to highly militarised areas where the army continue to control most aspects of daily life, and on a number of occasions returned refugees have been forced to cross the Guatemalan-Mexican border in flight from army attacks. The emergence since 1990 of the internally displaced Comunidades de los Pueblos en Resistencia (CPRs) in the Ixcán, Petén and highlands of the Ixil triangle signal a challenge to the army's counter-insurgency hegemony in the altiplano, given the CPRs' refusal to participate in the civil patrols or to live in model villages. However, army attacks against the CPRs continue, evidencing the fragility of gains and cautioning against an over-optimistic reading.

As Richard Wilson has argued, the army have so enmeshed themselves into indigenous culture in rural Guatemala, that any prospect of immediate 'demilitarisation' in the broadest sense of the word is unlikely.[89] The persistence of the civil patrols and the army's omnipotent presence in all rural development efforts mean that the militarisation of rural society in highland Guatemala has long since exceeded the boundaries of physical coercion alone. It is questionable indeed whether in the case of such a traumatised society subject to such wholesale penetration by military counter-insurgency operations it is meaningful to talk of demilitarisation in the terms of a peace settlement or its immediate aftermath. The impact of developments in civil society may yet prove the key to a slow and cautious process of change in civil/military relations in Guatemala. Nonetheless, given the numerous precedents which exist, a return to widespread repression cannot be ruled out.

The Guatemalan military is now firmly locked into the negotiating process. However, calls by the UN human rights expert appointed to Guatemala, Mónica Pinto, for the immediate abolition of the PACs have been repeatedly rejected by the high command whilst President de León himself has publicly reaffirmed his commitment to the PACs on numerous occasions. Under the March 1994 human rights accord, participation in the PACs must be voluntary. However, although undoubtedly the patrol system is not as omnipresent as it was in the mid-1980s, many who have attempted to leave have been subject to harrassment and murder.[90] In January 1995 de León announced that the PACs would become 'peace and development' committees, indicating the military's desire to retain structures of surveillance and control over the rural – and even urban – population.[91]

Given the history of cyclical violence in Guatemala and the manifest inability of the URNG to guarantee the physical safety of its members were they to disarm and attempt reintegration, the presence of the UN international peace-keeping force MINUGUA (agreed in January 1994 – see chapter eight) will be essential in the event of any future settlement.

Conclusions

Although the formal process of cease-fire, peace-making and (regime) transition is much more advanced in some countries of Central America than in others, it has nowhere reached a point at which a new, regular path of military behaviour and civil-military relations is clearly evident. As a result it would be misguided to talk yet of any 'consolidation' or firm pattern. Correspondingly, care should be exercised in drawing clear policy conclusions from experiences that are still underway, palpably fragile, and, on both internal and external fronts, liable to mutation and even reversal. Nonetheless, by early 1994 a number of broad tendencies can be identified.

Although, as stated at the outset, the Central American armies were preoccupied primarily with achieving settlements on a national basis, neither the absence of a regional war nor the quite differing approach taken by three US administrations should obscure a perceptible regional aspect to the process of peacemaking and transition. Indeed, it is possible to assert the existence of a 'knock-on effect' starting with Esquipulas (1987), taking off with the first substantial Nicaraguan ceasefire (March 1988), accelerating in late 1989 (the FMLN offensive in November; the US invasion of Panama in December), being consolidated with the defeat of the FSLN in the February 1990 elections, and reaching a natural – if scarcely 'logical' – peak with the 1991-2 Salvadorean settlement. The region's officer corps observing these developments must have drawn mixed and divergent conclusions, but if the Guatemalans – predictably the last in line – evidently sought to avoid repeating the Salvadorean experience, they surely gained a certain sense of confidence from the shifting local and international conditions. It may be that the January 1994 uprising in Chiapas put a brake on this, not least if one takes the plausible view that the region's conflicts have been pursued far more upon local considerations than as expressions of the shifting balance of world forces and ideologies. But even if this proves to be the case and Guatemalan 'exceptionalism' is further prolonged, it is unlikely to persist in the same form and will undoubtedly manifest the influence of developments in the surrounding states.

The process of ceasefire and transition has been shadowed by declining interest and involvement on the part of the US government. Indeed, with respect to the Clinton administration (1993-) there is a strong case for arguing that Central America was so low on the policy agenda that the military question was just as prey to congressional whim (as manipulated by Sen. Helms) as to any view in the State Department, let alone the White House. In the same vein, it would be misguided to assume that there was a coherent shift in US doctrinal influence on the armed forces, although in rapidly changing circumstances US military advisers sometimes plainly held and persuaded their audiences. Perhaps the most plausible scenario for the last years of the century is that which obtained during the 1960s and early 1970s, when US management of military matters was largely tactically determined at embassy and attaché level and without significant financial considerations. However, if there is now no guerrilla threat (or one that is massively reduced) at local level and no challenge emanating from Cuba, the region's armies have still been irreversibly transformed in some respects, not all of which are acceptable to Washington.

One signal trend in the current transition, no doubt related to the rapid decline in US military aid from 1980s levels, is that towards consolidation and diversification of the armed forces' institutional economic structures. Whilst the antecedents and extent of such corporate holdings vary greatly across the region, a shift in the nature of the military's interests is evident throughout. Whereas previously accumulation of wealth amongst the officer corps constituted a kind of 'primitive individualism', personal fortunes amassed through such semi-licit means as land purchases, logging deals and trade in emeralds, IPMs throughout the region are currently extending the institutional portfolio of the armed forces into the areas of manufacturing, finance and commerce. Whilst criticism of 'burguesías armadas' are not without justification, this institutionalisation might, in some circumstances, more accurately be seen as a guarantor of current efforts to demilitarise – as in Nicaragua, where the development of the IPM constitutes an attempt to attend to the welfare claims of large numbers of decommissioned personnel. Military demands for a *quid pro quo*, or at the very least some minimal financial guarantees, in exchange for reduction in numbers or substantive withdrawal from the public sphere are only to be expected; it is arguably preferable to give retiring officers an officially structured and sanctioned pay-off which at least provides a more plausible framework for official oversight. However, clearly it is not only desirable but also imperative that those officers found guilty of human rights violations receive no such benefits and are dishonourably discharged. If the traditional impunity of the region's military is truly to be reduced, then trials and punitive sanctions are the preferred, if not always the most politically acceptable, option in such cases.

Another consequence of the 1980s was the massive expansion of the military's involvement in cocaine and heroin trafficking throughout the region, a wholly less salubrious form of capital accumulation. Already significant in Central America by the end of the 1970s, *narcotráfico* took off in the subsequent decade, inevitably encouraged by the generalised climate of impunity prevailing across the isthmus. Such lawlessness was additionally fomented by the Reagan administration's drug-running operations to supply the contra which, by providing both sanction and substantial logistical support, aided those officers involved in cocaine smuggling to consolidate their hold on power. Particularly acute amongst the Guatemalan and Honduran armed forces – and almost *sui generis* in the case of Panama – the expansion of drug-trafficking by the military poses a serious threat to the formal command structure and *escalafón*, exacerbating factionalism amongst officers and inevitably increasing instability. This constitutes not only a threat to civil society but to the very foundations of the military institutions themselves.

Drugs are but one factor behind the climate of increased crime, violence and *delincuencia común* which has accelerated throughout the region with the end (or in the case of Guatemala, scaling down) of the civil wars. Whether rooted in motives of revenge (El Salvador) or a corollary of generalised socio-economic collapse (Nicaragua), the net effect of this phenomena has been to validate the official role of police forces in the maintenance of domestic order, even though police practice in many specific instances continues to provide considerable·cause for concern. In contrast to El Salvador, where guidelines governing the establishment and functions of the PNC were drawn up as part of the peace negotiations, the make-up and institutional remit of police forces elsewhere in the region is a function of various factors including: securing the demobilisation of rebel forces (Nicaragua), the abolition of the army (Panama), or the degree of control still exercised over the police by the armed forces (Honduras and Guatemala). In the present climate, the need for more stringent and efficient institutional regulation of the police is ever more apparent. However, the acute partiality and corruption demonstrated across the region by that very highest of legal institutions, the Supreme Court, raises the question of which bodies are indeed capable of carrying out this oversight. Perhaps the most noxious and enduring consequence of the civil wars of the 1980s is not, indeed, directly institutional at all but, rather, the influence they had on the outlook and behaviour of the societies affected well beyond those who participated or were directly prejudiced by the conflicts. In the immediate aftermath of the wars in Nicaragua and El Salvador both lawful and peaceable conduct were distinctly tenuous, and there was a profusion of armaments as well as a proclivity – as yet contained – for acts of revenge. However, in the still unresolved case of Guatemala one may readily refer to a 'militarised culture' – at least in many zones of the country – that extends well beyond current or former soldiers in the state and rebel armies. If Honduras has witnessed a strong reaction to this in the campaign to abolish conscription – one of the central expressions of military authority in civil society – it is notable that this has been resisted with unswerving resilience in Guatemala, not just for recruitment to the regular military forces but also for the salients they have driven deep into society via the *Comisionados* and the PACs. Here, then, one should beware the extension of the 'culture of war' generated by the awful exigencies of fighting to one that follows this experience but still prescribes behaviour in 'peacetime' that is based on the same brutal assumptions.

Notes

1. *Acuerdos de Chapultepec* (1992); Tulchin (1992); Vickers and Spence (1992); Walter and Williams (1992a).
2. As of late 1992 the military still controlled telecommunications; water and drainage; development support; national statistics and censuses; customs; civil aviation; and the post office.
3. Bacevich, Hallum, White and Young (1988), p. 44.
4. Walter and Williams, *op.cit.*, p. 78; Walter and Williams (1992b), p. 198. The Atlacatl Battalion had been involved (under different commanders) in both the El Mozote massacre and the execution of the Jesuits.
5. 'As the officers understood only too quickly, the ultimate sanction that the Americans could brandish – turning off the aid spigot – threatened to hurt the Americans themselves as much as it would the Salvadoreans, since the American fear of a communist El Salvador taking its place alongside Sandinista Nicaragua had become overriding.' Mark Danner, 'The Truth of El Mozote', *The New Yorker*, 6 December 1993, p. 61. The view of some US advisors that Salvadorean officers were deliberately keeping the war at an optimum level for their own financial needs is reported in Schwarz (1991), p. 21. If the US Congress's human rights conditions were largely inconsequential in terms of conditions within El Salvador, the restriction on the number of advisers, whilst often evaded, still impeded the influence and effectiveness of MilGroup, and advisers complained bitterly about it. See the comments of Col. John Waghelstein in Montgomery (1991), p. 11; Bacevich et al., *op.cit.*, p. 41.
6. The proposal to establish a mixed and provisional 'Gobierno de Amplia Participación' dated from 1983 and envisaged a military solution short of outright victory for the FMLN. Whilst for some time after its publication this objective might have been largely for propaganda purposes, it subsequently provided an authentic framework for guerrilla negotiations and strategic adjustments (Miles and Ostertag, 1991). The ERP, which switched the content of its title from Ejército Revolucionario del Pueblo to Expresión Renovadora del Pueblo, displayed an even sharper shift away from its radical origins than its sister-parties in the FMLN.
7. Americas Watch and American Civil Liberties Union (1982), p. 11.
8. For De Soto's explanation of his role – in the midst of negotiations – see Tulchin, *op.cit.*
9. For an impressionistic but persuasive depiction of the attitudes of leading conservative planters, see Paige (1993).
10. *Central America Report*, 18 June 1993; 13 August 1993; 17 September 1993.
11. *Ibid.*, 20 August 1993; 22 October 1993; 5 November 1993.
12. *Ibid.*, 16 November 1993; 10 December 1993.

13. Vickers and Spence, *op.cit.*, p. 13.
14. *Central America Report*, 7 May 1993; 8 October 1993.
15. The Constitutions of 1950, 1962 and 1983 provided the military with an unqualified internal security role. For example, clause 12, article 168 of the 1983 Constitution states: 'Disponer de la Fuerza Armada para el mantenimiento de la soberanía, el orden, la seguridad y tranquilidad de la República...' Amended on 30 January 1992, this clause now reads: 'Disponer de la Fuerza Armada para la Defensa y Soberanía del Estado, de la Integridad de su Territorio. Excepcionalmente, si se han agotado los medios ordinarios para el mantenimiento de la paz interna, la tranquilidad y seguridad pública, el Presidente de la República podrá disponer de la Fuerza Armada para ese fin. La actuación de la Fuerza Armada se limitará al tiempo y a la medida de lo estrictamente necesario para reestablecimiento del orden y cesará tan pronto se haya alcanzado ese cometido...' *Constitución de la República*, San Salvador, March 1992, pp. 63, 129. It is perhaps worth noting that it was the refusal of the high command to subordinate itself to the orders of the governing (civil-military) junta issued on 28 December 1979 that effectively sealed the polarisation over the following twelve months, leading to outright civil war.
16. The Chapultepec Accords state: 'the evaluation will take into account the record of each officer, including especially: (i) his history in terms of observing the legal order, with particular emphasis on respect for human rights, both in his personal conduct and the vigour with which he has corrected and penalised irregular acts, excesses or violations of human rights carried out under his command, especially if serious or systematic omissions are observed in this respect; (ii) his professional competence; (iii) his ability to adapt himself to the new reality of peace, within the context of a democratic society, and to promote democracy in the country, guarantee unrestricted respect for human rights and reunify Salvadorean society...' *Acuerdos de Chapultepec*, pp. 3-4.
17. *Central America Report*, 2 April 1993.
18. *Ibid.*, 15 January 1993; 5 February 1993.
19. Walker (1991), p. 81.
20. *Ibid.*, p. 86.
21. Both the Ministry of Interior and the Ministry of Defence were responsible to the joint FSLN National Directorate, of which Interior Minister Tomás Borge and Defence Minister Humberto Ortega were both members.
22. After initial rejection of the Arias plan, the Sandinista government signalled its willingness to compromise on the question of the internal political reforms stressed in the accords in exchange for an end to support by neighbouring states for insurgent forces and their backing for the plan agreed at Tela on 7 August 1989, which provided for voluntary demobilisation, repatriation and relocation of the contras by the end of the year and the moving forward of the Nicaraguan elections to February 1990.
23. A unilateral cease-fire was declared by the EPS as a result of the Sapoá talks but was later cancelled in 1989 in response to increased contra attacks in the run up to the 1990 elections.

24. Following the February 1990 polls, US Special Envoy Harry Shlaudeman and US Ambassador to Honduras Cresencio Arcos travelled to contra headquarters in Yamales, Honduras and told the insurgent leadership they must lay down their arms and demobilise before the USA would fund their transition to civilian life.

25. One observer maintains that a large number of draftees (who constituted some 40,000 members of the EPS) had deserted during the 1990 elections. See Child (1992), p. 89.

26. The percentage of the national budget devoted to defence had expanded from 20.4 per cent in 1980 to 34.1 per cent in 1985 and 41.3 per cent by 1987, a state of affairs which was unsustainable after 1988. In 1989 the military budget had been cut by some 30 per cent. Stahler-Sholk (1990); Walker (1991), p. 91. In addition, the suspension of Soviet and Cuban arms transfers since early 1989 had also affected the EPS's operational capacity.

27. *Central America Report*, 16 April 1993.

28. The 1986 Constitution prohibits the existence of any armed force apart from the EPS and the Sandinista Police within national territory: 'No pueden existir más cuerpos armados en el territorio nacional que los establecidos por la ley, la cual regulará las bases de la organización militar.' Art. 95, Constitución Política de la República de Nicaragua, *La Gaceta*, Managua, 8 January 1987.

29. Jaime Zeledón ('Comandante Bolívar') became police chief of Jinotega; members of the contra were also appointed as police chiefs in San Rafael del Norte and Yali, and as assistant police-chiefs in Pantasma and Wiwilí. *Central America Report*, 24 January 1992.

30. *Ibid.*, 17 July 1992.

31. *Ibid.*, 20 September 1991; 18 June 1993.

32. On 19 May 1990, a formal agreement was reached between the outgoing Sandinista government, the incoming Chamorro administration and the contra leadership (represented by Oscar Sovalbarro, 'Comandante Rubén') which pledged special assistance and development projects in return for demobilisation by the end of June. The demobilisation and reintegration, supervised by the CIAV, allowed the rebels to move into designated 'security zones' within Nicaragua prior to giving up their arms. Despite slow progress – many weapons handed in were old and rusty, indicating that a substantial portion of the contra's armaments had been salted away to hidden *buzones* – the vast bulk of the insurgent forces were successfully demobilised.

33. The Sandinista government had distributed some 50,000 AK-47s to its militia during the war and another 20,000 to civilian supporters between the election of February 1990 and the inauguration two months later. Child (1992), p. 110.

34. Despite calls from recontra leaders for the removal of General Humberto Ortega as Supreme Chief of the Armed Forces, the demands of the recontra were primarily economic and social rather than political. However, it should be noted that the February 1991 assassination of ex-contra leader and GN colonel, Enrique Bermúdez, in the car-park of the Intercontinental Hotel in Managua led to numerous protests from contra members, protests which increased when the subsequent police investigation failed to clarify the killing.

35. *Central America Report*, 16 July 1993.
36. The use of force in Estelí – where approximately 40 people, including civilians were killed – contrasts with the army's reaction to the July 1990 national strike called by the Sandinista Frente Nacional de Trabajadores (FNT), when the EPS eventually intervened to restore order but restrained from using direct force against the strikers.
37. *Central America Report*, 18 February 1994.
38. Contra members have now organised their own political party to pursue ex-contra demands through legal channels. The first national congress of the party, *Resistencia Nicaragüense*, was held on 4 December 1993 and was attended by more than 1,000 representatives of the *desmovilizados*.
39. Recontras of the Northern 3-80 Front led by José Angel Talavera ('El Chacal') demanding the removal of Humberto Ortega and Antonio Lacayo held nearly 40 Sandinista officials hostage and provoked a similar hostage-taking exercise in Managua by Sandinista supporters.
40. In a breath-taking piece of hyperbole, Helms's aid Deborah De Moss claimed in a 1992 report that Nicaragua was 'the most heavily militarised state in Central America'. *Central America Report*, 18 September 1992. It may be that De Moss's recent marriage to Chief of the Honduran Instituto de Previsión Militar, Colonel Héctor René Fonseca, had somewhat clouded her judgement with regard to the extent of militarisation elsewhere in the region.
41. *Central America Report*, 7 February 1993; CRIES (1993), p. 51. The visit of Cantarero López signalled the start of a gradual rapprochement between the EPS and other regional militaries: in November 1990 the EPS signed an agreement with the Honduran armed forces which provided for joint operations to fight arms trafficking and contraband along the border.
42. The Kremlin had turned down an offer to buy back weaponry supplied to the EPS. The IPM was set up with an initial budget of $5 million acquired through the sale of helicopters to Peru and Ecuador. *Central America Report*, 18 June 1993.
43. Most of the army's current business holdings were acquired through Laws 85 and 86, passed by the Sandinista government during the transition period in 1990. *Central America Report*, 24 June 1994.
44. The guerrilla groups are: Fuerzas Populares Revolucionarias 'Lorenzo Zelaya' – FPL – est. 1980; Frente Morazanista de Liberación Nacional – FMLH – est. 1979; Movimiento Popular de Liberación – MPL or Cinchoneros – est. 1980; and Partido Revolucionario de los Trabajadores Centroamericanos – PRTC – est. 1979. In 1983, together with the Honduran Communist Party (PCH), these groups formed the Dirección Nacional Unitaria (DNU). Despite some initial resistance, all four insurgent groups have now laid down their arms and switched their focus to the electoral arena, although they have little chance of breaking into what is essentially a two-horse race.
45. Although in theory the Head of the Armed Forces is selected by the President, in practice changes in the military hierarchy are decided internally, presented to the Executive as a *fait accompli* and then rubber-stamped by Congress.

46. Barry and Preusch (1986), p. 112.
47. Latin America Bureau (1985), p. 88.
48. On 14 May 1980, Salvadorean troops massacred approximately 600 civilians at the Sumpul river, Morazán, on the Salvadorean/Honduran border, Honduran troops preventing the fleeing refugees from crossing into Honduran territory. A few days prior to the massacre, the Honduran press had carried reports of a secret meeting in Ocotepeque, Honduras, between high-level military officers from Guatemala, Honduras and El Salvador: Comisión Nacional de Protección de los Derechos Humanos (1993), p. 39.
49. Alvarez promoted the formation of APROH (Asociación para el Progreso de Honduras), an anti-communist grouping of business and trade union leaders and key figures in both the National and Liberal parties. Past members of APROH include ex-President Rafael Leonardo Callejas and PN candidate for the 1993 poll, Oswaldo Ramos Soto.
50. *Central America Report*, 13 May 1994.
51. Article 1 of the *Ley Constitutiva de las Fuerzas Armadas* defines the same as 'una institución de carácter permanente, esencialmente profesional, se instituye para defender la integridad territorial y la soberanía de la República, para mantener la paz, el orden público y el imperio de la Constitución, velando por que no se violen los principios de libre sufragio y de la alternabilidad en el ejercicio de la Presidencia de la República', assigning responsibility for both external defence and internal security to the armed forces. *La Gaceta*, Tegucigalpa, 25 February 1975.
52. *Ibid.*, 14 June 1991 and 2 April 1993.
53. *Ibid.*, 2 April 1993.
54. A total of $32 million was cut from the governmental budget in 1991. Calls for a $3 million cut in military allocations were rejected. Military spending in 1991 officially represented 8 per cent of the national budget, but this figure was widely disputed. The official 1994 military budget is $40 million of a $961 million general budget, although the United Nations reportedly estimates the magnitude of the military budget at some $180 million. *Central America Report*, 14 June 1991 and 13 May 1994.
55. The assassination attempt against the son of ex-armed forces chief Regalado Hernández in January 1993 was widely suspected to be drug-related. See *Tiempo* (Tegucigalpa), 15 January 1993.
56. In 1991 the US State Department sponsored the opening of an office (Oficina de Responsabilidad Profesional, ORP) where individuals could make formal complaints against the police. The citizenry, not unsurprisingly, proved in the main unwilling to brave the Cuartel General to protest police brutality. They were hardly encouraged by the declarations of armed forces chief General Discua Elvir, who in 1991 added his voice to the debate over police reform stating, 'yo creo que la policía debería ser más violenta para que la respeten más'. *La Tribuna* (Tegucigalpa), 14 December 1991.
57. *Central America Report*, 12 August 1994.

58. The military budget allocation for 1995 previously stood at $35.2 million. The increase supported by Reina would bring this figure up to $49.2 million. *Central America Report*, 17 March 1995.

59. Denial has long since been a feature of Honduran politics. Both Suazo Córdova and his successor, President José Azcona de Hoyo persistently maintained there were no contra forces in Honduras, despite the effective occupation of large swathes of the departments of Danlí and Olancho for much of the 1980s. However, official protestations of innocence notwithstanding, in October 1987 a landmark judgement by the Inter-American Court of Human Rights gained Honduras the dubious distinction of becoming the first state to be found guilty in an international tribunal of carrying out disappearances against its own citizens.

60. Comisión Nacional de Protección de los Derechos Humanos (1993).

61. Panama is properly given as an example of 'imposition of democracy' in Whitehead (1991).

62. Article V of the 1977 Treaty reads: 'After the termination of the Panama Canal Treaty, only the Republic of Panama shall operate the Canal and maintain military forces, defense sites and military installation within its National Territory'. According to the Panamanian government, the USA spends some $750 million a year on Canal defence whereas anticipated fees for 1999 were $500 million. The 1991 security budget was $85 million. In September 1990 Vice-President Ricardo Arias Calderón declared, 'a military defence of the interoceanic canal similar to the proportions of the US is outside the concrete, practical and economic scope of Panama'. *Central America Report*, 21 September 1990. In May 1990 SouthCom commander General Marc Cisneros made a peculiarly engaging contribution to the anti-military campaign in stating, 'Panama doesn't need to have an army since there is no danger of invasion'. *Ibid.*, 8 June 1990. Although the FDP is abolished, the Fuerza Pública does not formally replace it, and is a new body.

63. *Ibid.*, 10 July 1992. Caution should be exercised in extrapolating from the referendum result. In March 1993 a poll found that 78 per cent of Panamanians wanted the USA to stay beyond December 1999, and only 17 per cent wanted all US forces out by 2000. Furlong (1993), p. 56.

64. The deficiencies of the constabulary force are well summarised in Rouquié (1987), pp. 120-177.

65. Conniff (1990), pp. 611-2.

66. The 1972 Constitution provided for elections every six years to an assembly composed of some 500 non-party *corregidores* who would meet once a year to elect the President, Vice-President and Jefe de Gobierno, who could simultaneously command the GN. In September 1972 Torrijos was elected 'Jefe Supremo de Panamá'.

67. Ropp (1992), pp. 213, 217.

68. Ropp estimates that some 45,000 poor workers were employed by the public sector by the mid-1970s, when central government borrowing – largely from private banks – was running at 5 per cent of GDP (against a regional average of 2 per cent). *Ibid.*, pp. 219-20. By the late 1970s *narcotráfico* was also

exercising an influence, but attention should be paid to the fact that by 1979 the GN-administered Colón Free Trade Zone was handling 7 per cent of Latin America's imports. For more anecdotal references to the political exploitation of Panama's shady economy, see LaRae Pippin (1964) and Kempe (1990). Such matters effectively require a suspension of academic protocols for referencing, but if Kempe (pp. 270-2) is right that maintaining the 'populist bureaucracy' at the end of the 1980s cost between $55 million and $65 million, this could certainly have been off-set by cocaine revenue.

69. Panama City rather resembles Beirut and Vienna in its importance as a regional intelligence/espionage centre. The coups of October 1968 and December 1969 are sometimes explained in terms of rivalry between the CIA and the US army's 407th intelligence battalion, and both bodies clearly had an interest in retaining Noriega's services during the 1980s. Under Noriega the FDP developed the UESAT (Unidad Especial Anti-Terrorista) anti-terrorist unit, the 'Machos del Monte' and 'Batallón 2000' elite groups.

70. Many human rights organisations claimed a greater number of casualties were caused, the matter acquiring importance within US politics as well as between the US and Panama. In December 1993 the Inter-American Human Rights Commission and the OAS accepted Panamanian demands for compensation, and although the US has not ratified the IAHR Accord, it is a member of the OAS, and rejection of its recommendations on this issue would imply a refusal to be bound by the OAS Charter's articles on human rights.

71. *Tico Times* (San José), 6 April 1993.

72. *Central America Report*, 30 April 1993. Panamanian relations with Peru soured considerably at the end of 1991 when Colonels Gonzalo González (CO of the Machos del Monte) and Heraclides Sucre (CO Batallón 2000), held responsible for the murder of fellow officers in the abortive coup attempt of October 1989, 'escaped' from 'house arrest' in Lima, where they were in exile. Peru (under the García government), Mexico, Ecuador and Cuba condemned the 1989 invasion. *Ibid.*, 22 November 1991.

73. Walter and Williams (1992b), p. 203. The police was initially planned to be only 4,000-strong.

74. *Central America Report*, 17 May 1991; 31 January 1992; 7 February 1992; Furlong (1993), pp. 26-7.

75. *Central America Report*, 4 September 1992.

76. Amongst several examples, the case of Máximo Pinzón and Luis Varela, respectively ex-chief of the FDP's intelligence unit and the leading suspect in the Spadafora murder, both subsequently in senior positions (chief of intelligence and chief of the homicide department) in the PTJ. Lt. Colonel Eduardo Herrera, the second of four directors appointed to the PN throughout 1990 and figurehead of the PN December 1990 mutiny, was Endara's favourite target and was jailed on at least two occasions for subversion without any trial or any more public evidence against him than existed against his erstwhile comrades who continued to hold posts.

77. The matter was quite serious, involving 150 officers and 500 US troops. Among the police's demands were a wage rise, guaranteed apolitical status, and full compensation for the relatives of those killed in the invasion. *Central America Report*, 14 December 1990.
78. Jonas (1991), p. 149.
79. For a critical assessment of the Cerezo period see Painter (1987).
80. WOLA (1989), p. 2.
81. Ricardo Córdova (1987); *Central America Report*, 15 November 1991. *Central America Report* gives the figures as 46,000 for the military and 17,500 for the police.
82. US military aid was first suspended in 1977 under Carter and was renewed in 1985 (when Guatemala received $0.5 million, compared to $136.3 million for El Salvador and $67.4 million disbursed to the Honduran military). During the Cerezo administration US military aid increased from $4.5 million in 1986 to $9.4 million in 1989, although the figure was reduced to $3.3 million in 1990. The total defence budget for the Guatemalan military in 1991 was $91 million. In 1993, US military aid had fallen to $0.4 million. *Central America Report*, 11 January 1991; Dunkerley (1994), p. 171.
83. CIIR Comment (London, 1993), p. 29.
84. The URNG's demands included: repeal of the 1985 amnesty, establishment of a Truth Commission; abolition of the civil patrols and obligatory military conscription; and the removal of the *fuero militar* so that military officers could be tried for common crimes in civilian courts.
85. The Mexico Agenda included: (1) human rights; (2) strengthening civilian power and the role of the military in a democratic society; (3) identity and the rights of the indigenous population; (4) constitutional reform and electoral processes; (5) socio-economic issues; (6) agrarian situation; (7) resettlement of population displaced by the armed conflict; (8) basis for incorporation of the URNG into national politics; (9) arrangements for a definitive cease-fire; (10) time-table for implementation, compliance and verification of the accords; and (11) signature of an Accord for Firm and Lasting Peace and demobilisation. *Central America Report*, 14 January 1994.
86. A pertinent reminder of the difficulties of investigation was the August 1991 death squad killing of José Mérida Escobar, chief of the police homicide division, who had implicated an army agent in the September 1990 murder of Mack. The Supreme Court recently ruled the case open again, despite the conviction of Sergeant Noel de Jesús Beteta to 30 years for the murder. This raises the possibility of a civil action against General Edgar Godoy Gaitán, former head of the Presidential Military Staff (EMP), suspected of ordering the killing. *Central America Report*, 18 February 1994.
87. Article 244 of the 1985 Constitution states that the main function of the armed forces is 'the maintenance of independence, sovereignty, national honour, territorial integrity, peace and internal and external security', reserving the task of internal security for the armed forces. *Constitución Política de la República de Guatemala* (Guatemala, 1992), p. 135.

88. *Central America Report*, 20 March 1992.
89. Wilson (1993a).
90. Solomon (1994). For more detail on the civil patrols see the survey carried out by the Human Rights Procurator's office; *Los Comités de Defensa Civil en Guatemala* (Guatemala, 1994).
91. In January 1995 Defence Minister Mario Enríquez signalled his approval in principle for the notion of forming PACs in the city. *Central America Report*, 27 January 1995.

CHAPTER 4

THE LEGACY OF CONFLICT:
REFUGEE REPATRIATION AND REINTEGRATION
IN CENTRAL AMERICA

Diana Pritchard

At first glance the large-scale repatriations occurring in recent years to Nicaragua, El Salvador and Guatemala appear as unequivocal evidence of the consolidation of regional peace and as a symbol of the end of conflict. This view seems credible when the current is compared to that of the 1980s, when tens of thousands of uprooted Central Americans fled violence in their countries to seek refuge across international borders. However, an analysis of the experience of those refugees, the processes of repatriation and the problems arising from resettlement belie such a simplistic interpretation. This chapter explores the relationship between refuge, repatriation and resettlement and regional peace, stability and economic restructuring.

The refugee question is analysed here as a central element in regional political change. This itself constitutes a challenge to the prevalent treatment of the refugee issue: typically, commentators underplay the importance of the uprooted in their analysis of regional conflict, perceiving them merely as its peripheral, unfortunate by-products.[1] However, the situation in Central America demands a different treatment.[2] The politicisation of the refugee question by key political and military actors in the region and the active role assumed by the uprooted themselves in political developments demands that the refugee issue be placed more centrally in analysis. Undoubtedly, mass exodus is a reflection of conflict, but it must also be seen as a catalyst for political change. As the refugee situation and the refugees themselves have influenced the evolution of political developments, so too the highly complex process of returnee reinsertion into society influences the prospects for future stability. While recognising that the problems and causes of displacement are similar for those staying or fleeing a country, analysis here is focused on cross-border refugee migrations rather than on the internally displaced, because of the national and international political implications generated by the former. Analysing the influence of the uprooted on political developments is pertinent to wider processes underway in the post-war context. Pacification and reconciliation are accompanied by the contentious process of reconstructing national political history. In this 'rewriting of history', the uprooted and repatriated struggle to be accorded their rightful place as significant historical actors, but do so in a context where other regional actors have polemically interpreted their roles. At one extreme, governments have perceived refugees as being, at best, illegal migrants, at worst guerrillas or subversives. To the extent that insurgent combatants claimed to represent 'the people', the notion of poor refugees as seedbeds of opposition was perpetuated. This view 'legitimised' the repressive and restrictive measures taken to contain these populations, when refugees were viewed within official circles as a security or foreign policy issue.[3] Such a notion continues to threaten the physical integrity of returnees to the extent that it informs policies of surveillance and repressive human rights practices.

Insurgent combatants have their social bases in the countryside and nurture support amongst peasant communities. However, the precise relationship between those fleeing their homes and the various insurgent forces is not at all clear; given the political sensitivity of the matter, it also presents acute methodological problems for investigation. Nonetheless, there exists significant evidence to indicate that many fleeing populations in El Salvador and Guatemala identified strongly with the guerrilla and supported its activities; in Nicaragua many refugees aligned themselves either with the ruling Sandinista forces or with the contra.[4] However, so too is it apparent that objective circumstances of the war made neutrality an increasingly dangerous stance. David Stoll's research on three towns in the Ixil region of Guatemala suggests that some indian communities, caught between two warring armies, ultimately opted for survival by associating with the stronger state forces.[5]

At the other end of the perceptual continuum, the displaced are viewed as 'victims' of conflict and as a 'problem' requiring humanitarian and emergency response. This approach, adopted by the United Nations High Commission for Refugees (UNHCR) and by some non-governmental organisations (NGOs), has been operationalised in the practical efforts of aid agencies to meet the immediate needs of refugees.[6] It has been important in gaining the necessary humanitarian 'space' to enable the agencies to reach target populations, but has perpetuated paternalistic practices concerning their assistance. In addition, such an approach largely ignores the actual and potential contribution of the displaced in political and economic developments.

In the past, these distinct interpretations of refugees had grave consequences for the thousands of uprooted who struggled for survival during times of war. For the future, if the fragile peace and stability in Central America is to be consolidated, these views need be modified through an assessment of the legacy of the refugee experience, a process to which this chapter aims to contribute.

Firstly, the situation during the 1980s will be outlined in order not just to contextualise the recent return population trends, but also to indicate how different experiences in exile gave rise to distinct patterns of repatriation and resettlement across the region.[7]

Fleeing Violence

Prior to the late 1970s, migrations in Central America were associated primarily with the search for improved income and standards of living: that is, for reasons unambiguously economic in origin. Most migrants were poor; victims of post-war developments in the agro-export economies of the region. The expansion of large estates producing coffee, beef and cotton for export led to the dislocation and progressive marginalisation of peasant producers. Agricultural modernisation, increasing demographic pressures and lower levels of productivity from their small subsistence plots forced peasant producers into the labour markets. Permanent and seasonal migration took place, both within any one country and throughout the region, including to Chiapas in Mexico, in search of agricultural work, principally harvesting agro-export crops. Other rural inhabitants migrated to the cities, contributing to an increasing rural-urban migration flow.[8]

Towards the end of the 1970s and continuing throughout the mid-1980s, political conflict and the emergence of armed insurgent movements in Nicaragua, El Salvador and Guatemala generated another type of migration. Widespread violence and political repression in El Salvador, Guatemala and Nicaragua became the motivating 'push factor', although individuals continued to leave for economic reasons, which were exacerbated in the context of war. Of all the countries in the region, El Salvador produced the largest exodus of refugees. During the early 1980s, the army mounted large-scale sweeps through the rural areas of the northern and eastern parts of the country in an effort to eliminate the gathering insurgency. During military operations in the countryside, local civilians were viewed by the military as supporters of the guerrilla. Determined to drain this mass support, the military executed thousands of people, confiscated property and torched homes and crops leading to the forcible dislocation of the rural population. By 1986, following an intensification of aerial bombardments, over one and a half million people had been displaced from their homes.[9] One million fled the country for fear, including individuals who were specifically targeted by death squad and military operations. Despite state violations of human rights and of the Geneva Conventions,[10] the USA provided a total of $1,019 million in military aid to El Salvador throughout the decade, reaching its highest level at $196.6 million for the year 1984.[11]

A massive displacement of over one million people occurred in Guatemala during what became known as the 'scorched earth' policy implemented between 1981-1982 under the regime of Lucas García (1978-1982). The government's counterinsurgency strategy was aimed at rural populations in order to break the guerrillas' base of logistical support. This involved the systematic destruction of livestock, crops and over 400 villages. The worst affected areas were the central and western highlands where up to 80 per cent of the (predominantly Mayan indian) population was displaced.[12] The detachment from their traditional land had profound implications for communities of ethnic Mayans, because of the centrality of land in economic, spiritual and cultural terms.[13] In Guatemala, as in El Salvador, displacement was not merely a byproduct of war: it was an explicit objective of the counterinsurgency. Although the massive scale of the violence has receded since the early 1980s, the targeting of opposition leaders, grassroots organisers, student activists and human rights campaigners continues to occur. Many have either been the victims of government security forces or have fled the country. Although the brutality of the Lucas García regime convinced the Carter Administration to suspend US military aid to the Guatemalan government in 1977, the sale of light weaponry and ammunition continued throughout the early 1980s.[14] US aid was formally restored after 1985 with the return to civilian government under Christian Democrat Vinicio Cerezo.[15] Human rights observance was poor under the Cerezo administration (1986-1990) and the government notably failed to bring the perpetrators of abuse to justice.[16] The arrival to the presidency of former human rights ombudsman Ramiro de León Carpio in 1993 failed to end the era of displacement.[17] A military offensive in the Ixcán generated a flow of hundreds of internally displaced indians into Mexico as late as February 1993.[18]

The situation in Nicaragua was somewhat different. Here, two distinct groups of displaced people existed during the 1980s, from the Atlantic Coast and from the Pacific region respectively. The majority ethnic group on the Atlantic Coast, the Miskito,[19] had historical links with Anglo-Saxon, rather than Hispanic culture.[20] These historical factors determined that the population would remain suspicious of the revolutionary insurrection occurring in the Pacific in 1978 and 1979 and ultimately of the Managua-based 'Spanish' (meaning *ladino* or mixed race) Sandinista Government. Prior to 1979 there was little local organisation in this region except for MISURASATA (Miskito, Sumu and Rama Sandinistas *Asla Takanka*), a pro-Sandinista organisation composed of Miskito and Sumu and *mestizos* (mixed race). However, initial hopes that the Sandinistas might bring improvements to the Atlantic Coast were superseded by indian mistrust once it became apparent that the initial policies of the FSLN (Frente Sandinista de Liberación Nacional) ignored the cultural differences and aspirations of the coastal groups.[21] Agrarian reform measures and literacy programmes in Spanish conflicted with existing livelihood, models of organisation and aspirations for respect of their culture of the coastal ethnic groups and represented an abrupt and unwelcome form of state intervention. The situation was exploited by US policy-makers and in 1981 the CIA (Central Intelligence Agency) began to recruit Miskitos to the contra.[22] Under threat of being arrested by the Sandinista authorities for aiding the contra forces, increasing numbers of Miskito fled to Honduras. There they received training and logistical support provided by the USA and were integrated into the Frente Democrático Nacional (FDN) of the contra. In 1982, an indian flight of some 22,000 was precipitated by the forcible removal of over 12,000 Miskito and 6,000 Sumus from communities in the Río Coco area on the border with Honduras. In order to clear this combat zone and prevent its use by insurgent forces, Sandinista forces burned seventy-two communities to the ground and killed livestock. Indians were relocated in newly constructed villages in Tasba Pri, some fifty miles away and in Abisinia, in the department of Jinotega.[23] (The flight of indians to Honduras was used to political advantage by Miskito leaders and the Reagan administration seeking to discredit the Sandinista Government.)

The other group uprooted in Nicaragua was comprised of *ladino* peasants on the Pacific Coast who were essentially caught in the crossfire between contra and government forces. They fled from their homes in central and southern regions of the Pacific region either to remote frontier lands, Costa Rica to the south or Honduras to the north. Some were successfully recruited by the contra because of the general disaffection generated among some sectors of the peasantry by initial Sandinista agrarian reform policies.[24] Others who chose to stay were relocated by the government away from the conflict zones.[25] In summary, displacement from the Pacific region of Nicaragua and to a lesser extent from the Atlantic Coast was unlike that which occurred in El Salvador and Guatemala; in Nicaragua, while contra tactics of 'low-intensity warfare' deliberately targeted the civilian population, state strategies of counterinsurgency were not directly aimed at the civilian populations as they were in Guatemala and El Salvador.

Uprooted populations face the traumas associated with the experiences of war, flight and loss, the effects of which lead to high levels of psychological disturbance among refugees. Those remaining within their country of origin generally take refuge with families in neighbouring villages or in more secure urban areas. Either way, they become the poorest sectors of society and, by increasing competition for limited local resources, often aggravate the economic situation in already marginal areas. In Guatemala, most of the internally displaced are Mayan indians who in many cases are forced into the anonymity of a 'silent refuge', shedding their distinctive indigenous clothes in order to remain unobtrusive.[26] In El Salvador, the lack of personal documentation of many of those displaced denied them access to government assistance. Constructing their makeshift dwellings along riverbeds and up hillsides, they swelled the slums of San Salvador.[27] Unlike those who fled across international borders, the internally displaced were subjected to government relocation and resettlement programmes, invariably accompanied by increased levels of militarisation. In Nicaragua, *asentamientos*, organised primarily for agricultural production, also formed militias against attacking Miskitos and contras.[28] In El Salvador relocated populations were also organised into civil patrols for defence, but here the objective was to impose military control over resettled communities.[29] Similarly, in Guatemala the displaced communities, relocated in so-called 'model villages' were obliged to organise into civil defence patrols (PACs). These were conceived by the army as a way to consolidate its control in remote highland areas and represented new power structures to which traditional community authorities have become subordinated.[30] In the judgement of Beatriz Manz they represent the most dramatic transformation within civil society of the counterinsurgency campaign.[31] The effective penetration of military rationale into the heart of indigenous communities through the mechanism of the civil patrols has been a complex process which has served, ultimately, to blur the distinction between state and civil society.

Only in exceptional instances have the internally displaced evaded governmental authorities. Like the *guindas* (in effect, mobile communities) that operated in semi-clandestinity in the combat zones of El Salvador during the early 1980s, the Comunidades de la Población en Resistencia (CPRs) survived in Guatemala by adopting semi-nomadic lifestyles.[32] At their most numerous they represented approximately 15,000 people and since 1993 some have established more open and permanently-settled communities.[33] Among those who fled to seek the protection of another state are those formally recognised as 'refugees' by the United Nations High Commissioner for Refugees (UNHCR) – a refugee being defined in the 1957 UN Convention on Refugees and its 1967 Protocol as an individual who flees with a 'well-founded fear of persecution for reasons of race, religion, nationality, membership of a particular social group or political opinion'. Such refugees are entitled to UNHCR assistance and protection. For the purposes of this discussion, 'refugees' is used to include the more numerous 'externally displaced' or *de facto* refugees who remain in exile as illegal and undocumented aliens but whose flight is nonetheless motivated by fear of political violence. In fact, in the context of Central America, establishing whether an individual is a migrant or refugee is far from straightforward. Some Salvadoreans who fled their country of origin as refugees found work in Guatemala, thereby becoming (at least technically) migrants, while many Guatemalans who seasonally migrated to work in southern Mexico became refugees in the early 1980s, when fear for their safety prevented their return.

Central American refugees include people from various social backgrounds. They can be divided into three broad categories. First, there are the well-educated middle class professionals who, as political activists, were singled out for political persecution. Typically, this group of political exiles sought asylum in Mexico and the USA and, benefiting from contacts in the host country, found relatively secure employment and adapted more easily to exile than did other groups. Typically, they talked of returning when political conditions changed. An unknown number have recently returned to their countries of origin, although data are insufficient to provide any estimate of numbers. A second group is the 'urban refugee'; this includes mainly young males from working class or lower-middle class backgrounds, many in El Salvador and Guatemala politically active in trade unions or grassroots organisations at which violence was directed. Those from Nicaragua included young males leaving to evade military service imposed in 1984.[34] They too sought protection in Mexico, the USA and Costa Rica, often aided in their journeys by family contacts. Once established in the host country, this group has tended not to return, contributing to the income of their families in their country of origin by sending remittances. A third and more numerous group of refugees are the poor peasants from El Salvador and Guatemala who were forcibly displaced during widespread violence in the rural areas. This group was predominantly comprised of women and children (many of the men were killed or recruited into the guerrilla or state forces) and remained within the region. The Miskito of Nicaragua can also be considered to fall within this group. While their exodus was qualitatively different from previous migrations of poor peasants within and from the region, these refugees followed traditionally established migration flows. Typically, Salvadoreans went to Honduras, Guatemalans to southern Mexico and Honduras and Nicaraguans to Costa Rica..

Estimates for numbers of uprooted Central Americans vary considerably and are notoriously difficult to establish, given the problems of border control. A generally accepted estimate is that during the 1980s an estimated fourteen per cent of the populations of Nicaragua, El Salvador and Guatemala were uprooted.[35] Approximately one million remained within their own countries as 'internally displaced'; a further million fled their countries of origin to seek exile in the USA, within the region and in Mexico and Belize.

The Politics of Exile

Refugee populations are characteristically impoverished and Central Americans who stayed within the region were no exception. This situation is reflected in their social indicators, particularly the high infant mortality rates and poor mental health encountered among the refugee population.[36] Conditions of some were worse than others because the extent to which their security, legal and socio-economic needs were satisfied differed according to whether they were recipients of international assistance, lived in camps or settlements or were dispersed throughout urban areas. Patterns varied considerably from country to country and according to the characteristics of the groups involved.

Refugee policies of host countries are formally defined by their legal obligations. All the countries in the region except Mexico and Honduras are signatories to the previously mentioned international agreements – the 1957 UN Convention and its 1967 Protocol – on refugees (Belize became a signatory in 1990). These agreements contain a limited definition of 'refugee' which fails to incorporate the victims of modern counterinsurgency strategies since it requires individuals to prove that they were specifically targeted for persecution. The 1984 Declaration of Cartagena provides a wider definition; however, despite the signing by all Central American states of the Declaration (which also confirms the basic principles regarding international protection and treatment of refugees), the Cartagena document is non-binding.[37]

National policies towards refugees are also influenced by economic and political considerations. During the 1980s, Mexico accepted the largest number of Central American refugees. It accepted not only the hundreds of thousands who were temporarily in transit to the USA, but also a semi-permanent refugee population of approximately 385,000 individuals. This population consisted mainly of Salvadoreans from urban backgrounds who lived mainly in Mexico's larger cities, and various ethnic groups of Guatemalan indians, mainly seasonal migrants and peasants who lived in the southern Mexican states. Only 3,500 Salvadoreans and 4,000 Guatemalans concentrated within forty border camps and two designated zones were granted asylum and assistance from the UNHCR. Life for those other unrecognised refugees dispersed throughout the southern provinces and in the cities was insecure on account of their illegal status. In order to dissuade new arrivals, in 1983 the Mexican government imposed a policy requiring refugees to obtain visas from Mexican consulates in their country of origin instead of being able to obtain temporary documents in Mexico. Deportation was a very real threat; in 1987 the Mexican authorities were deporting between 600 and 1,000 Central American 'illegals' per week.[38] These undocumented refugees were among the most vulnerable, subject to exploitation, high levels of unemployment and chronic ill health, hardships which numerous Church-based, national and international NGOs worked to alleviate.

Even under the auspices of international protection, refugees in the Mexican border camps experienced extreme overcrowding and, given their remote location, assistance efforts were often unable to provide for all their immediate physical needs.[39] However, their ability to reach self-sufficiency was restrained because of the already great demands of local populations for land. They were also frequently attacked by the Guatemalan military during border incursions and on one occasion, in April 1984, soldiers killed six refugees in the El Chupadero refugee camp. This incident precipitated the decision by the Mexican government to relocate refugees to settlements in Campeche and Quintana Roo to be integrated into rural economic development projects aimed at enabling them to gain a degree of self-sufficiency.[40] However, thousands of Guatemalan refugees refused to leave the border area because it was not only close to their homelands, but also offered the familiarity of cultural and kinship networks.[41] Reluctant refugees were forced to move after the Puerto Rico camp was burnt to the ground by Mexican soldiers in July 1984. Rather than leave the area, half the inhabitants fled to the Lacandona jungle, which since the Spanish Conquest has offered a sanctuary to Mayans, enabling their culture to remain intact.[42] The refugee migration created undesirable political consequences for the Mexican government. Aside from the border incidents, economic conditions in Chiapas, Mexico's poorest state, were exacerbated by the refugees' competition for resources, heightening local political tensions. The emergence of the armed insurgency of the Ejército Zapatista de Liberación Nacional (EZLN) in Chiapas in January 1994 only served to increase the suspicions of Mexican officials that Guatemalan refugees were spreading revolutionary ideas among the local Mexican population.[43]

In common with Mexico, Costa Rica has a tradition of providing political asylum to Central Americans. During the 1980s it played host to between 15,000 and 90,000 Salvadoreans and 1,000 Guatemalans of mainly working class and urban backgrounds, most of whom lived in and around San José.[44] The majority of refugees in Costa Rica were Nicaraguans, numbering between 70,000 and 100,000 in the mid-1980s (21,765 were assisted by the UNHCR in 1988).[45] This flood of refugees, paradoxically exacerbated by the Monge government's (1982-1986) anti-Sandinista foreign policy which enabled the contra to operate from within Costa Rican territory, coincided with a worsening economic crisis after 1982. In response to a rise in local xenophobia, the Monge government imposed restrictive labour legislation inhibiting the integration programmes favoured by the UNHCR and preventing recognised refugees from entering local urban labour markets. Recognised refugees subsequently became confined to the inactivity of the camps.[46] Many others remained as undocumented refugees.

In the 1980s, Honduras was dramatically transformed by the influx of refugees from its neighbours. By the middle of the decade it had received approximately 45,000 Salvadoreans and 1,800 Guatemalans, mostly of peasant origin. Initially thousands were dispersed within rural and urban areas and were assisted by church and nongovernmental organisations. The Honduran state, which does not recognise refugee status, responded by containing them in camps administered by the UNHCR, which included nearly 21,000 Salvadoreans and Guatemalans. Concerned to prevent refugees from viewing their camps as anything but temporary, refugees were refused farmland, engendering a high degree of economic dependency on external sources.[47] Honduras also received Nicaraguans from amongst the *ladino* population, including rightwing exiles incorporated into the contras forces. The military activities of the contra and their refusal to be relocated away from the border area precluded those resettled in the area from eligibility for UNHCR humanitarian assistance. Similarly, Nicaraguan Miskito indians who remained close to the frontier were denied assistance. This group remained within continuous Miskito territory amongst ethnic kin and were often able to resume their traditional trading activities. In smaller agricultural settlements some joined the contra voluntarily while others were forcibly recruited by Miskito insurgents.

Honduran refugee policy reflected its foreign policy stance and alignment to the USA. It was lenient towards refugees of Nicaraguan origin who fled the 'enemy' Sandinistas, while Guatemalans and Salvadoreans were treated as subversives allied to the guerrilla.[48] Nicaraguans had greater freedom of movement and men could work locally as labourers, while Salvadorean refugee camps were permanently patrolled and the refugees prevented from leaving, except in emergencies. Salvadorean refugees were harassed and in 1988 Honduran soldiers murdered refugees at Colomoncagua camp and Mesa Grande.[49] That Salvadoreans, under the international protection of the UNHCR, were attacked by the military of their host country serves to highlight the highly political nature of exile in the region.

Before July 1979, Nicaragua was a producer of political refugees, not a host country. Subsequently, although ex-Somoza sympathisers and disaffected Sandinista supporters departed, Nicaragua became host to 17,500 Salvadoreans, 500 Guatemalans and 500 other Latin American political exiles.[50] Between 1984 and 1988 only 1,808 of the Salvadoreans and 49 Guatemalans were attended by the UNHCR, but Nicaragua's liberal refugee policy, consistent with its government's commitment to support Central American revolutionary struggles, granted resident status to refugees and enabled them to integrate without discrimination from nationals into local productive activities. This promoted the functioning of self-help projects and enabled several refugee cooperatives to attain self-sufficiency.[51]

Guatemala not only produced but also received refugees: by 1985 there were an estimated 70,000 Salvadoreans living in the country with no legal recognition nor sources of assistance; most found work filling the vacuum left by departing indigenous workers. Belize had a relatively small refugee population of around 32,000, mostly Guatemalans, which represented approximately 20 per cent of the national population.[52] Given the relatively low national population density, refugees often gained *de facto* access to land alongside other immigrant farmers.[53] Geographical distance from the main theatres of conflict meant that Panama was host to the fewest refugees in the region; in 1985 it provided asylum to only 1,000 officially recognised Salvadorean refugees.[54]

The responses of refugees to these distinct conditions generated specific organisational and political outcomes. For undocumented refugees, where the fear of deportation was a real one, remaining anonymous was crucial, making them less likely to seek solidarity through organisational networks. Generally, it was within the refugee camps that collective responses to socio-cultural, economic and political problems developed. The development by refugees of their own active and functional organisations was a feature particularly of the camps in Mexico and Honduras.[55] For example, even in the context of difficulties of access to land, in the Cieneguita camp, Mexico, Guatemalan refugees of the Kanjobal ethnic group set up a corn collective, which financed grinders and enabled them to establish a women's mill cooperative.[56] The Permanent Commissions of Representation also emerged from these camps as a collective response to political demands of the refugees. Salvadorean refugees in Honduras maintained impressive internal community cohesion, organising around educational and productive activities. In 1988 they even staged an inter-camp fast to protest about their poor material conditions.[57] Salvadoreans outside the camps, such as those living in Nicaragua, were also organised: here they coordinated agricultural activities and service provision nationally amongst their communities.[58] Such activity served to defy the 'victim' image often ascribed to refugees and highlighted their resilience under conditions of considerable duress.

Yet some camp refugees, such as Nicaraguan *mestizo* refugees in Costa Rica and Honduras, were unable to develop even minimal organisational structures within their communities. This raises a question as to why some people actively resisted and shaped their situation in exile, while others submitted to it. A comparative study of Nicaraguan and Salvadorean refugees and internally displaced populations by Hammond points to various factors as being influential.[59] Circumstances of flight were important and the very random nature of counter-insurgency targeting of civilian populations meant that apathy provided no safe-haven: only collective action increased the chances of survival. In addition, the act of fleeing and the asylum process also constituted a political experience for some, by provoking reflection among individuals about their relationship as peasants to the government.[60] The experience of official hostility and economic deprivation during the period in exile was also conducive to the development of strong refugee organisation and was necessary in order to build or rebuild destroyed communities. Thus, the persistent threat of attack from the military, experienced by Salvadoreans in Honduras and Guatemalans in Mexico, reinforced the need to remain organised as a strategy for survival.[61] However, an important prerequisite for strong internal organisation appeared to be prior organisational experience. This goes further in explaining why the *mestizo* Nicaraguan refugees in Honduras and Costa Rica failed to develop organisational structures. Before their flight they had lived in isolation and had not learnt how to organise to defend their collective interests. Those among them who manifested leadership qualities tended to be ex-members of Somoza's

National Guard whose skills and track record were often inappropriate for the purposes of organising their compatriots around collective demands. By contrast, many of the exiled Salvadoreans in the Honduran camps and living in Nicaragua had prior political involvement or had been active in Christian base communities.

The Return

The socioeconomic and political problems of exile made repatriation an increasingly desirable objective for actors in the region. In general, refugees of professional, urban or peasant backgrounds who become incorporated into productive activities and labour markets in the host country tend not to return, particularly as the years advance. This is not the case for undocumented and poor refugees without access to land. For them, return offers the only opportunity to gain legal status and alleviate their dire conditions. The desire to return to their places of origin also has powerful psychological and emotional significance relating to identity. This is particularly the case for indigenous groups whose belief-systems revolve around traditional lands.

For international organisations the financial costs incurred by refugee populations are enormous. For example, in order to support a total of 200,000 refugees and returnees in the region, the UNHCR's expenditure for 1988 exceeded $33m.[62] Hence the emphasis, particular in light of the budget limitations facing UNHCR, to pursue so-called 'durable' (or cheaper) solutions for the refugee problem. This includes integration in the host country, resettlement in a third country or, most favourably, repatriation.[63] Displacement in the region has exacerbated poverty and the presence of refugees (and that of migrants) places a high burden on host countries. Not only do the areas refugees vacate become impoverished, but those to which they go become poorer because of the increased demands on resources. This requires greater expenditure on basic services, including health, education and housing.[64] Such socioeconomic factors directly or indirectly become political problems for host governments, creating opposition from local populations such as occurred in Honduras and Costa Rica and, as in Mexico, adding tension to a region which was itself experiencing severe economic and political problems.[65] The presence of refugees in areas surrounding national borders also translates into strategic concerns and affects relations between states (so apparent in the case of Nicaragua and Honduras during the 1980s). In the case of Costa Rica and Mexico, their reception of refugees embroiled them directly in the regional conflict and raised their stakes in the search for a resolution to the conflict through regional fora. Refugee producing countries also welcomed repatriation as evidence to the international community of restored stability and improved human rights.

The signature of the Esquipulas II regional peace settlement in 1987 (see chapter one) signalled the importance attached by the region's governments to a resolution of the displacement issue. A clause was included which made provision for guaranteeing the safe return and reintegration of nationals who had fled widespread violence in their homeland. It committed the five governments to 'give urgent attention to the flow of refugees and displaced persons brought about by regional crisis' and emphasised that voluntary repatriation would be promoted.[66] To the extent that there existed a consensus around the need to resolve the problem, the issue of the uprooted actually facilitated the global negotiation process.

The following section shows that return flows began in the mid-1980s during the conflict. It is maintained that return cannot be understood solely as a response to regional political changes. As in other parts of the world, repatriation, or *retorno* as refugees prefer to call the process, occurred most commonly by way of so-called 'spontaneous' movements of families or communities. In fact these *retornos* were achieved on the basis of information obtained through organised reconnaissance and the mobilisation of social or political networks (within the popular movements, the guerrilla or community structures) to gain information about conditions in the planned location of return. For the Miskito in particular, community and family sources proved valuable given the disinformation about conditions in Nicaragua which bombarded them via Honduran radio-waves.[67] In many cases, camp and settlement refugees negotiated terms and conditions for return. The demands, albeit specific to each group, were consistent in specifying the right to return and guarantees of security and development. These movements have maintained a degree of popular control over repatriation concerning dates, routes and final destinations. Repatriation has also taken place in 'official movements', under the auspices of the UNHCR which has organised returns by establishing tripartite commissions and agreements between governments of the countries of asylum and origin. Both spontaneous repatriations *en masse* and official repatriations received assistance from the UNHCR, NGOs or churches; others returning as families in so called 'individual repatriations' remain more vulnerable as regards their physical security and welfare.[68]

Table 4.1
Central America: Refugees[a] and Returnees (June 1993)

Country	Refugees	Returnees
Belize	8,940	-
Costa Rica	31,880	-
El Salvador	170	30,760
Guatemala	4,780	20,630[b]
Honduras	110	-
Mexico	50,200	-
Nicaragua	1,600	71,950
Total	97,680	123,340

Note: [a] UNHCR recognised refugees only
             [b] Figures from UNHCR cited in NCOORD *Newsletter*, February 1994.

Source: UNHCR, quoted in *CIREFCA Notes*, No. 3, August 1993

Nicaragua

The repatriation of Miskito and Sumu Indians to the riverine communities on the Atlantic Coast began in 1985 and was integrally related to the pacification of that region. This included the ceasefire and amnesty agreements between sections of the Miskito forces and the Ejército Popular Sandinista (EPS), and the emergence of locally elected mediating structures, the Peace and Autonomy Commissions, amongst indigenous communities. By 1985 Miskito combatants had increasingly come to acknowledge that indigenous rights were of no concern to the contras and that their alliance would not deliver political independence to the Miskito.[69] In addition, the Sandinista Government recognised the errors of its former stance towards the Atlantic Coast peoples and indicated a willingness to make concessions, initiating a two year consultation process to elaborate an autonomy statute for the region. This culminated in the Law of Autonomy which was incorporated into the national Constitution in 1987, establishing the rights of Atlantic Coast peoples to their own languages, religion and culture and increasing their control of the region's natural resources.[70] Once the autonomy process eliminated the main causes of the exodus, refugees wanted to return to use the lands they had traditionally farmed on Nicaraguan soil.[71] Return flows to other communities increased after the 1987 signing of the regional peace plan, creating a mechanism by which Nicaragua could cooperate with Costa Rica and Honduras to facilitate voluntary repatriation.[72] By the end of 1990, 32,500 Miskito and Sumus had returned to their original communities; 15,000 had returned under the auspices of UNHCR and 17,500 spontaneously. By 1991 the return of indigenous people to the Atlantic Coast was complete.

The repatriation of *mestizos* from Honduras reached significant levels only in 1989 and accelerated after the Sandinistas lost the national elections of February 1990. As such it occurred in response to political change, and in particular to efforts at economic reconstruction which are examined below. The flow of returning refugees was proportionally greater from Honduras than Costa Rica, suggesting that circumstances in exile were influential in decisions to return. Conditions in Honduras were generally less favourable than those in Costa Rica.[73] In response to the Presidential Decree of amnesty enabling refugees to become permanent residents (in effect between July 1990 and June 1991), 11,000 accepted. All Costa Rica's camps were closed and by late 1993 the Nicaraguan Government considered this repatriation to be complete.[74] The key characteristic of the Nicaraguan 'return' is of course the inclusion of other categories, including ex-members of the contra, whose numbers exceeded those of returning refugees.

El Salvador

The process of mass return to El Salvador began in October 1987 with the repatriation of 4,313 refugees from the Mesa Grande camp in Honduras. Twenty-four captures by the army subsequently occurred in the repopulated communities during the first five months, in violation of both the terms of Esquipulas II and government agreements with the refugees. The Salvadorean armed forces made frequent incursions into resettled villages, conducted military operations in close proximity and intimidated grassroots leaders in an apparent attempt to demoralise returnees. The government also withheld personal documentation from returnees, making those found without a *cédula* subject to arrest.[75] Despite this physical repression, returns to the zones of conflict continued. By 1991, over 30,000 people had returned in collective repatriations to El Salvador, including all those from Nicaragua and from the camps in Honduras, which were subsequently closed. An untold number remain in Mexico: their repatriation has occurred on an individual basis and is therefore difficult to quantify.

The returnees chose to return to El Salvador at a time when conditions were still precarious, rather than live under difficult camp conditions where their lives were frequently at the mercy of outside control. News of UNHCR budget cuts also increased their security concerns. In effect, they repatriated not because the war had ended but precisely because it was continuing,[76] although the specific stimulus was the internal return population movement which was gaining momentum under the co-ordination of grassroots organisations, such as the Coordinadora Nacional de Repoblación (CNR).[77] Repatriation also occurred at a time of government-sponsored repopulation programmes involving the internally displaced, part of official efforts efforts to consolidate control over populations and depopulated zones of conflict. Independent return movements were clearly perceived as a threat to this rural pacification strategy and after ARENA (Alianza Republicana Nacionalista) took office in 1989, offices of popular organisations, such as the CNR in San Salvador, were harassed.[78]

Most (68 per cent) of the *retornos* were collective 'mass repatriations' to seven departments, while individual returnees settled throughout the country.[79] Several factors made large-scale return the most appropriate for the Salvadorean refugees, including a strong sense of community derived from the collective experience in exile, and an increase in human rights abuses at the hands of the security forces which suggested that mass, collective return would afford greater protection. The confrontation they risked was minimised by their ability to mobilise support from the NGOs and secure international media coverage on the assumption that being more obtrusive increased their security. Each mass repatriation drew up a proposal for support from the government and UNHCR to secure the rights the refugees believed they were entitled to under international law. This constituted an assertion of their right to live in the place of their choice and to have access to the means of subsistence denied them by the counterinsurgency campaigns. Such demands were subsequently legitimated by the Central American Peace Plan.

The returns took place in the context of repeated attempts at negotiation and were characterised by tension and disagreements between the refugees, UNHCR and the Salvadorean government: a product of the returnees insistent demands and the highly politicised nature and context of the returns.[80] That they occurred at all reflects the high level of internal organisation of the refugees which in itself contributed to the overall process of pacification. To the extent that the first and subsequent returns were supported by labour unions, displaced peoples' organisations and Salvadorean Christian base communities, they formed part of a broad popular movement of opposition, as the following statement by a returnee demonstrates:

'We wanted to help, to become a social force in the struggle for peace and justice in our homeland. People wanted to return in an organised, massive way.'[81]

Though not openly taking sides in the civil war, the return of refugees from Honduras to the Salvadorean countryside can be interpreted as an attempt to provide solidarity to insurgent groups by establishing a friendly presence in the conflict zones.[82] For organised Salvadoreans who returned from Nicaragua in 1990, the desire to contribute to political struggle alongside the FMLN (Frente Farabundo Martí para la Liberación Nacional) against the government and military was an explicit motive.[83] Their increased numbers were of growing significance in the ongoing conflict.

Guatemala

Compared to Nicaraguans and Salvadoreans, the repatriation of Guatemalans to date has been low. According to the UNHCR about 20,000 refugees returned to Guatemala between 1984 and 1994, 11,000 of those during the last two years of this period. Most of the returns were collectively organised.[84] The process is perceptible, yet represents a small proportion of those refugees remaining in exile. This reflects the continuing volatility of the politico-military situation in Guatemala, the insufficient guarantees of security and the politically contentious issue of land tenancy.

In 1986, anticipating that the restoration of civilian government would signal large-scale repatriations, the government created the Special Commission for Assistance to Refugees and Internally Displaced (CEAR). This gave the military the main responsibility in organising repatriation, an involvement which was greater than in either El Salvador or Nicaragua. Nonetheless, tripartite agreements between the UNHCR and the Guatemalan government (which, significantly, excluded refugee representation) secured the return of 3,000 people between 1986 and 1989. These returnees were motivated by a combination of the desire to recover their original lands, the poor conditions in Mexico (camp fatigue) and certain religious attitudes (amongst returnees there was a proportionately high number of evangelical Christians).[85] The lack of improvement in the human rights situation meant that interest in repatriation diminished.

However, in response to the remaining refugees' desire to return to their places or origin and the need for coordinated political representation, the Permanent Commissions of Guatemalan Refugees in Mexico emerged during the late 1980s. These included representatives from each settlement, and were affiliated to associations of dispersed refugees. They manifested the development of cohesive inter-ethnic social organisation. The Permanent Commissions set about organising collective return movements and, after protracted negotiations with the Guatemalan government represented by CEAR, in October 1992 signed a comprehensive accord for return. This recognised the voluntary and peaceful nature of the return to locations of the refugees' choosing, reiterated government guarantees for their personal security and established mechanisms for verification and accompaniment by governmental and non-governmental organisations, both national and international. It also exempted returnees from association in self-defence groups (the civil patrols) for three years and created a framework by which the National Institute for Agrarian Transformation (INTA) would resolve the problematic issue of land acquisition or recovery.[86] The agreement heralded a series of collective independent returns initiated in January 1993 by the highly publicised return of 2,500 refugees to what became known as *Victoria 20 de Enero*.[87] As with the collective Salvadorean returns, these were the product of arduous struggles and as such represented a political victory for the Mayan refugees.

Although 1994 was designated in the 1992 agreements as the 'year of the return', the return never materialised. The self-styled coup (*autogolpe*) by President Jorge Serrano in May 1993 not only suspended the constitutional order, but also halted the repatriations. Nor did these resume as anticipated even after the subsequent election by Congress of former human rights ombudsman, Ramiro de León Carpio to the presidency in June 1993. In fact, human rights violations increased, being 68 per cent more frequent in the first half of 1994 than for the same period two years previously, most occurring at the hands of the civil patrols which remained totally unaccountable.[88] The killing of several returnees gave potential returnees objective cause for concern.[89] The return process also faltered because the government in 1994 redirected $20 million of the funds from FONAPAZ (Fondo Nacional para la Paz), created in 1991 to finance land purchases for returns and funded by Taiwan and the World Bank, in order to pay government salaries. Consequently, CEAR had no money with which to purchase land for returning refugees.[90]

Repatriation has been an issue integral to the formal peace negotiations. In Oslo in June 1994, agreement was reached between representatives of the governmental Peace Commission and the URNG (Unidad Revolucionaria Nacional Guatemalteca) on the resettlement of displaced populations, itself a significant step forward in a fairly moribund peace process. But, however laudable the measures relating to land acquisitions and development funding were, they changed nothing for the refugees because they were only to come into effect after the signing of the final peace agreement.[91] At present, the possibility of repatriation under conditions of an agreed peace settlement remains a distant prospect, particularly since the issue of the civil patrols continues to be highly contentious (see chapter three). The barriers to repatriation in this context remain considerable.

By the end of 1994 there were an estimated 44,000 recognised Guatemalan refugees living in Mexico in Campeche, Quintana Roo and Chiapas, together with an estimated 110,000 undocumented Guatemalan refugees throughout Mexico.[92] Circumstances in Chiapas remained highly insecure following the *zapatista* uprising in January 1994 and the drought of the same year. A vote in the Mexican Congress in 1994 redefining 'refugee' under Mexican law raised fears that, while assistance would still be extended to some, others not meeting the narrow definitions set down would face expulsion.

Reintegration and Socio-Political Insertion

Evidently, the problems facing forced migrants are not resolved immediately on their return, but are gradually addressed through the process of reintegration. This relates not only to economic reinsertion and material recovery, but also to processes of political and social reconstruction. Different groups of returnees had common and distinct experiences. Atlantic Coast returnees to Nicaragua were able to commence reconstruction in a context marked by minimal state interference. Tasks of emergency relief and reconstruction were conducted primarily by national and international NGOs. Not only was government presence and official intimidation absent but returnees were granted the means to protect themselves since, according to the Yulo Peace Agreement with the Miskito Kisan contras, former combatants were able to retain their arms. If constitutional and human rights were respected, political rights were also granted, enabling registered returnees to vote in the national elections held in February 1990. This motivated many more to return, particularly those who returned to the Pacific region. The UNO victory of February 1990 (55 per cent over the FSLN's 41 per cent), was not reflected in the newly created North Atlantic Autonomous Region (RAAN) where YATAMA (*Yapti Tasba Masrika Aslika*, or 'United for Mother Earth' in Miskito), a former Miskito contra group (and the last to disarm), took 22 seats, compared to the FSLN's 21 and UNO's two. In the South Atlantic Autonomous Region (RAAS), YATAMA took three seats, the FSLN 19 and UNO 23.[93] The high vote in the RAAN for the ex-contra suggests that the Sandinistas' codification of the autonomy law had failed to erase indigenous discontent with former policies. To a degree, the 1994 regional election results (see chapter two, figures 7 and 8) echoed this legacy of disaffection as much as they signalled an historical coastal sympathy with liberalism: in the RAAN the FSLN won 19 seats, the Constitutional Liberal Party (PLC) also obtained 19 and YATAMA suffered a reversal in its fortunes, securing only seven seats. In the RAAS the ratio was 13 to the FSLN, 18 to the PLC and five to YATAMA, with UNO gaining six seats.[94]

The situation was different in El Salvador because returnees in repopulated areas were subject to intense harassment and human rights abuses, and the access of returnees and NGOs to resettlements was barred. Intimidation extended to attempts to deny returnees their political rights through administrative irregularities relating to electoral documentation. Returnees were among the estimated 80,000 who were unable to obtain voting cards and the 100,000 denied a vote because their names were omitted from electoral lists in the 1994 elections. In contravention of all agreements concerning guarantees of safety and the demilitarisation of destination sites, returning Guatemalans, such as those in the *Victoria*, were subject to army intimidation, military exercises taking place nearby and helicopter overflights. Another serious threat to their personal security is posed by the civil patrols. At their most benign these have sought to prevent repatriation: in 1987 mayors from over 50 towns within Guatemala petitioned President Cerezo expressing their opposition to refugee returns.[95] In more sinister cases, the civil patrols were implicated in the murders of various repatriates. The presence of the UNHCR and other NGOs has proved a vital and necessary contribution to the fulfilment of guarantees of protection, particularly in more isolated areas.[96] In this context, the importance of accompaniment for future returns and the guarantees provided by MINUGUA – the United Nations Verification Mission in Guatemala – and of compliance with the commitments of the Comprehensive Agreement on Human Rights in Guatemala (signed March 1994) becomes clear.

Frictions have erupted elsewhere between returnees and other groups at a community level. In the Pacific region of Nicaragua, families of refugees who fled were typically identified as the enemy, a factor which accentuated the polarisation between those who stayed and the returnees, and discouraged the return of many until after the national elections in February 1990. This experience contrasts with that of the Atlantic Coast where communities typically fled and returned collectively and have not faced the same social barriers on return.[97] Here, the legacy of conflict is manifest in the disintegration of extended family networks according to returnees' response to the pacification process, which has created divisions within the wider Miskito community.[98] Similarly, Salvadorean returnees, in response to the harassment and intolerance encountered by a group repatriating from Colomoncagua, Honduras, felt compelled to publish a leaflet entitled 'An appeal to the national conscience: is it a crime to be a returned refugee?', in which they reminded compatriots that during exile they too had been subject to arbitrary acts of violence. Since local competition for limited resources has exacerbated or generated such local hostilities, governments and NGOs have acknowledged that an integrated community-based approach to reintegration projects is crucial to cementing community ties.

The way in which returnees relate to existing state and political structures is also conditioned by the way they themselves have been transformed during their experiences of asylum. Traditional forms of power within Nicaraguan Miskito communities, for example, have been significantly altered. Whereas power previously resided within the authority of the elders, headed by a leader (frequently a Moravian pastor), such forms have now been largely replaced by the Peace and Autonomy Commissions, elected bodies which were formed during the military conflict. These have developed as an intermediary mechanism for resolution of community disputes and problems and for representation before the regional government.[99] However, some observers remain concerned that the legacy of assistance provided by NGOs and national and international churches which have historically attended the coastal population has engendered a culture of dependency.[100] This has exacerbated problems of adaptation and demands that assistance and development projects be administered in such a way that the motivation and interest of the returnees in the reconstruction of their lives be stimulated.

Indigenous identities were also transformed by the sundering of people from their land. Whereas prior to the conflict, ethnic groups on the Nicaraguan Atlantic Coast did not hold a national/country allegiance which distinguished them from their Honduran kin, the experience of refugees in Honduras and the war have superimposed a Nicaraguan nationality on them. It is commonplace to hear Miskitos declare that they are Nicaraguans: a significant step towards nation-building.[101]

While some of the Salvadorean refugees had prior organisational experience, conditions in exile were conducive to the emergence of strong internal social cohesion and organisational structures. The impact on women was particularly significant; not only did objective circumstances dictate that women assume an activist role in community decision-making, but they were also targeted by specific NGO development projects. Contact with the UNHCR and other NGOs essentially gave refugees access to a transnational political 'space'. The refugees' effective appropriation of such universalist discourses as human rights in their organised struggles to return suggests that these organisations served as agents of change. In exile Salvadoreans emerged as proactive political subjects prepared to assert themselves as independent social actors. Their contribution to the repatriation process not only forced a reassessment of their relationship with NGOs, which subsequently redefined their aid and humanitarian approach to returning refugees as one of *acompañamiento*,[102] but also made a significant contribution to furthering the overall process of pacification. Projects such as Segundo Montes in Morazán, a settlement created by refugees returning from Colomoncagua, demonstrate how the economic and social affiliations nurtured in exile were reconstructed upon relocation, strengthening civil society.

The emergence of organisational networks within the Guatemalan refugees, epitomised by the Permanent Commissions, suggests how the experience of exile also politicised Mayan communities. They too have been exposed through contact with global NGOs to human rights discourses, to which they have successfully appealed for legitimacy in their negotiations for return. Beyond their objective of securing further returns, they have aimed to insert themselves into a broader movement asserting Mayan identity expressed through new groups within civil society, such as the Coordinadora de las Organizaciones de Pueblos Mayas de Guatemala (COPMAGUA) and the Asamblea de Sociedad Civil (ASC) seeking participation in the peace process between the government and URNG. Indigenous leaders have made clear their displeasure at their exclusion from peace talks, including the October 1994 meeting between the government and URNG on the Identity and Rights of Indigenous People.[103]

Exile also brought together Mayans from distinct regions and ethnic groups, a phenomenon the multi-ethnic composition of the *Victoria* return illustrated. If flight can be understood to have facilitated the survival of Mayan culture, important questions arise about the nature of transformed notions of identity. As with the Miskito, indigenous identity in Guatemala was previously a concept based on ethnic groups and, more particularly, on location. The return, constituting what Judith Zur has termed the 'symbolic re-appropriation of citizenship',[104] by extension represents the assumption of an essentially Guatemalan nationality. Mayan land, all the more sacred because of the amount of Mayan blood which has been shed on it over the past two decades and to which the refugees have for years been struggling to return, is firmly established under the jurisdiction of the Guatemalan state. This has necessitated a negotiation between the latter and the refugee *as Guatemalan citizen.*

As with the Salvadorean case, the legacy of radicalisation of hundreds of thousands of Guatemalans by their experience in exile is evident in their ability to retain and adapt on relocation the forms of collective organisation created in exile. The extent to which the organisational forms developed in exile are perpetuated upon relocation depends upon levels of internal cohesion and conditions of relocation. The *Victoria* resettlement quickly encountered problems as there was insufficient land to support the returning community, leading to divisions. By·contrast, the former cooperativists returning to their original lands of the Ixcán Grande have retained their former cohesion and solidarity. The experience of the transfer of the CPRs of the Ixcán to open settlements in 1993 also indicated that under new conditions the social structure developed in internal exile could be eroded.[105] Here, the location of resettlements created new commercial opportunities and the rationale for intense collectivised production diminished as families sought individualistic solutions to their problems.[106]

Economic Restructuring: The Development Imperative

Poverty in Central America was exacerbated during the 'lost decade' of war and economic and ecological crisis and the context of refugee return has been characterised by economic recession. The areas returnees tend to go to are the most affected by combat, where land is degraded, forests, croplands and villages have been razed and where large-scale military strategies have wreaked 'ecocide'. The disarticulation of the peasantry through displacement from their areas of traditional subsistence has also led to the adoption of farming techniques which over-exploit agricultural soils and degrade land.[107] In addition, prevailing economic conditions are marked by the social cost of the macro-economic structural readjustment programmes currently being implemented which reduce social service provision. In 1993, an estimated 68 per cent of the region's population lived below the poverty line.[108] On the Atlantic Coast of Nicaragua, unemployment was as much as 90 per cent in 1994.[109] In such circumstances, access to land is crucial for returning refugees.

While land in Central America has traditionally been the most important source of wealth, for the peasantry access to land guarantees their survival. In the absence of effective land reforms in El Salvador and

Guatemala, and with reversals in the distributive agrarian reforms enacted by the Sandinistas in the case of Nicaragua, land distribution remains highly concentrated throughout the region. The massive return of people to their country of origin has placed greater pressure on available arable lands, particularly since other groups, including internally displaced, demobilised combatants and war-victims, have often staked a prior claim. This has not been an issue for indigenous groups returning to the relatively underpopulated Atlantic Coast of Nicaragua since they were able to resettle on their traditional lands, but it has been an issue in the Pacific region. Agreements about land and credit formed part of the demobilisation pact reached between the UNO (Unión Nacional Opositora) government and the contra in 1990. The government's subsequent inability to fulfil those accords, together with the threat of a post-election reversal of the Sandinista's agrarian reforms, stimulated a resurgence of armed groups in the north of Nicaragua when political polarisation, neglect of these sectors and the explosive nature of the problem became evident.

In El Salvador, demands for access to land were also greater given the inclusion of other victims of war, demobilised FMLN and army combatants and government controlled repopulation efforts. The issue of land transfers was central to the process of peace negotiations. The December 1991 Chapultepec Accords confirmed that land would be redistributed to landless peasants and credit policies reviewed to favour small producers (see chapter eight).[110] Respect for tenancy of land in the conflict zones was also stipulated, thereby legitimising the claims of communities within the independent repopulation movement and granting them the political space in which to develop their own social and productive organisations. However, land transfers have suffered 'virtual paralysis', as UN Secretary General Boutros Boutros-Ghali lamented in September 1994,[111] threatening both the economic integration of the returnees and displaced and the social reunification on which the delicate peace is constructed.

In Guatemala, access to land is a competitive and politically contentious issue, exacerbated by population pressure and the government's 'repopulation' programmes for the internally displaced. For instance, in the Ixcán and Chacaj, the land that refugees left was declared 'voluntarily' abandoned, permitting the state to revert land to state ownership and repopulate the areas under national law.[112] Conflicts have erupted between *antiguos* and *nuevos*, of which the incident which occurred in October 1994 at the Finca Pocobastic in Huehuetenango is typical: the return of 28 Chuj families provoked an angry reaction from hostile residents of surrounding communities who threatened repatriates in order that they should not take their land. International accompaniment and mediation by UNHCR officials was required until the precise boundaries of the designated area were established.[113] Such confrontations will increase if the government fails to comply with its obligations to protect the right to land of those with titles and provide funds for the purchase of lands for returnees. Given that land concentration remains so skewed in Guatemala – 70 per cent of all farmlands are held by two per cent of the population – returnees will be at odds with their peasant compatriots unless development projects can be implemented which benefit both groups.[114] However, indigenous leaders have expressed concern at the intentions of Ramiro de León Carpio's government to transform the civil patrols into 'development committees'. They fear this is a pretext for the army to secure a presence in areas of refugee return through the disguise of soldiers as 'agents of development'.[115] Such a military-imposed solution is not conducive to social stability.

While the land issue remains central to the full integration of returnees and future prospects for peace, the material aspects of resettlement have been addressed through various development projects. Some 59 projects were created under the auspices of the International Conference on Central American Refugees (CIREFCA), convened in Guatemala City by the Central American governments and the UNHCR and operating between 1989 and 1994 with a budget of $157.2 million. This was directed to nationwide programmes such as the Quick Impact Projects, aimed at stimulating economic recovery in Guatemala, and activities directed at the socio-economic integration of a target population of 70,000 returnees, demobilised combatants and war victims in Nicaragua. CIREFCA also funded an electoral documentation project to enable returned Salvadoreans to exercise their suffrage in the 1994 general elections. Through its coordination efforts, CIREFCA has also promoted opportunities for dialogue and cooperation between opposing parties. It was also significant in being the first regional initiative to coordinate migration policy and tackle the problems of uprooted populations and returnees in an integrated fashion.[116] In a parallel process, NGOs have set up national coordinating mechanisms and played an increasingly prominent role in the implementation of development projects. Between them, the 100 international NGOs and 600 local NGOs operating in Central America have channelled US$250 million a year to the region,[117] establishing themselves as important regional actors. Whilst the scope of many of the development projects went beyond ameliorating the immediate needs of returnees to secure their insertion into productive activities, their long term viability is ultimately dependent on the prevailing macro-economic and ecological conditions of the region.

Another economic dimension of the refugee legacy relates to the implications of the net loss of 'human resources', the effects of which remain to be fully assessed. A quarter of a million young Central Americans migrated to the USA and Mexico. Northward migration flows were also accompanied by increased remittance flows south. In the case of Nicaragua, where funds also come from relatives in Costa Rica, these currently represent the largest source of foreign exchange after coffee; in 1994 the Salvadorean economy received some $870 million from relatives of nationals resident in the USA.[118] The significance of external remittances might suggest that uprooting is, perversely, some kind of 'default development strategy'.

Conclusions

Clearly, advances towards peace throughout the region have positively affected the refugees' prospects for return. However, to interpret their repatriation merely as a response to improved conditions of stability is to ignore the significance of the refugee issue in the search by regional actors for solutions to the conflict. In addition, such an interpretation negates the contribution of exiled populations themselves to these processes of conflict resolution.

The trend towards pacification in El Salvador and Nicaragua has meant that refugees from and repatriates to these countries are increasingly a disappearing phenomenon. Only in Guatemala, where a definitive peace settlement has yet to be reached, do issues of refugees and repatriation remain pertinent in the search for peace. Uncertainty generated by the faltering dialogue between the government and guerrilla, together with continued human rights abuse in Guatemala, has meant that the option of permanent settlement in Mexico has become an increasingly attractive alternative for some Guatemalans. The fate of those who choose not to repatriate rests mainly with the Mexican authorities, who have been reluctant to date to implement any measures that might discourage return flow trends. Nonetheless, the future of those Guatemalan refugees determined to remain in exile can be secured by continued provision of asylum by the Mexican government and fulfilment of pledges to facilitate the integration of refugees into the local economy. In a context of limited local resources, the continued support of international agencies and NGOs to further refugees efforts to achieve economic self-sufficiency will be vital.

For those Guatemalans who wish to return to their places of origin, the fear of persecution which inhibits repatriation can only be resolved through a definitive negotiated solution to the conflict and effective implementation of any settlement. Future returns therefore remain dependent on completion of the official peace process. Many refugees have also demanded the disbandment of the civil patrols, something repeatedly called for by the United Nations Special Expert on Guatemala, Mónica Pinto, but which the army has refused to sanction to date. The role of the international community in actively supporting the resolution of the conflict and implementation of the peace settlement will be decisive. Although a permanent NGO presence in Guatemala is unlikely, the international community's support of mechanisms – such as the local offices of the Human Rights Ombudsman – for the monitoring and verification of the government's commitments on human rights (especially in the more remote highland areas) is essential.

The last decade has been characterised by increasing poverty for the majority of Central Americans. While precarious circumstances in exile meant that poor refugees were among the most vulnerable of populations in the region, their return to their countries of origin has effectively resolved their legal status and fulfilled their desire to be back home. However, worsening economic conditions have often meant that returnees are unable to meet their own basic needs or even regain the meagre levels of subsistence characteristic of many families prior to exile. In many cases, returned refugees have joined others affected by the war – the internally displaced, demobilised combatants, war-wounded and orphans – in the frantic search for strategies to secure their survival. Perhaps remittances from refugees who have managed to integrate into the economic activities of their host countries, together with those from previous economic migrants, have provided some kind of default development strategy for the economies of these countries. However, the need for effective land reform and appropriate credit policies continues to be essential to ensure the successful reintegration of displaced populations in Nicaragua, El Salvador and Guatemala and stability in the longer term.

Notes

1. Fagen (1985); Child (1992); Booth and Walker (1989).
2. Elizabeth Ferris stresses how an examination of refugee policy provides insights into domestic policy and the manner in which local political structures articulate with international politics (Ferris, 1993).
3. Loescher (1988), pp. 295-320.
4. *Ibid.*; see also Pritchard (1988a); Hammond (1993), pp. 103-22.

5. Stoll (1993).
6. Ferris, *Op. cit.*
7. For comprehensive documentation of this period see Instituto Interamericano de Derechos Humanos (IIDH) (1992).
8. For an overview of migration in this period see *Ibid.* and Weaver (1994).
9. Edwards and Tovar Siebentritt (1991), p. 18.
10. This refers to the Protocol II Additional to the Geneva Conventions of 1949, to which El Salvador is a party.
11. The economic aid for the period 1980-1990 provided by the USA amounted to $2,837.6 million, increasing from $57.8m in 1980 to $508.9m in 1987. Dunkerley (1994), p. 145.
12. Oglesby (1991).
13. Mayan patterns of land inheritance reflect social organisation and ensure cultural continuity. Manz (1988).
14. Ferris (1987), p. 20.
15. US military aid amounted to $5.4m in 1986 and reached $9.4m in 1989; economic aid also increased from $20.3 million in 1985 to $146.2 million by 1989. Dunkerley, *Op. cit.*, p. 145.
16. Americas Watch (1990), p. 1.
17. Human Rights Watch/Americas (1994).
18. Gretta Tovar Siebentritt, 'From Refugee to Returnee', *National Jesuit News White Paper*, April/May (1994), p. 3.
19. Estimates of the ethnic make-up of the Atlantic Coast population vary: one source estimates that of an entire pre-war Atlantic Coast population of 250,000, the Miskito numbered 88,000, Sumu some 10,000, Afro-Americans (Creoles and Garifunas) 30,000, Ramas 800 and Spanish-speaking *mestizos* 120,000. Dunbar Ortiz (1986), p. 24.
20. The Atlantic Coast was a British protectorate during the seventeenth and eighteenth centuries, and the economic, political and cultural life of the ethnic groups on the coast had developed under British, not Spanish hegemony. The identification of the largest group, the Miskito, with Anglo-Saxon culture was enhanced by the arrival of missionaries from the Moravian Church in the mid-nineteenth century and the development of a US-dominated enclave economy on the Atlantic Coast throughout the twentieth century. Ortega (1991), pp. 8-9.
21. On Sandinista policy mistakes on the Atlantic Coast see Hale (1994) and Molieri (1986).
22. Reyes and Wilson (1992).
23. Hundreds of those unwilling to leave the Río Coco area, particularly Sumus, were kidnapped by the contra between 1981 and 1987. Instituto Interamericano de Derechos Humanos, *Op. cit.*, p. 79.
24. Bendaña (1991).
25. Barry (1990), pp. 35-7.
26. Oglesby, *Op. cit.*, p. 4.
27. Edwards and Tovar Siebentritt, *Op. cit.*, p. 22.
28. Barry and Serra (1988).

29. Edwards and Tovar Siebentritt, *Op. cit.*
30. Human Rights Watch/Americas, *Op. cit.*, p. 11.
31. Richard Wilson, writing about Q'eqchi communities, claims that civil patrols represent the penetration of military and state structures deep into indigenous culture (Wilson, 1993b).
32. Dunkerley, *Op. cit.*, p. 49.
33. National Coordinating Office on Refugees and Displaced of Guatemala (hereafter NCOORD), *Newsletter*, February 1995, p. 5.
34. Ferris (1987), p. 37.
35. CEPAL (1993), p. 9.
36. *Ibid*, p. 13.
37. See UNHCR (1994), p. 22.
38. Ferris (1987), p. 53.
39. Torres-Rivas (1985), p. 36.
40. Aguayo, Christense, O'Dogherty and Varesse (1987).
41. Torres-Rivas, *Op. cit.*, p. 38.
42. Dunbar Ortiz (1988), p. 18.
43. Manz, *Op. cit.*
44. However, only 200 Guatemalans were officially recognised by the Costa Rican government as refugees, Torres Rivas, *Op. cit.*, p. 41.
45. Barry and Serra, *Op. cit.*, p. 37.
46. Ambos (1987), pp. 4-71.
47. Torres-Rivas, *Op. cit.*
48. Diana Pritchard and Kia Ambos, 'From the Frying Pan into the Fire', *The Guardian*, 23 October 1987, p. 13.
49. Hammond, *Op. cit.*, p. 110.
50. Barry and Serra, *Op. cit.*, p. 10.
51. Torres-Rivas, *Op. cit.*, p. 75.
52. CIREFCA (1992), p. 7.
53. Torres-Rivas, *Op. cit.*, pp. 56-7. Paradoxically this contributed towards the 'hispanification' of the small Belizean populace (approximately 200,000) which had hitherto been predominantly English-speaking creole. However, it should be noted that refugees rarely gained formal title to land.
54. *Ibid.*, p. 33.
55. On Mexico see Hernández, Nava, Flores and Escalona (1993).
56. *Refugees* (May, 1991), pp. 12-14.
57. Hammond, *Op. cit.*, p. 115.
58. See Pritchard (1988a).
59. Hammond, *Op. cit.*
60. Basok (1990) pp. 281-97.
61. Hammond, *Op. cit.*, pp. 118-20.
62. Ferris (1993).
63. Harrell-Bond (1987), pp. 311-19.
64. CEPAL, *Op. cit.*, p. 13.
65. Manz, *Op. cit.*, p. 7.

66. The full text of 'Esquipulas II: Procedure for the Establishment of a Firm and Lasting Peace in Central America' is reproduced in Moreno (1994), pp. 191-8.
67. Ortega, *Op. cit.*, p. 199.
68. Instituto Interamericano de Derechos Humanos, *Op. cit.*
69. See Basok (1990) and Reyes and Wilson, *Op. cit.*, p. 147.
70. Barry and Serra, *Op. cit.*, p. 26.
71. Author's interviews with returnee Miskito Indians on the Río Coco, 1988.
72. Pritchard (1988b), pp. 37-8.
73. For a detailed comparison of the repatriation of the two groups see Basok, *Op. cit.*
74. Ministerio de Acción Social (1993).
75. Edwards and Tovar Siebentritt, *Op. cit.*, p. 116.
76. *Ibid.*, p. 128.
77. *Ibid.*
78. *Ibid.*, p. 130 and chapter 10.
79. CIREFCA, *Op. cit.*
80. Edwards and Tovar Siebentritt, *Op. cit.*, chapters 9 and 10.
81. 'Queríamos ayudar, convertirnos en una fuerza social en la lucha por la paz y la justicia en nuestra Patria. La gente quería regresar en forma masiva y organizada'. Quoted in Instituto Interamericano de Derechos Humanos, *Op. cit.*, p. 104.
82. Hammond, *Op. cit.*, p. 116.
83. See Loescher, *Op. cit.*; also author's personal interviews with refugees planning the return in Managua, Nicaragua, December 1989-January 1990.
84. NCOORD *Newsletter*, February 1995, p. 11.
85. Ferris (1993).
86. Bishops' Conference of Guatemala, *Accord of the Permanent Commissions of the Guatemalan Refugees in Mexico and the Government of the Republic of Guatemala*, 23 September 1992 (with additions 8 October), Guatemala.
87. *Central American Report*, 21 January 1994.
88. *Central American Report*, 22 July 1994.
89. Human Rights Watch/Americas (1994), p. 15.
90. NCOORD *Newsletter*, October 1994, p. 9.
91. *Central America Report*, 24 June 1994.
92. Ferris (1993), p. 207.
93. *Barricada*, 10 March 1994, p. 6.
94. *Central America Report*, 29 April 1994.
95. Ferris (1993), p. 209.
96. Instituto Interamericano de Derechos Humanos, *Op. cit.*, p. 99.
97. See Basok, *Op. cit.*
98. Hawley (1992), pp. 74-5.
99. Ortega, *Op. cit.*, p. 41.
100. *Ibid.*, p. 58 and Hawley, *Op. cit.*
101. Author's interviews with repatriated Miskito, Santa Isabel, RAAN, August 1988; see also Ortega, *Op.cit.*, p. 13.

102. Instituto Interamericano de Derechos Humanos, *Op. cit.*
103. *Central American Report*, 28 October 1994.
104. Personal communication with the author.
105. By 1993 the threats posed to the CPRs by military encirclement were reduced given the support of the popular movement, Church and international attention.
106. NCOORD *Newsletter*, February 1995, pp. 5-8.
107. Faber (1992).
108. CEPAL, *Op. cit.*
109. *Central American Report*, 4 April 1994.
110. *Acuerdos de Chapultepec* (1992).
111. *Central America Report*, 16 September 1994.
112. Ferris (1993), p. 210.
113. NCOORD *Newsletter*, December 1994, p. 6.
114. *Central America Report*, 9 August 1994.
115. *Central America Report*, 20 July 1994.
116. United Nations General Assembly (1994), A/49/534.
117. Ferris (1993), p. 220.
118. FUSADES and Banco Central de Reserva de El Salvador.

II: INSTITUTIONS

CHAPTER 5

EXECUTIVE-LEGISLATIVE RELATIONS
AND THE INSTITUTIONALISATION OF DEMOCRACY

Ricardo Córdova Macías

Several years after the installation of civilian governments via increasingly competitive electoral processes, Central America's fledgling democratic systems have begun to face a new set of problems linked to the institution-alisation and consolidation of democracy. Over the last few years, conflict between the executive and legislative branches has been a feature of the political process. Debate has centred on a number of areas: the organisation, competencies and operation of the legislative branch; the feasibility of transforming the presidential system into a parliamentary or semi-parliamentary system; the need for reform and decentralisation of public administration, and the strengthening of municipal autonomy; together with the need for constitutional reforms, improvement of electoral systems and machinery for increasing citizen participation. In recent years Central America has experienced problems particular to this stage of democratic consolidation which have been expressed as demands and conflicts around the reform of political institutions. Never before in the history of the region have so many blueprints for institutional reform been debated in such a short time.

Current debate on the need to redefine the role of the state has begun to examine in more detail the politico-institutional dimension and the issues of governability specific to this stage of the transition. This chapter will focus on political and institutional dimensions of the relationship between executive and legislative powers in Central America during the last few years, focusing in particular on the confrontation between the different branches of state in Nicaragua and the institutional crisis in Guatemala following President Jorge Serrano's *autogolpe* in May 1993. The attributes and operation of the Congress in Central American politics is reviewed and the agendas for its reform examined.

The Central American region has experienced politico-institutional conflict in the form of profound crises of governability which, in the cases of Guatemala and Nicaragua, have been expressed as conflicts of competence between the various powers of the State. The underlying problem is that of the legality and legitimacy of the state in societies undergoing transformation which in turn demands state modernisation. Evidently, political institutions and systems in Central America lack credibility. More generally, the region has experienced a crisis of governability because of the inability of the main political actors in politico-institutional arenas to resolve their differences and achieve a minimum consensus for political stability.

Executive-Legislative Relations in Central America

Between 1992 and 1994, Central America underwent several institutional crises involving conflict between the different branches of the state. This section examines the conflict of powers in Nicaragua and reviews the institutional crisis in Guatemala triggered by Serrano's *autogolpe* in May 1993 through to the *consulta popular* on constitutional reform of January 1994.

In the case of the Nicaraguan crisis, President Violeta Chamorro was in a vulnerable position after acceding to the presidency, as she had to reconcile two contradictory objectives: achieving an understanding with the Sandinistas in order to guarantee political stability, and maintaining cohesion within the right-wing coalition which had brought her to power. The back-drop to this state of affairs was a political system in which dialogue among the main political forces was unable to serve as a mechanism of consensus for overcoming the crisis. Although consensus and stability are the keys to governability, the hallmark of the Nicaraguan political system is the difficulty in reconciling the opposing positions of the country's leading political forces.

In the case of Guatemala, Serrano's *autogolpe* generated a crisis between the executive and the other powers. Fortunately the outcome was a peaceful one leading to a swift return to constitutional rule and the continuation of the democratic transition. Institutions such as the Constitutional Court, the Supreme Electoral Tribunal and the Human Rights Ombudsman played a major role in scotching this attempt to interrupt the constitutional order. Furthermore, social forces and political parties played a decisive role in the *Foro Multisectorial* and in the *Instancia de Consenso Nacional* (see below). Nevertheless, the crisis highlighted the difficulties of generating consensus amongst the various political forces subsequent to the restitution of the constitutional order. Dialogue between the country's main political actors has yet to produce a negotiated political solution to the armed conflict.

The Case of Nicaragua

In the aftermath of Violeta Chamorro's unexpected electoral victory in February 1990, questions were raised about the future governability of the Nicaraguan political system. As mentioned above, Chamorro needed to reconcile contradictory objectives: those of holding together her right-wing coalition and of reaching understandings with the Sandinistas to guarantee political stability. Both her inaugural speech and the *Protocolo de Transición* signed on 27 March 1990 indicated the government's desire for moderation and its search for an understanding with the Sandinistas.

The conflict between Chamorro's government and the coalition of parties which had brought her to power was manifest by July 1991, when the fourteen parties comprising UNO (Unión Nacional Opositora) requested her to implement the original UNO programme. The conflict deepened around the issue of property ownership: the Forum of the Second Phase of the *Concertación Económica y Social* promoted by the government in order to reach a consensus of government, business and trade unions on key socio-economic matters concluded its deliberations in August 1991, ending several months of intense national debate by approving a series of agreements to regulate property ownership in Nicaragua.[1] However, UNO disagreed with the Forum's conclusions, arguing instead for the repeal of the three main laws on property rights promulgated during the Sandinista regime. Potentially, this could have sparked a far-reaching socio-political conflict. The delegates of the private sector council (COSEP) refused to sign the agreements, which they argued favoured the Sandinistas. The Chamorro government, however, while not agreeing with the way property had been expropriated and allocated under the Sandinistas, decided that in order for national stability to be secured, it was necessary to back the *Concertación* agreements rather than entering into an all-out confrontation with the FSLN (Frente Sandinista de Liberación Nacional).[2]

The dissatisfied UNO deputies subsequently approved Law 133 on the 'Re-establishment and Stability of the Juridical Order of Private, State and Municipal Property', known as the Cesar Law. This ignored the executive's position and overturned Sandinista laws 85 and 86, passed during the transition period in 1990, which had provided guarantees for expropriated property. On 11 September 1991 the Chamorro government placed a partial veto on law 133 on the grounds of unconstitutionality. This further exacerbated the conflict between the two branches of state. The President justified the action, arguing that 'the fact that these laws [85 and 86] allowed improper repartition of state assets does not justify the use of similar mechanisms to repair the original wrong. The state possesses sufficient and lawful means to correct these abuses'.[3] The President was undoubtedly in a difficult position: if she failed to veto law 133 it would cause problems with the FSLN; if she did exercise the veto she risked causing a rupture both between the executive and the legislature and within her governing coalition. In December 1991 the Legislative Assembly accepted the presidential veto, thus legitimising the properties distributed under the Ortega government in the process known as the *'Sandinista piñata'*.[4] The veto improved government-FSLN relations, an alliance which was crucial for the government to maintain power and political stability. Another variable operating in this crisis was the freezing of $116 million in aid by the US Congress as the result of lobbying led by Senator Jesse Helms, who was demanding a faster return of properties confiscated under the previous regime to their former owners, which included 400 US citizens. Furthermore, Helms was lobbying for the removal of General Humberto Ortega as Commander-in-Chief of the army and an end to the Chamorro-Sandinista alliance.[5]

A second conflict erupted over the election of the Legislative Assembly's Governing Council for the 1993-94 period. An agreement between the faction of UNO known as the 'centre group' and the FSLN led to an escalation in political tension between the government and UNO. Clashes between the government and UNO deputies intensified until in December 1992 the Governing Council was forcibly disbanded and provisionally replaced by the executive, via Executive Decree No. 341-92. The president subsequently ordered police and military personnel to take over the site of the National Assembly and forcibly to control the entrance in order to prevent an occupation of Congress by hardline UNO deputies. Although the new governing council was elected on 9 January without incident, this marked the beginning of an unfolding institutional crisis. In February 1993 the stand-off between the Chamorro government and the UNO opposition was intensified by insistent denunciation of Antonio Lacayo, Minister of the Presidency and government 'strong man', for alleged corruption. Guillermo Potoy, Nicaragua's then Comptroller General, demanded that President Chamorro dismiss Lacayo, only to be himself relieved of his post by the Legislative Assembly, by that time dominated by Sandinistas and deputies close to the administration. Potoy's dismissal was denounced as a sign of the subordination of the legislature to the executive.[6] The parliamentary crisis continued to gather momentum with UNO hardliners issuing a 'Political Declaration' in which they accused the government of betraying their original political platform. These deputies subsequently declared themselves in open opposition to the government and in protest changed their name from UNO to APO – the Alianza Política Opositora.

The hardliners' communiqué charged that via Presidential Agreement 341-92, President Chamorro had awarded herself faculties and powers not conferred either by the constitution of Nicaragua or its laws, and had violated the principles of division, independence and sovereignty of the powers of the State. The communiqué laid the charge that the National Assembly had 'fallen under the control of the Sandinista fraction led by General Humberto Ortega, signifying that the State and Government of Nicaragua has been completely returned to those who were ousted by popular vote on 25 February 1990'.[7] The deputies charged that Chamorro had failed to fulfil her political commitment to UNO member parties, betrayed the UNO coalition and substituted their programme for the interests of co-government, acceding to the 'achievement of control and power by *Sandinismo* of all powers of the state and institutions of government'.[8] They concluded that their grouping 'has no other option but to go back into opposition with the same conviction and determination with which we fought against the dictatorship of the Sandinista Front'.[9] It is worth noting the proclamation stated that the dissidents would struggle to recover institutionality, constitutional order and the independence of powers as the essential basis of democracy. The 44 APO deputies subsequently abstained from participating in plenary sessions leaving the 39 Sandinistas and the seven UNO deputies allied with the government (the so-called 'centre group') in the Assembly. Thus, three years after her electoral triumph, the main political opposition faced by President Chamorro came from her former UNO allies. The most radical sector of APO demanded either that the President resign or alternatively that there be a plebiscite to shorten her mandate. The government in turn viewed this as an unambiguous attempt at destabilisation.

In April 1993 the possibility was raised of a *Diálogo Nacional* to serve as a mechanism for national reconciliation and overcome the institutional crisis rocking the country. To this end, meetings were convened between the executive, opposition, *Sandinismo*, the private sector and the trade unions. The *Diálogo Nacional* ushered in a new stage of closer relations between the government and UNO. However, it proved insufficient to solve the crisis. Indeed, the failure to reconcile the antagonistic positions of the main players subsequently led to serious criticism of the government for failing to implement agreements reached during the course of the *Diálogo Nacional*. One solution put forward was an early election. However, the crisis required more than early elections; it required some means by which to bring about the necessary consensus, involving dialogue and negotiation between the various political forces in the country. While elections might have altered the prevailing composition of political forces they would not necessarily have represented a solution to the political crisis facing the country.

The relationship between the government and the Sandinista Front was shaken somewhat by the President's speech given on 2 September 1993 to mark the fifteenth anniversary of the Ejército Popular Sandinista (EPS), when she announced her intention to remove General Humberto Ortega from his post as Commander-In-Chief of the EPS in 1994. This unexpected announcement caught the Sandinistas by surprise. During the latter half of November, following weeks of stalemate, negotiations between the government, UNO and FSLN recommenced. The UNO parliamentary bench subsequently accepted partial reforms to the Constitution, originally proposed by the FSLN, thus shelving UNO's initial proposal of convening a Constituent Assembly.[10] UNO then agreed to return to negotiations and, jointly with the FSLN, put forward a bill of constitutional reform to the Assembly.

From September 1992 to December 1993 the crisis had virtually paralysed the legislature. It was resolved on 9 December 1993 when 58 of the 92 deputies signed an historic agreement to reform the 1987 constitution. This aimed to provide a better balance between the powers of State, increasing the authority of the legislative branch at the expense of hitherto excessive presidentialism. In the course of the crisis resolution, the UNO split. Of the fourteen original partners in the coalition, only seven remained in January 1994. In this manner, a new 'national majority' was created in the National Assembly which afforded a majority to the FSLN. This resolution to the politico-institutional crisis signified the failure of the UNO project for a Constituent Assembly. It also implied a political realignment between the FSLN and moderate UNO sectors. These realignments marked the end of one stage and, according to one local think-tank, the beginning of a new one 'in which the opportunities available for each political group will be redefined within a changing institutional framework, beginning with the changes to the Constitution and ending with the 1996 elections which will close the stage now beginning and consolidate the alliances currently being formed'.[11]

On 10 December 1993 the Legislative Assembly adopted an amendment to the Nicaraguan Constitution authorising the approval of changes to the *magna carta* in one legislative sitting rather than in two, as had previously been the case. This measure opened the door to additional constitutional reforms. In essence, the reform package drafted in the FSLN and UNO negotiating committees sought to restrict the jurisdiction of the executive and to democratise the exercise of power. This project is supported by the President and 58 out of the 92 legislators. Several UNO deputies are violently opposed to the package.[12] In the FSLN view, 'the negotiation process which leads to reforms and the reforms themselves should contribute to a resolution of the country's political crisis; in order for all efforts to be focused on economic reactivation and the fight against poverty, resolution of the crisis is essential'.[13] In early January 1994 three quarters of the members of the National Assembly returned to their seats, thus normalising the function of the legislature. Essentially they sought to transfer the political battle to the legislature, in the hope of achieving an agreement between the different national political forces. During the course of the following months, the partial reform of the Constitution dominated the agenda. Some of the issues on the table included: the length of the presidential terms of office (a five year term was proposed instead of the existing six, together with a prohibition on reelection); the selection process for magistrates of the Supreme Court of Justice; the nature of the armed forces; property ownership; the faculties of the National Assembly; and executive-legislative relations.

The debate on constitutional reform also had an impact on the developing internal crisis within the Sandinista Front. During the first months of 1994 the new parliamentary alliance agreed a consensus agenda and by the middle of the year had approved the controversial *código militar* which institutionalised the subordination of the army to civil authority [see chapter three]. However, when it came to discussing the issue of constitutional reform, conflicts resulted both within the FSLN and also between the executive and the legislature.[14] Of the 170 constitutional articles initially targeted for reform, only 62 appeared in the final reform package. The proposed reforms aimed, firstly, to extend the democratisation of the state and its institutions, involving a correction of the imbalance of powers established in the 1987 Constitution, a return of exclusive legislative authority to the National Assembly and the reestablishment of the Assembly's authority over fiscal matters. Secondly, they aimed to examine the suitability of the socio-economic changes effected during the revolutionary decade. According to Carlos Fernando Chamorro, differences surrounding the issue of constitutional reform were a central factor in the internal crisis of the FSLN: 'When the possibility of constitutional reform and the need to seek negotiations with all political forces without preconditions was first broached in the Sandinista Assembly in August 1993, the initiative met with strong opposition.'[15] Subsequently,'what had begun as a crisis of political confidence between the party apparatus and the FSLN parliamentary bench became a thorough-going internal crisis.....the core of the conflict being a contradiction between those who perceived the reforms to be a step towards deepening democracy and those who saw them as a concession'.[16] Chamorro maintains that underlying these differences were two opposing views of power: 'an old-fashioned overall vision which refuses categorically to renounce authoritarian practices; and a more democratic, participatory vision of power, with checks and balances, where the popular movements can develop spheres of influence to capture government and move the transformation of society forward'.[17]

The Guatemalan Case

On 25 May 1993 news broke that the constitutional order had been suspended in Guatemala, a country where *coups d'état* were commonplace. What was novel in this particular case was that a civilian president, Jorge Serrano Elías, had decided to dissolve Congress, the Supreme Court of Justice and the Constitutional Court.[18] The coup was an indication of Serrano's inability to generate democratic consensus or maintain the constitutional order in Guatemala. The politico-institutional crisis which concerns us here has two distinct phases: the first commenced with the crisis of the *autogolpe* of 25 May and lasted until 6 June 1993 when Congress elected Ramiro de León Carpio, the then Human Rights Ombudsman, as the new president of Guatemala. The second phase was centred on the adoption of constitutional reforms in the *consulta popular* (referendum) of January 1994. The outcome of this politico-institutional crisis, which was resolved peacefully, facilitating a swift return to the democratic order, represented an important advance in the Central American political process.

From the *coup d'état* to the Election of de León Carpio as President

An examination of the background to the coup in Guatemala reveals a number of indicators of mounting ungovernability:

> – The breakdown in April 1993 of the parliamentary agreement between the opposition Christian Democrat party (PDCG), the Unión del Centro Nacional (UCN) and President Serrano's small Movimiento de Acción Solidaria party (MAS) which had guaranteed the adoption of laws and general governability during 1992

and the early months of 1993. This subsequently left the government without a parliamentary majority.

– Mounting criticism of Serrano, who was repeatedly accused of abuse of authority and misappropriation of funds; potentially this could have culminated in legal proceedings against the President.

– Accusations of corruption and impunity laid against some parliamentarians.

– The deadlock in the peace negotiations between the government and the URNG (Unidad Revolucionaria Nacional Guatemalteca).

– The stepping up of popular protest in response to the implementation of neo-liberal economic policies, particularly the increase in electricity prices.

– A wave of terrorist attacks against public and private buildings after June 1992 which contributed towards a generalised feeling of uncertainty and fear.

On 25 May President Serrano broadcast on national television and radio networks that he had decided 'temporarily and partially' to suspend the Constitution; to restrict constitutional guarantees; to dissolve Congress; and to change the incumbents of the Supreme Court of Justice, the Constitutional Court and the Procurators' offices. Indicating that his intention was not to remain in power beyond his constitutionally appointed mandate, Serrano stated that he would ask the Supreme Electoral Council to convene a Constituent Assembly within sixty days for the purposes of reviewing the Constitution. The President maintained that his *autogolpe* was justified by the need to purge the state of all forms of corruption. He berated the Congress and Supreme Court of Justice for their lack of credibility and prestige, and declared that during the previous two and a half years he had been subject to political blackmail by certain member of Congress which had made it impossible for him effectively to exercise his mandate. He was even more emphatic in denouncing Congress's ineffectual and obstructionist handling of preliminary hearings in cases where members of Congress were accused of corruption. Serrano accused the Supreme Court of political bias and the selective application of justice, which, he alleged, had weakened the rule of law.[19]

Also broadcast on 25 May were the 'Temporary Norms of Government'.[20] These stated that Congress was henceforth dissolved and that the President would assume legislative functions and govern via Presidential decree; that members of the Supreme Court of Justice and the Constitutional Court were to be dismissed and replaced by Presidential appointees; and that the Procurator General of the Nation was to be removed from his post as the Head of the Public Ministry. Existing municipal authorities, however, would remain in post. That same afternoon the Constitutional Court issued a resolution to the effect that the President's actions contravened the constitutional order and that the 'Temporary Norms of Government' decreed by the President of the Republic were therefore unconstitutional and their provisions invalid. On 31 May the Constitutional Court demanded that the ministers of government and defence support the ruling. The army, in response to the emerging civil-military consensus rejecting the *autogolpe* and, as ordered by the Constitutional Court, subsequently forced Serrano to step down. The army subsequently requested the Constitutional Court to oversee the return to the constitutional order.

On 4 June 1993 a proposal for a return to constitutional government was formulated by the Instancia Nacional de Consenso (INC), a body composed of representatives from the business sector, the main trade unions, the political parties, the cooperative sector and others. This contained five key points: a) the resignation of Gustavo Espina as Vice-President; b) the designation by Congress of a President and Vice-President; c) the formation of a transition government supported by a national consensus; d) an immediate purge and restructuring of the three branches of state: executive, legislature and judiciary and; e) reform of the Law on Elections and Political Parties. The same day, the Constitutional Court issued a resolution noting that the Guatemalan army had provided the necessary support to oblige Serrano to leave his post and ruling that Serrano's vice-president Gustavo Espina was disqualified from occupying the presidency on account of his participation in the *de facto* government and such illegitimate acts as the appointment of new magistrates of the Supreme Court. The resolution proposed that Congress should designate a replacement President and Vice-President to remain in office until the end of the existing presidential term. The following day, Gustavo Espina resigned from his post and the National Consensus Committee (INC) put forward a presidential slate to Congress. In an emergency session that same day, Congress decreed the posts of President and Vice-President vacant and proceeded to elect Ramiro de León Carpio as the new President to complete the presidential term (due to end on 14 January 1996).[21]

On balance, the Constitutional Court, officially dissolved by Serrano, played a leading role in the resolution of the crisis: it immediately ruled the presidential decree unconstitutional; it requested support from the ministers of defence and government to carry out the judgement of the court against Serrano; it cooperated with the executive in managing the return to the constitutional order; and it disqualified Vice-President Espina from the presidency and ordered Congress to elect a constitutional president.[22] The initial resolution of the Constitutional Court in response to the *autogolpe* sent a clear message; this was subsequently followed through by other decisions taken in an attempt to resolve the crisis and return to the constitutional framework. Similarly, the Supreme Electoral Tribunal (TSE) contributed by rejecting Serrano's request for a *consulta popular* or constituent assembly. The same was true for the statements made by the Human Rights Procurator. Civil society also played an important role in resolving the crisis, using the *Foro Multisectorial Social* and the *Instancia Nacional de Consenso* (INC) to campaign for a return to the constitutional order. As regards the role of the parties and Congress, Josef Thesing has maintained that essentially the parties were responsible for the development of the crisis of 1993 and specifically that during Serrano's second year of office the alliance of the UCN, MAS and PDCG was to blame for the progressive decline of public morale, politicising the judiciary, and widespread corruption which ultimately permeated the entire political system. This in turn contributed to the selective administration of justice which awarded impunity to the powerful; a highly irresponsible Congress which degenerated into a market place for votes; and an executive which supported unlawful business deals.[23] Essentially the Congress abused its function within the constitutional order, contributing to the erosion of democratic institutionality.

The *Consulta Popular* on Constitutional Reform

During the development of this crisis, Guatemalan citizens identified the culprits to be the President, Vice-President and Minister of Government, followed by the Congress and its members, the over-politicised judiciary and finally the political party system as a whole. This subsequently generated demands for a purge of Congress, the Supreme Court of Justice, and the executive. With the election of de León Carpio the most immediate stage of the crisis was resolved, but it soon became clear that the assurances given by Congress that it would clean up its act were false. The majority of congressional representatives argued that no legal mechanisms existed to make such a purge viable and they refused to resign their seats. Others even demanded a complete dissolution of Congress, a measure not contemplated in the Constitution.

In August 1993 President Ramiro de León Carpio publicly demanded the resignation of all congressional deputies, the dismissal of the Supreme Court magistrates and the adoption of a constitutional reform package (conditional on its support by a national referendum). The proposed package included the reduction of Parliament from 116 to 73 seats; the revocation of the right of members of Congress to a preliminary hearing in criminal cases; and the abolition of budgetary confidentiality for the three branches of the State.[24] In rhetorical terms, President de León referred to a national crusade against impunity and corruption and the purging of state entities in order to win back public confidence in state institutions. The President's announcement precipitated an institutional crisis following the legally questionable appointment on 5 September 1993 of a new legislative governing council by a parliamentary majority. The usurped president of the Congress took the matter before the Constitutional Court, which in turn decided to support him, effectively suspending the election of 5 September. The dispute in Congress was a result of growing polarisation within the Congress itself. A majority group of 70 congressional deputies (termed the *Gran Bancada*), maintained that a selective self-purge by Congress would only affect sixteen representatives. The minority group (which included those earmarked to be purged) and others sought the resignation of all 116 deputies in line with public opinion. The underlying issue was how to carry out the purge in a legal fashion. The possibility of shortening the legislative period and calling fresh elections was raised but subsequently rejected by the Constitutional Court.[25]

In response to Ramiro de León Carpio's public pronouncements, Congress had sought legal counsel from the Constitutional Court on the issue of whether or not it was legal for the president of one of the branches of the state to demand the resignation of members of another branch without recourse to established legal and constitutional mechanisms. In August 1993 the Constitutional Court gave its view on whether it was possible to reduce the existing constitutional period for which the deputies had been elected (1991-6); whether it was possible to bring forward the electoral process to elect a new legislature; and what the legal and constitutional mechanisms would be in such an eventuality.

However, the executive's preparations for a referendum on the question of congressional resignations were suspended when the Supreme Court of Justice awarded the deputies statutory protection from the Supreme Electoral Council, a somewhat dubious decision given that the

Presidential proposals for a purge also included the Supreme Court magistrates. At the same time the two blocks in Parliament agreed to declare a permanent Congressional sitting in order fully to discuss the proposed constitutional reforms. Various proposals were subsequently made: to reduce the presidential mandate to four years; to reduce the parliamentary mandate to four years with renewal of half the Congress every two years; to revise and modify the system of parliamentary immunity; to reform the procedure for election of the Supreme Court; and to reform the law on elections and political parties. In October the Supreme Court sent a court case to Congress requesting a hearing to determine whether or not de León Carpio had illegally issued unlawful resolutions.[26]

Decree 2-93, issued by the Supreme Electoral Tribunal on 1 October, called for a referendum (*consulta popular*) so that citizens could vote on whether or not they supported the President's request for the resignation of Congress, and his request for the resignation of the Supreme Court magistrates. The date for the referendum was fixed for Sunday 28 November 1993. Faced with Ramiro de León Carpio's proposed *consulta*, Congress produced a constitutional reform bill, adopted at first reading on 29 October, which would have given Congress the authority to separate the President from his office if Congress decided he was in violation of the law. The proposal, which met with widespread criticism from the President and many other sectors, signalled that the deputies were out of step with the general desire for reform, which aimed to reduce congressional privileges and authority, rather than increasing them, and to fight corruption and impunity.

On 1 November 1993 the Guatemalan Episcopal Conference invited the executive and legislature to hold talks in order to seek a swift solution to the institutional crisis. Within the framework of this dialogue, Congress suspended definitive adoption of its proposed constitutional reform package. In addition, the Constitutional Court provisionally suspended the Supreme Electoral Tribunal's decree 2-93 and consequently also suspended the *consulta* planned for 28 November. The aim of the Constitutional Court was to study whether the *consulta* violated the Constitution, which prohibits subordination of one power of state to another. Furthermore, the Court considered it opportune to evaluate whether or not this decision would cause irreparable harm to the institutional order.

Amidst great controversy regarding the Constitutional Court's deliberations, both sides continued to talk with episcopal mediation until on 15 November 1993 a commitment was reached to purge the three powers of the state, which included adoption by the legislature of a new package of constitutional reforms. The pact also made provision for the election of a new Congress by popular vote by mid-1994; in other words an early election, but only of congressional deputies. The new legislature, whose term of office would only last until completion of the presidential period on 14 January 1996, would then elect a new Supreme Court which would conclude the process of purging the state and full restoration of the legal order. A proposal for forty-five constitutional amendments was agreed, together with the convening of a *consulta popular* to approve the proposed reforms in early 1994. The measures were scheduled to come into force two months later, in March or April, if approved. In accordance with the law, some 120 days later (at the very latest in August) a new Congress would be elected whose deputies would take up their seats one month after the election and continue in office until 14 January 1996. Three days after swearing in, the legislature would call upon the selection committees to designate candidates for Supreme Court magistrates as well as for the Comptroller General of the Nation (to be elected and sworn in within thirty days, ie. during October). During the same period the executive would appoint the new head of the Public Ministry. The constitutional reforms included a reduction from five to four years for the terms of President, Vice-President, congressional deputies, departmental governors and mayors; from six to five years for Supreme Court magistrates; the removal of Congress's competence to hear preliminary proceedings against congressional deputies and the award of such competence to the Supreme Court; the reduction in the number of congressional deputies from 116 to 95 or 94, depending on the size of the population. The proposal to give Congress the power to remove the President in case of violation of the Constitution was rejected. In response the executive formally withdrew its demand for a referendum in November.[27] The constitutional reforms were provisionally adopted by Congress on 17 November and the Supreme Electoral Tribunal set the date for a referendum on 30 January 1994.[28] Some opposition sectors, such as trade unions, were against this compromise. However, essentially they questioned the procedure followed rather than the actual content of the reforms.[29]

In the event, the 'Yes' vote promoted by the President won the referendum of 30 January 1994. Guatemalan citizens thus approved 43 reforms to their constitution. Sixty-nine per cent voted Yes while thirteen per cent voted 'No', with eighteen per cent refusing either option, leaving their ballot blank. Political analysts were also surprised at the high level of abstentionism: 84.13 per cent of 3,439,331 citizens had voting rights but according to data from the Supreme Electoral Tribunal, only 545,916 (15.87 per cent of the latter) actually voted [see also chapter two, figure

2.1].[30] Such high abstentionism calls into question the legitimacy of the referendum. In fact the *consulta* was challenged by the popular sectors who felt the removal of magistrates and congressional deputies to be insufficient. They charged that reforms were undemocratic and unconstitutional and denounced the entire process as an insult to the population. Some sectors called for a 'No' vote, others for abstention, considering the deal to be little more than a pact between corrupt and illegitimate political leaders. President de León Carpio called for a 'Yes' vote, arguing that this was the only way out of the institutional crisis, a stance echoed by the general secretary of the Christian Democrat Party (PDCG), Alfonso Cabrera.

Discussion of the high abstention rate persists, although in general it is accepted that this was a response to the lack of credibility of the political system and institutions of State, complicated by the fact that the content of the reforms was unintelligible to the majority of the population. The Supreme Electoral Tribunal issued a communiqué on 4 February 1994 declaring the validity of the *consulta popular* held on 30 January and announcing the winning vote to be that of those citizens who favoured ratification of the Constitutional Reforms passed by Congress on 17 November 1993, with the following results: 370,044 votes in favour, 70,761 against, totalling 440,805 valid votes.[31]

Following the *consulta*, on 7 February 1994 President de León Carpio called on all sectors of society to sign a *Gran Acuerdo Nacional* to consolidate governability and build true democracy in Guatemala.[32] Gabriel Aguilera judged that the negotiation process (*concertación*) surrounding the *consulta popular* was positive, demonstrating the increasing capacity of social actors to seek negotiated solutions to conflict. However, he acknowledges that this was not the perception of other sectors of civil society who opposed the arrangement, viewing it as an élite pact removed from the interest of the majority, and suggests that this reaction reflected mistrust of a regime which had lost legitimacy.[33]

Congress: How it Operates and the Agenda for its Reform

Over the last few years the role of political institutions has been a focus of political debate in Central America. Particular emphasis has been attached to the role that a Congress plays, or should play in democratic transition. For example, for the United States Agency for International Development (USAID) one of the new strategic objectives of economic aid to Central America is 'to foster stable democratic societies'.[34] To this end, it is proposed to strengthen legislative processes and systems, to be achieved by 'strengthening institutional capacity to draft legislation, improving analytical and administrative capabilities via training, promotion of research and on-going dialogue around the central role which national assemblies play'.[35]

The following analysis of the powers and operation of Congress in Central America concentrates on common problems of the three post-war countries (El Salvador, Guatemala, and Nicaragua), examining political processes where peace has been attained by negotiation and in which increasingly competitive elections have been held.[36] Four elements will be analysed. First, the powers contemplated in constitutions. Secondly, the fulfilment or application of the powers established in the constitutions. Thirdly, some hypotheses will be advanced on the problems faced by legislative assemblies. Fourthly, a proposed reform agenda for an increase in the efficiency and legitimacy of the legislative body will be discussed. Most of the empirical evidence for this section is taken from the cases of El Salvador and Guatemala.

Powers of Congress

The Constitution of the Republic of El Salvador (promulgated in 1983, with reforms in 1991/2) establishes 38 functions for the Legislative Assembly (art. 131).[37] These can be synthesised in the following four functions:

- To legislate (decree and interpret laws, reform and repeal secondary laws, decree taxes and other levies on goods, services and income etc).

- To decree public income and expenditure.

- To operate checks and balances on the executive branch, principally by: receiving, approving or rejecting reports of the performance report of the executive as presented by its ministers; appointing special committees to investigate matters of national interest and adopting agreements or recommendations as necessary on the basis of the committees' reports; questioning ministers or their departmental heads and presidents of autonomous official institutions; recommending dismissal of ministers of state or officials of autonomous institutions to the President; preliminary hearings (*antejuicios*) of cases against government officials.

– To elect the following officials and bodies: Supreme Court of Justice, Supreme Electoral Council, Court of Accounts, Attorney General, Procurator General, Human Rights Ombudsman, National Council of the Judiciary.

Operating as a political forum might well be added as a fifth function. If a system is sufficiently representative then it allows for on-going discussion between different political positions, generating the necessary consensus and cohesion at key junctures to ensure governability. This essentially means creating opportunities in Congress to discuss matters of public interest. A democratic system requires a political process which is always open enough for citizens to understand how the country is being run. Therefore one of Parliament's roles is as a forum of political debate. It is important to note that pluralism is required beyond the discussion stage, as a modern parliament must be able 'to select and synthesize social demands and incorporate them into political alternatives'.[38] Analysis of the powers and *modus operandi* of Congress should be based on an assessment of these four functions, rather than merely examining the legislative function, understood as decreeing, amending and repealing laws. More than the legislative function is necessary if Congress 'is to be the political instrument of popular sovereignty'.[39]

Exercise of Congressional Functions

While all the above powers are enshrined in the Constitution, use is not always made of them; technical difficulties or lack of political will may inhibit their exercise or implementation. In the following paragraphs three different examples of the way in which the role of Congress is limited, compared to the role enshrined in the Constitution, will be discussed: budget adoption; monitoring of the executive branch; lack of an information policy.[40]

The Budget

In the Salvadorean case, although the Legislative Assembly has the power to decree a general budget, in practice the way the process of formulating and adopting the budget is structured gives Congress very little chance to modify it (it can reduce or reject certain proposed sums but not increase them).[41] Furthermore, a supplementary budget exists which in recent years has been as large or larger than the official budget; this does not have to be passed by the legislature. In addition, institutions like the Social Investment Fund (*Fondo de Inversión Social*) have special budgets which do not require the approval of the legislature.

In 1994, the congressional opposition came together to tackle this problem and in November presented a joint statement on budgetary matters.[42] This began by acknowledging that the budget was the product of a complex technical and political process in which congressional deputies participated only in the final stage, and alleged that without precise knowledge of the budget it was difficult for Congress to ratify it. The document identified a number of shortcomings, arguing that the legal framework of the budgetary system was obsolete, uncoordinated and inefficient, and highlighting the absence of an integrated budget for the different components of the public sector. It alleged that lack of co-ordination of economic and social policy made it impossible for Congress to take and implement the correct decisions, and charged that the existence of multiple supplementary budgets (in receipt of both external and domestic finance) was not only unconstitutional but also in contravention of the basic principles which should determine a modern budget: 'programming, balance, rationality, unity, transparency and flexibility'.[43] The document also lamented the fact that no legal mechanisms existed for follow-up and evaluation of budget administration to measure the effectiveness and social impact of expenditure, and concluded that 'the budget is merely a rehash of the old traditional formats and institutional vices which attempt to hide the true political situation with technical trickery'.[44]

Monitoring the Executive Branch

Currently, the democratic transition requires that Congress have supervisory control over the executive and the activities of the public administration in general. Various mechanisms for this exist: ministerial reports, special committees, questioning of government officials, preliminary hearings (*antejuicios*) and recommendations for dismissal. However, ministerial reports are little more than an anachronistic ritual – ministers merely read out the minutes of work carried out by their employees without any opportunity for questions by congressional deputies. In the case of questions to ministers, the deputy must specify to whom and in what form the question is to be asked. This is subsequently referred to the Committee for Legislation and Constitutional Points for confirmation and reformulation. The main constraint is that questions can only be asked after the minister in question has been previously advised and the question itself passed by a legislative committee. Such mechanisms are very far from constituting a modern system of checks and balances.[45]

The Lack of an Information Policy

The Salvadorean Legislative Assembly does not have a policy on public information. Furthermore, the last time minutes of legislative proceedings were published was for the period 1988-91. The lack of an information policy or a means for the public to have access to and follow debates in the legislature contributes to a widening of the gap between the people and Congress.

The Operation of Congress

This section will refer to five aspects which help to explain the limitations of the legislative branch in the Central American political process. Firstly, in historical terms the shortcomings of Congress is linked to the presidentialist nature of Central America's political systems. Furthermore, in the past the lack of political stability and conditions for democracy helped to restrict the preeminence of parliaments. In fact, the discussion of parliament's possibilities only began once the minimum democratic conditions and greater parliamentary pluralism were established during the postwar democratic transition.

Secondly, when the president has a parliamentary majority there is a tendency to neglect the supervisory function of Congress for lack of political will on the part of the party in government to push for a more balanced distribution of powers. It would appear that when the opposition has a majority in parliament there is a greater chance to impose checks and balances on the government; in some cases this can lead to confrontation between the different powers.

Thirdly, a key factor stemming from the lack of democratic conditions should be noted: in the past, political institutions elected by flawed and uncompetitive electoral processes have not been accustomed to act responsibly, nor obliged to be accountable to citizens. In other words, there was no link between voters and those elected to executive and legislature. Under today's new political conditions, the problems of representation and legitimacy are being tackled. Congresses must be seen to be democratically representative; representation is a complex phenomenon but its essence lies in a process of election of governing representatives who should be accountable for their actions. Legitimacy should not be confused with the term 'legality'; the latter implies that representatives are elected by a ballot among the citizenry in accordance with established legal norms. Legitimacy is understood to be the degree of support or consensus among the citizenry for a government which ensures compliance without recourse to force. Lipset sees legitimacy as the capacity of the system to promote and sustain the belief that the existing political institutions are the most appropriate for that society. Legitimacy is related to the population's belief that, in spite of their defects, existing political institutions are better than any others which conceivably might replace them.[46] However, although the prospects for the legitimacy of congresses have improved, it should not be forgotten that it is the way institutions function and the manner in which citizens perceive the work of Parliament and deputies which will increase legitimacy. In this transition stage, Borea's statement holds true, in the sense that parliaments are beset by problems of definition and that 'the image of what they should do and what they actually do have not coincided, leading to a gap which increasingly threatens their legitimacy'.[47]

Fourthly, the way in which deputies are elected does not make them accountable to the electorate. It is therefore important to discuss options for electoral reform which will bring candidates closer to civil society so that in an election everyone is clear who they are electing and with what mandate. At present voters cast their ballot without knowing the candidates or their programmes and there is a distinct lack of discussion of different proposals. However, increased citizen participation in electing deputies and greater Congressional legitimacy will not alone automatically guarantee greater effectiveness.

Fifthly, there is a certain tension in the relationship between political parties and parliamentary fractions which is linked to the issue of representation. The key question is: who do deputies represent, parties or citizens? Salvadorean political culture is based on the acceptance of parties 'controlling' their deputies and exerting party discipline. In other words the party 'is more important than the voter in determining legitimacy of representation'.[48] Some members of Congress maintain that they act as representatives of all the people without bowing to the command of the popular mandate ('*mandato imperativo*'),[49] but the solutions discussed tend to come from the political commissions of the parties. Each parliamentary decision concentrates and absorbs the efforts of the entire party leadership to such an extent that other party or Assembly activities are put on hold until the central problem is solved.[50]

Linked to the problem of the so-called *partidocracia* which tends to curtail development of the institutional system, is the fact that, as Rafael

Guido Béjar points out, there is little difference between the congressional representations of a party and full-time party officials, or between the parliamentary party and the party machine itself. The parties have turned parliament into an arena for clashes among the party apparatus; it is not yet functioning as a centre of autonomous power and as such cannot yet be considered a politically neutral space.[51]

The key to resolving this complex problem of representation and the role of Congress *vis-à-vis* the parties lies precisely in the role and operation of the parties themselves. There would be no problem if political parties were institutionalised, run democratically and coherent in their programmes. But the truth is that today political parties in Central America are in deep crisis. Two dangers should be noted here: firstly, when parties are weak, disunited and lacking in leadership, these qualities are reflected in the country's institutions and in political decision-making. The splits and internal crisis of the Salvadorean opposition during 1994, both within the PDC (Partido Demócrata Cristiana) and the FMLN, have affected the work of parliamentary fractions and of Congress overall. Secondly, with regard to the role of parties, it needs to be clear when parties are functioning according to internal democracy and when they are responding to the dictates of their higher echelons. The conduct of the parties is capable of distorting the functioning of democracy and its institutions [see chapter two].

This whole debate highlights the key question: what are the functions of the parties? They are currently faced with at least three challenges. First, internal reform is necessary. This applies to their methods of organisation and access to members and the electorate, their participation in national politics, and their methods of selecting party authorities and candidates. Secondly, as pointed out above, candidates must be answerable to civil society so that in an election it is clear who is being elected and with what mandate. Thirdly, it must be acknowledged that the crisis of the parties has affected their ability effectively to transmit voters' demands or concerns. This signals the need to find a new way of articulating party politics with the organisations and interests of civil society. To a certain extent civil society's rejection of the parties' monopoly on representation must be accepted as legitimate. Equally it must be accepted that political parties are indispensable mechanisms in the process of political representation. In other words, the existing parties need to redefine their relationship with civil society, accepting and opening up to society rather than reacting competitively.[52]

A Reform Agenda for Congress

The events which occurred in Guatemala cannot be dismissed simply as isolated cases of corruption. Rather, the *modus operandi* of Congress and the parties, together with the behaviour of some congressional deputies, led to a distortion of the function of parliament. In this section, attention is focused on the internal procedural rules of Congress.

The work of congressional deputies does not only depend on their innate capabilities and good will; in order for Congress to fulfil its function, changes to its structure and operation are needed. In order for the Assembly to become a modern institution able to respond to the challenges facing the country and the demands of the people, its internal procedure must be reformed.

In the Salvadorean case, prior to the March 1994 elections considerable consensus (albeit from different perspectives) existed around identifiable problems of the Congress and reform measures which needed to be taken.[53] These included:

– technical support in drafting and analysing bills and decrees; support for the different parliamentary groupings and congressional deputies in order to improve the quality of debate; specialist technical (but not political) support;

– a redefinition of the role of standing committees plus the guarantee of adequate support for their work;

– a general consensus that deputies were irresponsible and often badly prepared in many cases, and a recognition of the need for technical and administrative back-up for the work of the deputies;

– the need for committees to work to deadlines, and for these to be regulated;

– an overhaul of the organisational structure, removing inefficient upper echelons and creating modern management structures;

– the creation of new committees for municipal affairs, consumer protection etc;

– the elimination of customs exemptions to create more transparent administration of public funds;[54]

– the elimination of secret budget allocations;

– the setting up of departmental offices of the legislature;

– the publication of new laws fora other than just the *Diario Oficial*;

– the need for deputies to be permanently and closely linked to their constituencies;

– the development of a congressional information policy so that the Assembly can keep the country informed of what it does.

After the installation of the new legislature, the head of the FMLN parliamentary group denounced the absence of a legislative agenda to facilitate forward planning, charging that Congress had always been governed by total improvisation.[55]

In Guatemala a new role for Congress is currently emerging. The new representatives elected on 14 August 1994 took up their seats on 13 September and will conclude their term of office on 14 January 1996. This process was an important one, given the decline of Congress over the last years (and particularly in the preceding months) as well as the politico-institutional crisis surrounding the *autogolpe* which discredited many congressional representatives, complicating the return to governability. The new Congress faces huge challenges, the most serious being that of how to rebuild public confidence in the institution. Eventually it will have the responsibility of implementing any legal changes stemming from a peace agreement between the government and the URNG (Unidad Revolucionaria Nacional Guatemalteca). The high level of abstention in the August 1994 election highlights the need to legitimate political institutions and authorities if the democratic system is to be consolidated effectively.[56]

More specifically, one Guatemalan think-tank has proposed the following reforms to the Congressional Rules of Procedure:[57]

– Legal instruments to guarantee efficient implementation of Congress's legislative authority.

– Legal instruments to guarantee effective congressional oversight of the budget which ensure that the budget is consistent with the government's year-plan, politically consistent and technically viable.

– Legal instruments to guarantee that the constitutional attributes are exercised. This should apply not only to budget supervision but also aspects such as: questioning ministers, particularly in order to clarify the degree of consistency of public administration, to identify shortcomings and promote greater ministerial responsibility in the public eye; appointment of committees to investigate specific matters of public administration which are of national interest, incorporating a procedure of hearings where representatives from interested sectors of the population can be admitted.

– Legal instruments to guarantee transparency in the drafting and execution of the congressional budget.

– Legal instruments to guarantee appropriate procedures for *antejuicios*.

– The conformation of the Governing Council, the Standing Committee and the Committees of the Congress of the Republic and the setting of their powers which takes into account the occasional, justifiable need for reshuffles.

– The elaboration of consensual mechanisms which allow for the adequate operation, registration and composition of parliamentary groups.

– The setting up of a Disciplinary Committee to rule on cases of abuse of parliamentary privilege and conflicts of interest, with powers to impose the relevant disciplinary sanctions.

– The provision of a suitable mechanism for efficient and institutionalised assessment procedures (consultancies etc.).

– The establishment of an adequate system of remuneration for deputies which is linked to productivity and active, efficient participation.

– The establishment of efficient consultation mechanisms open to all sectors interested in the matters dealt with by the Congress.

It should be noted that the transformation of the presidentialist system into a parliamentary or semi-parliamentary system has also been discussed. An example of this is the April 1992 proposal by Alfonso Cabrera Hidalgo, general secretary of the Guatemalan Christian Democrat party, for reform of the presidential system.[58] This proposed a parliamentary system of government to ensure more effective representation of the population in national decision-making and the formation of alliances to balance and legitimise the exercise of political power. Even prior to Serrano's *autogolpe*, the inability of the political class to solve the country's socio-economic problems was identified as the root cause of the crisis of political legitimacy, prompting attempts to strengthen and consolidate the process of democratisation. Alfonso Cabrera proposed reform to the Constitution and to the Law on Elections and Political Parties to transform the presidentialist system into a parliamentary one which would, firstly, lend flexibility to public administration, in the sense that if a government failed to fulfil its electoral mandate then it could be replaced via institutional and legal means, without having to wait five years until the end of its term of office and without resort to *coups d'état*. Secondly, it would provide greater transparency of public administration; the financial affairs of state enterprises could be publicly discussed and details of their operation kept in the public domain in order to eradicate corruption. Thirdly, reform to the electoral law would enable broad and genuine parliamentary representation of majorities and minorities and the attainment of a national consensus on matters of major importance. This debate on presidentialism versus parliamentarianism is only just beginning in Central America. It is likely that discussion of the suitability of these systems for the countries of Central America will increase in the forthcoming period.

Conclusions

By way of conclusion, four aspects are referred to here. Two are related to politico-institutional conflicts in Central America in recent years, the resolution of which has involved discussion of constitutional reforms; the other two relate to the powers and operation of Congress and the agenda for reform of the legislature. With regard to executive-legislative relations in the two conflicts analysed (Guatemala and Nicaragua), in the first instance I would underscore the difficulty these political systems have encountered in generating the means for dialogue or negotiation among the main political forces which would enable sufficient consensus to safeguard governability in these societies in transition. In the Salvadorean case, the most important part of the peace process, as stated by President Cristiani himself in his Chapultepec speech, was the method adopted to end the war, i.e. the search for consensus. Cristiani's speech stressed that the *process* of dialogue was as important as the final result.[59] While it is true that the negotiation was possible because of a strategic military balance in which neither side was able to inflict outright military defeat on the other, it should not be forgotten that the main lesson of the war is that no one force alone is able to determine the destiny of a country. In this sense, I would agree with Rafael Guido Béjar that a central problem for the governability of El Salvador is that of defining and continuing to operate within those terms which made consensus and ultimately the signing of the peace accords possible.[60] Consensus is not the same as unanimity. The search for consensus is a process of political engineering through which all participants in a decision-making process agree to accept a particular solution, even though some might continue to think differently. What matters is the commitment to abide by the decision, even though not all involved may be satisfied. Consensus is a mechanism to ensure stability which is essential for decisions of outstanding national importance and in times of crisis.

In the Nicaraguan case, as Rodolfo Cerdas states in chapter two, 'the persistence of armed groups – contras, *recompas*, *revueltos* etc. – indicates not only the problems involved in incorporating different armed sectors into civilian life, but also the serious difficulties the political system faces in effectively opening up to include the different groups that comprise the Nicaraguan political scenario'. The substantial difficulties different business, political and trade union sectors find in resolving their differences through dialogue and negotiation is a serious problem. The Nicaraguan political system has been characterised by difficulties in reconciling the opposing positions of the country's main political, social and economic forces.

In the case of Guatemala, Serrano's *autogolpe* generated a crisis between the executive and other powers which fortunately had a peaceful outcome involving the return to the constitutional order and continuation of the democratic transition. The institutions themselves, such as the Constitutional Court, the Supreme Electoral Council and the Human Rights Procurator, played a critical role in ensuring the failure of this attempted break with the constitutional order. Furthermore, social forces and political parties played a singularly important role both in the *Foro Multisectorial* and the *Instancia Nacional de Consenso*. However, the crisis highlighted the obstacles to consensus among the leading political forces once order was restored. As Josef Thesing notes, in some senses the panorama became even more complicated because President de León Carpio had neither his own party nor the usual democratic legitimation of being voted in by the people. He was therefore reliant on generating consensus and support from the country's major organised sectors in order to govern.[61] A negotiated solution to the armed conflict continues to impede dialogue between the protagonists in Guatemala.

To sum up, some countries in the region have experienced a crisis of governability as a consequence of the main politico-institutional actors' inability to settle their differences and attain a minimum consensus to guarantee political stability. A second feature is the crisis of legitimacy of political systems and institutions. In the course of the democratic transition, significant sectors of the population have become disenchanted with politics, the parties and the political system itself. Governments must therefore demonstrate their capacity to mediate and seek consensus, involving dialogue with all sectors of the population. Consensus is vital for stability in periods of crisis such as the current stage of transition. A style of government is required that considers the opinions of others and seeks to build consensus and agreements which consolidate the democratic transition. The improvement of real and effective participation of the people in the building of a new democratic society is equally crucial.

It must be recognised that what occurred in Guatemala was not merely the result of a few isolated cases of corruption; rather, the way in which Congress, political parties and some members of Congress operated discredited the role of Congress overall. Here I would stress the urgent need to reform the rules of procedure governing the legislatures in Central America. The review of the powers and operation of Congress, on the basis of the five functions mentioned above, reveals the shortcomings and limited role of the legislature in the democratic transition and as an instrument of the popular will. It is interesting to speculate as to why institutional crises have occurred in Guatemala and Nicaragua but not in El Salvador, when the issues at stake have been broadly similar. Two important differences should be noted: firstly, in El Salvador the president enjoyed a near-majority in Congress and his own party was both strong and disciplined. Secondly, over the last few years El Salvador has experienced a positive process of consensus-building among the political parties, for example, the case of COPAZ – Comisión para la Consolidación de la Paz – in the implementation of the Peace Accords. This has been reflected in the National Assembly. In other words, the role of parties and Congress as mechanisms for generating socio-political consensus has generally been positive in El Salvador.

Following the Salvadorean elections of March 1994, the new legislature was installed on 1 May. A number of major challenges have faced the new Congress. Firstly, the pressing need for the legislature to reform its own structure and functioning. Secondly, following the withdrawal of the

United Nations Observer Mission in El Salvador (ONUSAL) and the expiry of COPAZ, the Legislative Assembly will be the only body for *concertación* in the country. This will mean that members of Congress will have to act in accordance with national rather than party interests. Lastly, the legislature was responsible for the appointment of magistrates to the new Supreme Court of Justice and the Supreme Electoral Council.

The development of a new political and institutional framework in line with the peace agreements capable of meeting the challenges of reconstruction and reconciliation required the appointment of skilled and committed people. In the case of the appointment of the Supreme Court magistrates, congressional opinion was divided. The right wing – ARENA (Alianza Republicana Nacionalista) and the PCN (Partido de Conciliación Nacional) – ranged against the rest of the opposition which united to negotiate as a block.[62] The election of Supreme Court magistrates required the approval of a two-thirds congressional vote. Division led to impasse and the country was without a Supreme Court of Justice for nearly a month until the two sides reached an agreement on the main issue of contention – the appointment of the Court's president.

This test case manifested how complex and difficult a process it is for members of Congress to learn the parliamentary game and coalition-building strategies. It also illustrated how hard it was to create compromise between the different party groups in Congress on such vital issues. However, it should be noted that this was the first time in Salvadorean history that a Supreme Court was selected by means of debate in the legislature and proposals from civil society, instead of from a slate put forward by the executive. The Bar Association and the *Consejo Nacional de la Judicatura* (CNJ) also played a vital role. The outcome of the election was a positive one and the new Court is likely to assume an independent role, having rejected the continuism of the past and politicised appointments to the judiciary. The election also represented an important victory for the opposition (ARENA controls the executive and has a simple majority in the Legislative Assembly, but does not control the two-thirds required for selection of the Supreme Court).

The challenge for consolidation of the fledgling democracies in Central America demands redefinition of the terms of the relationship between political parties and civil society. Political institutions have to be more responsible and efficient and citizen participation must increase at all levels of the government and civil society. The most important challenge for the citizens of Central America throughout the following years will be to democratise the running of government institutions, political parties and the organisations of civil society.

Notes

1. INCEP, *Reporte Político*, No. 63, Guatemala, August 1991.
2. See COSEP (1991a, 1991b and 1991c).
3. INCEP, *Reporte Político*, No. 64, Guatemala, September 1991.
4. [Editor's note] A *piñata* is a papier-maché toy full of sweets which is ceremoniously burst at children's parties. The term – implying a bonanza – was applied to the distribution of properties which occurred during the transition period after the Sandinistas lost the election of February 1990.
5. General Humberto Ortega subsequently stepped down as army Commander-in-Chief (see chapter three).
6. INCEP, *Reporte Político*, No. 79, Guatemala, February 1993.
7. UNO (1993).
8. *Ibid.*
9. *Ibid.*
10. The sectors of UNO working to promote a Constituent Assembly were supported by the Catholic hierarchy, particularly Cardinal Obando y Bravo.
11. 'Nicaragua: nuevo escenario político (¿y el económico?)', *Envío* (Managua), No. 145 January-February 1994, p. 145.
12. INCEP, *Reporte Político*, No. 89, Guatemala, January 1994.
13. 'Objetivos de la Reforma Constitucional para el FSLN', *Barricada* (Managua), 12 October 1993.
14. See Chamorro (1994-1995), p. 22-24.
15. *Ibid.* [Editor's translation].
16. *Ibid.* [Editor's translation].
17. *Ibid.* [Editor's translation].
18. For further analysis of Serrano's *autogolpe* see: Poitevin (1993); Aguilera (1993); Thesing (1993); Aguilera (undated mimeo).
19. The full text of President Serrano's 25 May broadcast message can be found in INCEP (1993).
20. For details of the Temporary Norms of Government see *Ibid.*
21. De León was elected in the second round of voting, polling 106 ballots of the 115 members present.
22. Thesing, *Op. cit.*, p. 13.
23. *Ibid.*, pp. 22-3.
24. INCEP, *Reporte Político*, No. 86, Guatemala, September 1993.
25. On 30 August 1993 the INC presented a proposal for purging and restructuring Congress, involving the whole-scale purge of the three branches of the state, beginning with Congress, where sixteen deputies whose behaviour had allegedly compromised the legislature as a whole were to resign; the simultaneous resignation of the Supreme Court magistrates; and the continuation of the purge in the Executive branch.
26. These charges had first been brought by a lawyer called Víctor Manuel Len; INCEP, *Reporte Político*, No. 87, Guatemala, October 1993.
27. INCEP, *Reporte Político*, No. 88, Guatemala, November 1993.

28. For the text of the constitutional reforms see Tribunal Electoral Supremo (1993).
29. INCEP, *Reporte Político*, No. 89, Guatemala, January 1994.
30. INCEP, *Reporte Político*, No. 90, Guatemala, February 1994.
31. INCEP, *Reporte Político*, No. 91, Guatemala, March 1994.
32. INCEP, *Reporte Político*, No. 90, Guatemala, February 1994.
33. Aguilera (undated mimeo), pp. 15-16.
34. USAID (1991) [Editor's translation].
35. *Ibid.* [Editor's translation].
36. See Córdova Macías (1993); Aguilera (1994).
37. A recent ASIES study identified 88 constitutional functions of the Guatemalan Congress. This study defines the Guatemalan system as semi-parliamentary; see ASIES (1994).
38. *Ibid.*, p. 22.
39. *Ibid.*, p. 20.
40. For discussion of the operation of the Guatemalan Congress see ASIES (1994); ASIES (1993); Cruz Salazar (undated).
41. This limited congressional role in budget adoption is common to most countries in the region. On Nicaragua see 'El lado oscuro del presupuesto', *Envío* (Managua), No. 154, November 1994, pp. 3-16.
42. 'Visión estratégica del presupuesto general de la nación. Elementos de análisis para una proyección hacia el futuro', mimeo (San Salvador, 25 November 1994).
43. *Ibid.* [Editor's translation].
44. *Ibid.* [Editor's translation].
45. In the Guatemalan case, art. 166 of the Constitution establishes that 'neither the Congress in plenum, nor any other authority may limit the deputies' right to ask questions, nor qualify or restrict such questions...Any deputy may put additional questions deemed pertinent and which relate to the matter or matters contained in the question'; *Constitución Política de la República de Guatemala* (Guatemala, 1992), p. 108 [Editor's translation].
46. Lipset (1959).
47. Borea (1994) [Editor's translation].
48. Guido Béjar (1994).
49. Art. 125 of the Constitution establishes that 'the deputies represent all the people and are not bound by any *mandato imperativo*'.
50. Guido Béjar, *Op. cit.*, p. 23.
51. *Ibid.*, pp. 23-4.
52. See Maihold (1994), p. 220.
53. On the consensus for reform of the Legislature prior to the March 1994 elections see: 'Candidatos a diputados por el FMLN combatirán corrupción en Asamblea', *La Prensa Gráfica*, 21 January 1994; 'MNR en pro de reformas internas en Asamblea', *La Prensa Gráfica*, 11 March 1994; 'FMLN pedirá fondos de partida secreta para comisiones', *La Prensa Gráfica*, 1 February 1994; CEDEM (1994).

54. Despite various calls for the elimination of customs exemptions, on 30 April 1994 parliamentarians adopted a decree which allowed them to import goods to the value of $16,000 (limited to a single vehicle) during their term of office. The acting president of the Treasury Committee explained that these reforms aimed at greater transparency in deputies' use of customs exemptions. See 'Franquicia de $25 mil a diputados', *El Diario de Hoy* (San Salvador), 9 September 1994.

55. 'En Asamblea prevalece la improvisación, Quinteros', *La Prensa Gráfica*, 19 October 1994.

56. ASIES (1994).

57. See ASIES (1993).

58. INCEP, *Reporte Político*, No. 71, Guatemala, May 1992.

59. See 'ADIOS A LAS ARMAS. Paz para El Salvador', *El Día* (Mexico), 17 January 1992, p. 6. [capitals in original].

60. Guido Béjar (1993), pp. 20-24.

61. Thesing, *Op. cit.*, p. 17.

62. This included the Partido Demócrata Cristiano (PDC), the FMLN, the Convergencia Democrática and the Movimiento Unificado (MU).

CHAPTER 6

JUDICIAL REFORM IN CENTRAL AMERICA:
PROSPECTS FOR THE RULE OF LAW

Rachel Sieder and Patrick Costello

'The significance of the justice sector lies in its basic role as a guarantor
of rights and arbiter of conflicts among citizens and between the public
and the state'.[1]

During any transition to democratic rule, the institutional structures of
democratic governance must be developed and stabilised. A fundamental
aspect of this process is the establishment and strengthening of the rule of
law, by which, in a liberal democracy, we understand a system of
guaranteed and enforced rights and obligations applying universally to all
citizens. The rule of law is both a mechanism whereby limits on the
exercise of state power are ensured and accountability of rulers is
guaranteed, and a set of rules which regulates relations between society
and the state and between individual citizens. As Pilar Domingo has noted,
'the connection between an operative legal system and a democratic
process is highly relevant, precisely because of the emphasis on the
principles of law-abidance and rights protection which lie at the heart of
constitutional democracy'.[2] In order for a democratic order to become
consolidated, the rule of law must become an accepted requirement of
governmental practice and of everyday life.

The current transition in Central America involves extensive reform
of the judicial system as part of a broader process of state restructuring in
the wake of the generalised regional conflict of the 1980s. Viewed in
comparative perspective, the state apparatus in the region has traditionally
been among the least efficient in Latin America, long characterised by
patronage networks, clientelistic mechanisms of distribution, corruption
and subordination to powerful internal and external interests. While
successive constitutions have aspired to the most advanced forms of
constitutional democracy, extreme socio-economic and power inequalities
mean that the application of justice and the benefits of constitutional rule
have tended, at best, to be highly partial. Impunity has generally been the

norm for many, generating quite justifiable popular perceptions that there is one law for the rich and powerful and another for the poor. This gap between formal rules and practice presents a significant obstacle for the construction of a system based on the rule of law.

The outcomes of current changes are by no means conclusive and both structural preconditions and past experience counsel a cautious reading. However, it should be recognised that the time span for effective judicial restructuring and the establishment of the rule of law is generally much longer than the period in which political agreements on minimal democratic procedures and arrangements in the transition process are agreed upon; there is no predictable or linear development between establishment of institutional frameworks and internalisation of the rule of law. Conjunctural events can often be as, if not more, important than institutional redesign in generating public confidence.

There are a number of basic principles which should be used to judge any legal system. Firstly that of legitimacy: the judiciary should be seen to be legitimate by the majority of the population. Secondly, there needs to be accessibility for all citizens. Thirdly, judicial independence: the system should have autonomous decision making power. Fourthly, fairness: the legal system should ensure the exercise of universal legal principles, such as the presumption of innocence. A fifth factor is efficiency: the system should expedite cases in a manner which guarantees speed and which is manageable in terms of cost, while protecting such universal principles as the right to defence and other due process guarantees. Lastly, the judicial process should be accountable or 'transparent'.

Examining the cases of El Salvador, Guatemala and Honduras, it is proposed here to assess the progress of and prospects for current reform of the justice sector (with particular reference to the area of criminal justice) and to evaluate the implications of the changes effected to date for the process of democratic transition and state restructuring. While recognising that the justice system is divided into a number of constituent parts, those which set the norms (Congress, executive) and those which have specific functions within the system (police, courts, Public Ministry, Human Rights Ombudsman etc.), it is proposed here to focus on the functional components, or judicial apparatus.

The problems facing the justice system in Central America can be divided primarily into those of a political and those of a technical nature. The principal political problems affecting the system are: lack of judicial independence and domination by the executive; subordination of civilian authorities to military power; and a tradition of impunity for human rights abuses carried out by the military and security forces. Previous efforts at

reform have tended to focus on the technical problems of justice administration and ignore these more fundamental aspects. However, without a
significant shift in the balance of forces and the existence of sufficient
political will, effective reform of the justice system will remain unrealised.
The separation of powers is a key element in attempts to establish
governmental legitimacy and the rule of law. However, Central America
is no exception to the general tendency in Latin America whereby the
judiciary, in common with most other branches of government, is
dominated by the executive.[3] The weakness of legislatures throughout the
region is reflected to this day in a pattern of governance through executive
decree rather than through legislation.[4] A highly politicised judiciary
closely identified with the executive has tended to be the norm. In addition,
the politicisation of judicial appointments has resulted in a high turnover
of appointees, severely undermining both independence and institutional
continuity. Current initiatives throughout the region aim to increase
judicial independence by reforming selection and appointment procedures
for all levels of personnel, extending periods of tenure for judges and
increasing the financial autonomy of the judicial branch.

The historical tendency of the armed forces in Latin America to
dominate civilian authorities has been particularly marked in Central
America, where lack of democratic traditions and the weight of the
military in the political system have characterised the post-independence
period. In the current transition it is by no means assured that the power of
the armed forces in Central America has been decisively reduced or that
democratic practices have taken root. Law enforcement in the region has
traditionally been distinguished by its militaristic nature, with both police
and criminal investigation procedures largely controlled by the armed
forces. The current trend towards establishing civilian control over these
areas has met with differing degrees of success across the region.

Given the legacy of extreme human rights abuse which characterised
Central America in the 1980s, a critical test of the judicial system in any
post-conflict order must be, first and foremost, its ability to guarantee the
basic human rights of all citizens. This implies acting as a check on
excesses of governmental power and coercive force, and as a guarantor of
constitutional and universal rights and freedoms. The criminal justice
system is central to this mediating role, addressing as it does the most
serious individual and social conflicts. Essential to the transition towards
more democratic rule is the subordination of military and police authority
to civilian control and to the rule of law. However, any attempt to
prosecute the security forces – long accustomed to impunity for their
abuses – is fraught with peril. The debate over accountability for past

abuses is one of the most complicated and controversial aspects of the judicial transition in Central America.

The technical problems facing the justice system are of a secondary nature, but have a significant and negative impact on the rule of law. Typically, the judiciary is weak, lacking in resources and infrastructure and staffed by inadequately trained personnel. Delay in the processing of cases has reached crisis proportions in Central America; in the three countries examined here, the overwhelming majority of the prison population has never been sentenced. This is due both to inefficient, complex and outdated legal institutions and procedures and to widespread corruption. Although the right to legal defence is enshrined in the constitutions of the region, in practice this is often denied. Trials are lengthy, conducted through written means rather than orally, and the investigative stage is often completed largely in secret.[5] In this sense, then, the judicial system has traditionally been one of the least transparent or accountable aspects of government. Modernisation of the courts, trial proceedings and legal codes, together with reevaluation of systems of public defence, are amongst the specific concerns of current reform initiatives, particularly those promoted in the region by USAID (United States Agency for International Development).

A second problem is that of police inefficiency in tackling rising crime. Although the powers of the police have traditionally been extensive, police functions have been linked to internal surveillance and counter-insurgency rather than effective criminal investigation. The militarisation of police forces throughout the region meant there was often little connection between police and the courts. Modern techniques of criminal investigation are sorely lacking and convictions have tended to be secured on the basis of extra-judicial confessions rather than on the provision of material evidence. Efforts to demilitarise the region's police forces have been accompanied by concerns to modernise techniques of criminal investigation. In addition, the rising crime rate in post-war Central America has generated demands from local business sectors for more efficient systems of crime detection and prevention.

Pressures for reform of Central American legal systems are the result of a number of converging forces, both domestic and international in origin. After the murder of the four US churchwomen in El Salvador in 1980, the USA began to support judicial reform efforts in Central America, Congress in 1983 allocating funds for improving the Salvadorean courts and police. Subsequently, in response to the 1984 Kissinger Commission Report, judicial and police improvement programmes were initiated throughout Central America and the Caribbean. During the 1980s

Administration of Justice (AOJ) programmes, and more recently 'Rule of Law' (ROL) programmes, emerged as a major component of USAID's efforts to support 'fledgling democracies'.[6] Since the end of the Cold War, the debate around human rights in Central America has become less ideological, allowing for a certain convergence of demands for legal reform from a wide range of governmental and non-governmental sectors. There is a broad consensus amongst both domestic and international actors on the need to guarantee the peace and ensure that there is no repeat of the widespread and systematic abuse of human rights which characterised the region during the 1980s. In addition, the conflict of the 1980s combined with the end of the Cold War has made the Central American left reassess the value of the civil and political rights traditionally associated with liberal models of democracy.

Secondly, whereas the 1980s were characterised by the mobilisation of the revolutionary left to secure political control of the state by armed means, the 1990s is characterised by the increased mobilisation of civil society around citizenship demands and a growing awareness amongst the population of their democratic rights. This is reflected in a number of areas which have far-reaching implications for reform of the judicial system. For example, the growing mobilisation around indigenous rights (primarily in Guatemala, but also, to a much lesser extent, in Honduras) signals the need to incorporate an 'indigenous perspective' into any attempts at reform. Perceptions of justice and law enforcement are culturally relative and this must be taken into account when assessing the viability of any proposed change. The increased demand for women's rights has resulted in pressure for certain reforms of the legal system, particularly with regard to the questions of domestic violence, incest, sexual abuse and rape, along with demands for anti-discrimination legislation. Additional areas where the mobilisation of civil society has far-reaching implications for legal reform are those of environmental and children's rights.

A third element exerting pressure for change is the process of economic liberalisation and structural adjustment currently underway in the region. Elements of the domestic business sector, international investors and the US government have all highlighted both the ineffectiveness and the corruption of the judiciary and pressed for a number of reforms. A revised judicial system provides a mechanism to advance programmes of economic integration, for example by establishing clear rules regarding the content and definition of property rights and laws of copyright. The question of property rights, especially of land tenure, is of particular importance in the current transition in Central America: guarantees of land to ex-combatants in El Salvador and Nicaragua and to the internally displaced and returning refugees in El Salvador and Guatemala are at the heart of the respective peace settlements; in Honduras, the effective abolition of the agrarian reform in 1991 was but one manifestation of a far-reaching process of structural adjustment. Another area where the pressures for change are significant is that of labour legislation; reforming labour codes allows for increased flexibility of employment practices to favour new kinds of capital investment in the region, such as assembly or *maquila* operations. It is largely for this reason that international financial institutions have also recently focused on reform of the judicial sector in Central America as part of wider efforts to promoted 'good governance'.[7]

Honduras

In Honduras, the transition to constitutional rule in 1981 did not correspond to what is understood here by democratisation. Indeed, the return to elected government was followed by an accelerated period of militarisation and the worst human rights abuses in recent history. Since 1990, partly in response to international and regional shifts, the dominance of the military over civilian authority and civil society has increasingly come under question. However, despite significant institutional reforms and improvements in the observance of human rights, the rule of law and democratic governance remains far from consolidated.

Judicial Independence

The first constitution of the Central American federation in 1826 formally declared the independence of the judiciary. However, from the earliest period of post-colonial rule in Honduras, the judiciary was the weakest branch of government. Judicial office was considered 'booty' to be distributed by whichever group was in power. Judges did not receive any remuneration until 1844 and the almost constant state of war throughout the nineteenth century meant that at times it was difficult even to constitute the Supreme Court.[8] In the first half of the twentieth century, the overwhelming influence of the US fruit companies on the nation's economic and political life had a negative impact on the judicial system. In the north coast banana enclaves, public officials often received two salaries, one from the state and one from the companies; this was usually sufficient to ensure a blind eye was turned to company infractions of domestic legislation. Even when efforts were made to force compliance with legal requirements, the weak fiscal base of the state and the overwhelming influence of the companies invariably tipped the scales in favour of the latter.

The tradition of dividing up judicial posts as public spoils between and within political parties has been particularly explicit in Honduras, facilitated in part by the relative stability of a bipartisan political system and the predominance of patronage mechanisms throughout society. Such practices have undermined even the nominal independence of the judiciary and have periodically led to acute conflict. For example, in 1985 a dispute within the ruling Liberal Party led to the removal of all nine Supreme Court magistrates by Congress, which then proceeded to appoint a new Supreme Court. This was rejected by the executive, which continued to recognise the original tribunal, resulting in the *sui generis* situation whereby two Supreme Courts existed simultaneously. The head of the new Court was subsequently imprisoned on the orders of President Suazo Córdova and the situation was only finally resolved when a political agreement was reached between the competing Liberal factions to elect a new Court.[9] More recently, Oswaldo Ramos Soto, the 1993 Nationalist presidential candidate, was appointed president of the Supreme Court in 1990 by his rival, President Rafael Leonardo Callejas (1990-94), principally in order to limit the former's proselytising activities. Lack of judicial independence is also linked to lack of financial autonomy. Although the 1982 Constitution stipulated that three per cent of the national budget should be allocated to the judiciary, this has never in fact been complied with. In 1989 the judiciary received some 1.6 per cent of the national budget; in 1991, 1.03 per cent; and in 1993, 1.76 per cent.[10]

The Honduran Supreme Court is made up of three chambers: civil, penal and that relating to labour law, each consisting of three magistrates. There is no constitutional chamber at present; the full complement of nine magistrates decide on constitutional matters when they fall outside the specific remit of the three *salas*. However, proposals for the creation of a *Sala de lo Constitucional* are currently being promoted by, among others, the Presidential Commission for Modernisation of the State[11] and supported by the Inter-American Development Bank.[12]

In 1992 there were ten appeal courts, 64 lower courts and 325 magistrates courts (*juzgados de paz*) in Honduras.[13] Political considerations have traditionally been paramount in the selection of the judiciary at all levels. At present, Supreme Court magistrates are selected by a simple congressional majority for a period of four years, corresponding to the Presidential term of office. This has meant that each new executive tends to appoint a sympathetic Supreme Court immediately upon its inauguration. Appeal Court judges and lower court judges are named by the Supreme Court. In 1987, the Honduran Supreme Court and USAID signed an agreement which included a government commitment to implement a 1980 judicial career law to ensure a more independent and objective judiciary. The gradual application of this law since 1991 has yet to demonstrate a marked improvement; a USAID evaluation published in June 1993 concluded that there was considerable uncertainty over whether the Honduran government had the political will to implement the new merit system for appointing and promoting judicial personnel.[14] Since 1993, proposals for constitutional reform to extend the tenure of Supreme Court magistrates, broaden the nomination process, and introduce a two-thirds congressional vote for selection have been under discussion. It is hoped that such changes will reduce political influence over the judiciary.[15] Such measures would undoubtedly represent a significant improvement on current practice. In addition, USAID is currently financing a sector-wide planning body for the judicial sector (*Comisión para la Reforma del Sistema Judicial*) in order to increase the efficiency of reform efforts. However, in 1994 USAID itself acknowledged that the conservative orientation of the commission had not led to innovative leadership.[16] Important though such measures are, they are unlikely automatically to guarantee the efficacy of the judiciary.[17]

Equality of Access

Public access to legal defence and to the legal system in general is sorely deficient in Honduras. Despite the fact that the universal principle of right to defence is enshrined as a constitutional right, in practice the poor have limited access to adequate legal representation. A survey carried out in 1987 by the University of Florida found that some 24 per cent of a sample of detainees had never had any public defence.[18] While over 50 per cent of the population is rural and lives in dispersed communities, some 86 per cent of all Honduran lawyers, half the appeal courts and 42.9 per cent of the lower courts are based in the two major cities, Tegucigalpa and San Pedro Sula.[19] In 1990, there were only fifteen public defenders for indigents in the entire country.[20] By 1992 this had increased to 29, with over half based in Tegucigalpa.[21] Some magistrates in the current Supreme Court (1994-)[22] have recently expressed interest in extending and decentralising the system of public defenders, particularly to rural areas with a high concentration of indigenous population.[23] However, in the context of a shrinking national budget, it is unlikely that sufficient funds will be forthcoming to provide adequate coverage.

The slowness, inefficiency and lack of transparency of the courts and trial system undoubtedly contribute to a state of impunity. Trials are divided into *sumario*, the investigative stage, and *plenario*, the trial and sentencing stage. The latter generally consists of a cursory judicial review of the evidence collected during the *sumario* stage, followed by sentencing. While in theory the *sumario* stage of the trial should last no more than one month, a 1987 survey by the University of Miami found that average trial time was anything between eight and 23 months.[24] Defendants are often uninformed of the charges against them and, in general, the entire investigative process is characterised by secrecy and arbitrariness. It is common practice for those able to stand bail to be provisionally released and for criminal proceedings against them not to be pursued to the *plenario* stage, effectively granting impunity for the crimes in question. The great majority of those detained in prison have not been sentenced, many being incarcerated for periods exceeding the maximum penalty for the crime of which they were originally accused.[25]

A number of recent measures offer some prospects for improvement; it is hoped that the introduction of a new penal procedures code (in the process of drafting at the time of writing), which includes a number of important measures including the introduction of oral and public trials, will remedy some of the deficiencies of the criminal process, speed up trial proceedings and increase transparency. In addition, USAID is currently supporting a programme of supernumerary judges with the aim of tackling the backlog of cases in the tribunals.

Public Ministry

One of the most far-reaching changes of recent years was the creation of the Public Ministry. This was proposed by the April 1993 Ad-hoc Commission on judicial and police reform[26] and approved by Congress on 9 December 1993, just prior to the inauguration of the new Liberal government of Carlos Roberto Reina. Public prosecution was previously one of the weakest links in the judicial system; in 1986, Honduran prosecutors (*fiscales*) had no support staff, no offices, desks or even office supplies and had to take their work to their own private offices.[27] Functions of the Public Ministry were covered by a 1906 statute regulating the courts and in the figure of the *Procurador General*, created in 1961. However, in practice the Public Ministry was subordinate to the Supreme Court, lacked autonomy or organic unity and had virtually no role in the criminal investigation process. Under the civil law tradition, criminal investigation was the responsibility of the prosecuting judge resulting, in practice, in inefficiency and delay.

The Ad-hoc Commission recommended the creation of a single public ministry with functional and administrative autonomy under the control of the figure of Attorney General (*Fiscal General de la República*). The new ministry is responsible for both criminal investigation (previously overseen by trial judges and carried out by the militarily-controlled police force), criminal prosecution and guarantee of due process.[28] The Attorney General is selected by a two-thirds congressional majority for a seven year term. The new Attorney General was elected in March 1994, and only after Congress approved a working budget for the new institution the following May was the ministry able to commence operations. It covers a broad range of areas and departments include: forensic anthropology services; the DIC (División de Investigaciones Criminales); the Public Prosecutor's office against corruption (*Fiscalía contra la corrupción*); the Human Rights Prosecutor's office (*Fiscalía de derechos humanos*); and the anti-narcotics section (although at the time of writing the narcotics department had yet to be set up).[29] Special prosecutors also cover the areas of defence of the constitution; defence of the environment; consumer protection; and protection of minors and disabled.[30] Reform to the constitution to include the figure of the Public Ministry is envisaged in the near future.

At the outset of his term of office, Attorney General Edmundo Orellana Mercado numbered among his priorities anti-corruption measures; action on the cases of forced disappearance (see below); and institutional organisation of the ministry itself.[31] Popular expectations were initially high. Throughout the latter half of 1994, a number of high profile accusations of corruption were made against members of the previous government, including ex-President Rafael Leonardo Callejas. However, in December 1994 the Special Prosecutor against corruption, René Suazo Lagos – widely accused of political bias – resigned after disputes with Orellana Mercado. His resignation was seen as a setback for President Reina's political agenda of 'moral revolution'. Given the resources and expertise required for effective investigation of fraud cases, it seems likely that progress in securing prosecutions may fail to match expectations raised by the creation of the new ministry. Arguably, the functions of the Public Ministry are too broad and it should prioritise the areas of criminal justice and penal law rather than dissipating its energies across a wide range of activities. However, its constitution is undoubtedly an important advance towards securing the rule of law and a more effective system of criminal justice.

Human Rights

A key test of judicial independence is its performance in periods of human rights abuse. While human rights violations in the early 1980s never reached the levels of Guatemala or El Salvador, the practice of forced disappearance was employed by irregular groups controlled by the armed forces against both left-wing government opponents and other Central Americans living in the country. However, the judiciary significantly failed to safeguard the fundamental and constitutional rights of those forcibly detained. In July 1988, in a landmark case, the Inter-American Court of Human Rights found the Honduran state guilty of violating the American Convention on Human Rights by causing the disappearance of Angel Manfredo Velásquez Rodríguez. In sentencing, the court signalled the failure of the judicial system to protect human rights in the early 1980s or effectively to investigate and sanction those guilty of such crimes.[32] The judgement established the legal obligation on the part of the Honduran state to prevent abuses of human rights; to carry out serious investigations with the means at its disposal; to identify those responsible; to impose sanctions; and to compensate the victims of abuse.

The role of the National Commissioner for Human Rights in recent years has been significant. This office was created by presidential decree in June 1992 as part of the wider project of state modernisation and is responsible for respect and defence of human rights by the state and individual citizens. In the current programme of institutional strengthening, regional offices are being set up with international support and legislation is under consideration to formalise the Commissioner's Office either by special statute or by including it in the Constitution, with the aim of improving the financial resources at its disposal.[33]

The 1993 report on the disappeared by National Commissioner for Human Rights, Leo Valladares, signalled the responsibility of the armed forces for the forced disappearances of the early 1980s. It denounced the failure of civil institutions to protect human rights during the period, highlighting in particular the shortcomings of the judiciary, and found that judges had abdicated their democratic authority and constitutional control of legality, failing to undertake investigations or to provide guarantees such as *habeas corpus* and thereby encouraging a state of impunity for human rights abuses.[34] The report recommended judicial proceedings to establish the truth about the disappearances and prosecute those responsible. Action on the cases of those disappeared in the early 1980s is one of the major challenges currently facing the Honduran judicial system. As Valladares stated in his report; 'Honduras's democratic institutions must prove to the nation's citizens that they function effectively and are not mere formalities. It is time to take concrete steps'.[35] It remains to be seen how much will be achieved: both the Attorney General and the Human Rights Prosecutor at the Public Ministry have given assurances that they are committed to pursuing judicial proceedings in the cases of the disappeared, although both recognise that collection of material evidences at this stage will be a difficult and painstaking task.[36] Nonetheless, some advances in following up the Commissioner's report have been made: in November 1994 a report published by a commission of *fiscales* implicated a number of military officers, including General Reynaldo Andino Flores, the current Minister of Defence, in six cases of forced disappearance, and in early December 1994 the Attorney General announced that charges would be brought against military officers found to be responsible for the disappearance and murder of student Nelson Mackey Chavarría, whose remains were exhumed in the same month. However, the impediments to securing convictions are great; many judges remain unwilling to pursue cases against military officers and witnesses are often fearful of testifying.

Despite significant recent advances, the armed forces remain largely unaccountable to civilian authorities and continue to enjoy near-total impunity. Even in cases where there is abundant evidence to convict, members of the military are invariably not brought to account. The armed forces have refused to let the civilian courts judge its members and the resort to military jurisdiction has traditionally provided the armed forces with a mechanism to guarantee their own impunity.[37] Military courts are effectively independent from the judicial system, judges are appointed by military authorities, and victims unable to press charges. In 1987, the assassination of Supreme Court magistrate Mario Reyes Sarmiento by an agent of the FUSEP (Fuerzas de Seguridad Pública) – apparently in an altercation when the agent asked the judge for his documents – resulted in a show-down between the judiciary and the military, the then president of the Supreme Court ordering that the accused be tried in the civilian courts, whilst the high command of the armed forces claimed military jurisdiction. In this case, the highest judicial power in the country was unable to prevail over the military. One of the first steps of the new Supreme Court elected in January 1994 was to clarify the constitutional position on competing military and civil jurisdictions. However, the trial of military officers for human rights abuses in civilian courts remains the exception rather than the rule.

Demilitarisation and Police Reform

Honduran politics has long been characterised by the weakness of civilian authorities and the predominance of military power. In particular, the control of the military over the police forces, intelligence gathering and criminal investigation has weakened the judicial system and contributed to the effective impunity of the armed forces. Recent changes indicate a slow shift towards greater civilian control; yet it remains to be seen whether current reforms will have a decisive impact on the traditional impunity of the military.

Following the revolt by the National Police against the Liberal government of Villeda Morales in 1959, the military-controlled police corps was abolished and replaced by a Civilian Guard subordinate to the Ministry of Government and Justice. However, this was destroyed after Villeda Morales was removed by a military coup in 1963 and the CES (Cuerpo Especial de Seguridad), a new police force under the control of the armed forces, was set up. This subsequently became the FUSEP in 1975, constituted as a fourth branch of the Honduran military.[38] Despite the existence of a separate graduation and ranking system for police officers, the FUSEP Commander has always come from the army, as have the majority of high-ranking officers in the force.[39] The militarisation of the police increased during the 1980s, and the criminal investigation department of the FUSEP, the DNI (Departamento Nacional de Investigaciones), was signalled as responsible for many of the human rights abuses which took place throughout the decade.[40] Torture and other forms of degrading punishment were commonplace, both for those detained for politically-related offences and for common criminals. The constitutional limit of 24-hour incommunicado police detention was regularly violated.[41]

In March 1993, after a wave of violent crimes and corruption scandals in which members of the DNI were implicated, President Rafael Callejas created the Ad-hoc Commission to examine questions of judicial and police reform. The Commission's report, published a month later, recommended the abolition of the DNI and the creation of a new Division for Criminal Investigations (DIC), located within the Public Ministry and directly responsible to the Attorney General. A high level group was also set up to study the future of the FUSEP. The DIC effectively constitutes a judicial police force, i.e. a professional, technical investigative corps subordinate to the courts. This had long since been a demand of the judiciary. Effectively, it means the separation of public order and crime prevention (which remains the responsibility of the FUSEP) from criminal investigation after the event. The DNI was finally disbanded in June 1994. During the latter part of 1994, the DIC was still in training and criminal investigation had been temporarily (and somewhat controversially) assumed by the FUSEP. According to Attorney General Orellana Mercado, some 200 DIC agents had been recruited by August 1994 and it is expected that by August 1995 some 700 agents will be operating in the field.[42] In contrast to the case of El Salvador, where members of the previously militarily-run Special Investigation Unit (SIU) have been incorporated into the new National Civilian Police (PNC), no ex-DNI agents were included in the DIC.[43] However, the institutional consolidation of the DIC is far from assured and more resources and international support will be needed if it is to function effectively.

To date, the FUSEP remains a branch of the armed forces. Throughout 1994 a general consensus appeared to have developed that the FUSEP would eventually pass to civilian control, although there existed little agreement about the manner or time-frame in which this would occur.[44] Some progress can be noted; in November 1994 Congress approved the transfer of the Treasury Police from military to civilian control, despite protests from the FSP high command.[45] The armed forces have signalled their support for the transfer of the police to civilian control, but this is conditional on the police corps remaining intact and a commitment to budget increases being secured.[46]

El Salvador

The judiciary in El Salvador, traditionally inefficient, corrupt and highly politicised, was further subordinated to military power during the course of the twelve year civil war. Police functions, historically tied to the needs of a particularly coercive form of rural capitalism, became a central support of the counter-insurgency. Although considerable international funding was directed towards improving the judiciary during the 1980s, impunity of the military and security forces for human rights abuses remained the norm. The Chapultepec accords signed in December 1991 and new institutions created in the wake of the peace settlement have provided an unprecedented opportunity for comprehensive reform of the judicial system. However, depoliticisation of the judiciary has by no means been secured and further measures are needed if due process and the rule of law are to be guaranteed.

The Salvadorean judiciary has never been independent of the executive or legislature. Before 1991, Supreme Court magistrates were selected by a simple congressional majority for a five year term. Legislatures dominated by the far-right ARENA (Alianza Republicana Nacionalista) party selected the Supreme Courts in 1984 and 1989, effectively ensuring the dominance of ARENA over the judiciary. It was also a highly centralised legal system: the Constitution of 1983 concentrated authority in the hands of the President of the Supreme Court, who as President of the *Sala de lo Constitucional*, enjoyed powers of constitutional review. The Court was also granted the right to appoint and remove lower court judges (under the 1962 Constitution this had previously been carried out by the legislative assembly). Lower court judges and justices of the peace were usually chosen on the basis of their political affiliation rather than their legal expertise; in municipalities throughout El Salvador, local ARENA party leaders continue to serve as justices of the peace.

Judiciary and Counter-Insurgency

A poor judicial system was made systematically worse by the civil war. The criminal justice system, never particularly efficacious, effectively collapsed with the onset of the conflict. Military authorities refused to cooperate with the courts, often directly obstructed investigations and rejected even minimal limits on their methods of interrogation and detention. Throughout the civil war the judicial system consummately failed to challenge the impunity of the military, which refused to submit to the rule of law. When attempts at investigation of human rights abuses were attempted, judges, lawyers and court officials were subject to bribery, intimidation, and physical attack, such as the assassination attempt made in 1980 on the judge investigating the killing of Archbishop Romero. In other instances, the Supreme Court systematically blocked attempts to investigate political killings, further strengthening impunity.[47]

Throughout most of the 1980s, certain constitutional guarantees were suspended under a state of emergency, decreed in 1980, 1984 and 1989. Article 30 of the 1983 Constitution authorised the use during states of exception of special military courts under the control of the Ministry of Defence to try civilians accused of political crimes. Recourse to these courts meant the virtual elimination of rights of due process, especially the right to an independent and impartial hearing. Under the terms of the state of emergency decrees, detainees could be held for months in incommunicado detention, during which the right to counsel was systematically denied. This gave the Security Forces ample opportunity to extract extrajudicial confessions which were permitted to form the sole basis for convictions, effectively institutionalising coerced confessions.[48] The state of emergency was only lifted in March 1990. In theory, all constitutional rights have been in place since this date.

Efforts to reform the judicial system began at the behest of the United States at the height of the civil war, following the murder of a number of US citizens in El Salvador by the security forces and the manifest failure of the Salvadorean judiciary adequately to investigate the cases. The approach adopted by the USA identified weaknesses in the legal system, rather than military intransigence, as responsible for the failure to end human rights abuses. The judicial reform effort was critically important in securing continued congressional approval for aid flows (both military and economic) to El Salvador throughout the conflict. Following the election of Napoleón Duarte in 1984 and a 1985 amendment to the Foreign Assistance Act, funds were channelled to the AID Administration of Justice I programme (AOJ). This had four separate components. Firstly, the Commission to Investigate Criminal Acts, commonly referred to as the Special Investigative Unit or SIU, was set up in July 1985 in order to develop an effective criminal investigation capacity for difficult human rights cases. The SIU was the most important element of AID's programme and received some $1.5 million a year.[49] However, the dependence of the unit on the military severely limited its ability to undertake effective investigations. The SIU was independent of the courts and Attorney General's office and, although officially under the jurisdiction of the Justice Ministry, its operations were directed by and responsible to military officers. Using the justification that, under the Penal Procedures Code, only the Security Forces counted as auxiliary organs of the judiciary – and therefore alone were able to bring evidence before the courts – SIU detectives were drawn exclusively from the ranks of the Security Forces and remained active members subject to military discipline and dependent on the armed forces for career advancement. The SIU had one of the best equipped forensic laboratories in the region, but its location within the Joint Command of the Armed Forces did little to encourage the confidence of either citizens or trial judges in its ability to provide impartial forensic evidence. The unit was widely condemned for its lack of independence and repeated failure properly to investigate human rights violations.[50] A second component of the AOJ programme was the financing of a judicial protection unit to protect witnesses in high profile human rights cases. However, this proved almost wholly inactive and was only used in the 1984 trial of the five National Guardsmen accused of the 1980 killing of the four US churchwomen and the February 1986 trial for the Sheraton Hotel murders. Thirdly, AID set up the Revisory Commission on Salvadorean Legislation (CORELESAL), which was mandated to study all aspects of the judicial system and existing codes and propose draft legislation. CORELESAL moved slowly and its achievements were minimal; AID cut off its funding in June 1991, a year ahead of schedule and transferred its work to the Justice Ministry.[51] Lastly, a Judicial Administration and Training programme was funded by AID; this concentrated on updating court equipment and administrative procedures, and on training judges, justices of the peace and other court personnel.

Between 1984 and 1990 AID provided some $13.7 million to the judicial reform programme in El Salvador.[52] However, given that it focused on technical problems rather than addressing the lack of political will for reform, the project inevitably achieved little. In over a decade of civil war in only two cases (both involving US citizens) had convictions been secured against military officers for abuse of human rights.[53] In 1990, the US government reported that after six years of US assistance, El Salvador's judicial system still lacked the ability to deliver fair and impartial justice because, at the time, the Salvadorean government lacked the commitment to do so.[54]

Peace Accords: Constitutional Reform

In December 1991, UN-mediated peace negotiations culminated in the signing of a peace accord which ended the civil war. However, while the negotiating process achieved far-reaching results in terms of reform of the armed forces and security services, agreements for institutional reform of the judicial sector were less extensive, in part due to inadequate preparation and lack of expertise on the part of the FMLN (Frente Farabundo Martí para la Liberación Nacional) and a distinct lack of political will on the part of the ARENA government of Alfredo Cristiani (1989-1994).

The constitutional reforms aimed to depoliticise the judiciary, increasing its professionalism and independence by reforming selection procedures at all levels. Supreme Court magistrates are now selected by a two-thirds legislative majority for a term of nine years. Their terms are staggered so that one third comes up for renewal every three years, with the effect that no single legislative assembly can select the entire Court. Supreme Court magistrates are chosen from a list drawn up by the National Council on the Judiciary (Consejo Nacional de la Judicatura – CNJ) and half the candidates must come from the bar associations. While the 1983 Constitution had provided for a National Council on the Judiciary, enabling legislation was not passed until 1989. The 1991 reforms broadened both the composition and the mandate of the Council.[55] Members of the CNJ are selected by a two-thirds congressional majority. The first CNJ was chosen in April 1993, but initially support from the Cristiani administration was lukewarm and the Council faced the active opposition of the Supreme Court of Gutiérrez Castro (1989-1994). Since 1993 the CNJ has become more active in training judges and identifying corrupt and inefficient judicial authorities. Other changes to the Constitution effected in 1991 included the amendment of article 30 so that military courts could no longer claim jurisdiction over civilians, and the inclusion of a requirement for six per cent of the national budget to be mandated to the judiciary.

While the constitutional reforms represented a considerable advance, they failed to address the centralisation of powers in the Supreme Court. El Salvador's judicial system represents perhaps the most extreme case of verticalism and concentration of powers in Latin America. The Supreme Court is responsible for jurisdictional functions, serving as the highest court of appeal and ruling on the constitutionality of legislation.[56] It also administers and oversees the entire justice system and licenses lawyers and notaries to practice.[57] As a result of the 1991 reforms, the CNJ now proposes candidates for lower court judges and justices of the peace, yet powers of appointment and dismissal remain with the Supreme Court, severely limiting the independence of all judicial appointments.[58] In addition, the CNJ's members remain subject to dismissal by the Supreme Court.

The Truth Commission

Judicial reform was more extensively addressed in the March 1993 report of the United Nations Truth Commission, mandated to investigate past human rights abuses and make recommendations to prevent their future recurrence.[59] The Commission named individuals and institutions responsible for human rights violations, including the entire military high command, and in this respect made a significant impact on the tradition of impunity for such crimes. The report criticised the judiciary, stating that it had actively contributed to impunity and human rights abuses during the civil war, and singled out Supreme Court President Mauricio Gutiérrez Castro for unprofessional conduct in the case of the El Mozote massacre and for his failure to cooperate with the Truth Commission's investigations.[60]

Recognising the insufficiency of the constitutional reform achieved by the peace accords, the Commission's recommendations called for extensive decentralisation and reform of the justice system. Amongst the proposals put forward were the transfer of administrative responsibility for the judiciary to the CNJ; the empowerment of the CNJ to appoint, sanction and dismiss lower court judges (thus removing this power from the Supreme Court); and the removal of the power to authorise and suspend lawyers from the Supreme Court. The report also called for lower court judges to be permitted to admit writs of *habeas corpus*; for improved judicial training, and for the strengthening of due process guarantees.[61] Many of the measures proposed required further constitutional reform. However, despite the Commission's recommendations, the legislative assembly failed completely to decentralise the CSJ's power to appoint, sanction and dismiss judges when proposals for constitutional reform were discussed in April 1994.

Perhaps the most controversial recommendation of the Truth Commission was its call for the voluntary resignation of the entire Supreme Court elected in 1989, judged to be so vitiated that it would be unable to deliver justice in the cases examined. The Supreme Court (supported by much of the Salvadorean right) responded with paid advertisements in the national press accusing the Truth Commission of political bias and of acting in an unconstitutional fashion injurious to Salvadorean sovereignty.[62] The armed forces were similarly forthright in their condemnation.[63]

Almost immediately after the publication of the Commission's report, a broad general amnesty law was passed, effectively ensuring that none of those signalled as responsible would be brought to trial. The amnesty explicitly extended to the judicial system, defining a number of violations of due process guarantees as 'political' crimes, and covers civil as well as criminal responsibility, denying victims and their families the right to establish accountability and seek redress through the courts for abuses committed before January 1992. Non-governmental human rights groups and the opposition Democratic Convergence challenged the amnesty's validity, charging that a self-decreed amnesty was unconstitutional. However, the Supreme Court repeatedly voiced its support for the new law and failed to review its constitutionality, claiming the matter to be outside its competence. The resulting failure to enforce accountability for past human rights violations considerably weakened the Salvadorean judicial system and respect for human rights.

Public Ministry

Another institution subject to reform as a result of the peace accords was the Public Ministry. This previously included the Attorney General's office

(Fiscalía General de la República) and the Public Defender's office (Procuraduría General de la República); in 1992 these were joined by the Human Rights Ombudsman's office (Procuraduría para la Defensa de los Derechos Humanos – PDH), created in July 1992 as a result of the peace accords.[64] The constitutional reforms mean that each head of a branch within the Public Ministry is now selected by a two-thirds congressional majority, rather than by simple majority as previously occurred. The terms of office are for three years and re-election is possible. Dismissal can only occur by a two-thirds congressional vote.

The Attorney General's office – responsible for state prosecution services – was largely inactive throughout most of the 1980s, following the murder in February 1980 of Attorney General Mario Zamora.[65] The Human Rights Prosecutor (Fiscalía de Derechos Humanos), located within the Attorney General's office, was notable for its almost total inefficacy throughout the 1980s. Even today, the Attorney General's office has been widely criticised for its inefficiency and susceptibility to political pressure.[66] The Public Defender's office, which has regional offices in twelve of the country's fourteen departments, is responsible for providing legal representation for indigents in a wide range of instances, including civil, criminal and labour matters. In 1993, the Public Defender's office dealt with 14,827 cases and the departmental offices another 8,292 cases – a total of 23,119 cases in one year.[67] However, as in nearly all Latin American countries, the Public Defender's office fails to meet the considerable demand for legal aid. If the institution is to be strengthened, more and better trained public defenders, increased funds and greater efficiency are required.

It was partly the failure of existing institutions to guarantee human rights that prompted the creation of the office of Human Rights Ombudsman. This has extensive and broad responsibilities for guaranteeing respect for human rights, including oversight of judicial compliance with due process guarantees (although it has no powers to prosecute), automatic rights to inspect detention centres, and the mandate to recommend legislative reforms to promote human rights.[68] By December 1994, regional offices of the PDH had been opened in Santa Ana, San Miguel, San Vicente, La Libertad, Morazán, Chalatenango and Zacatecoluca. The constitutional mandate assumes that the Ombudsman will assume many of the oversight functions carried out by the UN Observer Mission (ONU-SAL) in the transition period. However, initially the institution received less than enthusiastic support from the Cristiani government, and only in the final year of their mandate did ONUSAL's Human Rights Division begin to concentrate attention and resources on the institutional strengthening of the PDH.[69] The first Ombudsman, Christian Democrat Carlos Molina Fonseca, appointed in February 1992, was widely condemned by non-governmental human rights organisations for not taking a more proactive role in the defence of human rights.[70] Although Molina Fonseca has asserted that the PDH should be 'a conciliatory, not an inflammatory institution',[71] unless the Ombudsman's office is seen to take more decisive action in cases of human rights violations, citizen confidence in this new institution will not develop and it runs the risk of becoming yet one more in a long line of ineffective state institutions. Much will depend on the direction given by the new Ombudsman, originally scheduled to be elected in February 1995. However, the postponement of the election by the legislative assembly until the end of the following month and the refusal of ARENA to sanction the appointment of the candidate preferred by non-governmental human rights organisations did not bode well in this respect. Indeed, the manner in which both the Ombudsman and the Supreme Court were selected indicated that the two-thirds congressional requirement lends itself more to political negotiation between the parties in the legislative assembly than to depoliticisation of the administration of justice *per se*.

Criminal Investigation

Before the peace settlement, the Salvadorean security forces – El Salvador's Security Forces, the National Police (PN), National Guard (GN) and Treasury Police (PH) – responsible for much of the worst death squad activities during the early 1980s, were all classified as 'auxiliary organs' for the administration of justice. However, they consistently failed to present reliable evidence to the courts, regularly covered up the involvement of their members in human rights abuses and were responsible for frequent violations of the rights of detainees, including the widespread use of torture. There was little or no coordination between the security forces and the Attorney General's office, even though the 1983 Constitution stated that the latter was responsible for overseeing criminal investigation. Through ICITAP (International Criminal Investigative Training Assistance Program), the USA channelled funds to El Salvador with the aim of training the police to secure evidence rather than relying on forced confessions. However, ICITAP had a negligible impact on police abuse of human rights.

The peace accords abolished the old Security Forces and transferred responsibility for criminal investigation to the Attorney General. In practice, the institution responsible for carrying out criminal investigation is the new civilian police force (Policía Nacional Civil – PNC). Both the Ministry of Justice and the Attorney General's office had argued for the creation of a judicial police force separate from the PNC and answerable to the Attorney-General,[72] but the FMLN was unwilling to see an investigative body formed outside the PNC, fearing the emergence of a parallel organisation not subject to the same stringent legislative controls. However, there was a significant failure in the initial stages to prepare PNC cadets for specialised divisions, especially criminal investigation. In a highly controversial move, the government and the FMLN negotiated an agreement in December 1992 for the widely criticised Special Investigative Unit (SIU) along with the PN's anti-narcotics section, the Unidad Ejecutiva Antinarcotráfico (UEA), to be incorporated into the Policía Nacional Civil, breaking the spirit of the accords. Screening of SIU and UEA personnel was condemned by ONUSAL and others as inadequate. Notwithstanding the subsequent dismissal of a number of these agents on the recommendation of ONUSAL, followed by the resignation of the entire anti-narcotics division in protest in the early months of 1995, considerable concern continues to exist that inclusion of the SIU and UEA, together with the incorporation of significant numbers of the Policía Nacional, has provided a foothold for the military within the PNC and reduced the prospects for the establishment of an impartial and independent criminal investigation body under civilian control.

The PNC, deployed throughout El Salvador between March 1993 and December 1994, is a significant improvement on the previous security forces. New training doctrines emphasise citizens' rights and emphasise the need for minimal use of force. However, increasing accusations of human rights abuses by PNC agents have provided cause for concern. Although in part this is a consequence of a rapidly expanding police force and a civilian population more willing to denounce abuses, accusations of arbitrary practices, such as failure to observe due process guarantees, have been attributed to deficiencies in PNC training.[73]

Current Prospects

In the wake of the peace accords, international funding to the judicial sector has increased. In September 1992, AID officials signed a grant agreement with the Salvadorean government for a new five-year $15 million judicial reform project ('Judicial Reform II'). This aims to link technical support to Salvadorean efforts at institutional restructuring, strengthening planning and coordination mechanisms and promoting consensus around the need for judicial reform before commencing large-scale projects.[74] Considerable emphasis is also placed on training of judges and the introduction of a merit-based judicial career structure.[75] Training efforts are also focusing on the Attorney General's office and on public defenders, but results to date have been mixed.[76]

Since 1991, AID funds have been channelled through a small-scale legal reform unit, the Technical Support for Judicial Reform (ATJ), a dependency of the Justice Ministry. The unit's first priority was to draw up a new Criminal Procedures Code which introduces significant changes, such as separating the investigative and sentencing functions currently carried out by the same trial judge, the introduction of oral and public trials, and a revision of the jury system.[77] These measures all aim to strengthen constitutional and fundamental human rights guarantees for detainees, laying particular emphasis on the presumption of innocence.[78] Many guarantees are explicitly strengthened by a new public defence law passed in August 1992 which outlawed the admissibility of extra-judicial confessions. However, media attention on an alleged increase in common crime since the end of the war has produced an increasingly unfavourable climate for promoting and ensuring the rights of detainees and few steps have been taken to date to implement the new law. The new Penal Code and Penal Procedures Code remain subject to final approval by the current legislative assembly (1994-96) before they reach the statute book.

Despite considerable legislative and institutional advances, change in judicial practice has been slow. Criminal investigation and observation of due process guarantees, such as *habeas corpus*, remain sorely deficient. Testimony continues to carry more weight than material evidence and public prosecutors often fail to fulfil their legal obligations to investigate crimes.[79] The right to defence is still systematically violated and many in prison have never had access to counsel. Almost 90 per cent of the prison population have never been brought to trial.[80] Despite initiatives at increased collaboration, there is still little coordination between the police and the courts: in some cases local judges have failed to respond to PNC requests for search or arrest warrants, despite adequate documentation; in others, many police investigations are rendered legally invalid by failure to observe due process guarantees.[81] Corruption, biased rulings and failure to investigate crimes often reflect the political affiliations of either the appellants or the judges. ONUSAL has repeatedly criticised judicial practice and called for reforms.[82]

Although human rights violations have decreased since the end of the civil war, accountability has not markedly improved. Politically motivated killings continued throughout 1993 and 1994 and were generally not seriously investigated, usually remaining unsolved. In December 1993, after the murders of FMLN commanders Francisco Velis and Heleno Castro Guevara, the United Nations Secretary General declared the creation of the Joint Group for the Investigation of Politically Motivated Illegal Armed Groups (better known as the Grupo Conjunto). In its July 1994 report, the Grupo Conjunto claimed that common crime was being used as a cover for political murder, and detailed the links between organised crime (including bank robberies, drug trafficking and car theft) and death-squad structures linked to the military.[83] The report recommended the setting up of a special unit to deal with this phenomenon within the criminal investigation division of the PNC and stressed the need for improved coordination between the PNC, the Attorney-General's office and the courts.[84]

The selection of a new Supreme Court on 27 July 1994 appeared significantly to improve the prospects for change. The two-thirds requirement necessitated a compromise between ARENA, FMLN and Christian Democrat congressional deputies and, despite deadlock for over a month, the Court finally appointed was the least politicised in Salvadorean history.[85] However, to date the new Court has been slow to take decisive action to advance pending reforms of the judicial system, implement the Truth Commission recommendations, or purge the judiciary of corrupt judges. Although the CNJ in September 1993 denounced 121 judges for corruption and abuse of power, and ONUSAL in November 1993 presented a list of some fifty judges charged with corruption, during its first hundred days in office the new Supreme Court dismissed only three judges and suspended three more.[86]

While the acute politicisation of the judiciary characterising the 1980s has somewhat lessened, the legislative battle to appoint the new Supreme Court and the new Human Rights Ombudsman revealed the degree to which judicial appointments at the highest level are still considered as political spoils by the parties. Under the constitutional reforms, a third of the court must be renewed every three years and three of the justices to be rotated out in 1996 are all sympathetic to the left. A new legislative assembly, also to be elected in the same year, will nominate their replacements, raising the possibility that ARENA could increase its influence over the CSJ if it improves its position in the legislature. If ARENA achieved a two-thirds majority in the legislative assembly, the party would effectively be able to strengthen its grip over all sectors of the administration of justice by imposing its preferences in elections for the

Human Rights Ombudsman, CNJ, Attorney General and Chief Public Defender.

Guatemala

The criminal justice system in Guatemala has long been notable for failing to punish the perpetrators of human rights abuses and thus deter future violations. Since the return to constitutional rule in 1986, the absence of significant change in this area has raised questions regarding the nature and validity of the democratic transition.

The failure of the system is rooted in two separate historical problems. Firstly, since its very constitution during the colonial period, when lawyers were the main representatives of the Spanish Crown, the legal system has been alienated from the majority indigenous population.[87] The historical legacy is that 'the system of administration of justice is part of a state which historically responds to the culture, values, customs and interests of the non-indigenous population'.[88] The second problem is the absence of separation of powers within the state. Historically, the executive and particularly the military, have both been involved in and have influenced judicial functions. Over the last forty years, the logic of counter-insurgency has effectively placed the military 'above the law'. Judicial reform in Guatemala can only be effective to the extent that it tackles these two deeply rooted structural problems. The use of these criteria provides a way of assessing the myriad constitutional, procedural and material reforms that have been implemented since the 1985 Constitution was promulgated by the military regime of Mejía Victores (1983-1985).

The blurring of judicial and executive roles began during the colonial era. Apart from the political role of lawyers as representatives of the Crown, mayors had jurisdiction over penal matters including the power to organise *ad hoc* (non-indigenous) citizens' militias, and the administration of gaols. Recognition of the rights and (more importantly) obligations of the indigenous population was restricted to the office of the *Protector de los Indios*. This function was later assumed by the office of *Procurador de la Audiencia*, which was responsible for the meting out of severe sentences (torture and flogging) to *indígenas* who contravened Spanish law.

Independence brought scant improvement. In 1837 the support of indigenous peasants for the conservative revolt led by José Rafael Carrera indicated the distance between liberal democratic theories of the rule of law and the reality for the majority of the population. The spark for revolt was Gálvez's attempt to replace the Hispanic system of private courts and multiple *fueros* with the Livingston Codes which reorganised the legal system in an effort to make all equal before the law and introduce modern judicial forms (such as trial by jury) in rural areas. However, widespread illiteracy and clearly delineated class divisions meant that the introduction of the new codes in effect increased the vulnerability of the rural poor and reduced the autonomy of indigenous communities. Under Carrera, measures were introduced which represented, in essence, a return to the Hispanic tradition of *fueros especiales*. This (in theory at least) offered some minimal protection to the indigenous population, albeit of a highly authoritarian and paternalist nature.[89]

Numerous Constitutions have been passed in the post-independence period (1875, 1879, 1935, 1945, 1956, 1965, 1985), together with Criminal Codes (1877, 1889, 1898, 1973); reforms and laws which often contradict each other. The resulting complexity of legal institutions and regulating statutes is characterised by vulnerability to executive decree at one extreme and local justice at the other. While formal equality before the law has been enshrined in the legislation, the collusion of local judges with the 'private justice' of local, economically powerful actors, and the use of police forces to guarantee state power – for example during the regimes of Estrada Cabrera (1898-1920) and Ubico (1931-1944) – have meant that for the majority of Guatemalans, the rule of law has been little more than a juridical fiction.

Counter-Insurgency and Justice

The 1954 coup which ousted the elected regime of Jacobo Arbenz (1951-1954) had a number of immediate repercussions on the justice system. The new Head of State, Colonel Castillo Armas, began directly to nominate local judges and created special tribunals for political suspects.[90] After the 1963 coup by Colonel Peralta, the 1956 Constitution was replaced by executive Charter, restricting rights of *habeas corpus*. At the same time, the strategy of 'disappearance' began to be systematically employed by the armed forces against the guerrilla insurgency in the east of the country. A Presidential Guard was set up linking military and security forces throughout the country and Military Commissioners were appointed in rural areas to gather information on and control 'subversive activities'. In this sense, then, the military were directly responsible for the investigation and punishment of 'crimes'. During the elected regime of Méndez Montenegro (1966-1970), the President criticised the police as responsible for multiple tortures and assassinations in the preceding decade. However, attempts at reform were unsuccessful and disappearances increased during this period. By 1970 the police force and army were directly linked under the framework of the Centro Regional de Comunicaciones, militarising the police still further.

The height of judicial subservience to counter-insurgency dictates occurred during the eighteen months of General Ríos Montt's rule (1982-83). The 1965 Constitution was suspended and the magistrates of the Supreme Court were replaced by the deans of private universities. Decree 46-82, issued in July 1982, created special tribunals authorised to impose the death penalty for a wide range of political crimes via summary trials. In the space of fifteen months, some fifteen people – who were not present at their own trials – were executed on the basis of verdicts from these tribunals.[91] The new Supreme Court magistrates were silent about the arbitrary character of these verdicts. The investigations which brought the evidence for convictions came from military intelligence (G2) and the Security Directorate of the Presidential Guard (Estado Mayor Presidencial – EMP). The EMP was identified by Amnesty International as the 'centre of the Guatemalan government's programme of "disappearances" and political murder'.[92] In rural areas, the countrywide introduction of paramilitary civilian patrols under military command left vast areas of the country under direct military jurisdiction without any effective alternative recourse.

Transition?

The democratic election of a civilian president and the promulgation of a new constitution in 1985 raised hopes of some kind of transition to a state under the rule of law. The constitution itself appeared to offer significant improvements, creating a new Supreme Court chosen partly by Congress and partly by a commission of legal professionals.[93] In contrast to both El Salvador and Honduras, where jurisdiction over constitutional matters is exercised by the Supreme Court, in Guatemala a separate Constitutional Court was established to rule on the constitutionality of judicial decisions and legislative decrees. In an attempt to promote judicial independence, the new Constitution stated that two per cent of annual state revenues should be allocated to the judiciary. A Human Rights Ombudsman to investigate and report on cases of violations was created and also included in the 1985 Constitution. The Ombudsman is selected by a two-thirds Congressional majority for a five-year term. Branches of the Ombudsman's office were set up in all 21 departmental capitals in Guatemala. Other substantive reforms included the abolition of the Police Investigations Unit,[94] replaced by a new Special Investigations and Drugs Brigade (BIEN) and the expulsion of 600 police agents for serious violations.[95]

These reforms were sufficient to draw in significant amounts of development assistance, particularly from USAID, to support the overhaul of the criminal justice system. Funds were supplied to equip and run the offices of the Human Rights Ombudsman, and in 1987 the USA began authorising grants (totalling over $7 million by 1991) for improving the administration of justice in Guatemala.[96] These funds were administered through the Harvard Law School's Center for Criminal Justice. The programme achieved some initial results through pilot courts experimenting with the introduction of public, oral hearings, and in training some judges. However, AID acknowledged that the follow-up project, signed in September 1988, 'never really got off the ground'.[97] In July 1990, the Harvard Program was terminated and its director, Philip Heymann, criticised the lack of will on the part of senior military and civilian authorities to prosecute the perpetrators of human rights violations. In a statement to the US Congress, referring to the murder of twelve students in August and September 1989, Heymann stated: 'I told the then Minister of Defence [General] Gramajo that Harvard would not stay if there was no clear sign of a willingness to investigate such political terrorism. To the best of my knowledge, nothing was done, not the slightest effort was made to mount a vigorous and determined investigation of the student killings'.[98] Guatemala holds the dubious distinction of being the only country in Latin America where USAID has decided to terminate a judicial reform project because of manifest lack of progress.

A second US-funded reform effort was directed through the Justice Department's ICITAP programme. The programme provided courses for police, judges and prosecutors to teach them 'to use physical evidence to corroborate witness and victim testimony rather than to rely solely on confessions'.[99] Yet, after the training of hundreds of police officers, little has changed in the process of criminal investigation and there is much evidence to suggest that the police themselves are carrying out torture, murder and disappearances, particularly in the case of street children, where the interest of high profile international non-governmental organisations (NGOs) has played a significant role in exposing the involvement of the police.[100]

By 1990, the United Nations Special Expert was reporting that reform of the criminal justice system was essential to guaranteeing the rights and integrity of the individual Guatemalan citizen, a statement testifying to the failure of the reforms already undergone.[101] Further evidence of this failure came from events subsequent to the murder of sociologist Myrna Mack Chang in September 1990. This case has been documented in detail elsewhere,[102] but it is worth noting that Mack's murder was a high profile political killing aimed to silence her investigations into the plight of internally displaced people in the country at a time when the government was trying to gain large amounts of aid for projects to help these people. In a subsequent court case, Noel de Jesús Beteta, at the time of the murder a low-ranking member of the Security Directorate of the Presidential Guard (EMP), was sentenced to thirty years in prison. However, before sentence was passed, the chief police investigator on the case was murdered, eight different judges worked on the investigation stage alone, and the Appeals Court closed the case against Beteta's military superiors.

The Myrna Mack case was one of the highest profile cases in Guatemalan legal history. In addition to the interest of international NGOs, it attracted UN comment via the reports of the special expert,[103] and US government censure via the State Department Country Reports.[104] In most other human rights cases, where the victims were indigenous peasants without access to police or courts and where the only local authorities were the civil patrols and the military garrisons, little has been achieved beyond condemnation by human rights NGOs.[105]

The failure of constitutional and USAID-promoted reform reflected the lack of political will to initiate far-reaching reforms and was a consequence of the continuing involvement of the executive and military at the heart of the judiciary. Partly as a consequence of this state of affairs, the majority of the indigenous population lacks access to any system of legal representation. The representation of the indigenous population within the justice system itself is minimal; in 1989 a mere five per cent of Guatemalan Justices of the Peace were indigenous, while no legal officials above this rank were indigenous.[106]

Separation of Powers

Since 1986, the continuing influence of the military over the judicial system in Guatemala has been reflected in the failure of civilian governments to investigate and prosecute the crimes of their military predecessors. The structures of repression in place prior to the transition to constitutional rule have remained largely intact. Military impunity has been reinforced since 1986 and the influence of the armed forces over the criminal justice system has continued, for the most part, unchallenged.

This influence is most evident at the level of the police, which is legally responsible for criminal investigation. In the capital, the open coordination of police and military commands in the Sistema de Protección Civil (SIPROCI) was condemned in the 1992 report of the UN Special Expert.[107] During 1993, SIPROCI was replaced by the Hunapú, a joint command force also operating within the capital. After further UN condemnation, this too was abolished, but military 'advisers' continued to be assigned to all heads of police departments. According to Americas Watch, testimony of a high ranking former police officer has suggested that military intelligence (both G2, or D2 as it is now known, and the Security Directorate of the Presidential Guard) have infiltrated the National Police's Department of Criminal Investigations.[108]

Even if demilitarisation of the police were to be achieved, there would still be a need for professionalisation of the force: police officers are poorly paid, have little practical or legal training, and are consequently vulnerable to corruption and manipulation. During his period as Human Rights Ombudsman (October 1989 – April 1993), Ramiro de León Carpio played an important role by challenging the police monopoly on criminal investigations in cases of human rights abuse. However, both his predecessor and his successor have used the position less effectively, suggesting a continuing institutional weakness in the area of criminal investigation.

With regard to the judiciary itself, four years after the return to civilian rule Americas Watch declared that 'the Guatemalan judiciary remains crippled by a combination of sloth, corruption and, perhaps most decisive, fear of the consequences should it seek to touch the military's impunity in matters of human rights'.[109] The process by which judges are selected remains highly politicised: Supreme Court and Appeal Court magistrates are chosen by Congress for a five-year period, and political considerations are paramount. The plenum of the Supreme Court in turn names First Instance judges and Justices of the Peace.[110] Most of the appointed judges have previous experience in civil rather than criminal law and, in general, training of judges is inadequate.

The Public Ministry, headed by the Attorney General, is responsible for overseeing cases and for state prosecutions, yet there is strong evidence of infiltration of the Ministry by the Presidential Guard.[111] In 1988, the Harvard project reported that less than five per cent of defendants are ever convicted and concluded that neither the courts not the Attorney General's office could properly investigate and prosecute criminal cases.[112] The reintroduction of the right to submit petitions of *habeas corpus* in 1986 has made little difference to the numbers of people who 'disappear'. Criminal defence lawyers are only available to those who can afford a private lawyer; otherwise, legal defence services are provided by law students who have to undertake such tasks as part of their training and who often have negligible interest in the cases themselves. As with police reform, the removal of military and executive influence over the judiciary is a necessary first step which needs to be supplemented by structural reforms, such as: the introduction of the '*carrera judicial*' as envisaged in the 1985 Constitution to ensure selection of the judiciary on the basis of merit; the restructuring of the Public Ministry to ensure a more activist role; and the strengthening of the office of Human Rights Ombudsman.

Equality of Access

The concentration of both police and judiciary in the cities, and particularly in the capital, is an indication of the marginalisation of the largely indigenous rural population from the criminal justice system. In 1986, 71 per cent of National Police personnel were based in Guatemala City, along with eight of the sixteen appeal courts; twelve of the forty-eight First Instance judges and thirteen of the seventy-four Justices of the Peace.[113] Under the 1985 constitution, the local administration of justice by mayors was rejected and the judiciary created a series of District Courts (*juzgados comarcales*), each to cover two or more municipalities. However, a 1986 survey found that in 246 municipalities there were no Justices of the Peace and local judicial power was exercised by the mayor.[114] The impunity of civil patrol chiefs, identified as responsible for most of the murders in rural areas, is also a natural consequence of the lack of national coverage of the judiciary. In many areas of the country, the military is the most visible authority of the state. Where warrants for the arrest of suspected killers have been issued, they have remained largely unacted upon due to the inability of the judiciary or police to encroach on the territory of the civil patrols.

However, even if Guatemala's countryside were demilitarised and the civil patrols and military commissioners abolished (as has repeatedly been called for by successive UN Special Experts),[115] the judiciary would remain a distant institution for most indigenous Guatemalans. Until 1994, the conduct of trials was based on the inquisitorial model, the trial stage consisting of the reading of a written file by a sentencing judge who then convicted or acquitted behind closed doors. Decisions were often taken without testimony being taken from witnesses and the secrecy with which the entire process was conducted effectively meant there was little opportunity for public scrutiny. Trials based on written Spanish documents had little transparency for a largely illiterate rural population, many of whom do not speak Spanish. In 1986 only two courts in the entire country had a budget for interpreters and most courts relied on employees knowledgeable in the local language. Given that the vast majority of judges are non-indigenous, the verification of accurate translation proved almost impossible.[116]

This series of structural problems has been compounded by massive ignorance of the law. Attempts to remedy this situation via human rights education has been met with repression by the army and civil patrols. For example the CERJ (Consejo Etnico Runujel Junam), an NGO set up in 1988 specifically to promote the understanding of constitutional rights in indigenous areas, has suffered the murder and/or 'disappearance' of nineteen of its activists since it was founded.

Prospects for Reform

After the constitutional crisis occasioned by former president Serrano Elías's attempted dissolution of Congress and the Supreme Court in 1993 was resolved by the Constitutional Court's approval of Ramiro de León Carpio as President, there has been a revival of judicial reform and a return of USAID to Guatemala, which is currently administering a $5 million project in this area. One reason for this renewed interest was the congressional approval of a new Code of Criminal Procedures at the end of 1992. This code came into effect in July 1994. This was partly a response to 1990 UN recommendations and, potentially at least, could provide a means to tackle many of the problems outlined here. The code gives the Public Ministry part of the responsibility for initial criminal investigations, further challenging the police monopoly in this area. The Public Ministry is currently undergoing reform to enable it to perform this role effectively. The new code introduced mixed oral/written trial proceedings, including the presence of witnesses to give testimony, and gives increased public access to ensure greater scrutiny. The code requires the creation of a professional public defence system by the judiciary. Additional provision has been made for the case of failure to provide *habeas corpus*. In addition to the new code, there have been other reforms. Under Police Chief Cifuentes and Interior Minister Moscoso, military 'advisers' to police departments were removed and the Security Director-ate of the Presidential Guard (known as the *'archivo'*) was disbanded and a special police unit was set up to investigate human rights violations.

However, after the experience of failed reform under Cerezo, over-optimism about the effects of the new reforms would be misplaced. At present, the infrastructure for their thorough implementation simply does not exist. In addition, increasing access to a public system of oral/written trials will have little effect on those areas militarised by the continuing existence of civil patrols, who exercise *de facto* control over all state institutions in those localities. Other reforms have already run into trouble: police chief Cifuentes and Interior Minister Moscoso were both removed from office, in February and March 1994. It is widely suspected that the *archivo*'s files were simply transferred to military intelligence (D2).

The continuing power of the military to intervene, albeit extra-judicially, in affairs of criminal justice was starkly illustrated by the assassination on 1 April 1994 of Epaminondas González Dubón, President of the Constitutional Court. It was widely suspected that the murder of the highest judicial authority in the country was linked to the Myrna Mack case; it seems that the Court was about to make a ruling on the constitutionality of closing the case without investigating the crime's intellectual authors.[117]

The limits to judicial reform in Guatemala, then, are set by the extent of military impunity. Impunity continues to be internationally criticised in Guatemala; an OAS (Organisation of American States) delegation in December 1994 stated that 'the consequences of impunity go beyond the rights of victims, creating a climate that affects the security of the population, promotes corruption, and is incompatible with a state of law'.[118]

Impunity will only be tackled by a Truth Commission to identify what happened in cases of violations and provide recommendations which would prevent a repetition of the events. Unfortunately, the history of attempts to set up such a commission is itself marked by impunity. In November 1984, a commission was created by the *de facto* government of Mejía Victores to investigate cases of disappearance. After four months it concluded that there were no disappeared in Guatemala. In April 1987, the civilian government set up a second commission to investigate the whereabouts of disappeared individuals. After several months, families of the disappeared were informed that their relatives were dead. A third commission, set up as an internal entity of the human rights ombudsman's office, failed to report on its findings.[119]

On 23 June 1994, as part of the peace negotiations between the government and the URNG (Unidad Revolucionaria Nacional Guatemalteca), a new agreement was signed to establish the terms of reference of a Truth Commission that would clarify the events of the past as well as formulating specific recommendations to prevent such events in the future.[120] The accord represents the only hope for an end to impunity in Guatemala, yet prospects for its success look doubtful. In particular, the work, recommendations and report of the Commission will not 'individualise responsibilities' nor will they 'have legal objectives or effects'. In other words, individuals will not be named and the agreement has already decided that the Commission will make no recommendations on prosecutions, in effect sanctifying impunity for human rights violators before it even begins its investigations. In addition, the Commission will only begin its work after the signing of a peace accord. This still looks a long way off in Guatemala: in December 1994, after a year of intensive negotiations, agreement had been reached on only two points of an eleven point agenda.

The breakthrough in the peace negotiations resulting in the signing on 24 March 1995 of an accord between the URNG and the government of Guatemala on indigenous rights and identity has raised prospects for future improvements in the administration of justice. Provisions set out in the accord include: promotion of the official use of indigenous languages to increase awareness amongst the indigenous population of their rights; the provision of training programmes in indigenous languages for judges and court interpreters; the development of training courses for Public Ministry officials and judges to increase awareness of indigenous customs; the increased provision of legal aid and legal interpreting facilities for indigenous communities; and a reform of the municipal statute to allow greater recognition of local custom in municipal administration.[121] However, while the prospects for the rule of law in Guatemala are probably better now than they have ever been, the failure to identify the individuals and structures which continue to prevent the effective exercise of the rule of law means that the results of judicial reform will continue to be limited.

Conclusions

Current prospects for a gradual improvement in the rule of law are perhaps better than at any previous period in recent Central American history. It is now generally accepted that the problem of justice is a fundamental problem of democratic transition: whereas previously analyses of judicial shortcomings tended to be depoliticised and almost exclusively technical in their prescriptions, the legal system (and indeed institutional reform in general) now tends to be viewed much more in terms of its function in ensuring that basic human rights guarantees are observed and in guaranteeing the essential features of a democratic order. In the present conjuncture, then, the initiatives for judicial reform outlined above represent an important window of opportunity for change. However, although regional trends can be identified, prospects for the rule of law are far from uniform: in Guatemala, the absence of an effective transition and the acutely disproportionate balance of forces currently negotiating a peace settlement give little indication that *de facto* (if not *de jure*) intervention by the armed forces in the judicial process will be markedly reduced in the near-future. In Honduras, significant advances have been made but new institutions remain far from consolidated. El Salvador perhaps represents the most far-reaching case of change, the constitutional reforms secured as an outcome of the negotiated peace indicative of a real shift in the balance of power, but even here reform of the judicial system has been relatively limited and insufficient to secure consolidation of the rule of law.

During the 1980s, US support for judicial reform in the region was situated within a highly polarised ideological context and was firmly identified with supporting the so-called 'fledgling democracies' – the three countries examined here. Since the end of the Cold War, US interests in the region have shifted away from geo-politics and now focus on furthering economic liberalisation and securing regional stability – objectives which demand substantive reform to the existing legal system. Whereas previously even cosmetic reforms to the judiciary served a purpose (at least in propaganda terms), today the policy emphasis is on securing an impartial and – more importantly – effective judiciary. However, in many instances this has meant attacking the position of former US allies in the region, particularly those sectors within the armed forces who have traditionally enjoyed a monopoly over criminal investigation services and exercised their effective right of veto over the judiciary. Partly in consequence, US policy is often inconclusive or highly unpredictable.

Although the record of judicial reform in Central America is distinctly mixed, in recent years improvements of both a procedural and substantive nature have been made in all three countries examined here. The creation of new institutions, such as the human rights ombudsman, and the reform of the Public Ministries throughout the region represent significant advancements; the introduction of oral trial proceedings and public access to trials could yet prove to be one of the most far-reaching reforms to date, holding out the prospect of far greater transparency and accountability than previously evident in the judicial process. The current willingness of the international community to support these reform initiatives as an integral part of the peace processes (national and regional) provides grounds for optimism. However, a number of limitations continue to exist: firstly, the resources available for the effective implementation of new legislation and the operationalisation of the respective institutions remain insufficient.

Providing effective legal defence and extending the territorial reach of legal services will inevitably involve increased costs, and the challenge of consolidating new institutions as state budgets are repeatedly cut back is considerable.

Secondly, judicial reform can only be successful to the extent that parallel institutions are developed and strengthened. Among the most important of these is the legislature, traditionally one of the weakest and most ineffectual organs of state throughout the region (see chapter five). The pervasiveness of clientelist practices, corruption and patronage mean that securing professionalisation and depoliticisation of the judiciary across the region will necessarily be both difficult and slow. Evidently, another parallel institution which must undergo significant reform if the rule of law is to become a reality is the armed forces. This involves not just the relinquishing of control over criminal investigation services, but also extensive structural reforms to the military itself.

Only an extensive and effective purge of state institutions (both civil and military) will decisively challenge clientelism and impunity. In this respect the role of 'truth commissions' in increasing accountability, transparency and the prospects for the rule of law has been stressed here. The current transition depends on an end to impunity and the reinforcement of accountability. The jury is still out in the case of Honduras, the passing of the amnesty in El Salvador effectively blocked the possibility of prosecutions, considerably weakening the universality of the rule of law; the current prospects in Guatemala appear even less favourable, given the terms agreed for the truth commission.

Central America has a tradition of powerful military institutions and weak and ineffective structures of governance. The judiciary has generally been far removed from the reality of most citizens' daily lives. The new judicial institutions signalled here have opened up important oppositional spaces, yet perceptions of the judiciary must change if those spaces are fully to be taken advantage of. In the first instance, improving access to the legal system involves local education initiatives to increase awareness of legal rights and of the legal system in general. The work carried out by non-governmental organisations continues to be critically important in this respect; for example, the work of the Consejo Etnico Runujel Junam (CERJ) in Guatemala, which has focused on increasing public awareness of the constitutional right not to serve in the civil patrols. Shifts in popular perceptions often depend in part on the position adopted by incumbents in key posts – for example, the activist stance adopted by Ramiro de León during his period as Human Rights Ombudsman in Guatemala – but ultimately hinge on a significant reduction of traditions of abuse and impunity. The Salvadorean PNC has secured considerable public confidence precisely because it signifies a break with past practice. However, the increasing levels of immiseration experienced by the majority of the region's population may mean that priorities in the current transition focus on securing justice in socio-economic, rather than civil and political terms. It is also pertinent to raise the question of the extent to which the liberal constitutional order, with its individualist conception of rights, is relevant to all sectors of Central American society; while much research in this area remains to be carried out, collective conceptions of rights held by certain indigenous groups throughout the region may indeed signify and demand a quite different judicial order from the one referred to here.

Notes

1. Salas and Rico (1993), p. 7.
2. Domingo (1994), p. 7.
3. For a typology of the Supreme Courts in Latin America and an assessment of their relative independence see Verner (1984), pp. 438-506.
4. For an examination of this phenomenon in the case of Mexico see González Oropeza (1994).
5. For a more extensive discussion of the shortcomings of the penal system in Latin America see Binder (1993).
6. USAID, Centre for Development Information and Evaluation (1994), p. 4.
7. For a polemical assessment of 'good governance' see Leftwich (1993).
8. Salas and Rico (1989a), p. 28.
9. *Inforpress Centroamericana*, 11 April 1985; 13 June 1985.
10. Salas and Rico (1989a), p. 111; AID (1992), p. 2; figures for 1993, personal interview with Supreme Court Magistrate Blanca Valladares, Tegucigalpa, 11 August 1994.
11. This project is part of the Commission's programme for strengthening the rule of law and civil society (*fortalecimiento del Estado de derecho y la sociedad civil*), see Comisión para la Modernización del Estado (1994), p. 13.
12. Personal interview, Rafael Valladares, Commission for Modernisation of the State, Tegucigalpa, 29 August 1994.
13. AID, *Op. cit.*, p. 5.
14. USAID, Center for Development Information and Evaluation (1993).
15. Personal interviews with Miguel Angel Rivera Portillo, President of the Supreme Court, Tegucigalpa, 9 August, 1994; Efraín Moncada Silva, Minister of Government and Justice, Tegucigalpa, 9 August 1994. The current package of constitutional reforms is promoted by the Presidential Commission for Modernisation of the State; see also Secretaría de Estado en el Despacho de Gobernación y Justicia (1992).
16. USAID, Center for Development Information and Evaluation (1994), p. 21.

17. In Chile, Supreme Court magistrates hold life tenure (one of the changes currently being considered in Honduras). Yet during the worst years of the Pinochet dictatorship in Chile, the magistrates, despite having been selected under democratically elected regimes prior to the 1973 coup, made no effort to protect human rights; see Correa Sutil (1993).
18. Salas and Rico (1989a), p. 92.
19. *Ibid.*, p. 93; AID, *Op. cit.*, p. 6.
20. Espinal Irías (1990), p. 106. From 1988 to 1991 the salaries of these public defenders were paid by AID; United States General Accounting Office (GAO) (1993), p. 16.
21. AID, *Op. cit.*, p. 29.
22. All members of the Supreme Court of Justice are nominated by the President of the Republic at the start of his term. In 1994, Liberal President Carlos Roberto Reina nominated a new Supreme Court.
23. Personal interview, Blanca Valladares, Magistrate of the Supreme Court, Tegucigalpa, 11 August 1994.
24. Salas and Rico (1989a), p. 150.
25. In 1986 the average time spent awaiting trial in Honduras was a year and a half, while some 24 per cent of the prison population had been jailed for more than two years without trial; Salas and Rico (1993), p. 40. Supreme Court Magistrate Blanca Valladares estimated that the number of prisoners who had not been sentenced was approximately 6,000 in 1994; personal interview, Tegucigalpa, 11 August 1994.
26. The April 1993 Ad-hoc Commission report on judicial and police reform identified a number of weaknesses in the legal system including impunity; judicial corruption; lack of public confidence and recourse to 'private justice'; violation of the principle of presumption of innocence (incarceration without trial); and narcotrafficking. A number of proposals were put forward in the report, including measures to de-politicise and professionalise the judiciary; the implementation of anti-corruption measures; and the carrying out of a judicial 'audit' under the auspices of the Supreme Court to speed up the backlog of cases; Ad-hoc Commission (1993).
27. Salas and Rico (1993), p. 27.
28. 'El Fiscal General de la Nación velará por el respeto de los derechos y las garantías constitucionales, investigará los delitos y descubrirá a los responsables, tendrá la obligación irrenunciable de ejecutar la acción penal pública, iniciará acciones contra los servidores públicos que falten a la ley...', Ad-hoc Commission (1993), p. 2.
29. Attorney General Edmundo Orellana Mercado stressed that narcotics would be transferred to the Public Ministry only once the judicial police force (DIC) was fully operational; personal interview, Tegucigalpa, 16 August 1994.
30. Personal interview, René Velásquez Díaz, General Director of Public Prosecutors, Tegucigalpa, 30 August 1994.
31. *Ibid.*
32. Inter-American Court of Human Rights (1988), para. 147, p. 33.

33. In 1994, the national budget allocated to the National Commissioner's office was only 674,000 lempiras, approximately $78,000; personal interview, Leo Valladares, National Commissioner for Human Rights, Tegucigalpa, 9 August 1994.
34. CEJIL and Human Rights Watch/Americas (1994), p. 124.
35. *Ibid.*, p. xii.
36. Personal interviews, Attorney General Edmundo Orellana Mercado, Tegucigalpa, 16 August 1994; Human Rights Prosecutor, Sonia Dubón de Flores, Tegucigalpa, 17 August 1994.
37. Article 90 of the Constitution states that military crimes (those included in the Military Code) are to be handled by the military courts; this article has been interpreted by the armed forces as giving their courts jurisdiction over cases of human rights abuses where their members are implicated.
38. República de Honduras (1976).
39. This is a source of considerable conflict between police officers and army officers, a point made by Leticia Salamón. See Salamón (1994b), p. 9.
40. See for example: Americas Watch (1989); Amnesty International (1992a); CEJIL and Human Rights Watch/Americas, *Op. cit.*
41. Americas Watch (1989), especially chapter IV.
42. Personal interview Attorney General Edmundo Orellana Mercado, Tegucigalpa, 16 August 1994.
43. According to the Commander in Chief of the FUSEP, the US Justice Department's police training programme ICITAP (International Criminal Investigative Training Assistance Program) recommended the inclusion of some DNI agents into the DIC but this was rejected. Some FUSEP officials are reportedly involved at present in training prosecutors at the Public Ministry in criminal investigation techniques, personal interview with Colonel Roberto Lázarus, Tegucigalpa, 17 August 1994.
44. In August 1994, Colonel Roberto Lázarus, Commander in Chief of the FUSEP, estimated that the entire process would take approximately a year to a year and a half; personal interview, Tegucigalpa, 17 August 1994.
45. *InterPress Service News Cable*, 5 November 1994. FUSEP Commander in Chief Colonel Lázarus expressed his opposition to the piecemeal transfer of the police force to civilian control, favouring the transfer of the entire corps in a single operation; personal interview, 17 August 1994.
46. *Ibid.*
47. One example was the December 1988 removal by Congress of the Christian Democrat Attorney General for his role in the extradition request for Alvaro Saravia, an associate of Major D'Aubuissón then living in Miami, in connection with the killing of Archbishop Romero. The Court subsequently proceeded to rule the extradition request invalid.
48. Limits for incommunicado detention were reduced throughout the 1980s, according to the terms of subsequent emergency laws. For more detail see Americas Watch (1991a), chapter five.
49. Lawyers Committee for Human Rights (1993a), p. 23.

50. A 1989 report alleged the existence of an unwritten agreement between President Duarte (1984-89) and Defence Minister Vides Casanova to the effect that the SIU would not investigate crimes in which the armed forces were implicated without the President's specific recommendation; Lawyers Committee for Human Rights (1989), p. 50.

51. For a resume of CORELESAL's activities see CORELESAL (1991).

52. Americas Watch (1991a), p. 81.

53. In both cases, the rape and murder of the four US churchwomen and the Sheraton Hotel murders, the victims were US citizens and pressure from the US Embassy to resolve the cases was intense.

54. United States General Accounting Office (GAO), *Op. cit.*, p. 3.

55. In December 1992 a new law for the CNJ was passed. The eleven members include: two lawyers proposed by the Supreme Court; two of the most senior lower court judges; three practising lawyers nominated by the bar associations; three law professors and one member of the Public Ministry. The influence of the Supreme Court in the selection of the CNJ remains considerable; Spence and Vickers (1994), p. 7.

56. Some sectors within the Salvadorean legal community have called for powers of constitutional oversight to be removed from the Supreme Court and transferred to a separate Constitutional Tribunal, as in the case of Guatemala: Fundación de Estudios para la Aplicación del Derecho (FESPAD) (1994), p.16; personal interview, Felix Ulloa, Director of the Instituto de Estudios Jurídicos de El Salvador (IEJES), San Salvador, 13 July 1994.

57. The last legislative assembly (1989-1994) transferred the Supreme Court's right to bar lawyers from practising to a new Consejo Nacional de la Abogacía y Notariado. However, the current assembly (1994-) has yet to ratify this reform (a prospect which appears increasingly unlikely) and consequently the power to bar lawyers continues to be held by the Supreme Court.

58. For more detail on the 1983 Constitution and its effect on the organisation of the judiciary see Fundación de Estudios para la Aplicación del Derecho (FESPAD), *Op. cit.*

59. The Truth Commission selected a number of cases of human rights abuse, selected for the seriousness of their repercussions or as representative of certain systematic practices; see United Nations Truth Commission (1993).

60. *Ibid.*, p. 156 and pp. 163-165. On the Mozote massacre see Danner (1994).

61. *Ibid.*, chapter V. See also United Nations (1993a).

62. See for example *Diario Latino*, 29 March 1993.

63. Col. Julio César Grijalva, commander of the First Infantry Battalion, lent his public support to the President of the Supreme Court, calling him 'the voice of national dignity' and, referring to the Truth Commission's title ('From Madness to Hope'), stated – apparently without irony – 'if fighting Communism is madness, then we prefer to remain insane'; *Proceso*, No. 556 (San Salvador), 24 March 1993.

64. For more detail on the history of the Public Ministry see CORELESAL (1990a).

65. This followed a television speech by ARENA leader Major Roberto D'Aubuissón in which called on security personnel to go beyond the law to fight subversion and named Zamora as one of many 'subversives'; Americas Watch (1991a), p. 38 and p. 77.
66. Lawyers Committee for Human Rights (1993a), p. 18; see also United Nations (1993b), p. 35.
67. Programa Centroamericano: Servicios Legales, Derechos Humanos y Administración de Justicia (1994), pp. 5-6.
68. Within the PDH there are five deputy ombudsmen, with responsibility for human rights, children, environment, women and the elderly, respectively; República de El Salvador (1992b).
69. A cooperation agreement between ONUSAL and the Procuraduría de Derechos Humanos was signed in July 1993.
70. Progress on generating reform proposals has been mixed; the Ombudsman's legislative proposal for a new public security law was rejected by both ONUSAL and local human rights NGOs as injurious to fundamental human rights; Procuraduría para la Defensa de los Derechos Humanos (1994); *Proceso*, No. 596, 26 January 1994; personal interview with Florentine Meléndez, Human Rights Division, ONUSAL, San Salvador, 20 July 1994.
71. Personal interview, Carlos Molina Fonseca, San Salvador, 15 July 1994.
72. Fiscalía de Derechos Humanos (1992).
73. See United Nations (1994a) and (1994b).
74. In contrast to the 1980s, AID now acknowledges that addressing the attitudinal and political obstacles to reform is an essential first step; United States General Accounting Office (GAO), *Op. cit.*, p. 4. However, AID remains distinctly unwilling to work with local legal advocacy and human rights non-governmental organisations.
75. Personal interview, Linn Hammergren, Head of Judicial Reform Project, AID, San Salvador, 7 July 1994.
76. Lawyers Committee for Human Rights (1993a), p. 99.
77. For an earlier draft proposal of the Penal Procedures Code see CORELESAL (1990b).
78. During the Cristiani administration, the Justice Ministry (under René Hernández Valiente) generally supported AID-promoted measures to improve constitutional guarantees, such as the new Criminal Procedures Code. However, the rest of the judicial sector, particularly the Supreme Court under Gutiérrez Castro, actively opposed them.
79. United Nations (1994c); Procuraduría para la Defensa de los Derechos Humanos (1993).
80. United Nations (1993b), pp. 32-8 and 44.
81. Stanley (1993), p. 14; Procuraduría para la Defensa de los Derechos Humanos (1993).
82. See for example United Nations (1994c).
83. *Central America Report*, 5 August 1994.
84. United Nations (1994) *SC/5947*, 23 November (New York).

85. José Domingo Méndez, the new President, a finance lawyer who has never previously held public office, is untainted by the corruption scandals which beset the previous Court.
86. *Central America Report*, 18 November 1994.
87. Salas and Rico (1989b).
88. *Ibid.*, pp. 12-13.
89. Woodward (1993), p. 53 and chapter five.
90. These tribunals were organised within the *Comité de defensa nacional contra el comunismo*.
91. Salas and Rico (1989b), p. 43.
92. Amnesty International (1981).
93. The selection system for the Supreme Court in Guatemala is one of the most complicated in Latin America. The Court, comprising nine magistrates, is elected by the Congress following a mixed system whereby four are elected by the Congress and the remainder from a list of thirty nominees determined by a judicial nominating commission composed of representatives of law schools, bar associations and the judiciary itself; Salas and Rico (1993), p. 35.
94. 'La disolución del Departamento de Investigaciones Técnicas, se dio como resultado del incumplimiento sistemático de los fines para los cuales fue creado, pues en muchos casos sus funciones investigativas no se realizaron en forma legal, idónea y técnica', Policía Nacional (1986).
95. It should be pointed out that these police officers were expelled without any trial and were subsequently transferred to military intelligence units.
96. Figures from USAID (1985).
97. *Ibid.*, p. 10.
98. Written statement presented before the Western Hemisphere Sub-Committee of the House of Representatives, July 1990.
99. US Department of State, Bureau of Public Affairs, 'Criminal Justice and Democracy in the Western Hemisphere', April 1989, quoted in Americas Watch (1991b).
100. Amnesty International (1992b).
101. UN report paraphrased in USAID (1985), p.12.
102. See Lawyers Committee for Human Rights (1992) and (1993b).
103. 'The judicial investigation into the political assassination ... of Myrna Mack Chang...has made laborious progress because of repeated pressure and threats against police officers and judges involved in the investigation'; United Nations (1992a), para. 149.
104. United States Department of State, *State Department Country Reports: Guatemala* (1992 and 1993).
105. The major exception is the case of Chunimá, where the ex-civil patrol chiefs were sentenced in July 1993 to thirty years for the murder of two men and wounding of another. The first warrant for their arrest was issued in January 1991, but it took enormous international pressure and the intervention of the Inter-American Court of Human Rights to secure their arrest in August of the same year.
106. Salas and Rico (1993), p. 38.

107. United Nations (1992c), para. 190.
108. Americas Watch (1993).
109. Americas Watch (1990), p. 74.
110. In a survey sponsored by the United Nations in 1987, two-thirds of all Guatemalan lawyers and one third of all judges considered that political relations and friendships were more important than experience and ability in determining appointments; Salas and Rico (1989b).
111. In January 1990, Edgar Ligorría Hernández, head of criminal investigations at the Public Ministry, presented himself to the mother of one of Noel de Jesús Beteta's victims as Beteta's lawyer. At the time, Beteta was working for the Presidential Guard; Americas Watch (1993).
112. USAID (1985), p. 7.
113. Salas and Rico (1993), pp. 100 and 174.
114. *Ibid.*, p. 100.
115. United Nations (1992c), para. 193; United Nations (1994g), paras. 158 and 162.
116. Salas and Rico (1989), p. 97 and p. 174.
117. Human Rights Watch/Americas (1994), p. 37.
118. *Cerigua Weekly Briefs* (Mexico City), 20 December 1994.
119. From 'Proposal of the Civil Society Assembly on the Commission for the Clarification of the Rights Violations during the Armed Conflict', *Central America Report*, 1 July 1994.
120. 'Accord on the Establishment of the Commission for the historical clarification of human rights violations and acts of violence which have caused suffering to the Guatemalan people', *Central America Report*, 1 July 1994.
121. URNG/Government of Guatemala (1995).

III: INTERNATIONAL DIMENSIONS

CHAPTER 7

PACIFICATION AND RECONSTRUCTION
IN CENTRAL AMERICA:
THE INTERNATIONAL COMPONENTS

Laurence Whitehead

When viewed from the standpoint of global strategy, the Central American
crisis of the 1980s is too easily reduced to a merely local exemplar of late
Cold War regional clashes. Equally, when viewed from an 'area studies'
perspective, acute awareness of the local specificities of the crisis
sometimes obscures from view the overall international conflict and its
logic. This chapter seeks to navigate a course between these twin mis-
perceptions. It draws attention to the local factors affecting the timing and
course of the crisis, and to their partial lack of correspondence with the
timetable of bi-polar conflict. It also highlights those characteristics of
isthmian politics which proved relatively favourable and which facilitated
the process of peace-making. These characteristics also generated
widespread international support for subsequent reconstruction (relative,
that is, to the poor outcome of other regional conflicts). But both these
observations need qualification, and the regional experience must still be
situated in the context of the victory of the West in the Cold War.

The timing of ideological and military polarisation in Central America
coincided rather precisely with the intensification of what was at the time
called 'the New Cold War', and what with hindsight can be labelled the
final round of the old Cold War, which occurred between the Soviet
invasion of Afghanistan in December 1979, and First Secretary Gorbachev's espousal of the doctrine of universal human values in 1986/7. The
high point of the 'New Cold War' was reached in 1982/3, when President
Reagan launched his 'star wars' initiative and labelled Moscow 'the evil
empire'. This was also the period of maximum violence and uncertainty in
the Salvadorean civil war. The military crisis peaked slightly earlier in
Guatemala, and a little later in Nicaragua, but even so the synchronism
between regional and global processes was striking. With hindsight we can
see that in Central America the logic of military escalation began to give
way to a logic of negotiation as early as 1983 (the successful US 'rescue
mission' to Grenada precipitated an important shift in perceptions of the

balance of forces), but this was a slow and uncertain process, at least until the signing of the Esquipulas peace agreement of August 1987.[1] By that time Gorbachev's assault on traditional Soviet foreign policy was gathering momentum[2] and the most assertive phase of the Reagan administration's efforts to rebuild US self-confidence had been completed. (The 'Irangate' scandal was just beginning to sap the President's strength.)

Between Esquipulas and the electoral defeat of the Sandinistas (in February 1990) the West won victory after victory in the last phase of the global Cold War. Hardly anyone foresaw in 1988, or even at the beginning of 1989, that before Nicaragua went to the polls communist regimes would be displaced throughout east-central Europe, and that even the Berlin Wall would be torn down. Until that dramatic last phase in the collapse of the Soviet bloc, it was generally assumed that a succession of long-lasting regional conflicts would be wound down through negotiations still conducted within an essentially bi-polar framework. (This, for example, was the basis on which the Angolan conflict was to be settled, and the rationale underlying Vietnamese troop withdrawal from Cambodia.) Not all regional conflicts were to be ended by means of political settlement, however. Afghanistan, for example, was too far gone for that, and in an outcome that proved to be of more than local significance, Soviet forces were destined to suffer a humiliating retreat, a communist counterpart to what US troops had experienced in Vietnam. Much closer to our regional concerns, the US invasion of Panama of December 1989 underlined the essential post-Cold War reality facing the Central American isthmus: once again there was only one superpower with overwhelming military supremacy in the region. (Illusions that in certain circumstances Cuba's armed forces might be capable of countering Washington's firepower in the Caribbean had already been shaken by Grenada; Panama shattered any residue of such fantasies, and the Gulf War dramatised US technological supremacy still further.)

Since February 1990 both Central America and the world have been trying to find their way in a new post-Cold War world. One of the distinguishing features of isthmian affairs is the fact that, notwithstanding the West's overall victory and the USA's renewed position of military and ideological (if not so clearly economic) leadership, the framework guiding pacification and reconstruction in Central America largely corresponds to the agreements negotiated before the end of global bi-polarity. Despite US unilateralism in Panama, the emerging Central American settlement is strongly multilateral in conception and implementation. Admittedly Moscow (and Berlin, and even Havana) have virtually disappeared from the Central American map of external reference points, but the same is not true of Brussels, or London, or Mexico City. Moreover, linkages between Central American governments (including some that were established during the period of heightened regional polarisation) have emerged intact, and now provide a significant basis for dialogue between regional and extra-regional actors. (This is one reason why it would be artificial to insist too heavily on isolating the 'international' from the 'local' components of the pacification process.) We also witness a strong presence of non-governmental organisations and actors, nearly all of which derive most of their resources and influence from their extra-regional connections. In sum, therefore, the international components of the post-Cold War settlement in Central America are considerably more complex and diverse than one might guess from the raw facts of Western triumph in the global Cold War, and of renewed US ascendancy in the Caribbean basin. Despite the striking synchronicity between the successive stages of the global New Cold War and the various phases of the Central American conflict, this outcome confirms that a distinctive regional process has always been at work, a process which cannot merely be analysed as little more than a local reflection of a global power struggle.

This chapter develops on these themes under the following headings: (i) disentangling the interplay between global and regional processes; (ii) the Central American conflict as a divisive issue in the internal politics of the USA; (iii) the motives and conduct of such external mediators as the Contadora Group, the EU (European Union),[3] and the UN (United Nations). These international factors require close attention, not least given the widespread and largely justified view that the isthmus has an exceptionally 'dependent' or 'penetrated' political structure, where domestic forces are unusually subject to influence, pressure, and even direction from outside. Even so, in the conclusion it is argued that, compared to most other areas of regional conflict during the late Cold War period, Central America has benefited from having some relatively autonomous and effective sources of local political leadership, which contributed actively to shaping the peace process. Facing the threat of an externally imposed resolution of the crisis that would jeopardise Central America's precarious sovereignty, isthmian elites responded by crafting a compromise *salida* which could mobilise countervailing international assistance around the theme of non-intervention and international respect for legality.

Disentangling the Global/Regional Interplay

The Sandinistas did not plan to come to power at the start of the 'New Cold War'. As their name suggests, they were engaged in a long revolutionary process which had its distant origins in nationalist resistance to a US military occupation of their country that preceded the Bolshevik seizure of power. Admittedly both Sandino, and more particularly his Salvadorean counterpart, Farabundo Martí, worked in alliance with Moscow at the beginning of the Stalinist era. More importantly for this analysis, the 1970s generation of Central American revolutionaries was strongly influenced by the Cuban Revolution. Indeed, Fidel Castro's authority was required in 1977 to bring the rival Nicaraguan guerrilla movements together in a nine man *frente*, a critical step towards a successful insurgency. Castro was similarly influential in unifying and thereby strengthening the guerrilla movements of El Salvador and Guatemala. Nevertheless, it was the decomposition of the Somoza regime, and the associated radicalisation and polarisation of opinion in the other two countries that determined the timing of the onset of the regional crisis. These were essentially isthmian political processes (perhaps somewhat assisted by the post-Vietnam syndrome that overshadowed the Carter administration). They were hardly coordinated with Moscow (which, until the last minute, had scant expectation that any of Castro's guerrilla protégés could actually make a second revolution), and even in the case of the Cuba link it remains to be established whether Castro saw any connection between his activities in Africa and the timeliness of a revolutionary offensive in Central America. The best assumption is that external allies of the Sandinistas and their associates responded as best they could when it turned out that after many failed attempts, this time the revolutionary bandwagon really was underway.

Suppose the Sandinista victory had occurred at some other point in the global Cold War, could the regional conflict have been contained and de-ideologised? Or was an aggressive US reaction virtually inescapable, whatever the context, given the intimate nature of Cuban influence over the Sandinista leadership, Central America's strategic and symbolic importance to Washington and US policy-makers' ultra-sensitivity to any possibility of a 'second Cuba'? Lyndon Johnson's response to the Dominican insurrection of 1965, and the Nixon/Kissinger reaction to Allende's electoral victory in Chile in 1970, indicated that for at least as long as the Vietnam War continued, a fierce US reaction was to be expected. The CIA-sponsored destabilisation of Arbenz in Guatemala in 1954 pointed in the same direction. If there was a brief 'window of opportunity' for the Sandinistas it was probably limited to the short period between the collapse of the US-supported government in Saigon (mid-1975) and the Iranian Revolution (which was well underway by the Spring of 1979). This was, it should be recalled, the period when Cuba had sufficient leeway to launch various military initiatives in Africa. By the time the New Jewel Movement came to power by means of a coup in Grenada (13 March 1979) the US backlash against what was already regarded as Cuban and Soviet adventurism was clear.

Nevertheless, it should be remembered that even as late as mid-1979 a substantial array of Nicaraguan and external political actors clearly believed that it was possible to replace the Somoza regime with a revolutionary coalition that would be capable of enjoying a renegotiated relationship with Washington. These forces deserve to be remembered here, because many of them reappear as significant actors in shaping the pacification process after 1987. When the USA sought approval for the Organisation of American States (OAS) for the despatch to Managua of an international force, ostensibly to separate the two sides in the civil war and enforce a negotiated solution, the majority of Latin American governments refused to approve what some saw as a potential repetition of the Dominican Intervention. (As a result of the 1965 OAS intervention in the Dominican Republic, the popular insurgents had been kept out of office for the next twelve years.) Thus, such key governments as those of Mexico, Costa Rica, Colombia and Venezuela preferred to block an international force, and instead to assist the Sandinista-led coalition in overthrowing the Somoza dynasty by force. The State Department (under the gentlemanly, but soon-to-resign Cyrus Vance) acquiesced to this alternative, which also won the support of such key Nicaraguan political actors as the Chamorro family, the Catholic church, Virgilio Godoy's fraction of the Liberal party, and many businessmen.

In view of the eventual outcome – in 1990 Violeta Chamorro was elected President to displace the Sandinistas and curb their Revolution – we are inescapably driven to ask why a decade earlier a broad-based anti-Somoza coalition, with the Sandinista front as its backbone, could not fulfil the hopes and expectations of its moderate backers, and strike some kind of a deal with the Carter administration that would have kept Central America at least partially insulated from the maelstrom of the Second Cold War. However, this is not the place to undertake a systematic analysis of that issue. Just two points must suffice here:

– Despite Sandinista efforts to portray themselves as a broad front, driven into confrontation with the USA by US intransigence, the *comandantes* were in reality so strongly predisposed towards a Castroite view of the world that there was little chance of them seriously engaging in compromise in the wake of their military victory.[4] In any case, the Carter administration was already under so much pressure from the right that it would have been an untrustworthy partner in any such alliance. This reflected deep geo-political realities.

– Somoza's regime had acted in many respects as a 'regional *gendarme*' for US security interests in the vicinity of the Panama Canal. After Carter secured the ratification in 1979 of an agreement with General Omar Torrijos, under which the Canal would eventually revert to the Republic of Panama, the destruction of the Guardia Nacional in Nicaragua by a pro-Cuban military organisation greatly accentuated the worries of the US security establishment. Moreover, the Sandinista victory was secured with the active participation of insurgents from other Central American countries. Thus, no matter what sober realism one tries to project backwards onto the Sandinista leadership (and they were in a state of acute overconfidence in the aftermath of their victory), it is very difficult to see how they could effectively have assuaged the fear in Washington that their revolution was bound to destabilise reactionary despotisms in El Salvador and Guatemala, and could only have the effect of leaving the Canal route perilously exposed. In short, since Nicaragua was not an island that could just be sealed off by naval encirclement, the military lobby in Washington was always likely to advocate other forceful measures to contain and de-radicalise the revolution, and these were almost bound to seem unacceptable to the Sandinista leadership.

Even so it is still possible to construct scenarios of détente and liberal tolerance within Washington which could theoretically, under very favourable circumstances, have headed off the regional confrontation (rather as Dwight Morrow headed off an escalation of US-Mexican tensions in the late 1920s). But although such scenarios were perhaps possible, they were extremely improbable, and in the event the breakdown of relations between Carter and the Sandinistas was heavily over-determined, particularly when the Iranian revolution is factored ino the equation.

Although all this may seem like a very speculative argument concerning a now rather distant history, it still needs to be addressed if we are to evaluate the conduct of external actors in the current pacification process. If there had been near universal consensus that all responsibility for the outbreak of the crisis rested with the FSLN (Frente Sandinista de Liberación Nacional) then there would have been less willingness to accept a significant and persisting Sandinista voice in the peace agreement, and in the post-1990 settlement. But since blame for the origins of the crisis is more widely apportioned by many knowledgeable observers, the Sandinistas retain some legitimate authority, and the pacification process is accordingly somewhat more balanced than the post-Cold War 'correlation of forces' would require. Reagan sought from the Sandinistas the kind of 'unconditional surrender' that had characterised Washington's victories in the Civil War and the two World Wars, and in Grenada and Panama. So the fact that President Bush's Secretary of State settled for much less requires careful explanation.

Was the threat of revolution in Central America in itself a major component of the Second Cold War, or was it no more than an unfortunate sideshow? Again, an exhaustive analysis is beyond the scope of this chapter, but a good case can be made that, notwithstanding genuine US security fears in the Caribbean, Central America was more a convenient arena for theatrical displays of US resolve than a central element in the bipolar conflict of the early 1980s, which rather was concerned with the strategic balance in Europe, the security of oil supplies from the Middle East, and perhaps also with the fragility of the financial mechanisms integrating the western capitalist system. Central America was marginal to all these issues. The Reagan administration's efforts to justify its centrality by invoking fear of a 'domino' process running right through Central America and into Mexico were not generally considered very credible, not even by large sections of political opinion within the USA.[5] If the Central American conflict had truly represented a core element of threat to the Western Alliance in the new Cold War, then following the West's overwhelming victory in that conflict, Washington would have come under much more pressure to impose a punitive settlement.

Can we at least conclude that it was the winding down of the global Cold War that largely determined the timing and strategic significance of the Central American peace process, if not its specifically multilateral and negotiated contents? My impression is that the Central American left had radically scaled back its hopes and ambitions by 1986, well before the new direction in Soviet policy had taken a clear form. The timing was strongly affected by the rhythm of US electoral politics. By securing easy re--election for a second and final term in November 1984, Reagan had ensured that the 'roll-back' of communism in Central America would last longer than the local insurgents were in a position to resist, at least on a massive scale. So it became necessary for the Sandinistas (and even for the FMLN – Frente Farabundo Martí para la Liberación Nacional) to shift towards a search for some kind of negotiated end to the conflict. In global and ideological terms they were 'strategically defeated' well before the endgame stage of the Cold War. It was by no means a foregone conclusion that the eventual outcome would take the relatively accommodating form of the Esquipulas II Agreement (see chapter one). If the Republicans had not suffered a net loss of eight Senate seats in the November 1986 mid-term elections, the Reagan administration might well have weathered the Irangate scandal and successfully blocked a compromise peace. The US alternative was to escalate the contra war until it reached a definite resolution, which would have to be attained before Reagan was due to relinquish office for the last time, i.e. in January 1989. In practice, the Oliver North operation needed to reach a culmination well before the 1988 presidential election campaign was underway. The hardline Republicans thus needed a clear victory in Nicaragua before the end of 1987, and they came quite close to achieving one.

Finally, in this section, how does the West's victory in the global Cold War intermesh with the regional peace process since 1990? Most commentators list a rather standard set of answers to this question. It has been said that the discrediting of Soviet and Cuban Marxism has disoriented and demoralised many on the Central American left, who could have maintained their revolutionary commitment in the face of mere defeat (they always knew the balance of forces was against them), but not when their utopia was revealed as ideologically bankrupt. It has been said that, once again (as prior to the Good Neighbour Policy) US regional ascendancy – military, economic, and political, if not diplomatic – blocked off all but the most limited experiments in regional diversity. It has also been said that, having secured this victory, Washington no longer has much incentive to put further resources into the reconstruction of the isthmus. Other more conflictual zones of conflict claim a higher priority, and insofar as post-war Central America does receive international assistance, US policymakers expect a large proportion of that to come from those US allies who criticised US unilateralism in the region, and claimed they knew a better way to solve its problems. All these claims need careful evaluation as more evidence becomes available. For now it needs only to be noted that they tend to confirm what has been indicated throughout this section, namely that from beginning to end the regional conflict needs to be disentangled from the global rivalry in which it became embedded. In particular, this chapter will emphasise two distinguishing features of the Central American conflict: the breadth and depth of international resistance to US unilateralism in the region; and the unexpected capacity of Central American leaders to co-operate in forging an alternative *salida*. To pursue this argument further we should now consider more closely the domestic motives and conduct of the various external actors, starting with the USA.

Central America as a Source of Domestic Divisiveness within the USA

It is impossible to account for relative US forbearance towards radical challengers in the isthmus, either before or during or after the acute phase of the regional conflict, unless we attach very considerable weight to the distinctive dynamics of Central America as a specifically domestic issue within the US political process. (Here it needs to be recognised that at best there is no more than a 'loose fit' between the perceptions of Central American realities that compete for attention in the USA, and the ways those realities are apprehended by most Central Americans themselves or the – again distinct – ways they are perceived in Europe, the Contadora countries, etc.)

In part this was a debate about the 'Vietnam Syndrome', with the Reaganites seeking to demonstrate in a new arena that the anti-war movement had applied double standards, romanticising the communist insurgents and undermining if not actually betraying western-led forces of freedom. In the wake of the Vietnam débâcle, the Reaganites felt that many in the US administration and media had lost the will to defend either US national interests or the West's moral superiority, and as a result Washington had courted a succession of further foreign policy setbacks by opportunistic opponents – in Angola, in Iran, in Afghanistan, and of course also in Nicaragua.[6] The solution was to restore US self-confidence both in its power (future adventurers would take on the USA at their peril) and in the essential moral superiority of its international stance. The achievement of that goal would require theatrical displays of will-power in appropriately chosen hotspots, combined with very energetic campaigns to convince domestic US opinion that such reassertionism was justified and necessary. Domestic critics and doubters would need to be defeated and discredited since they were viewed as among the most dangerous allies of any foreign challengers. Such a reorientation of domestic opinion would require the invocation of a good deal of patriotism. Foreign allies and external friendly critics were not be allowed to blunt the force of this domestic campaign, which would depend to a considerable extent for its success on selling a persuasive image of the issues at stake to a normally rather uninformed and inward-looking US public.

The stance of the US anti-war network was, of course, more or less the mirror image of all this. The USA was too powerful, and was once again projecting its power overseas for an unjust cause. Moreover, the Reagan offensive was directed as much against enlightened internationally minded liberals within the USA as against external enemies. If the US public was scourged by Reagan's patriotism and militarism, the country would not only commit further atrocities abroad, it would also fall into a new dark age of McCarthyism and illiberalism at home. The most immediate danger was that US forces would once again be committed to a programme of foreign interventions that would not only be unjust in their own terms, but also misjudged in the sense that as they proceeded the USA would become bogged down, unable to achieve worthwhile results abroad, or to conduct an honest evaluation of its mistakes at home. For the opponents, as much as for the advocates, of Reagan's policies it was necessary to market a persuasive, and in the last analysis perhaps even an oversimplified and distorted, image of the issues at stake, in order to block these evils. However, opponents of the Reagan policy initially had incentives to portray a rather more realistic and accurate account of conditions in Central America than the hardliners in the US administration. In part this was simply because at the outset of the Central American conflict the allies available for the USA to work with were not of a kind likely to emerge well from any honest public scrutiny. (Later on, however, Washington put together increasingly broad coalitions of more respectable Central American allies, whereas some of the administration's critics became increasingly embattled, and were at times driven back into making excuses for less than admirable activities of the insurgents).[7] The major anti-Reagan forces also had another incentive to portray Central American realities with some degree of accuracy. Their domestic credibility was immensely reinforced by the fact that a wide range of international groupings that could in no way be dismissed as Communist dupes – Catholic bishops, the European Parliament, practically all the civilian governments in Latin America, etc. – kept indicating support for US liberal positions. Despite assiduous efforts by the US administration it proved extremely difficult to drive a wedge between these various 'moderate' opponents of the Reagan stance in Central America, which tended to remain rather united in their analysis of the real issues at stake on the isthmus, and in their disbelief in US overstatements and distortions. At the heart of this whole network of restraint was the Democratic majority in the US Congress.

It is only necessary to glance at other international crisis points where no such restraint exists, to see how critical a factor this must have been in shaping US policy. On the Middle East, for example, the pro-Israel forces in Congress and the media have never been counter-balanced, with the result that US power has been deployed forcefully and systematically on one side of the scales in that region. Closer to our area, there was no pro-Noriega lobby or current of opinion within the USA, once his protector, Bill Casey, died and the CIA (Central Intelligence Agency) came to regard him as a liability. As a result, after 1987 the Panamanian dictator's capacity to resist the development of US power was feeble, even though he controlled the full military and economic resources of the Panamanian state and could present himself as the prime legatee of Panamanian nationalism, and despite the fact that many of his local opponents within Panama could plausibly be dismissed as *compradores* and oligarchs.

The conflict within the USA over its Central American policy dated back to the Carter administration, but became more heated (and acquired its essential form) as a result of the National Security Council's November 1981 decision to fund a counter-revolutionary force in Nicaragua with the aim of ousting the Sandinistas. This decision pitted the Reagan administration against the Democratic majority in the Chamber of Representatives, and it raised deep constitutional issues concerning the congressional power of the purse, versus the executive's duty to respond effectively when US national security was at risk. The January 1984 Kissinger Commission Report represented an early effort to find common ground on which the two branches of government could co-operate. But following Reagan's re-election in November 1984, his hardline advisers believed they had secured a strong enough popular mandate to dispense with the need for domestic compromise. They saw the chance to wrongfoot congressional liberals by securing a complete victory in Central America before the 'great communicator' finally left office at the end of 1988. They thought that if they could secure such a victory, they would restore the executive supremacy over foreign policy-making that had been impugned by the Vietnam War. US capacity for leadership would be permanently strengthened, not only in this regional conflict, but more generally. The stronger the USA was seen to be, the less it would need to use its power.

In addition to this constitutional motive for Reagan's assertiveness, (and of course the ideological factors which have generally received most attention), there was another very practical reason why his advisers were willing to take big risks in order to achieve a quick result in Central America.[8] The contra forces had grown so large, and had become so visibly the major instrument of US pressure against Nicaragua, that their future became a matter of central concern to US policy makers. Reagan could not disband them with the Sandinistas still in power, nor could he very well leave office with the contras still dependent on funding from a

Congress that would be most unlikely to sustain them thereafter. (In the event Reagan's final budget request to Congress included $270 million to support the contras for just one year – a bid that was answered by the authorisation of a heavily conditional $36 million.) This is the essential background to the Irangate scandal, which arose after the administration had raised $54 million for the contras from assorted allies with no Nicaraguan interests of their own ($32 million from the Saudis, with a request for another $100 million pending, $10 million from Brunei, $10 million from the Iranian arms deal, and $2 million from Taiwan). The Reagan administration had tried to press ahead with its interpretation of US national interests against the explicit instructions of Congress (as Poindexter minuted on 9 June 1986 'The President is ready to confront Congress on the constitutional question of who controls foreign policy'), and the mid-term 1986 election (in which the Republicans lost control of the Senate for the first time since 1980) ensured that the executive would no longer be allowed to get away with such unconstitutional procedures.[9]

As a result of Irangate, the US executive lost the initiative in Central American policy-making, and the 'impasse' which had blocked the possibilities of a peaceful settlement was cleared.[10] The Reagan administration was caught off-balance by the Esquipulas Peace Agreement, because its key officials were engaged more or less full-time in protecting themselves from perjury charges, and had even less time than usual for monitoring events on the isthmus. In any case, the opportunity for securing a decisive military victory had been lost. Henceforth it would only be possible to sustain a Central American policy provided the suspicions of a Democrat-controlled Congress were allayed. Henceforth the USA would have to fall into line (however reluctantly) with the bi-partisan and multilateral approaches that Reagan had so firmly resisted for the first six years of his term. This was the changed domestic context, without which subsequent pacification processes in Central America would be inexplicable.

Once Congress had assured itself that Reagan's ascendancy had ended, it faced the unfamiliar and difficult challenge of negotiating the framework of an alternative policy that would be sufficiently strong and effective to defeat Reaganite charges of capitulationism, but that would also wind down the conflict, demobilise the contras, and build bridges with America's 'moderate' critics in Central America and elsewhere. This was not a task for which Congress was particularly well-designed at the best of times, and particularly not an easy task in the face of a still truculent administration, a quite ideologically polarised US public opinion, and an unpredictable and intractable situation on the isthmus. Between August 1987 and the end of

1991, the US Congress (helped by the Esquipulas process and, after January 1989, by the deal-making skills of President Bush's new Secretary of State, James Baker) proved remarkably successful in meeting these challenges, and thus in overcoming the ideological and constitutional conflicts which had crippled Washington's Central American policy-making for the previous decade.[11] After the end of 1991, however, some of the traditional vices of fragmented and short-sighted decision-making reappeared, due both to the declining salience of regional issues once the Salvadorean Peace accord had been signed, and also to the reversals of position attendant on the replacement of Republican by Democratic control over the executive once President Clinton was elected. The Republican recapture of both houses of Congress in the mid-term 1994 elections now threatens to further dissipate Washington's isthmian achievements.

Between 1987 and 1991 the peace process in Central America was mirrored by a painful process of negotiation and reconciliation between estranged factions within the US political class. Just as the Central American political elites began to curb and demobilise their militant supporters, so also centrist Republicans under the leadership of James Baker manoeuvred to distance the Bush administration from the ideologues of the Reagan period, in tacit alliance with Democratic power brokers in Congress from Jim Wright onwards, who sought to re-establish a broad-based congressional consensus that would shelter the party from accusations of irresponsibility and betrayal in the face of the United States' declared regional enemies. The life was draining out of the solidarity movement in the USA throughout this period, in part because Irangate shifted the focus from blocking US intervention (an issue which could arouse mass protest) to the constitutional and judicial arenas (where US legal culture operates as a powerful substitute for political activism). Many of those most concerned with the welfare of ordinary people in Central America were, if not enthusiastic about Washington's grudging endorsement of the peace process, at least relieved that a third Republican turn in the White House presaged nothing worse. (There are analogies here with the Ford-Carter transition from the excesses of Nixonism.) The US Catholic network, which had played such a prominent role in resisting Reagan's policies in the early 1980s, naturally fell in with a Central America-based peace initiative, not least because liberation theology was also on the retreat, resolutely combatted by Pope John Paul II and most of the isthmian hierarchy.

James Dunkerley, in his generally excellent reconstruction of the chronology of the pacification process, offers some perceptive observations about the contrast between US influences on the Nicaraguan peace negotiations (1987-9), which were for the most part negative and even obstructionist, and the more supportive role played by Washington in the 1990-91 negotiations in El Salvador.[12] However, he overlooks one element that I believe to be crucial; at the very height of the FMLN's November 1989 offensive (indeed on the day in which the insurgents moved into the wealthy *barrios* of the capital and trapped twelve Green Berets in the Sheraton) as many as 194 members of the House of Representatives voted in favour of making portions of the 1990 military aid allocation ($85 million) conditional on the investigation of the previous week's murder of the Rector of the University of Central America (UCA) and five other Jesuit priests. Of course, 215 Congressmen opposed such conditionality and it was defeated, but this was an extraordinarily significant vote nonetheless.[13] (I would assume that the precise balance of the vote reflected a deliberate decision by Congressional leaders to signal that they had a majority for cutting military aid to Salvadorean military clients practising human rights abuses, but that they were not going to use that majority in a way that might be misinterpreted by the insurgents, or might backfire against them in the eyes of US public opinion). To my mind, in terms of US domestic politics the killing in cold blood of the Jesuits (a decision of the Salvadorean High Command, allegedly taken in the presence of, and without demur from, President Cristiani) represented the decisive discredit of Reagan's strategy in El Salvador, just as the Irangate scandal destroyed his maximalist strategy in Nicaragua. James Dunkerley attaches great importance to the FMLN's demonstration of its continued strength and resolve, and this was no doubt a powerful factor inducing the Salvadorean regime to seek peace thereafter. But as far as US domestic politics were concerned, on its own the FMLN offensive would have had the effect of stiffening the resolve to fight back, had it not been for the way that the military chose to strike out. Between 1981 and 1990 the Salvadoreans had received $1,000 million in military aid from the US taxpayer, notwith-standing their complicity in the assassination of Archbishop Romero in 1980. For US opinion in general, and US Catholic opinion in particular, it would be almost intolerable to allow such a situation to continue any longer after the same military establishment had repeated the offence a decade later.

Of course the US congressional response was not to favour an FMLN victory, but rather to seek a compromise peace settlement. On the Bush administration's side, this involved complex and frustrating negotiations with their murderous clients, negotiations in which many senior officials found themselves dangerously close to complicity in covering up what they had discovered about the Jesuit killings.[14] On the side of the congressional Democrats and their NGO (Non-Governmental Organisation) allies, it involved a somewhat comparable, although much more filtered, minuet with the FMLN and its political associates. This is much less well documented, but I am inclined to accept the interpretation of one close observer from within the Bush administration,[15] who told me that though he was no admirer of Senator Dodd and Co., he had to recognise that a major factor in inducing the FMLN to strike a deal by the end of 1991 was the 'civilising' influence of congressional liberals and the US solidarity movement. Rebel leaders realised that after the end of the Cold War this was the only kind of international support they could still rely on, and that it was based on a concern for peace and justice that differed from the priorities of a previous category of their backers. If the insurgents lost this last source of solidarity then (like, say, Sendero Luminoso) they faced the possibility of utter annihilation. Realisation of this made it necessary for the FMLN to try to live up to some of the awkward expectations of their US liberal friends.

Until 1990 the administration in Washington had viewed with suspicion most attempts by third parties to mediate, or even to interpose their good offices in the cause of regional pacification. The tendency had been to perceive such initiatives either as covert efforts to boost anti-USA forces (a suspicion apparently justified by the 1981 Franco-Mexican declaration recognising the FMLN as a legitimate actor, but also extended to most attempts to treat the Nicaraguan government as an internationally recognised authority, which it in fact was); or failing that as misguided attempts to do good, which would in practice only have the effect of encouraging Central American rebels to resist, and of strengthening the inclination of US liberals in Congress to make trouble and encroach on the executive's foreign policy-making prerogatives. However, from the beginning of 1990 all this changed. Having successfully deployed unilateral force to capture Noriega, witnessed the dismantling of the Berlin Wall, and secured the electoral defeat of the Sandinistas, the Bush administration no longer viewed the Central American insurgents as a security threat, and no longer feared that international do-gooding would hamper its relationship with Congress. On the contrary, as we shall see in the next section, the European Union, the Contadora Group,[16] and the United Nations could now be tapped both for economic assistance and for political support in pacifying the isthmus, thus reducing the burden on an over-loaded Washington. Perhaps the most significant indication of this new stance was the November 1990 creation in Washington of a 'Partnership for Democracy and Development in Central America' (PDD) involving the 24 member states of the OECD (Organisation for Economic Cooperation and Development) in regional reconstruction through joint action, and the multilateral coordination of aid (the PDD held its third plenary in Tokyo in March 1993). This was launched as a US initiative and signalled that the USA's allies would no longer be acting in competition with the administration in Washington. It also signalled that executive-congressional differences had been largely overcome.

It is commonly stated that US aid to the isthmus has been held at disappointing levels since 1990, and by many yardsticks this is no doubt true.[17] However, it should be noted that even in 1993 the USA was still supplying over 60 per cent of the Overseas Development Assistance received in the region (down from 77 per cent in 1985), so it is hardly surprising if US leadership remains intact.[18] In fact Central America is still receiving about 50 per cent of all US cooperation commitments in Latin America, and still conducts almost half its trade with the USA.

On the positive side, then, the slow and painful process of surmounting US internal divisions over isthmian affairs has created the possibility of pursuing a more constructive policy, acting in co-ordination with regional and international opinion, and beginning to address the bitter legacy of destruction arising from over a decade of regional conflict. Washington has already played a distinctly positive role in the Salvadorean peace negotiations, and it might potentially do more of the same in Guatemala, if the peace process there gathers momentum. Some observers also claim that there has been a shift in the traditionally subservient nature of the relationship between Central American elite groups and their North American sponsors. It is argued that the regional origins of the peace process, and the success of efforts at Central America-wide cooperation, have produced a greater maturity and self-confidence within the region, and that this is reflected in the more respectful attitudes displayed by many policy makers in Washington.

However, such optimistic interpretations should not be pressed too far. Although Oliver North was narrowly defeated in his bid for a Senate seat in November 1994, the Republicans as a whole captured both houses of Congress, and Senator Helms has therefore regained the strategic position of Chairman of the Senate Foreign Relations Committee, with oversight over key appointments and policy initiatives in the isthmus. Even before that victory, Helms had succeeded in making a resumption of US aid to Nicaragua conditional on the payment of compensation to those US citizens who were expropriated by the Sandinistas (many of them ex-Somocistas). More generally, throughout the 1990s the US Congress has been keener to suspend aid as a punishment for democratic backsliding, than to provide support as a reward for improved civic performance. In consequence there is a widespread perception in Central America that the region's deep problems have not been fully appreciated in Washington, and that there are still few restraints on the hegemonic power's traditional inclination to push its demands to the limit, with scant concern for the local repercussions.

External Mediators

Given the regional hegemony exercised by the USA, and its propensity to view the isthmian conflict in national security terms, the scope for external mediation was heavily constrained until the end of the Cold War. What is remarkable, however, is the persistence and determination of various other international actors in the 1980s, all of whom sought to interpose themselves between a Washington viewed as inclined to resort to unilateral military action, and a Central America incapable either of defending itself effectively, or of ceasing to provide an invitation to US intervention. No single mediator was ever strong enough to have much impact alone, but collectively and successively these mediators did help to tip the balance in favour of a peaceful settlement, not least because they retained a foothold within the US political establishment, via their contacts with the Democratic majority in Congress, and with the liberal US media. In this section we shall very briefly discuss the initiatives for a peaceful settlement put forward by the Contadora Group of Colombian, Mexican, Panamanian and Venezuelan foreign ministers (which faded after 1986), then the European Community, and then the United Nations, but all three should be seen as acting in conjunction, and in association with a range of other international actors (NGOs, party internationals, the Catholic church, etc.) in order to steer the region away from a worse confrontation.

Contadora
Although the Contadora Group had its heyday in 1983-86 it merits attention here, both because of its early pre-eminence and its role in paving the way for the Esquipulas settlement[19] and because it reappears in the 1990s – organisationally in the form of the Group of Three (Mexico, Colombia, and Venezuela, this time without Panama) – and conceptually, through its stress on multilateralism, the acceptance of the 'juridical fiction' of state sovereignty, and the reliance on treaties and internationally supervised negotiations as the privileged instruments of pacification. The weaknesses of this strategy are easy to pinpoint, of course. It involved treating an ideologically polarised conflict which spilt over national boundaries and

sucked in great powers as if it were composed entirely of negotiable differences of interest separating entities which were all discrete and authoritative within their jurisdictions, and which agreed on the primacy of international law. The remarkable fact is that, a decade after this quixotic formula was first proposed (a decade in which most of the original authors of the Contadora approach lost office, or were discredited by domestic economic failures or political scandals), these juridical fictions not only live on but claim the allegiance of virtually all those who originally had scorned them. They now provide a rallying point for isthmian, international, and US moderates alike; and they strengthen the hand of the recently elected new generation of Central American political leaders in Guatemala, Honduras, Costa Rica, and perhaps even Panama, in their efforts to curb the excesses of the respective old guard. Most strikingly of all, even ARENA (Alianza Republicana Nacionalista) and the FMLN (or the Ortegas and UNO – Unión Nacional Opositora), largely accept the principles of Contadora as the basic framework for compromise and conciliation.

The main force underpinning the Contadora formula was the intense and sustained pressure coming from within Central America. A wide variety of leadership and popular groups demanded a settlement and were quite prepared to swallow a few juridical fictions in order to gain one. Without that driving force, the treaty framework would have been discarded long before (as draft settlements of the Angolan, Mozambican and Afghan conflicts, for example, have all been cast aside). With that impetus behind it, on the other hand, the spirit of Contadora proved almost indestructible. When Mexico faltered, Colombia took up the baton, and when all the four regional powers lost heart the Central American Presidents breathed new life into the formula. All this time the European Community provided a stable framework of encouragement, through the annual ministerial meetings organised under the San José process (ever since the 1984 Treaty of Luxemburg). And the moment the UN Secretary General, Javier Pérez de Cuéllar, realised that the US veto on mediation in the Security Council had been lifted, the UN rushed in to embrace the state-centric juridical approach to pacification which provides that body with its essential *raison d'être*. At the most critical periods this diplomatic and political activity was reinforced by the far from negligible economic incentives provided by the San José agreement of 1980 (under which the two oil exporting founders of Contadora provided the oil importers of Central America with a 25 per cent discount on their energy bills, distributed on a non-discriminatory basis to all the four states in contention). So up to 1986 Contadora should not be under-estimated. It also provided most of the groundwork for the Esquipulas settlement with the exception that, reflecting isthmian war weariness, President Arias added the irresistible prospect of a permanent cease-fire, and verifiable steps towards democratisation and the protection of human rights.

However, turning to the post-1990 period, it is the role of the European Community, under the San José process, and of the United Nations, via ONUCA (United Nations Observer Group for Central America) and ONUSAL (United Nations Observer Mission in El Salvador), which require our special attention. These are the two international channels of mediation and reconstruction which have had the most to contribute, and which still have the potential to offer more.

The European Community
The 1984 Treaty of Luxemburg, which gave rise to the San José process, was a remarkably bold and assertive initiative for the European Community (EC) to undertake in the face of resistance from the Reagan administration, and at the height of the new Cold War. Few would have anticipated that it would hold together so well, last so long, and have such a positive record to report, a decade later. Viewed from Europe, Latin America may well seem the most favourable setting in the so-called 'Third World' for the application of those political and diplomatic formulae in which the EC developed a comparative advantage (multilateralism, peaceful resolution of disputes within a framework of international law, economic convergence and integration, etc.). If Europe is to establish itself as a major and unified actor in global politics it is through the promotion of such formulae that its influence is most likely to be felt. Of course it cannot be stressed too heavily that the search for a re-definition of Europe's global role is still at an early stage. As far as Latin America is concerned, the sub-continent is a low priority and the EC, now renamed the European Union (EU) (see footnote 3) is unlikely to pay too high a price for the application of its distinctive policies in this area of the globe rather than elsewhere.

Nevertheless, provided the price is not too high there are some good reasons why the architects of an emerging external policy for a more unified Europe would have considered Central America a promising arena for action. A key motivation would be to demonstrate to a sceptical audience in Europe that it is possible to achieve worthwhile progress in the promotion of values held widely throughout the EU, through the disinterested application of common European policies.[20] The relatively tractable condition of Latin America makes it a suitable focus for such efforts. Moreover, although the sub-continent is of the most marginal economic or strategic significance for the EU, it does have a significant hold upon the

European political and cultural imagination. The episodic reasons for that hold (passions aroused by human rights violations, or civil wars, that stir memories of recent European history) may now fade, but there are also structural reasons that should prove more durable. These include shared languages and religious traditions, the widespread presence of emigrants from Europe, and the existence of strong historical ties which are kept alive through such agencies as the international party organisations (Christian Democracy, the Socialist International, etc.) and quite intense programmes of educational and cultural exchange.

To achieve visible results in Latin America as a whole would require an input of EU resources far in excess of what is likely to be available. From this standpoint, then, it was almost a matter of good fortune for the (then) EC that one small sub-region of the continent presented itself to world opinion as in particularly acute need of solidarity and targeted external assistance. The aftermath of the Sandinista revolution catapulted Central America into world headlines and played up precisely those themes on which an emerging EC would be best placed to take a stand. From 1984 onwards the foreign ministers of the Community have established a remarkably high profile, and have sustained a complex programme of support for reconciliation and reconstruction on the Central American isthmus. In contrast to the USA, the EC obviously had no intention of sending force, of violating international law, or of discriminating between sovereign states on purely ideological grounds. Moreover the EC's prolonged absence from the Central American scene made it far less responsible than the United States for the circumstances that had led the region into crisis. So although a few critics assumed that European initiatives must be motivated by hegemonic aspirations, these were clearly paltry by comparison with the vested interests that could be associated with US policy.

The main cost to the EC of its involvement in the San José process was not the limited financial commitments involved, but the investment of scarce foreign ministerial time and resources, in particular when their efforts risked offending Washington. Yet if the new Europe was to assert itself as an autonomous global actor, some divergences with the USA would have to be courted and sustained. From that perspective Central America offered a relatively favourable opportunity, since US opinion was deeply divided (with many Democrats closer to Brussels than to the White House in their definition of the issues); since a successful European policy could hardly be rated a mortal affront to the United States; and since a surprisingly diverse array of European governments were able to convince themselves of the merits of a distinctive common policy. In the event, the

Esquipulas Peace Plan offered substantial vindication of the European diagnosis of the regional crisis. But fortunately for the EC the USA was not humiliated and the outcome was satisfactory to both parties. With hindsight an unkind but not entirely fanciful way of characterising the San José process in the 1980s would therefore be to say that joint western interests were best served by the adoption of a 'carrot and stick' policy, and that through a process of tacit co-operation the EC acquired the function of offering the carrots leaving the USA free to concentrate on administering the sticks. It is unlikely that such an international division of labour could have emerged through premeditation, but it developed rather naturally from the distinctive military and geopolitical orientations of the two parties and from the very different profiles of the interests they had at stake in the sub-region.

The key significance for Europe of the San José process was that it offered an unusually favourable context for the Community to present itself as a disinterested actor. From the military and geo-strategic viewpoint the EC was disinterested in that it lacked both a capacity and a need for force projection. From the economic viewpoint it was disinterested in that the financial costs of the policy were quite modest and the economic interests at stake were minimal. (Note, for example, that whereas the USA spent the 1980s designing preferential trade schemes such as the Caribbean Basin Initiative, the EC bent its comparable energies to the Lomé accord, from which Central America was excluded. However, since 1 January 1992 Central America has been the beneficiary of a Lomé-style agreement with the EU, following the adoption of a special General System of Preferences or GSP scheme which extends duty-free entry to the EU market to a number of Central American agricultural products).

Finally, from a demographic viewpoint, the emerging Europe's relationships with Africa, Asia and the Middle East may well be dominated by the wish to restrict uncontrolled migration. This becomes an even higher priority for European policy-makers as the spectre of mass emigration from the USSR and Eastern Europe looms. But so far as Central America is concerned, if there is continuing out-migration it will be to the USA and not to Europe. Here too, then, the EU is uncharacteristically disinterested.

One distinctive feature of the EU's cumbersome and formalised decision-making procedures is that it not only takes a long time to set any given co-operation agreement in motion, it also takes just as long to change course or deviate from past commitments. After eleven years of build-up, the San José process has now acquired considerable inertia.[21] Not even the upheavals in eastern Europe are likely to interrupt its pre-established course. Since 1984 the custom of holding regular annual summit meetings at foreign ministerial level has become ingrained. The tenth Inter-ministerial Meeting between the Member States of the EU and Central America was held in Athens in March 1994 and the eleventh in Panama in February 1995. Belize, Colombia, Mexico and Venezuela also participate in the process, so that potentially as many as 25 Foreign Ministers may be involved (the EU had 15 members on 1 January 1995). In February 1993 Central America and the EU signed a third generation Framework Agreement for Co-operation. These regular summits tend to lock the EU into its commitments. Gradually the European Union is becoming an ever more important source of aid for Central American development (see Table 7.1). Moreover this economic aid is being administered under a system of political supervision at the highest level, which pays close attention to human rights and social welfare. (These aspects were carefully considered at the Athens meeting, for example.) Yet European political conditionality does not involve the kind of high level unilateral threats to cut aid that win so much popularity in the US Congress. Just as the Central Americans used to express frustration over the EC's unresponsiveness to crisis conditions on the isthmus, other regional lobbies have begun to protest that their immediate needs are greater and yet Central America seems to have acquired pre-emptive rights. In fact it is as difficult to make the EU slow down as to make it speed up. This is a marked contrast with Washington's policy-making style, which favours the rapid development of resources to tackle whatever may be judged the crisis of the moment, but which often lacks the stamina to achieve follow-through when a crisis goes off the boil.

Over the medium run we can anticipate that two conflicting forces are likely to shape EU relations with the isthmus. The force of inertia will tend to sustain and even somewhat increase the levels of European support committed so far, whereas European strategic self-interest will argue for a redirection of attention towards higher priority problems. The Central Americans will argue, with good reason, that having followed much of the advice they received from Europe they are now entitled to claim their promised rewards.

On the positive side the European Commission has budgeted 2.9 billion ecus (approximately $3.71 billion) for aid and co-operation with Asia and Latin America over the 1991-5 cycle (an 82 per cent rise over the previous cycle) and has stressed the need to restore Latin America's share of a growing aid budget. Within that budget Central America has received highly preferential treatment (worth about 150 million ECUs, or $180 million dollars, in 1993). The sums remain modest, of course, but the Commission points to various features that make this assistance particularly worthwhile. On a *per capita* basis Central America already receives more economic aid from the European Union than any other region of the world, and under the fourth generation *acuerdo marco* envisioned for the late 1990s this assistance should rise further. Such aid is given in the form of donations, priority goes to aiding the poorest countries, and targeting the poorest strata of the population. Food aid, aid for reconstruction, emergency relief and aid to refugees are favoured (hence the concentration on Central America). Moreover in addition to the EU's direct expenditure on co-operation, many individual European countries also have substantial unilateral aid programmes with large Central American components. The OECD's Development Assistance Committee estimates total European Union official development assistance to Central America at US $352 million in 1992 (for a cumulative total of US $2,393 million 1980-1992). The entry of Austria and Sweden into the Union in 1995 will reinforce these flows at a time when US development aid to the isthmus is continuing to plummet. Taking both bilateral and multilateral sources of aid into account the EU countries claim to be devoting 0.5 per cent of their GNP to Third World co-operation, and there are plans to raise this to 1.0 per cent in the next few years. (Compare the 0.2 per cent spent by the USA – mostly on a handful of strategic clients – and the 0.3 per cent spent by Japan, although this is now also rising rapidly.)

Table 7.1
European Commission Cooperation with Central America (in US $ million)

	1985	1990	1991	1992	1985-92
Development Aid	36	105	108	119	724
Economic Cooperation	1	19	10	16	54
Humanitarian Aid	1	15	14	26	87
Total Cooperation	38	140	132	˙ 160	865

1985-1992 Total Cooperation:	Costa Rica	28
	El Salvador	136
	Guatemala	107
	Honduras	62
	Nicaragua	240
	Panama	8
	Regional Organisations in Central America	284
	Total Cooperation	865

Note: Does not include bilateral aid from individual European aid budgets.
Source: IRELA (1994b), p. 53.

Moreover, on the political side, the European Commission can point to at least three distinctive features of its isthmian policies which seem to dovetail with the sub-region's particular needs. First, EU policies are formally non-discriminatory, which is why Nicaragua was never subjected to European sanctions and indeed even Castro's Cuba remains technically eligible for assistance. This was very important during the 1980s, when US policy sought to benefit El Salvador and penalise Nicaragua, but when EU non-discrimination helped keep alive the institutions of Central American co-operation. The second feature, then, is that the EU believes it has a special mission to encourage schemes of regional integration such as have been repeatedly attempted in Central America ever since its independence. Thirdly, European experience suggests that progress on the relatively technical questions of regional economic integration can promote much broader goals – reducing militarism and the threat of local wars; eroding ideological polarisation; widening the basis for political toleration and pluralism; strengthening constitutional and representative government and the rule of law; and forging an extra-national sense of loyalty and identity. The EU believes that it has established an attractive model for other once strife-torn regions to imitate, and that Central America is well-placed to benefit from this European experience. (This belief may help explain some of the more eccentric features of the Commission's policy, such as the stress on the establishment of a Central American parliament.)

With the defeat of the Sandinistas, the peace agreement in El Salvador, and the negotiations in Guatemala, many in Europe and the United States believe that the Central American crisis has finally gone off the boil. The inhabitants of those three troubled republics may be forgiven for taking a more cautious view, but here we are concerned with international perceptions. There would have to be a very major and spectacular setback to the Esquipulas process to convince outside observers that Central America had plunged back into the abyss. By far the most likely prospect for the next few years is that, however unpleasant conditions on the isthmus may continue to be, European opinion will regard Central America as having slipped well down the hierarchy of regional trouble spots compared to the recent past. The urgency of its reconstruction needs will be thought to rank far behind those of the former Yugoslavia, the other states of East-Central Europe, the ex-USSR, the Mahgreb, the Middle East, and much of Africa. Moreover, all of those just-mentioned regions are of far more direct economic and political concern to the emerging Europe than Central America, which already has a patron and protector in the form of the USA. Even within Latin America, Central America's claims to priority have come under challenge, notably when the European

Commission admitted the Dominican Republic and Haiti to the Lomé accord, in 1989, and when it extended duty free access to tropical products from Andean countries, in 1990, to assist in their anti-narcotics programmes. It was only in 1992 that similar benefits were finally extended to Central America.

The United Nations

With the ending of the Cold War, the USSR and other members of the UN Security Council were no longer likely to veto collective peace-keeping initiatives. The Secretary General of the United Nations (UN) therefore became involved in mediation much later than the other actors considered here, but (particularly in El Salvador) the UN has subsequently become a major and rather effective participant in the pacification process. The UN first became involved in Central America in late 1989, when the UN Observer Group in Central America (ONUCA) was set up, charged with observing the compliance of the Central American governments with articles 5 and 6 of the Esquipulas II agreement. ONUCA was wound up in early 1992, by which time ONUSAL (the observer mission in El Salvador) took centre stage. ONUSAL helped repatriate refugees and assessed the human rights situation, in addition to verifying compliance with demilitarisation commitments and overseeing elections.

ONUSAL was a significant innovation for the UN in various respects. It represented the first time that a UN peace-keeping mission was deployed before a cease-fire; it was the first time that a human rights verification component was included in a UN peace-keeping mission; it was the first such mission headed by a civilian; and it had more of a peace-building component than any earlier UN mission, which necessarily involved a relatively high degree of intrusiveness into what had hitherto been considered purely domestic matters.[22] In other words, Central America provided the UN with a suitable arena to try out the new strategies of international peace-keeping that were emerging as its blueprint for the post-Cold War world.

In fact UN Secretary General Javier Pérez de Cuéllar took a direct and personal interest in the problem of isthmian pacification, which as a Peruvian he felt he understood relatively well. In April 1990 Pérez de Cuéllar's efforts at sponsoring a settlement in El Salvador bore their first fruit, when the government and the FMLN signed an agreement in Geneva, establishing the bases for a resumption of dialogue. UN sponsorship continued until the signing of the Chapultepec Peace Agreement in January 1992. Since then such high officials as Marrack Goulding, Alvaro de Soto, and even Boutros Boutros-Ghali have flown to El Salvador to renegotiate timetables and settle conflicts over interpretation of the Chapultepec Accord, thereby keeping the peace process on track. Both UN executives were actively assisted by a four nation group known as the 'Friends of the Secretary General' (Colombia, Mexico, Spain and Venezuela) which exerted influence on the various local power contenders to keep the peace process on track. (For example, the FMLN regarded the Spanish government as trustworthy, so Madrid's good offices helped overcome certain problems with the Salvadorean guerrillas.) The UN has also participated in the Guatemalan peace negotiations, which started in March 1990, but have yet to give rise to a treaty (although both sides achieved a framework agreement at Puebla in March 1994). Through its Plan Especial de Cooperación Económica para Centroamérica the UN has mobilised resources amounting to $470 million, and recently identified new projects worth $90 million. Some $220 million of this funding is earmarked for assisting Central American refugees (see chapter four).

Although the OAS is part of the UN system, it is important to note the contrasts between the global and the regional organisations. Liisa North reports the findings of her Canadian research group on UN peace-keeping in Central America as follows: 'We would urge great caution in proceeding towards involving the OAS (Organisation of American States) in peace-keeping activities. The UN attempted to collaborate with the OAS in Central America, specially through CIAV/OAS (Commission for International Verification and Support), which was mandated to assist in the demobilisation of the Contras in Nicaragua. However, the OAS component quickly became mired in controversy due to its alleged lack of respect for the norms of impartiality. In general, greater OAS involvement raises a number of serious questions that range from the use of military personnel from countries with recent records of gross and systematic human rights abuse to US dominance in that organization'.[23] Such charges notwithstanding, however, it should be noted that the role of the OAS in monitoring the fairness of electoral processes throughout Latin America has been both extensive and positive.

Conclusion

All these international actors were drawn into attempts to resolve the Central American conflict, and persisted in supplying high-level mediation backed by substantial commitments of material resources, because of the risks to international security if regional tensions were not abated, but also because they considered that isthmian political elites had the capacity to construct a 'model' settlement. Efforts from within the region to negotiate a durable *'salida'* inspired a degree of international confidence, and kept the external mediators 'locked in' until pacification was achieved. (Contrast, with say, Somalia.) Thus the final section of this chapter will survey the Central American regional component of the pacfication process, an essential element in shaping international responses to the crisis.

In the late 1970s region-wide crisis was first triggered and then intensified by a collapse of the always fragile local capacity for political mediation and conflict resolution, first in Nicaragua (following the assassination of Pedro Joaquín Chamorro in 1978), then in El Salvador and Guatemala (as the knock-on effects of the revolutionary upsurge in Nicaragua polarised those societies). Within each of those three countries centrist political groupings were split, marginalised, and subjected to violent intimidation. Even demilitarised Costa Rica's highly developed political resources were for a short period mobilised mostly to bring down the Somoza dynasty, if necessary through violence. These isthmian political dynamics accentuated the region-wide conflict and governed its timing, which did not just reflect trends in the Cold War more generally. The collapse of political intermediation in Central America elicited a variety of international responses. In the USA the incoming Reagan administration chose directly to deploy US power and resources in order to block the advance of the revolutionary left, even at the risk of further undercutting the sovereignty and autonomy of the region's moderate political forces. In Latin America and Western Europe this elicited a counter-response, initially focused partly on solidarity with the embattled (but legally recognised) Sandinista administration and its allies. By 1982, however, all the Latin American and European emphasis was centred on preserving Central America's threatened political sovereignty, and on pressing for a negotiated settlement to the region's internal wars, before they became further internationalised. This was the rationale for both Contadora and the San José process, both of which presupposed the re-emergence or reconstitution of an authoritative and autonomous 'political centre' within the region.[24]

In most regional conflicts it has not been possible to count on any such mediating force.[25] Neither in South-East Asia, nor in the major sub -regional conflicts in Africa, have civilian political and social elites achieved or retained the capacity to play such a role. By contrast, in Central America this potential was never completely lost, and after 1986 an effective centre re-emerged both to contain and de-radicalise the revolutionary left and to fend off the militarist and interventionist right.

The external actors reviewed in this chapter were only able to secure the settlement that eventually emerged because of the resilience, autonomy and ingenuity of this sector of the Central American political class. One key element was provided by the Costa Ricans, who were of course never intimidated, polarised, or subordinated to external control to anything like the extent prevailing in the four militarised states of the isthmus.[26] A somewhat related factor was the persistence, even in the worst moments of the crisis, of norms of inter-state co-operation and mutual recognition on a range of non-political issues of mutual interest. Thus, Central American finance ministries and central banks never ceased to operate conjointly on technical questions, international transport and communications were for the most part co-operatively maintained, and so forth. Such regional institutions and practices provided a basis for higher level political, and eventually even military, co-ordination as the peace process gathered momentum. The European Community's institutionalisation in 1984 of annual summits at foreign ministry level reinforced this capability, which later became enshrined in a series of presidential summits and internationally binding agreements negotiated after 1986 under the Esquipulas framework. But the reconstitution of an effective political centre should not be viewed solely in terms of inter-governmental relations. This potentiality was powerfully reinforced by the interplay of a series of prominent non-governmental agencies and institutions operating throughout the region – notably the Catholic church, but also the party internationals, networks of human rights and social activists, the media and the professions. Elements of the regional business community have also played a part.

In short, despite the severity of the regional crisis precipitated by the overthrow of the Somoza dynasty, Central America possessed a certain range of structural advantages which created the potential for a comparatively successful and internally-led *salida*. These advantages included a shared history of regional co-operation, and even to some extent of a shared isthmian political identity; a political class experienced in brokering accommodations in deeply divided societies; and popular traditions of nationalism and political involvement which militated against externally imposed solutions, and which generated an authentic capacity for local political representation. External support for pacification and reconstruction in Central America was forthcoming not just because of the gravity of the isthmian crisis of the early 1980s, but also due to a well-founded belief that this sub-region, more than other conflict-torn areas of the Third World, had the local potential to overcome its violent political antagonisms and to achieve a peaceful reconstruction of its society and economy. Such external hopes of pacification have been largely vindicated since 1990, but the tasks of reconstruction are still far from complete, and continued external support and understanding are therefore still needed.

Notes

1. US military aid to Central America peaked at $238 million in fiscal year 1984. It declined to $107 million by 1990, and half that in 1993.
2. This is traced in, for example, Adams (1992).
3. [Editor's note] – after the Maastricht Treaty of 1 November 1993, the European Community became the European Union.
4. See the testimony of Roger Miranda, chief aide to General Humberto Ortega until his defection in 1987; Miranda and Ratliff (1993).
5. This is a point I have previously made; see Whitehead (1983). A somewhat extended version appears in Larkin (1988).
6. Patrick J. Buchanan, Director of Communications in the Reagan White House, defended Oliver North in June 1987 by charging that 'the Liberal wing of the Democratic Party has made itself the silent partner – the indispensable ally – of revolutionary communism in the Third World', *Newsweek*, 13 July 1987.
7. For anti-administration logic carried to its ridiculous extreme, see Chomsky (1985). The main targets here are all those who are even slightly less intransigent than Chomsky himself, however uncomfortable with US policy they may be.
8. At Oliver North's trial in 1989, the US Government submitted various 'admitted facts' which shed some light on the risks being contemplated. For example, it was admitted that in late August 1986 a Noriega representative proposed to assassinate the Sandinista leadership, in exchange for a promise to clean up Noriega's image and lift the US ban on arms sales. It was also admitted that although declining this offer on legal grounds, in mid-September North met with Noriega in London and elicited an alternative offer of immediate Panamanian actions against an oil refinery, an airport, and the Puerto Sandino off-load facility. It is not known what would have happened if the Sandinistas had not shot down a C-123 on 5 October, and thus triggered the first stage of the Irangate scandal. My own opinion at the time was that US policy was leading up to a confrontation that would probably trigger a US military intervention in Nicaragua (I gave a lecture at a Warwick University Workshop on US policy in Central America on 1 November 1986 which was published; see Whitehead, 1987). However, the investigations concerning Irangate have never pursued this theme.
9. Curiously, the best study of Irangate (Draper, 1991) inexplicably ignores this election result, and is written as if the scandal would have taken the same course even had the Republicans retained their control of the Senate, an assumption I would strongly question.

10. Di Palma and Whitehead (1986) described the minimum requirements for a political settlement, and identified the principal impediments up to mid-1985, emphasising in particular the re-elected Reagan administration's determination to make no concessions. This key obstacle to a negotiated settlement was dissolved in the course of 1987, as I have recorded in Whitehead (1988).

11. In May 1989 Bush's Secretary of State, James Baker, met with Gorbachev's Foreign Minister Edvard Shevardnadze in Moscow to negotiate bi-polar cooperation for the settlement of outstanding regional conflicts. Before leaving Washington, Baker took great care to secure bipartisan agreement from Congress on his Nicaraguan policy, without which his Moscow negotiations would have been in vain.

12. 'We can contrast the nature of the Salvadorean negotiations of 1990-91 – when an essentially domestic treaty was brokered internationally and depended heavily upon Washington's conditional withdrawal of funds – with those for Nicaragua in 1987-9 which took the form of an international treaty that possessed important domestic implications, required direct internal agreements for its success, and was forced through with great difficulty, since Washington (not a signatory) maintained funds to the rebels in open defiance of one of the treaty's core clauses' (Dunkerley, 1993, p.36).

13. On the very day of this vote another event occurred of great relevance to the theme of this section (although not a Central American event as such). President Bush vetoed the Moynihan amendment, which would have prohibited 'soliciting or diverting funds to carry out activities for which US assistance is prohibited'. In other words, Bush vetoed a law passed by both Houses which aimed to preclude any future Irangate-style operations to circumvent congressional power of the purse constraints on executive control of US foreign policy. This highlights the immense importance of Central America as a domestic constitutional issue.

14. Doggett (1994) reconstructs all that has been unearthed so far, using the Freedom of Information Act and the documents declassified up to November 1993 under pressure from Congressman Jim Mokely.

15. Interview with US ambassador Peter Romero, Quito, Ecuador, 3 June 1994. Between 1989 and 1993 Romero was at the State Department, and was closely involved in both the Nicaraguan and the Salvadorean peace negotiations.

16. The Contadora initiative for a peaceful settlement in Central America was initiated in January 1983, the Contadora Group consisting of the foreign ministers of Colombia, Mexico, Panama and Venezuela. A list of proposals for a regional peace settlement – including control of arms supplies; removal of foreign advisers; creation of demilitarised zones; prohibition of activities destabilising neighbouring countries; and prohibition of any political or military intervention in another state – was formally presented to Central America's foreign ministers in June 1984. However, sustained opposition by the US government to the Contadora proposals and differences among the Central American governments ensured their impact was limited. See Bagley, Alvarez and Hagedorn (1985).

17. For example, the US aid appropriation for El Salvador fell from $230 million in fiscal year 1993 to only $94 million in fiscal year 1994, and then fell even further to only $69 million in fiscal year 1995. The 1995 appropriation for Nicaragua fell to $57 million, and the disbursement may well prove far less than that. For Guatemala the 1995 figure is only $43 million, and for Honduras only $39 million.

18. Following the guidelines proposed by the Sanford Commission, and in keeping with Washington's new enthusiasm for promotion of democracy, US aid to the region is now formally subject to a form of democratic conditionality which is supposed to be monitored by tripartite commissions in each country. Despite the establishment of these bodies, I have seen no evidence that they can influence aid disbursements either positively or negatively. See Sanford Commission (1989).

19. The main respect in which Esquipulas went beyond Contadora was in its stress on the necessity for internally democratic processes.

20. I have sketched a country-by-country assessment of European motivations in Whitehead (1992). My overall interpretation was that the absence of significant direct European entanglements or even major interests in the region was precisely what made Central America such an attractive arena for a Community initiative. These were small, poor economies where a modest amount of economic aid might produce a large effect and, notwithstanding Reaganite rhetoric, the crisis was manageable (not something that could be said of most Third World problems). It had been artificially inflamed, and so would respond well to a modest dose of conciliation. A low cost but high visibility initiative would do much to enhance the credibility of the European integration process. As a 'disinterested' promoter of pacification and reconciliation, the European Commission would gain status *vis-à-vis* individual European chanceries, any of which could achieve relatively little acting 'in isolation' (p. 4). However, the San José process was the product of a very specific and time-limited conjuncture. Following the end of the Cold War and the disintegration of the former Soviet bloc, most of the factors which in the early 1980s had prompted an uncharacteristic European concern over the affairs of Central America have ceased to operate.

21. See IRELA (1994a).

22. See in particular Liisa North's chapter in Klepak (1993).

23. *Ibid.* p. 174. MacFarlane and Weiss have attempted to theorise from this case, suggesting that regional organisations are not well-suited to peace-keeping; MacFarlane and Weiss (1994).

24. For a generally well-balanced account see Child (1992).

25. For an interesting attempt to specify the key elements of contrast between UN pacification efforts in Cambodia and El Salvador see Munck and Kumar (1995).

26. The pre-history of the Esquipulas peace plan remains to be written. In addition to the input from the EC and Contadora, President Vinicio Cerezo of Guatemala also took the lead for a while. On the Costa Rican side, the narrow victory of Oscar Arias in the 1986 presidential election certainly played a part. What is less well-recognised is the role of the Soviet ambassador to Costa Rica,

Yuri Pavlov, whose recently published memoir (Pavlov, 1994) says less than it might about his role, from the earliest days of the Gorbachev period, in pioneering the new Soviet strategy for resolving regional conflicts. The role of the Chilean Christian Democrat adviser, John Biehl, in alerting Costa Rican leaders to the new possibilities arising from the change of leadership in Moscow, also deserves more attention than it has received so far.

CHAPTER 8

UN VERIFICATION:
ACHIEVEMENTS, LIMITATIONS AND PROSPECTS

Stephen Baranyi

The conclusion in January 1994 of a Framework Accord for peace negotiations between the Guatemalan government of Ramiro de León Carpio and the URNG (Unidad Revolucionaria Nacional Guatemalteca) in January 1994 raised hopes that the 'firm and lasting peace' envisaged in the Esquipulas II Agreement seven years previously might yet become a reality in this, the most intractable of Central American conflicts. Expectations exist that verification of the Human Rights Accord (signed March 1994) by the United Nations (UN) might end gross violations of human rights, that UN leverage will help the parties to the negotiations reach further agreements, and that through its presence the UN might promote reforms to the armed forces and other institutions, as has been the case in El Salvador.

However, an element of caution is in order. Guatemala's recent history is one of alternation between failed reformist projects and reactionary responses. The recent failures of the Cerezo (1986-1990) and Serrano (1990-1993) governments to broaden their democratic projects beyond limited political liberalisation suggest that with or without UN involvement, the reforms necessary for lasting peace will be most difficult to implement in Guatemala.[1]

A key factor underpinning this historical pattern is the balance of power between those who have tended to oppose profound democratic reforms (a reactionary coalition led by sectors of the armed forces, the business sector, as well as traditional political party elites) and those who have tended to push for structural changes (a reformist coalition led by the URNG, popular and indigenous sectors, certain intellectuals and parts of the Catholic church). This balance of power remains tilted against the reformist coalition, particularly on the military plane, where the 1,000-odd fighters of the URNG have long been strategically outweighed by the 44,000-strong armed forces.

The contemporary record of the United Nations also suggests the need for a cautious assessment. At the beginning of the 1990s, many believed

247

that the end of the Cold War would allow the UN to attain the grand objectives laid out in its Charter or at least provide effective peace services in various war-torn societies across the globe.[2] Since then, the controversy surrounding Operation Desert Storm in the Persian Gulf, the uneven record of UNTAC (United Nations Task Force for Cambodia) in Cambodia, and the fiascos of UN missions in Angola, Rwanda, Somalia, the Western Sahara and the former Yugoslavia, have challenged us to reevaluate our thinking on the new generation of UN 'peace' missions.[3] Yet in order to understand and enhance the prospects for peace in Guatemala, we must go beyond recognition of recent UN failures to identify factors which may improve the chances of success in the future.

One way of pinpointing these factors would be to review the interpretations of UN peace operations offered or suggested by different strands of social theory. This deductive approach could provide useful insights, but would perhaps be out of place in a volume of this nature.[4] This chapter therefore adopts the inductive route by looking at recent UN experiences in two cases which are broadly comparable to Guatemala, namely Nicaragua and El Salvador, explaining the UN's record in each case, and teasing out their implications for MINUGUA, the Verification Mission in Guatemala.

Before examining the UN's role in Nicaragua from 1989 to 1990 in particular, it may be useful to return to the mid-1980s and recall that one of the cornerstones of the Esquipulas II Agreement, signed by the five Central American heads of state in August 1987, was the principle of 'simultaneity'. By enshrining this norm, the five signatory governments committed themselves to implementing, according to the same schedule, measures leading to war termination, democratisation, development and regional integration. The three governments involved in armed confrontations with internal forces (El Salvador, Guatemala and Nicaragua) were supposed to begin processes of dialogue with the insurgents, leading to their reincorporation into society in exchange for reforms outlined in general terms in Esquipulas II, but subject to further negotiation by the belligerents. These processes were supposed to be facilitated and monitored by the International Commission for Verification and Follow-up (CIVS), on which the five Central American governments, the members of the Contadora Group, the UN and the OAS (Organisation of American States) each had a seat.[5]

Reality, of course, unfolded quite differently; instead of occurring simultaneously, the management of the armed conflicts took place sequentially, beginning with Nicaragua from 1989 to 1990, then El Salvador from 1990 to 1994, and Guatemala from 1994 onwards. This sequence reflected the fact that by the turn of the decade, the Nicaraguan conflict was quite 'ripe for resolution', the war in El Salvador had just escalated, while the protracted conflict in Guatemala showed no signs of abating.[6] It also reflected the priority accorded by the Central American governments and by the Bush Administration to ridding themselves of the 'contra problem', then in resolving the Salvadorean war, which had flared up with the FMLN's offensives in 1989 and 1990. Finally, this sequence probably reflected the pragmatic calculation, on the part of senior UN officials, that instead of risking the UN's reputation by tackling all three conflicts at once, it would be wiser to take them on one by one, beginning with the easiest and moving towards the most intractable, while building up the necessary infrastructure, knowledge and credibility along the way. With the benefit of hindsight, we can now assess how the UN actually fared first in Nicaragua and then in El Salvador, analysing the factors which explain its mixed record in both cases. Finally, we can examine what has been learned along the way, and how these lessons might be effectively applied in Guatemala.

ONUCA, ONUVEN and CIAV in Nicaragua

When the CIVS was disbanded by the Central American presidents in January 1988, after tabling a report highly critical of most states' compliance with the Esquipulas II Accord, the issue of verification was left unresolved. Agreement eventually converged around a UN role in the verification of the limited security commitments in Esquipulas II, but the modalities of such a mechanism remained unclear. In that Accord, the signatories had committed themselves to: (i) prevent the use of their own territory by organisations seeking to destabilise any of the governments in Central America and (ii) to refuse to provide them with, or allow them to receive, military and logistical support. In 1988 the Hondurans and the Nicaraguans each proposed that a UN verification mission with enforcement capabilities be mandated to prevent, by force if necessary, any obstruction of the Accord by the Nicaraguan Resistance based in southern Honduras.[7]

In January 1989 the UN Secretary-General responded in no uncertain terms that the Honduran and Nicaraguan proposals ran against the principles of UN peace-keeping and that political agreements between the belligerents (and not just the five states which had signed the 1987 Accord) would have to precede any UN attempt to verify the security commitments.

This debate evolved until agreement was reached on a three-pronged solution: one UN mission would monitor elections in Nicaragua; another UN mission would monitor compliance with the security provisions of Esquipulas II; and a joint UN-OAS mission would promote the voluntary demobilisation of the Nicaraguan Resistance. These agreements led, respectively, to the creation of the UN Observer Mission to Verify the Electoral Process in Nicaragua (ONUVEN), the UN Observer Group in Central America (ONUCA) and the Commission for International Verification and Support (CIAV).

ONUCA was established by Security Council Resolution 637 of 7 November 1989, which mandated it to verify that the security provisions of Esquipulas II were not being violated by any of the five Central American states.[8] The first ONUCA contingent was sent to the region in early December to lay the groundwork for the deployment of 260 Military Observers, an Air Wing, a Naval Unit, a Medical Team and administrative staff. Headquarters were established in Tegucigalpa, Honduras, while Liaison Offices, Verification Centres and Operational Posts were set up in each country. By the new year patrols were becoming acquainted with the physical environment and meeting with officials at national and local levels.

Meanwhile ONUVEN had deployed to Nicaragua in August 1989 to facilitate and monitor the processes leading up to the national elections, as well as the elections themselves in February 1990. At the same time, CIAV had been in the region since September 1989 trying to persuade the contras to demobilise voluntarily. CIAV was endowed with little power and few resources until after the elections, when it was put in charge of the civilian aspects of contra demobilisation. As such, ONUVEN and CIAV were the peace-building components of the joint UN-OAS coordinated approach to conflict management in Nicaragua.

One month after the February election, the Security Council authorised the expansion of ONUCA's mandate and strength to allow it to take delivery of the weapons and military equipment voluntarily handed over by the contras. An 800-man light-infantry battalion was provided by Venezuela to offer some security for what became known as 'Operation Home Run', and by mid-April ONUCA was able to conduct its initial demobilisation operations in Honduras. In April 1990 the so-called Definitive and Effective Ceasefire Agreement was signed in Managua, and the Security Council authorised a further expansion of ONUCA's mandate to allow it to monitor the separation of forces, the concentration of contra forces inside Nicaragua and their voluntary demobilisation afterward.

ONUCA deployed to designated Security Zones as Sandinista Army units withdrew and as the contra began relocating its combatants. Ceasefire talks had gone through several cycles, implementation was postponed by serious crises, and so it was not until after the Managua Protocol on Disarmament was signed on 30 May that real demobilisation began, after the government had presented concrete plans for reductions in troop size to the armed forces (Ejército Popular Sandinista – EPS) and the distribution of lands to former contra combatants. Yet by the end of ONUCA's expanded mandate period on 29 June 1990, over 20,000 contra fighters had been demobilised, over 16,000 small arms had been handed over, and over 400 crew-served weapons had been turned over to ONUCA for demolition.

If we consider the large number of combatants demobilised voluntarily in such a short period by such a small mission, Home Run was an impressive success despite the crises and delays.[9] Logistically, the knowledge acquired and the infrastructure established by ONUCA before Home Run proved useful for planning the Operation, concentrating ONUCA personnel in Nicaragua and Honduras, providing order inside Security Zones and destroying weapons. Politically, ONUCA was compelled – by the relative military weakness of its forces compared to contra and Sandinista Army units and by the traditional norms of peace-keeping – to secure and maintain the consent of both sides for all parts of the operation. This proved difficult in the case of the contras, since ONUCA's initial mandate had been explicitly state-centred and since CIAV officials, in a well-intended attempt to induce contra demobilisation before the elections, had alienated contra leaders and jeopardised the UN's pretence of impartiality. Yet ONUCA managed to rebuild confidence in the UN by shuttling contra commanders to and from ceasefire talks and by ensuring that a solid juridical basis for its role in contra demobilisation came out of those bilateral negotiations. The timely and objective investigations which ONUCA carried out during the demobilisation crisis that occurred in May 1990 consolidated confidence in its effective impartiality.

Beyond this, peace-keeping was facilitated by ONUVEN's contributions to a transparent election in Nicaragua, by the good offices of the UN Secretary-General's Personal Representative, and by CIAV's initial handling of the social and economic aspects of contra reintegration into Nicaraguan society. Despite these efforts, however, ONUCA and CIAV left loose ends which threatened to unravel into a major crisis by 1991. ONUCA did not manage to destroy more than a fraction of the weapons held by the contras. Some of these turned up in the hands of the *re-contras*, *re-compas* and *revueltos*[10] who took up arms again to protest failures by the government and CIAV-OAS to provide land, housing, security or other goods promised to demobilised combatants. In the early 1990s, these problems threatened to undermine the peace forged by peace-keepers and peace-makers. By 1994 a degree of macro-economic and political stability had been established, but the country remained plagued by violence and serious social conflict.[11]

The inadequacy of peace-building measures partly reflects the fact that provisions for land, housing and other goods which could enable demobilised combatants to meet their basic needs were negotiated hastily from February to May 1990, and that little attention was paid to the reform of broader state institutions (the army, the judiciary, the police, etc.) that would greatly affect the lives of former combatants. In turn, this lack of specificity in the Nicaraguan peace accords stemmed from the Sandinistas' enduring power and their ability to impose their view that these institutions had already been reformed by the Revolution and that subsequent changes would be negotiated with the newly-elected Chamorro government, not with US-funded 'mercenaries'.

The difficulties encountered from mid-1990 onwards also reflect the coordination problems which arose between ONUCA and CIAV-OAS, rooted in the differences between the UN and the OAS. These tensions were heightened by the inadequacies of the socio-economic peace-building efforts undertaken by CIAV-OAS, but it seems inaccurate to blame the OAS alone for these problems. The economic chaos which Nicaragua found itself in by 1990 would have made it difficult for any international mission to resolve existing conflicts; moreover, some of the structural adjustment measures applied by the Chamorro government, on the advice of the IMF (International Monetary Fund) and the World Bank, may have actually aggravated existing social tensions. As such, the ONUCA-ONUVEN-CIAV complex managed, but did not resolve, the conflict in Nicaragua. Yet even in the improbable case that the Security Council had authorised ONUCA forcibly to demobilise the contras, it is unlikely that such an enforcement mission would have fared better than ONUCA did under the constraints of consent, non-use of force and impartiality. Indeed, it appears that the initial success of Home Run was largely due to the strict respect for these norms shown in the practices and eventual (if not initial) mandating of ONUCA. In addition to the exhaustion of the warring parties on the ground, ONUCA's successes were also rooted in ongoing and impartial peace-making activities by the UN and other mediators, in the political peace-building accomplishments of ONUVEN and the socio-economic peace-building efforts of CIAV. That the latter did not eliminate the roots of armed conflict does not point to the failure of peace-keeping. Rather, it highlights the difficulties of resolving deep conflicts through short-term peace-building measures, particularly in the context of harsh stabilisation and structural adjustment policies.

ONUSAL in El Salvador

In May 1991 the Security Council authorised the establishment of ONUSAL as an 'integrated peacekeeping operation'. Although it was mandated only to supervise compliance with the Human Rights Accord signed in July 1990, the mission, initially staffed by 135 personnel, was authorised to observe all peace agreements that might be reached by the government and the FMLN in the future.[12] Years earlier, during the escalation of violence generated by the FMLN's offensives, there were several suggestions that UN forces might be used to enforce peace in El Salvador: in December 1989 the five Central American presidents called for the demobilisation of the FMLN by CIAV, and one year later the Chief Military Observer of ONUCA, General Augustín Quezada Gómez, suggested that his operation could be deployed to El Salvador even before a ceasefire, a possibility which the presidents endorsed at their December 1990 summit. Yet these options were rejected by the UN Secretary-General, who stood by the classical peace-keeping parameters spelled out to the Central Americans in January 1989. The FMLN also rejected the broadening of ONUCA's mandate in El Salvador and insisted on the creation of a new UN mission with *integrated* verification and peace-building functions, headed by a civilian official and not by a military officer.

Against this backdrop, the UN-mediated talks proceeded slowly, punctuated by US congressional pressure on the government of El Salvador to negotiate in good faith, the signing of the Human Rights Accord in July 1990, the request by both parties that the UN deploy a mission to supervise compliance with that Accord before a ceasefire, escalated fighting in November 1990, further pressure by Washington for compromise and intense peace-making efforts by UN officials. By February 1991 the UN had established a small Preparatory Office to prepare the ground for deploying an observer mission, and negotiations had resumed in Mexico. Three months later the Secretary-General requested Security Council approval for early deployment, thus facilitating another breakthrough in the talks and the signing of the Mexico Accords in late April 1991. Because of renewed fighting in El Salvador and delays in New York, ONUSAL only began operating in July 1991, but by the fall its activities were contributing to wider peace-making efforts. During earlier rounds, the

Preparatory Office had already cooperated with ONUCA in transporting FMLN leaders out of the country for the talks, thereby building FMLN confidence in the impartial capacities of UN peace-keepers. These activities continued while the verification activities of the ONUSAL Human Rights Division deepened confidence in the UN and in the possibilities for peace: although ONUSAL's August 1991 report was more critical of the state's acts of repression and inability to protect human rights, it also took official views into account and criticised FMLN violations. ONUSAL's November 1991 report stressed that despite recent progress, only an end to the war would open the door to fundamental improvements in the country's human rights situation.

Together with the pressure from certain elements in the USA and from the 'Friends of the Secretary-General' (Colombia, Mexico, Spain and Venezuela), UN activities in the field and at the negotiating table contributed to more breakthroughs: in September 1991 the New York Agreement was signed, on 31 December the parties reached a ceasefire agreement and in December 1991 they signed the Chapultepec Accord, officially putting an end to the civil war.

In February 1992, ONUSAL was expanded with Security Council authorisation to include a Military Division with 375 personnel and a Police Division with about 300 members. The Military Division co-ordinated and supervised the ceasefire and the relocation of over 9,000 FMLN and 63,000 armed forces personnel to agreed-upon points and zones, but problems soon arose. The main difficulty was that the FMLN refused completely to relocate its forces inside the zones, primarily because the government had changed the name of two security forces, the National Guard and the Treasury Police, instead of disbanding them as the accords had suggested – but had not spelled out in detail. The FMLN also complained that the government had failed to begin transferring land to demobilised combatants and other potential recipients as had been agreed.

The Under-Secretary General for Special Political Affairs, Marrack Goulding, rushed to El Salvador to defuse the crisis, yet it was not until late June that all armed forces and FMLN units had been completely relocated to designated points. By July the FMLN had acceded to the demobilisation of 20 per cent of its forces, while the government moved ahead on measures ranging from the *de facto* dissolution of the National Guard and Treasury Police to the establishment of foundations for the Policía Nacional Civil (PNC). In September 1992 the Ad Hoc Commission recommended that over 100 senior Armed Forces officers be transferred or discharged for human rights abuses or other acts of gross misconduct. By the end of September another 20 per cent of FMLN forces had been demobilised and the government had moved ahead on the dismantling of Civil Defence Units and of two rapid deployment infantry battalions (BIRIs). One month later another 20 per cent of FMLN forces was demobilised while further progress was made on the creation of the PNC and the implementation of the Ad Hoc Commission's recommendations.

By 17 December 1992, the last 40 per cent of FMLN combatants had been demobilised and the Frente was legalised as a political party. By the end of the year most FMLN weapons had been destroyed by ONUSAL, another BIRI had been dismantled, the first PNC class was being trained in the new National Academy for Public Security and the government had discharged or transferred some of the officers identified as human rights violators by the Ad Hoc Commission.[13]

Despite the extreme tensions and immense difficulties associated with these processes, no serious breaches of the ceasefire occurred during 1992. Still, UN mediation was required on numerous issues, and senior officials from the Secretariat (backed by the USA and the Friends of the Secretary-General) had to intervene directly in at least five instances. Together with ONUSAL officials, they kept the process on track by upholding the spirit of the accords while showing impartiality towards the antagonists and flexibility on the timing of implementation. Their ability to promote peace-building processes such as the creation of the PNC, reforms to the Armed Forces and the management of land transfer disputes greatly facilitated progress in the demobilisation phase. As a result, the Military Division was gradually reduced to 103 observers by February 1993 and 22 observers by May 1994.

Of course, major problems lingered. As in Nicaragua, both sides retained weapons: the FMLN (Frente Farabundo Martí para la Liberación Nacional) hid light arms in secret caches while the armed forces left arms with former Civil Defence Unit members – in addition to preserving the substantial military assets to which they were entitled under the accords. Many former members of disbanded security forces joined the PNC or the armed forces. By May 1994, the dissolution of the National Intelligence Directorate – historically the central agency of the surveillance and repression system – and its effective replacement by the State Intelligence Organ had still not been adequately verified.[14]

Although human rights violations decreased after the ceasefire, a resurgence of death squad style killings in mid-1993 prompted the government to accept the establishment of a Joint Group for the Investigation of Politically-Motivated Illegal Armed Groups, as originally proposed by the Truth Commission. In July 1994 the Joint Group concluded that illegal armed groups continued to exist and carry out politically-motivated killings; that some of these groups might be linked to agents of the state as well as to organised crime; and that continued strengthening of the PNC and deeper reforms of the judiciary were necessary to follow through with the systematic investigations, prosecutions and punishment required to put an end to the use of violence for political ends.[15]

The Human Rights Division of ONUSAL has also drawn attention to the deficiencies of the judicial system due to excessive centralisation of power, inadequate resources, partisanship and corruption. The judiciary is probably the institution which has most effectively resisted reforms under the peace process. Still, the selection of a new Supreme Court of Justice by the Legislative Assembly in July 1994, however messy and protracted, has kept the door open for more significant judicial reforms in the future.[16]

Progress on socio-economic issues has also been uneven. In February 1993 the tripartite Forum for Social and Economic Coordination agreed to a number of steps which could bring the country's labour practices into line with international labour standards. Yet in April 1994, the outgoing Legislative Assembly hastily passed a series of Labour Code reforms which ignored many of these prior agreements; since then, the new government of President Calderón Sol has signalled its desire to press ahead with these more limited reforms, which include replacing the Forum with a much weaker Superior Labour Council.[17] Similarly, although new timetables for land transfers were agreed to in October 1992 and May 1994, by mid-1994 only 24 per cent of potential recipients had received the land titles promised to them under the accords.[18]

It may still be too early to draw definitive conclusions about the transition in El Salvador or about UN contributions to its elemental processes, but it is possible to highlight certain patterns. Any objective analysis should recognise that the changes implemented so far, despite their depth, do not amount to the 'negotiated revolution' heralded by the Secretary-General in 1992. No revolutionary shift in domestic power relations has yet been accomplished: land and capital remain concentrated in the hands of traditional economic elites, the vast majority of the population remains economically marginalised, the armed forces' capabilities and autonomy remain substantial, and human rights violators remain effectively immune to prosecution and punishment for their crimes. Many of the promises made to ex-combatants (on both sides) have not yet been fulfilled and the country remains awash with arms. In this context, there is a possibility that after ONUSAL leaves the country and international attention shifts elsewhere, unfulfilled provisions of the peace accords could lead to a resurgence of violence akin to that experienced since 1990 in Nicaragua.[19]

The liberal democratic institutions enhanced under the peace accords do, however, represent a vast improvement over past authoritarian practices: they allow popular sectors to organise themselves freely, and the political opposition to express its ideas in the media and the Legislative Assembly as well as to influence key decisions such as the selection of the new Supreme Court; and they allow the Attorney General's Office, the National Civilian Police and the office of the Human Rights Ombudsman to contest the practices of impunity. By safeguarding a space for popular sectors and opposition parties to keep issues such as judicial and land reform on the policy agenda, this liberal democratic framework also diminishes the likelihood that the transition which has occurred to date might be reversed.

The contribution of ONUSAL to this incomplete transition highlights both the importance and the limitations of UN 'active verification', a concept apparently coined by ONUSAL officials to describe what they have attempted in El Salvador.[20] In principle, active verification goes beyond the monitoring of given accords by facilitating their implementation through ongoing peace-making as well as through the identification and active promotion of specific measures within the spirit of the accords. While the coordinated efforts of ONUCA, ONUVEN and CIAV included peace-making and facilitation, integrated missions such as ONUSAL should theoretically be better placed to deliver a more active and coherent package of international conflict management services.

The Salvadorean case partly confirms this assumption. The initial record of ONUSAL shows how the deployment of a carefully-mandated, structured, and staffed human rights verification mission can facilitate the conclusion of a complex set of peace accords in a country deeply divided by civil war. The expanded mission's record from 1992 to 1994 shows that the integrated use of military, police, human rights and socio-economic verification with continued mediation and the active promotion of reforms can keep a fragile process on track and lead to major institutional changes and attitudinal shifts. ONUSAL's accomplishments during this period also show how the adherence to the classical norms of UN peace-keeping – namely maintaining UN impartiality and the consent of the signatories, and shunning the use of force as a way of protecting UN functionaries or of ensuring compliance with given agreements – can produce positive results in certain contexts.[21]

Yet ONUSAL's experience shows how even an integrated, active verification mission which attempts to adhere to the classical norms of UN peace-keeping can be limited in its impact. Four limitations are worth noting in this respect. First, the UN's rush to have the 'final' peace accords signed by the end of 1991 (which was the end of UN Secretary-General Pérez de Cuéllar's term) was useful in pressing the parties to make necessary compromises, but resulted in areas like judicial reform and the economic elements of national reconstruction being left quite vaguely defined. Second, by upholding the provisions for the FMLN's demobilisation by the end of 1992, the UN effectively facilitated the diminution of the FMLN's leverage *vis-à-vis* the government and the Armed Forces. This conjunctural factor exacerbated the UN's *de facto* deference to the government which was, after all, ONUSAL's host as the duly constituted authority of a sovereign state.[22]

Third, at several critical junctures (for example when it criticised but subsequently accepted the March 1993 amnesty and when it endorsed the first round of the 1994 elections), ONUSAL seems to have prioritised the objective of keeping the process on track over the objective of denouncing non-compliance with the accords. To be fair, it must be noted that the UN's priorities were influenced, at least in these instances, by the fact that both parties accorded higher priority to keeping the process on track than to fighting impunity or electoral irregularities retroactively.

A fourth fundamental limitation is the tension between short-term peace-building measures like the Land Transfer Programme and the wider market-oriented macro-economic policy context. Senior officials in the UN Secretariat have acknowledged that:

'Without stabilization, the implementation of the peace agreements could well be ephemeral. Strict adherence to the economic programme, on the other hand, might well jeopardize the peace process. There is therefore a crying need for these two processes to be harmonised so that they support rather than work against each other.'[23]

The difficulty, as these officials and others have noted, is that in practice some of the structural adjustment measures implemented (on the advice of international financial institutions) by the two administrations of ARENA (Alianza Republicana Nacionalista) – Cristiani (1989-94) and Calderón Sol (1994-) – have tended to undermine, not complement, peace-building measures promoted by ONUSAL. The government's commitment to fiscal discipline, for example, has meant that important peace-building programmes have come to depend on external financing and have, as a result, been jeopardised by under-funding. The most worrying cases in point are the programmes for the reintegration of ex-combatants into society: failure to compensate ex-combatants from both sides provoked several occupations of the Legislative Assembly and serious clashes with security forces in 1993 and 1994. As the FMLN noted in August 1994, failure to assign sufficient resources to these programmes 'could become a source for greater frustration and social instability, as occurred in Nicaragua'. This concern has also been recently expressed, albeit in more nuanced terms, by the UN Secretary-General.[24] In a broader context, the need for policy measures additional to the implementation of the peace accords would appear vital. Only through a more equal distribution of land assets and adequate provision of technical assistance and credit can problems such as rural poverty, falling rural wages and accelerated environmental degradation be tackled. Further land reform therefore remains critical to long term economic growth and stability in El Salvador.

MINUGUA in Guatemala

On 19 September 1994, after a lengthy tug-of-war between the UN Security Council and General Assembly over which body should mandate the field mission for Guatemala, the General Assembly passed Resolution A/48/267. This confirmed the provisions of the March 1994 Comprehensive Agreement on Human Rights and the recommendation by the UN Secretary-General that the primary task of the UN Verification Mission in Guatemala (MINUGUA) should be to verify and facilitate compliance with the Agreement.[25] The Verification Mission's mandate is not retroactive: its responsibility is limited to verifying that the Human Rights Agreement is respected from the time of MINUGUA's deployment on 20 September 1994 onwards. According to the terms of the Human Rights Agreement, the Mission is supposed to focus on civil rights (such as the rights to life, security and physical integrity of the person, due process and individual liberties) as well as universally recognised political rights. In so doing, MINUGUA is supposed to pay special attention to the situation of the 'most vulnerable groups in society' and to sectors such as refugees and internally displaced persons which have been directly affected by the war. It is recognised that culturally appropriate guidelines will have to be established for the Mission's work with indigenous persons and communities, given the predominantly indigenous character of Guatemalan society, and of these vulnerable sectors in particular.

Another fundamental characteristic of MINUGUA is that it is mandated to strengthen national institutions which are already working (or should be working) to promote respect for human rights. The primary targets of this institution-building function are governmental agencies including the National Police, the judiciary, the Public Prosecutor's Office, as well as the semi-autonomous Human Rights Ombudsman's Office (PDHG) and non-governmental organisations. MINUGUA will be staffed by almost 300 international personnel in its initial phase, that is: 220 civilian personnel in charge of human rights verification, technical assistance, public information and administration; 60 civilian police observers; and ten military liaison officers. The Office of the Director, Leonardo Franco, is based in Guatemala City. Franco is backed by a Deputy Director and by principal advisors on human rights, legal, military and police affairs as well as indigenous peoples' issues. Eight regional offices are being established: one each in the capital, Cobán, Huehue-tenango, Quetzaltenango, Santa Cruz del Quiché, Santa Elena, Sololá, and Zacapa; five sub-regional offices will also be established. These offices will be staffed by teams which will include a regional coordinator, a legal officer, three human rights observers, three police observers and a military liaison officer.

The last aspect of the Human Rights Mission which is worth noting is that, as suggested in the 10 January 1994 Framework Accord, MIN-UGUA's mandate and structure will be broadened to include the verification of additional accords once a final peace agreement is signed.[26] Like the development of ONUSAL in El Salvador, it is expected that the signing of further accords on matters such as police and military reform, the demobilisation of combatant forces, land transfers, the identity and rights of indigenous peoples, and particularly the signing of a Final Accord for a Firm and Lasting Peace, will lead to the addition of new divisions and units in MINUGUA to oversee and facilitate compliance with those agreements.

There is little doubt that the decision to deploy MINUGUA represents a major breakthrough in the Guatemalan peace process, equal in importance to the signing of the January and March 1994 accords as well as to the establishment and functioning of the Assembly of Civil Society (ASC) since then. Yet if MINUGUA is to fulfil its human rights promotion objectives, facilitate the peace talks and help attain the ultimate goal of a firm and lasting peace, there are four major challenges which will have to be faced head on.

The first challenge will be to help close the gap between accords signed at the negotiating table and compliance with those same accords. Although the Human Rights Agreement was meant to go into effect immediately after it was signed, in July the Human Rights Office of the Archbishop of Guatemala reported 787 violations of the rights to life, liberty and physical integrity of the person, in the first six months of 1994. In September, the Human Rights Ombudsman's Office reported that 325 violations of civil rights had occurred since the signing of the Human Rights Agreement. The URNG (Unidad Revolucionaria Nacional Guatemalteca) is certainly responsible for some of these violations, yet these other sources concur that the state, especially the security forces, is directly or indirectly responsible for the majority of civil rights violations.[27] Closing this gap will only be possible if MINUGUA rigorously carries out its verification activities and actively promotes institutional strengthening to prevent grave human rights abuses and impunity in the future. The Salvadorean experience suggests that maintaining the advisory services of the UN Independent Expert as a complement to a field mission can bolster independent and rigorous human rights verification.

The gap between the peace accords and the reality on the ground is one of the factors which led to the *de facto* suspension of the talks in July and August 1994. Indeed, despite the calendar agreed to in March 1994 as well as efforts by the UN Moderator and the government to keep the talks going, the URNG refused to return to the table until there was a clear demonstration of the government's will to comply with the Human Rights Accord and the international community's willingness to verify compliance *in situ*. Almost immediately after the General Assembly passed Resolution 48/267, UN Moderator Jean Arnault announced that talks would soon resume.

Another major factor holding up the talks was the dissatisfaction on the part of both the URNG and the ASC, with the agreements signed in Oslo in June 1994. On 17 June, the parties signed the Accord for the Resettlement of Populations uprooted by the Armed Conflict, which sets out a framework for the resettlement and reintegration into society of those who fled the country or were internally displaced as a result of the war.[28] The agreement which sparked the most controversy, however, was the Accord on the Establishment of the Commission to Clarify Human Rights Violations and Acts of Violence that have Caused the Guatemalan Population to Suffer, signed in Oslo on June 23. This agreement provides for the establishment of a three-person body under the aegis of the UN, after the signing of the Final Accord, to investigate violations which have occurred in the 34-year armed conflict. Although it reaffirms the 'right of the Guatemalan people to know the full truth' set out in the March Accord, it only provides for the identification of institutions responsible for violations and, as such, provides a weak basis for the prosecution of individuals.[29]

The 23 June Accord was seen as weak in comparison to both the proposal submitted by the ASC before the talks and the agreement which formed the basis for the Truth Commission in El Salvador. The weaknesses in the Accord on the Clarification Commission and delays in the deployment of the UN verification mission provoked an outcry from human rights organisations and other sectors of civil society. Ten thousand people marched in Guatemala City during the first week of July to demand the immediate deployment of the UN mission. Meanwhile Monsignor Rodolfo Quezada Toruño, President of the ASC and former Conciliator of the peace talks, criticised the international community for being more interested in keeping the talks going than in promoting meaningful agreements.[30]

These responses highlight a second challenge the UN and the broader international community will have to face in order to reach their objectives in Guatemala, namely the challenge of getting robust agreements, not just any agreements, out of the peace talks. Although it is ultimately up to the parties to decide when to sign agreements, pressures from the international community – particularly from the UN and the Group of Friends of the Peace Process, which includes the USA, Colombia, Mexico, Venezuela, Norway and Spain – greatly affect their incentives to reach accords, as shown by the impact of international pressure during the Oslo round. The Salvadorean experience also reminds us that a delicate balance must be maintained between maintaining pressure on the parties to negotiate in good faith and forcing them to sign accords which could undermine the cause of peace in the long run.

The third major challenge facing MINUGUA and the international community is to apply the lessons of ONUCA and ONUSAL to ensure that successful verification and institution-building are not undermined by inadequate reinsertion and reconstruction measures or by a broader macroeconomic policy framework which places too much emphasis on market-oriented reforms. The absence of clauses on economic and social rights in the Human Rights Accord and in the initial mandate of MINUGUA represent missed opportunities to strengthen the international juridical foundations for managing this tension. However, the presence of the economic and social aspects of the agrarian situation on the negotiating agenda, the emphasis on sustainable development and the involvement of beneficiaries as agents in planning and implementing programmes within the framework of the Resettlement Accord, as well as the aim of expanding MINUGUA into an integrated peace-building mission suggest that the parties and the UN are aware of this issue. What remains to be seen is what they will do to manage the tension between short term peace measures and market-oriented reforms in practice.

The final major challenge facing MINUGUA is that of adapting the experience of the UN in other contexts to the particularities of Guatemalan society. The explicit recognition that special methods will have to be developed to work with indigenous peoples is a promising sign in this respect, as is the emphasis placed on strengthening national institutions such as the Office of the Human Rights Ombudsman and non-governmental human rights organisations. The provisions for working with national institutions from the outset represent an advance on the Salvadorean experience, made possible by the prior existence and respected trajectory of national institutions such as the Ombudsman's office. In turn, the importance assigned to working with indigenous peoples reflects the unique salience of indigenous peoples in Guatemala, the high level of consciousness and organisation of some Guatemalan indigenous peoples, and the recognition by the UN system of the need to address their specific situation, including their cultural rights. Finally, by incorporating voices other than those of the belligerents into the peace process, the provision for an Assembly of Civil Society also represents a step ahead of the Nicaraguan and Salvadorean negotiating experiences. The ASC has already demonstrated its capacity to build consensus around serious proposals on complex issues such as the rights of indigenous peoples. These advances are promising, but we will have to wait and see whether the parties and the international community take sufficient advantage of these openings and rise to the challenges inherent in promoting peace in the unique context of Guatemalan society over the next years.

Beyond Incomplete Transitions?

The above case studies of UN experiences in Nicaragua, El Salvador and Guatemala suggest several modest conclusions about the factors which shape the success of UN peace operations, at least in societies where statehood and sovereignty are not complete fictions – as they seem to have been in less promising contexts like Bosnia and Somalia. In the Central American context, one can conclude that a fundamental factor explaining the relative success of the UN's role has been its adherence to the classical norms of peace-keeping, namely to the principles of consent, impartiality and non-use of force except in self-defence. Although there is some truth in the view that the UN was able to avoid the use of force because of the existence of a minimum of order and consensus, one should not forget that the UN resisted calls by governmental authorities to use force in Nicaragua and El Salvador, and that the UN played a crucial role in constructing the frameworks for peace which eventually made the resort to force unnecessary. The non-use of force principle could be tested in Guatemala, but it is worth noting that MINUGUA's mandate does not envisage a departure from the norms spelled out to the Central American presidents in 1989.

The second fundamental factor explaining the UN's relative success in Central America has been its adherence to the axiom that peace-making should not be separated from peace-keeping and peace-building. The structural differences between the coordinated operation in Nicaragua and the integrated mission in El Salvador show that significant learning took place from 1989 to 1991, within the UN and in Central America, about how to ensure a synergy between mediation, verification and the facilitation of more far-reaching peace-building measures. The fact that the UN plans to follow the ONUSAL model of an integrated, civilian-led mission in Guatemala confirms the basic wisdom of this axiom. Finally, the retention of a New York-based Moderator and a UN Independent Expert for human rights in addition to MINUGUA shows that the Salvadorean experience also taught the UN that an integrated field mission should be complemented by external good offices and monitoring.

Yet these cases also demonstrate that, despite the UN's adherence to the classical norms of peace-keeping, its role within the Nicaraguan and Salvadorean transitions was problematic in three fundamental ways. First, though more attention was paid to the promotion of comprehensive and meaningful agreements in El Salvador than in Nicaragua, UN pressure for the conclusion of accords by the end of 1991 has had very negative consequences for the prospects of lasting peace in El Salvador. One hopes that the temptation of hastily brokering incomplete accords will be avoided in Guatemala. Second, despite its attempts to adhere to the norm of impartiality and an impressive record of investigating and denouncing patterns of non-compliance, the UN has tended to privilege keeping peace processes on track over rigorous verification. This tendency, which converges with the UN's tilt towards sovereign authorities, was accentuated by the early demobilisation of the guerrillas – especially in El Salvador. It may be difficult to avoid this problem in Guatemala, where the balance of power so clearly favours the armed forces. As such, it is worth noting that a hasty demobilisation of the URNG would accentuate this problem, but that external monitors like the UN Independent Expert could help counter-balance these subtle biases towards keeping the process on track and favouring the state.

Third, while the UN has applied lessons learned in Nicaragua to its operations in El Salvador, there is still a real possibility that its relative successes in the smallest Central American republic might also be undermined by incomplete peace-building. The extension of ONUSAL's mandate beyond the original deadlines of May and November 1994 suggests that the UN does not wish to repeat the mistakes of its premature pullout from Nicaragua. ONUSAL's increasing emphasis on strengthening the national institutions which could carry on its functions after the UN pulls out in 1995 is also positive in this respect, as is the even greater emphasis that MINUGUA is supposed to place on institutional strengthening. Yet these advances could be tragically undermined by a failure to face the tension between peace measures and prevailing macro-economic policies. Insofar as the conflicts in Central America are rooted partly in struggles over economic and social matters, it is worth asking whether, unless the UN confronts the tension between peace-building and market reforms head on, it may leave the region having disarmed the guerrillas but not eradicated the causes of war.

Notes

1. Ortega Pinto (1994). See also Barry (1992) and Dunkerley (1988), particularly chapter 9.
2. Boutros-Ghali (1992). See also Mackinlay and Chopra (1992) and Weiss (1993).
3. Bennis and Moushabeck (1992). For comparative assessments of recent UN peace missions, see Human Rights Watch (1993) and Amnesty International (1994). Background data on recent and current UN operations can be found in United Nations (1990) and *Peacekeeping and International Relations*, especially XXII, No.6 (November/December 1993), p. 19.
4. For a preliminary discussion along these lines, see Baranyi (1994).
5. This discussion of the processes which shaped the UN's early peace-making role in Central America is based on Opazo Bernales and Fernández V. (1990), Child (1992) as well as Baranyi and North (1992).
6. Of course, this is a matter of judgment. Yet it seems accurate to argue that in the Nicaraguan case, by 1989 the externally-sponsored Resistencia Nicaragüense (RN or contra) had been almost defeated on the battlefield and its middle-level leaders had indicated a willingness to bargain with the Sandinista government, itself greatly weakened by the war and by the collapse of the USSR; that in El Salvador, a similar point of 'ripeness' was reached only in 1991, after the FMLN's offensives, the killing of the Jesuits and the shift of US policy away from its alliance with the Armed Forces; and that the conflict in Guatemala has only recently been moving towards a similar 'ripeness for resolution', due less to any change in the battlefield situation than to a recognition by both the armed forces and the URNG that little more can be gained through military means, and that many of their objectives can be attained through negotiation. The concept of 'ripeness' is borrowed from Zartman (1985).

7. See the secondary sources in note 5 above. For primary sources, see Baranyi and North (1992).

8. ONUCA was authorised to 'monitor on a regular basis areas reported to harbor bases and camps of irregular forces..., monitor on a regular basis land, sea and air borders across which military operations might be carried out or assistance of the kind excluded might be provided...[and] investigate immediately any complaint received from one of the five governments ...'. See United Nations (1989).

9. For a similar judgment, see Klepak (1994).

10. *Revueltos* refers to groups of contra and demobbed Ejército Popular Sandinista soldiers who have joined forces and taken up arms.

11. Centro Nicaragüense de los Derechos Humanos (CENIDH) (1994) and Asociación Nicaragüense Pro-Derechos Humanos, various issues of *Reflexión*. See also Americas Watch (1991c).

12. The discussion of the processes leading to the establishment of ONUSAL and of its performance to mid-1992 is based on Acevedo (1992). See also Karl (1992) and Baranyi and North (1992), especially pp. 23-33.

13. See Vickers and Spence (1992); Holiday and Stanley (1993); Munck (1993).

14. United Nations (1994e), paragraph 17. See also Montes (1994).

15. The Joint Group's report is reproduced in *Inforpress Centroamericana*, 11 August 1994 and 18 August 1994. See also United Nations (1994d).

16. See United Nations (1992b); United Nations (1994f), especially paragraphs 67-72, and United Nations (1994e), especially paragraphs 51-60.

17. El Salvador Information Project (1994).

18. United Nations (1994e), paragraph 67.

19. Spence and Vickers (1994).

20. 'Intervención del Director de la División de Derechos Humanos de la Misión de Observadores de las Naciones Unidas en El Salvador', speech delivered by Diego García Sayán to the 50th Session of the UN Commission of Human Rights, Geneva (24 February 1994).

21. For a similar assessment, see Sarti Castañeda (1994), especially pp. 82-4.

22. Some participants believed that ONUSAL in fact tilted the other way. Retired General Mauricio Vargas, who was on the governmental team during the peace negotiations and remains influential behind the scenes, argued in mid-1994 that ONUSAL had been 'more complacent' with the FMLN and 'harder on' the government, to which the Chief of Mission at the time, Mr. Ter Horst, replied that this was only natural since 95 per cent of the commitments in the accords related to government action. Nonetheless, this author agrees with those who conclude that, in the final analysis, ONUSAL was compelled by circumstances to accept the government's actions even when it denounced actions such as the amnesty law which violated the spirit of the accords.

23. De Soto and Del Castillo (1993), p. 2.

24. FMLN (1994). See also United Nations (1994a).

25. See United Nations (1994h), Resolution A/48/267 and 'Acuerdo Global sobre los Derechos Humanos', reprinted in *Inforpress Centroamericana*, 7 April 1994.

26. 'Acuerdo marco para la reanudación del proceso de negociación entre el Gobierno de Guatemala y la Unidad Revolucionaria Nacional Guatemalteca', in *Inforpress Centroamericana*, 13 January 1994.

27. See 'Informe del primer semestre de 1994 de la Oficina de Derechos Humanos del Arzobispado', in *Inforpress Centroamericana*, 28 July 1994; the summary of the PDHG's report in 'La interminable espiral de la violencia', *Inforpress Centroamericana*, 8 September 1994 and United Nations (1994g).

28. *Inforpress Centroamericana*, 23 June 1994.

29. See *Inforpress Centroamericana*, 30 June 1994.

30. The Bishop stated that the international community was 'only interested in a ceasefire, not in seeing a resolution of the substantive issues which are considered to have originated and fuelled the armed conflict', Edward Orlebar, 'Guatemala Rights Agreement Fails to Take Root', *Financial Times* , 29 July 1994.

IV. CONCLUSIONS

CHAPTER 9

CONCLUSIONS

Rachel Sieder

The absence of the acute levels of armed conflict and ideological polarisation that characterised Central America during the 1980s has meant that current prospects for a gradual improvement in the rule of law and the strengthening of a liberal democratic order are perhaps better than in any previous period. In the wake of the civil wars, both regional and international actors have come to view institutional reform of the state and political system as necessary to ensure the observance of basic human rights guarantees and the construction of a more democratic order. However, as has been indicated throughout this volume, Central America's democracy is still in formation and the process of transition and consolidation in a region characterised by the absence of democratic traditions and the fragility of existing institutions is necessarily both slow and difficult.

The initiatives towards political and institutional restructuring outlined in this volume would have been unthinkable twenty years ago. Present developments are fundamentally a product of the revolutionary challenge to the political and socio-economic *status quo* which occurred in Nicaragua, El Salvador and Guatemala during the late 1970s and 1980s. As indicated in the third section of this book, they are also intimately bound up with shifts in the international environment since the late 1980s.

From the end of the Cold War, US interests in the region have shifted from the geo-political towards the geo-economic. To the extent that furthering economic liberalisation and securing regional stability demand the absence of conflict and an efficient institutional framework, the international environment is now more favourable to the development of democratic systems in Central America. However, given that many of the decisive changes essential for democratisation involve challenging long-term allies of the USA, particularly within the region's military, US policy towards Central America is often, at best, inconclusive or highly unpredictable. The effects of the current economic policies of the US and the international community on regional prospects for democratisation are even more debatable (see below).

Just as the civil wars of the 1980s were highly internationalised in character, the role of extra-regional actors proved equally important in the multiple transition process outlined in the introductory chapter of this volume. While no common regional 'transition prototype' is discernible, the demonstration effect of developments in any one country (and particularly their international dimensions) on others has been considerable.

A critical factor in the Central American transition explored in previous chapters has been the innovative role played by the United Nations in national and regional peace processes. In the post-Cold War period, the willingness of the international community to support certain reform initiatives as an integral part of conflict resolution and post-conflict restructuring has helped strengthen local efforts towards democratisation. The renegotiation of institutional responsibilities – such as reducing the role of the military or strengthening the powers of congress *vis-à-vis* the executive – has generated considerable political conflict and the role of the respective United Nations missions in mediating this has been an appreciable one. While not without its flaws, the role of ONUSAL (UN Observer Mission in El Salvador) in the implementation of the Salvadorean peace accord has been central in supporting the construction of democratic local institutions, such as the civilian police force. The UN's profile in Guatemala through MINUGUA (UN Verification Mission in Guatemala) will be equally essential for the successful implementation of those accords signed to date.

Governability *versus* Democracy

The essential principles underpinning any liberal democratic order are those of effective representation of citizens by their rulers and accountability of rulers and ruled alike. It is a truism that governability is a necessary but not sufficient condition for democracy; whereas governability essentially refers to managing the *status quo*, 'democracy' implies an ideal – a vision of the future. Central America is in one sense more 'governable' today than it was in the mid-1980s at the height of the armed conflicts; the zero-sum conceptions of politics adhered to by local and international actors have been replaced by a greater (though far from uniform) disposition to compromise. However, effective representation, particularly of the marginalised sectors of society, and full accountability of the state and its agents have yet to be realised. What then are the prospects that a democratic system of rule built on the principles of accountability and effective representation will develop in Central America?

As indicated throughout this book, a number of changes are essential for the consolidation of democracy in the isthmus: first, the development of a new democratic role for the armed forces and the effective subordination of military to civilian power. The military have traditionally dominated the region's politics, an authoritarian pattern which was reinforced and transformed during the conflicts of the 1980s. A reduction in political intromission by the armed forces is a necessary precondition if the institutions charged with democratic representation – such as political parties and congress examined in this volume – are to fulfil their mandate. Reform necessarily involves extensive structural reforms to the military itself. In addition, as indicated in chapter six, accountability of the military for their actions is essential for the strengthening of the rule of law in Central America, a region where the absence of democracy was for so long characterised by military abuse and lack of accountability of the armed forces.

One key reform stressed in this volume is that of separating the military from functions of internal security. As outlined in chapters three and six, considerable advances have been made throughout the region, particularly in El Salvador and (to a lesser extent) Honduras. However, these gains are presently being threatened by a region-wide trend to involve the army in the fight against a wave of rising crime. The nature and causes of the current increase in crime have yet to be exhaustively analysed, but contributing factors include worsening economic conditions, widespread and rapid demobilisation of army and guerrilla forces and a surfeit of arms throughout the region. In El Salvador, the report of the United Nations *Grupo Conjunto* also indicated the involvement of organised interests within the private sector and the military in the increase in crime.[1] During the early months of 1995, troops were mobilised to augment police forces in San Salvador and Tegucigalpa, threatening a remilitarisation of domestic security functions. Army troops were also deployed to patrol the streets of Guatemala City throughout March 1995 to supplement the largely ineffectual (militarily controlled) police force's efforts to maintain public order.[2] The question of how crime and public order are dealt with in a transitional period is evidently a critical one and something that must be taken into account when drawing up plans for the institutional redesign of the police force and the military.

Secondly, to the extent that the judicial system ensures accountability and the enforcement of universal democratic rights and obligations, effective judicial reform is the cornerstone of democratic consolidation (see chapter six). However, this can only be successful to the extent that parallel institutions, such as the military and congress, are reformed. The pervasiveness of clientelist practices and patronage within state structures throughout the region means that securing professionalisation and depoliticisation of the judiciary will necessarily be both difficult and slow. Throughout the region, the legislature has traditionally been one of the weakest and most ineffectual organs of state (see chapter five). The recent focus on corruption scandals in both Honduras, where the Public Ministry has accused many congressional deputies – including ex-President Rafael Leonardo Callejas – of malfeasance, and El Salvador, where the charges levelled by right-wing commentator Kirio Waldo Salgado against members of the governing ARENA (Alianza Republicana Nacionalista) party have split the right, give scant indication that the nature of parliament or of parliamentary protocol has changed substantially in recent years.[3] In Guatemala, attempts to purge Congress resulted in the abortive *autogolpe* of May 1993 and subsequently the constitutional changes initiated by President Ramiro de León Carpio in January 1994. However, the unprecedentedly low turn-out for the January referendum on constitutional reform (a mere sixteen per cent of registered voters), and the twenty per cent turnout for the congressional elections the following August, indicated widespread disillusionment with both the performance of the legislature and prospects for its meaningful reform. Despite President Ramiro de León's much heralded 'purge' of congress, there is little indication that Guatemala's *partidocracia* have assumed a more effective representative role.

If institutional reform is to be effective it is vital that it occur not merely at national but also at local level. The links between national and local developments will be a central focus of efforts at democratic consolidation during the next few years; for example, measures such as changes in selection procedures for the Supreme Court (see chapter six) must eventually generate positive changes in the administration of justice at local level if they are to have lasting effect. Recognising the importance of reform at the level of local communities, the accord on indigenous rights and identity signed by the URNG (Unidad Revolucionaria Nacional Guatemalteca) and the Guatemalan government on 31 March 1995 as part of the peace process sets out the need for local judicial reform, containing such clauses as the creation of legal aid services for indigenous peoples, the promotion of training programmes for judges in indigenous languages and the recognition of customary law in the administration of municipal affairs.[4] However, the challenge of consolidating new institutions in a context of a shrinking state budget is a particularly complex one, and concerted and continued international support will be required to ensure that such reforms are effectively carried out in Guatemala and throughout the region.

Thirdly, in order for patterns of clientelism and impunity to be decisively broken, an effective purge of state institutions (both civil and military) is an imperative. The role of 'truth commissions' (see chapters three and six) is central in this respect; only by uncovering the truth about past abuses of state power can accountability be determined, transparency increased and the prospects of securing justice improved. If institutions created in the wake of the regional conflict are to take a more pro-active role and inspire public confidence in the rule of law, a qualitative change in past practice has to occur. Ultimately, strong institutional development will only be guaranteed by a thorough 'weeding out' of elements responsible for previous violations and the development of new institutional doctrines. While most observers would reject the prosecution of all those implicated in past abuses as both politically and practically unfeasible, the success of the current transition will depend on the manner in which the question of impunity is addressed and accountability reinforced.[5] This problem is not exclusive to Central America; in very different contexts societies as diverse as South Africa, Rwanda and Northern Ireland are currently grappling with similar dilemmas.

Fourthly, the contributions in this volume discussing political parties (chapter two) and executive-congressional relations (chapter five) have highlighted the instability and lack of permanence of political parties and alliances in the region. In order for an institutional framework of governance separate from sectarian party interests to be consolidated, parties need to develop a new and less instrumentalist relationship with the institutions of state, particularly the legislature. However, changing the ingrained patterns of a traditionally highly authoritarian political culture will inevitably be a slow and gradual process. In general terms, the fragile political parties and party systems are currently unable adequately to mediate and represent the different group interests of Central American society. Carlos Vilas has noted the vigorous nature of interest groups in Central America – particularly within the private sector, and to a lesser extent the trade unions – despite the weakness of political parties[6]. A key question in rebuilding political regimes is how movements (popular and otherwise) and parties relate to each other. Democratisation in the absence of effective representation of interest group demands is likely to fuel alienation and disenchantment with the political system as a whole, a phenomenon referred to by Rodolfo Cerdas in chapter two as 'el desencanto democrático'. Reform of political parties and the party system are therefore essential to facilitate greater representativeness and permanence of the political system.

Accountability and Representation

Liberal democracy is defined in large measure by the principle of accountability. Problems of accountability still loom large throughout Central America: of executive and legislature to the electorate; of the military to the judicial process; and of the political parties to civil society. The political system continues to lack transparency and to suffer the problems of clientelism and corruption. Although the role of congress is significantly more important to the political process than it was a decade ago, the traditional supremacy of the executive over the legislature tends to be reinforced by the weakness and instability of the party system, while accountability is further weakened by the current absence of a direct link between congressional representatives and their respective electorates.

In addition, as Cerdas notes in chapter two, the introduction of structural adjustment policies throughout the region at the behest of international financial lending institutions such as the International Monetary Fund and the World Bank in recent years has tended to make economic decision-making increasingly centralised and less open to debate. The ability of national congresses to link social and economic policy has become highly restricted as decision-making over economic affairs is located extra-nationally or occurs exclusively between international lending agencies and the executive. The social costs of structural adjustment in the region have been high and, precisely because they provoke strong opposition, such programmes have tended to be imposed from above without any significant attempt to arrive at a negotiated consensus.[7] Bresser Pereira, commenting on this phenomenon notes 'in the end society is taught that it can vote but not choose'.[8] The continued erosion of governments' ability to respond effectively to citizens' demands is likely significantly to undermine representative institutions and reduce the prospects for 'good governance' in Central America.

While the tradition within political science represented by writers such as Schumpeter, Dahl and Huntington stresses institutional definitions of democracy – interest group representation through elections – it has been argued throughout this volume that electoral mechanisms alone are insufficient to guarantee democracy in Central America.[9] In the past, the lack of representative institutions of government together with socio-economic inequality has led to polarisation and rupture in the region and change needs to be far-reaching if the return to such a cycle is to be prevented. The central question remains that of how to incorporate marginalised sectors into the political and economic system. This is particularly important in the case of groups which developed an autonomous voice throughout the 1980s, such as women, indigenous groups and marginal urban dwellers existing within the informal sector of the economy. If democracy is to be consolidated, such sectors must find effective representation and participation through political parties and the institutions of state, contributing to the reform of those structures and institutions in the process.

Politics in Central America today is marked by the loss of an emancipatory vision, a phenomenon far from exclusive to the region. Mobilisations around discreet issues and moves in favour of local autonomy are some of the more evident political corollaries of the decline of revolutionary politics among the forces of the left in the region. Gilles Bataillon has described this phenomenon as the emergence of 'restricted identities' and notes that the multiplication of what he refers to as 'micro-civil societies' has resulted in the fragmentation of political demands.[10] This in turn is linked to a worsening economic situation and the deepening of socioeconomic inequalities. Such developments present new dilemmas for questions of representation and accountability in the political sphere. Christian Anglade includes minimum socio-economic rights in his base-line definition of democracy and argues that 'the ignoring of basic social needs by governments is a reflection of the lack of political representation of those who are socially excluded'.[11] Without questioning the veracity of this statement, the question must be raised of the extent to which – in the context of a globalising economy and highly dependent local economies – any government in Central America can exercise autonomy with regard to social and economic policy.

Traditionally, the Central American region has been characterised by powerful military institutions, a high degree of intervention by powerful external actors and weak and ineffective structures of governance. The end to the civil wars and current institutional reform initiatives have opened up important oppositional spaces in Central American politics, yet popular perceptions must change if those spaces are to be utilised to the full. Such a process involves slow and gradual education of citizens to increase awareness of their democratic rights and a gradual process whereby the legitimacy of government is established. Whether or not prevailing conditions will allow the space for such developments has yet to be seen.

Notes

1. The report of the Grupo Conjunto is reproduced in *Central America Report*, 5 August 1994.
2. *Noticias de Guatemala*, 31 March 1995 (Mexico City).
3. See *Central America Report*, 11 November 1994 and 18 December 1994.
4. URNG/Government of Guatemala (1995).
5. See Sieder (1995).
6. Handal and Vilas (1993), p. 123.
7. See Pelupessy and Weeks (1993), especially the chapter on Nicaragua by Oscar Catalán Aravena.
8. Bresser Pereira, Maravall and Przeworski (1993), pp. 9-10.
9. Dahl (1971); Huntington (1968); Schumpeter (1976).
10. Bataillon et al. (1994), p. 10.
11. Anglade (1994), p. 238. Anglade includes equal civil and political rights; minimum socio-economic rights and accountability in his minimum definition of democracy.

BIBLIOGRAPHY

Acevedo, C. (1992) 'Balance global del proceso de negociación entre el gobierno y el FMLN', *Estudios Centroamericanos*, Año XLVII, Vol. 47, Jan-Feb 1992, No. 519-520.

Acuerdos de Chapultepec, mimeo (San Salvador, 1992).

Adams, J. S. (1992) *A Foreign Policy in Transition: Moscow's Retreat from Central America and the Caribbean 1985-1992* (Durham, North Carolina: Duke University Press).

Ad-hoc Commission (1993) *Informe de la Comisión Ad-hoc de Alto Nivel para las reformas institucionales, que garanticen la seguridad y la paz social en Honduras*, mimeo (Tegucigalpa, April).

Aguayo, S., H. Christense and S. Varesse (1987) *Los Refugiados Guatemaltecos en Campeche y Quintana Roo: Condiciones Sociales y Culturales. Instituto de Investigaciones de las Naciones Unidas para el Desarrollo Social* (Geneva: United Nations Research Institute for Social Development, UNRISD).

Aguilera, G. (undated) '*Democracia y la cuadratura del círculo, la crisis política en Guatemala*', mimeo.

Aguilera, G. (1993) 'Guatemala, El Carrusel de los Golpes', *El Día Latinoamericano*, 14 June 1993.

Aguilera, G. (1994) *Guatemala, los temas sustantivos en las propuestas para la paz* (Guatemala: Facultad Latinoamericana de Ciencias Sociales, FLACSO).

AID (United States Agency for International Development) (1992) *Diagnóstico sobre la administración de justicia en Honduras* (San José: USAID).

Alcántara, M. (1992) 'El sentido del sistema político democrático en los países de América Latina ¿Democracias inciertas o democracias consolidadas?', in R. Steichen (ed.), *Democracia y Democratización en Centroamérica* (San José: Editorial de la Universidad de Costa Rica).

Ambos, K. (1987) *The Central American Refugee Crisis: a study of the refugee situation and refugee policy of Costa Rica, Honduras and Nicaragua*, Refugee Studies Programme, Oxford University, mimeo (Oxford).

Americas Watch (1989) *Honduras: Without the Will* (New York: Americas Watch).

Americas Watch (1990) *Messengers of Death: Human Rights in Guatemala, November 1988-1990* (New York: Americas Watch).

Americas Watch (1991a) *El Salvador's Decade of Terror: Human Rights since the Assassination of Archbishop Romero* (New York and Washington: Americas Watch).

Americas Watch (1991b) *Guatemala: Getting Away with Murder* (New York: Americas Watch).

Americas Watch (1991c) *Fitful Peace: Human Rights and Reconciliation in Nicaragua under the Chamorro Government* (New York: Americas Watch).

Americas Watch (1993) *Clandestine Detention in Guatemala* (New York: Americas Watch).

Americas Watch and American Civil Liberties Union (1982) 'Report on Human Rights in El Salvador', 20 July 1982 (Washington DC: Americas Watch).

Amnesty International (1981) *Guatemala: A Government Program of Political Murder* (New York: Amnesty International).

Amnesty International (1992a) *Disappearances in Honduras: A Wall of Silence and Indifference* (London: Amnesty International).

Amnesty International (1992b) *Children in Fear* (London: Amnesty International).

Amnesty International (1994) *Peace-keeping and Human Rights* (London: Amnesty International).

Anglade, C. (1994) 'Democracy and the New Rule of Law in Latin America', in Ian Budge and David McKay (eds.), *Developing Democracy* (London, Thousand Oaks and New Delhi: Sage Publications).

ASIES (Asociación de Investigación y Estudios Sociales) (1993) 'Propuesta de Reformas a la Ley Orgánica y de Régimen Interior del Organismo Legislativo', in ASIES, *Reconversión de los Partidos. Su reto ante la Crisis* (Guatemala: ASIES)

ASIES (1994) *Los Retos del Nuevo Congreso* (Guatemala: ASIES).

Asociación Nicaragüense Pro-Derechos Humanos, *Reflexión* (various).

Bacevich, A., J. Hallum, R. White and T. Young (1988) *American Policy in Small Wars: The Case of El Salvador* (Washington: Institute for Foreign Policy Analysis, John F. Kennedy School of Government).

Bagley, B., R. Alvarez and K.J. Hagedorn (eds.) (1985) *Contadora and the Central American Peace Process: Selected Documents* (Boulder, Colorado: Westview Press).

Baloyra, E. (1987) *Comparing New Democracies: Transition and Consolidation in Mediterranean Europe and the Southern Cone* (Boulder, Colorado: Westview Press).

Baranyi, S. (1994) 'Beyond Traditional Peace-keeping? Caveats from International Theory and from UN Experiences in Central America', *Estudios Internacionales*, Vol. 9 (1994).

Baranyi, S. and L. North (1992) *'Stretching the Limits of the Possible: United Nations Peacekeeping in Central America'*, Aurora Papers 15, Ottowa Centre for Global Security (Ottawa: Ottawa Centre for Global Security).

Barricada (Managua) (various).

Barry, D. (1990) *'Evaluation of the Impact of UNHCR's Assistance Program for Returnees'*, unpublished mimeo (1990).

Barry, D. and L. Serra (1988) *Refugiados, repatriados y población desplazada* (Managua: Coordinadora Regional de Investigaciones Económicas y Sociales, CRIES).

Barry, T. (1992) *Inside Guatemala* (Albuquerque, New Mexico: Inter-Hemispheric Education Resource Center).

Barry, T. and D. Preusch (1986) *The Central America Fact Book* (New York: Grove Press).

Basok, T. (1990) 'Repatriation of Nicaraguan Refugees from Honduras and Costa Rica', *Journal of Refugee Studies*, Vol. 3, No. 4 (1990).

Bataillon, G. et al (1994) *Centroamérica entre Democracia y Desorganización: Análisis de los Actores y de los Sistemas de Acción en los Años 1990* (Guatemala: Facultad Latinoamericana de Ciencias Sociales, FLACSO).

Bendaña, A. (1991) *Una Tragedia Campesina* (Managua: Editora de Arte).

Bennis, P. and M. Moushabeck (1992) *Beyond the Storm: A Gulf Crisis Reader* (Edinburgh: Canongate).

Binder, A.M. (1993) *Justicia Penal y Estado de Derecho* (Buenos Aires: Ad-Hoc).

Blachman, M.J. and K.E. Sharpe (1992) 'The Transitions to "Electoral" and Democratic Politics in Central America: Assessing the Role of Political Parties', in Louis W. Goodman, William M. Leogrande and Johanna Mendelson Forman, *Political Parties and Democracy in Central America* (Boulder, San Francisco and Oxford: Westview Press).

Booth, J. (1989) 'Elections and Democracy in Central America: A Framework for Analysis', in Booth, John A. and Mitchell A. Seligson (eds.), *Elections and Democracy in Central America* (Chapel Hill and London: University of North Carolina Press).

Booth, J.A. and M.A. Seligson (eds.) (1989) *Elections and Democracy in Central America* (Chapel Hill and London: University of North Carolina Press).

Booth, J. and T. Walker (1989) *Understanding Central America* (Boulder, San Francisco and London: Westview Press).

Borea, A. (1994) *La difícil democracia en América Latina: desafíos y respuestas* (San José: ICEP).

Boutros-Ghali, B. (1992) *An Agenda for Peace: Preventative Diplomacy, Peacemaking and Peace-keeping* (New York: United Nations).

Bresser Pereira, L., J. Maravall and A. Przeworski (1993) *Economic Reforms in New Democracies* (Cambridge: Cambridge University Press).

Bulmer-Thomas, V. (1991) *A Long-Run Model of Development for Central America*, Research Paper No. 27 (London: Institute of Latin American Studies, 1991).

Casáus Arzú, M.E. (1992) 'El retorno al poder de las élites familiares centro-americanas 1979-1990', *Polémica*, No. 18 (Sept-Dec).

CEDEM (Centro para Estudios Democráticos) (1994) 'The role of the new Legislative Assembly in the division and balancing of powers', CEDEM Seminar Bulletin, 29 January 1994 (San Salvador: CEDEM).

CEJIL (Center for Justice and International Law) and Human Rights Watch/ Americas (1994) *The Facts Speak for Themselves: the Preliminary Report on Disappearances of the National Commissioner for the Protection of Human Rights in Honduras* (New York and Washington: CEJIL).

CENIDH (Centro Nicaragüense de los Derechos Humanos) (1994) *Derechos Humanos en Nicaragua, Informe anual Abril 1993-Abril 1994* (Managua: CENIDH).

CEPAL (Comisión Económica para América Latina) (1993) *El Impacto Económico y Social y las Migraciones en Centroamérica* (Santiago de Chile: CEPAL).

Central America Report (Guatemala City) (various).

Cerdas, R. (1993) *El desencanto democrático. Crisis de los partidos y transición democrática en Centroamérica* (San José: Red Editorial Iberoamericana Centroamérica).

Cerigua Weekly Briefs (Mexico City) (various).

Chamorro, C.F. (1994-1995) 'Nicaragua: reformas constitutionales y crisis del Sandinismo', *Tendencias*, No. 36, December 1994-January 1995 (San Salvador).

Child, J. (1992) *The Central American Peace Process, 1983-1991: Sheathing Swords, Building Confidence* (Boulder and London: Lynne Rienner Publishers).

Chomsky, N. (1985) *Turning the Tide: US Intervention in Central America and the Struggle for Peace* (Boston: Pluto Press).

CIREFCA (Conferencia Internacional sobre Refugiados Centroamericanos) (1992) *The Second International Meeting of the Follow-up Committee*, mimeo, 7-8 April 1992 (San Salvador).

CIIR (Catholic Institute for International Relations) Comment (1993) *Guatemala: Transition from Terror* (London: CIIR).

Comisión Nacional de Protección de los Derechos Humanos (1993) *'Los Hechos Hablan por Sí Mismos': Informe Preliminar Sobre los Desparecidos en Honduras, 1980-1993*, mimeo (Tegucigalpa).

Comisión para la Modernización del Estado (1994) *Documento preliminar: programa de modernización del Estado para el período 1994-1998*, mimeo, February (Tegucigalpa).

Conniff, M. (1990) 'Panama since 1903', in Leslie Bethell (ed.), *Cambridge History of Latin America*, Vol. VII, *Latin America Since 1930. Mexico, Central America and the Caribbean* (Cambridge: Cambridge University Press).

Córdova, R. (1987) *'Los Efectos Económicos de la Militarización en la Región Centroamericana (1979-1986)'*, Occasional Paper No. 20 (Miami: Latin American and Caribbean Center, Florida International University).

Córdova Macías, R. (1993) *El Salvador: las negociaciones de paz y los retos de la postguerra* (San Salvador: Instituto de Estudios Latinoamericanos).

CORELESAL (Comisión Revisora de la Legislación Salvadoreña) (1990a) *Problemática de la Administración de la Justicia en El Salvador*, mimeo, December (San Salvador).

CORELESAL (1990b) *Exposición de Motivos y Anteproyecto de Reformas al Código Procesal Penal*, mimeo, August (San Salvador).

CORELESAL (1991) *Terminación de labores e información del trabajo realizado por la Comisión Revisora de la Legislación Salvadoreña*, mimeo, October (San Salvador).

Correa Sutil, J. (1993) 'Chile and Transition', in Irwin P. Stotzky (ed.), *Transition to Democracy in Latin America: The Role of the Judiciary* (Boulder and London: Westview Press).

COSEP (Consejo Superior de la Empresa Privada) (1991a) *'Consideraciones en torno al derecho de la propiedad en Nicaragua'*, mimeo, August (Managua).

COSEP (1991b) *'Acuerdos de la Segunda Fase de la Concertación Económica y Social'*, mimeo, August (Managua).

COSEP (1991c) *'Porqué el COSEP no firmó el documento de la concertación'*, mimeo, August (Managua).

CRIES (Coordinadora Regional de Investigación Económicas y Sociales) (1993) *Centroamérica '93: Anuario* (Managua: CRIES).

Cruz Salazar, L. (undated) 'La posibilidad del juego parlamentario en el marco de la actual Constitución de la República', in ASIES (Asociación de Investigación y Estudios Sociales) (undated) *Democracia, Gobernabilidad y Sociedad Política* (Guatemala: ASIES).

Daalder, H. (1990) 'The Reach of the Party System', in Peter Mair (ed.), *The West European Party System* (Oxford: Oxford University Press).

Dahl, R.A. (1971) *Polyarchy, Participation and Opposition* (New Haven: Yale University Press).

Danner, M. (1993) 'The Truth of El Mozote', *The New Yorker*, 6 December, 1993.

Danner, M. (1994) *The Massacre of El Mozote* (New York: Vintage Books).

De Soto, A. and G. Del Castillo (1993) 'An Integrated International Approach to Human Security. El Salvador: A Case Study', unpublished paper, April.

Diamond, L., J. Linz and S.M. Lipset (eds.) (1989) *Democracy in Developing Countries: Latin America* (London: Adamantine Press; Boulder, Colorado: Lynne Rienner Publishers).

Diario Latino (San Salvador) (various).

Di Palma, G. and L. Whitehead (eds.) (1986) *The Central American Impasse* (London and Sydney: Croom Helm).

Doggett, M. (1994) *Death Foretold: The Jesuit Murders in El Salvador* (Washington, DC: Georgetown University Press).

Domingo, P. (1994) *Rule of Law and Judicial Systems in the Context of Democratisation and Economic Liberalisation: A Framework for Comparison and Analysis in Latin America*, Documentos de Trabajo No. 25 (Mexico: CIDE).

Draper, T. (1991) *A Very Thin Line: The Iran-Contra Affair* (New York: Hill and Wang).

Dunbar Ortiz, R. (1986) *La Cuestión Miskita en la Revolución Nicaragüense* (Mexico: Editorial Línea).

Dunbar Ortiz, R. (1988) 'Guatemalans in Lacandona', *Refugees*, No. 53, May (Geneva: United Nations High Commissioner for Refugees (UNHCR)).

Dunkerley, J. (1988) *Power in the Isthmus: A Political History of Modern Central America* (London: Verso).

Dunkerley, J. (1993) *The Pacification of Central America*, Research Paper No. 34 (London: Institute of Latin American Studies)

Dunkerley, J. (1994) *The Pacification of Central America* (London and New York: Verso).

Edwards, B. and G. Tovar Siebentritt (1991) *Places of Origin: The Repopulation of Rural El Salvador* (Boulder, Colorado: Lynne Rienner Publishers).

El Día (Mexico) (various).

El Diario de Hoy (San Salvador) (various).

El Salvador Information Project (1994) *Prospects for Progressive Labor*, San Salvador, 18 July 1994.

Envío (Managua) (various).

Espinal Irías, R. (1990) *El Sistema de Justicia en Honduras* (Tegucigalpa: Edivasa, Editorial Valle).

Ethier, D. (ed.) (1990) *Democratic Transition and Consolidation in Southern Europe, Latin America and South East Asia* (Basingstoke and London: Macmillan Press).

Faber, D. (1992) 'Imperialism, Revolution and the Ecological Crisis in Central America', *Latin American Perspectives*, Vol. 19, No. 1.

Fagen, R. (1985) *Forging Peace: The Challenge of. Central America* (San Francisco: Policy Alternatives for the Caribbean and Central America, PACCA).

Ferris, E. (1987) *The Central American Refugees* (New York: Praeger).

Ferris, E. (1993) *Beyond Borders: Refugees, Migrants and Human Rights in the Post-War Era* (Geneva: World Council of Churches, WCC).

Financial Times (London) (various).

Fiscalía de Derechos Humanos (1992) *Propuesta para la creación de un Organismo de Investigación del Delito*, borrador (San Salvador, February 1992).

FMLN (Frente Farabundo Martí para la Liberación Nacional)(1994) 'Evaluation of the Process of Implementation of the Peace Accords', *FMLN circular*, mimeo, 12 August (San Salvador).

FESPAD (Fundación de Estudios para la Aplicación del Derecho) (1994) *Diez Años de Constitución: un balance y una perspectiva. Organo Judicial* (San Salvador: FESPAD).

Furlong, W.L. (1993) 'Panama: The Difficult Transition Toward Democracy', *Journal of Inter-American Studies*, Vol. 35, No. 3.

Gils, B., J. Rocamora and R. Wilson (eds.) (1993) *Low Intensity Democracy: Political Power in the New World Order* (Boulder and London: Pluto Press).

González Oropeza, M. (1994) 'Justice by challenge: the administration of justice and the rule of law in Mexico', unpublished paper presented at the conference *Mexico under Zedillo*, Institute of Latin American Studies, London, November.

Guido Béjar, R. (1993) 'El Centro político y la reproducción del consenso', *Revista Tendencias*, No. 23, September (San Salvador).

Guido Béjar, R. (1994) 'Parlamento y partidos políticos', *Revista Tendencias*, No. 33, September (San Salvador).

Hale, C.R. (1994) *Resistance and Contradiction: Miskitu Indians and the Nicaraguan State, 1894-1987* (Stanford: Stanford University Press).

Hammond, J. (1993) 'War-uprooting and the Political Mobilisation of Central American Refugees', *Journal of Refugee Studies*, Vol. 6, No. 2.

Handal, S. and C. Vilas (1993) *The Socialist Option in Central America: Two Reassessments* (New York: Monthly Review Press).

Harrell-Bond, B. (1987) 'Refugee Issues', *Third World Affairs*, pp. 311-319

Hawley, S. (1992) *'Return of the Miskito and Sumu to their Country of Origin'*, Refugee Studies Programme Oxford, mimeo (Oxford).

Hernández, A., N. Nava, C. Flores and J. L. Escalona (1993) *La experiencia de refugio en Chiapas: nuevas relaciones en la frontera sur mexicana* (Mexico: Academia Mexicana de Derechos Humanos).

Higley, J. and R. Gunther (1992) *Elites and Democratic Consolidation in Latin America and Southern Europe* (Cambridge: Cambridge University Press).

Holiday, D. and W. Stanley (1993) 'Building the Peace: Preliminary Lessons from El Salvador', *Journal of International Affairs*, Vol. 46, No. 2.

Human Rights Watch (1993) *The Lost Agenda: Human Rights and UN Field Operations* (Washington: Human Rights Watch).

Human Rights Watch/Americas (1994) *Human Rights in Guatemala during President de León Carpio's First Year* (New York: Human Rights Watch).

Huntington, S.P. (1968) *Political Order in Changing Societies* (New Haven: Yale University Press).

INCEP (Instituto Centroamericano de Estudios Políticos) *Reporte Político*, Guatemala (various).

INCEP (1993) *La Crisis Político-constitucional de Guatemala: del Golpe de Estado de Jorge Serrano a la Presidencia Constitucional de Ramiro de León Carpio. Documentación nacional e internacional del período 25.5-17.6.93*, Temas y Documentos de Debate No. 45, May-June (Guatemala).

Inforpress Centroamericana (Guatemala) (various).

Inter-American Court of Human Rights (1988) *Caso Velásquez-Rodríguez*, mimeo (San José: Inter-American Court of Human Rights, IACHR)

IIDH (Instituto Interamericano de Derechos Humanos) (1992) *Exodos en América Latina: la migración por violencia Centroamerica 1980-1990* (San José: IIDH).

IRELA (Instituto de Relaciones Europeos-Latinoamericanas) (1994a) *Diez Años del Proceso de San José* (Madrid: IRELA).

IRELA (1994b) *A Triple Renewal for Central America? Elections, Integration and Economic Development*, Dossier No. 48 (Madrid: IRELA)

Jonas, S. (1991) *The Battle for Guatemala: Rebels, Death Squads and US Power* (Boulder and London: Westview Press).

Karl, T.L. (1992) 'El Salvador's Negotiated Revolution', *Foreign Affairs*, Vol. 71, No. 2, Spring.

Kempe, F. (1990) *Divorcing the Dictator: America's Bungled Affair with Noriega* (London: I.B. Tauris).

Klepak, H.P. (ed.) (1993) *Canada and Latin American Security* (Laval, Quebec: Méridien).

Klepak, H.P. (1994) 'Peacekeeping in Central America', in David A. Charters (ed.), *Peacekeeping and the Challenge of Civil Conflict Resolution* (New Brunswick, Canada: University of New Bruswick, Centre for Conflict Studies).

La Gaceta (Tegucigalpa) (various).

La Gaceta (Managua) (various).

La Nación (San José) (various).

La Prensa Gráfica (San Salvador) (various).

La Tribuna (Tegucigalpa) (various).

LaRae Pippin, L. (1964) *The Remón Era* (Stanford: Stanford University Press).

Larkin, B.D. (ed.) (1988) *Vital Interests: The Soviet Issue in US Central American Policy* (Boulder and London: Lynne Rienner Publications).

Latin America Bureau (1985) *State for Sale* (London: Latin America Bureau).

Lawyers Committee for Human Rights (1989) *Underwriting Injustice: AID and El Salvador's Judicial Reform Programme* (New York: Lawyers Committee for Human Rights).

Lawyers Committee for Human Rights (1992) *Guatemala: an interim report on the investigation of the murder of Myrna Mack* (New York: Lawyers Committee for Human Rights).

Lawyers Committee for Human Rights (1993a) *El Salvador's Negotiated Revolution: Prospects for Legal Reform* (New York: Lawyers Committee for Human Rights).

Lawyers Committee for Human Rights (1993b) *Decision in the Myrna Mack case: a question of command responsibility unresolved* (New York: Lawyers Committee for Human Rights).

Leftwich, A. (1993) 'Governance, democracy and development in the Third World', *Third World Quarterly*, Vol. 14, No. 3.

Ley Constitutiva de las Fuerzas Armadas, *La Gaceta* (Tegucigalpa, 25 February 1975).

Lipset, S.M. (1959) 'Some Social Requisites of Democracy: Economic Development and Political Legitimacy', *The American Political Science Review*, Vol. LIII, No 1.

Loescher, G. (1988) 'Humanitarianism and Politics in Central America', *Political Science Quarterly*, Vol. 103, No. 2.

Lowenthal, A. (ed.) (1991) *Exporting Democracy: The United States and Latin America* (Baltimore: Johns Hopkins University Press).

MacFarlane, S. N. and T. G. Weiss (1994) 'The United Nations regional organisations and human security: building theory in Central America', *Third World Quarterly*, Vol. 15, No. 2.

Mackinlay, J. and J. Chopra (1992) 'Second Generation Multinational Operations', *The Washington Quarterly*, Vol. 15, No. 3.

Maihold, G. (1994) 'Representación política y sociedad civil en Centroamérica', in M. Carballo Quintana and G. Maihold (eds.), *¿Que será de Centroamérica? Gobernabilidad, legitimidad electoral y sociedad civil* (San José: Fundación Friedrich Ebert).

Malloy, J.M. and M. Seligson (1987) *Authoritarians and Democrats: Regime Transition in Latin America* (Pittsburgh: University of Pittsburgh Press).

Manz, B. (1988) *Refugees of a Hidden War: the Aftemath of Counterinsurgency in Guatemala* (Albany: State University of New York Press).

Miles, S. and B. Ostertag (1991) 'The FMLN: New Thinking', in A. Sundaram and G. Gelber (eds.), *A Decade of War: El Salvador Confronts the Future*

(London: Catholic Institute for International Relations).

Ministerio de Acción Social (1993) *Plan de Acción CIREFCA 1993-1996. Documento concertado entre el Gobierno y las ONGs con el apoyo del sistema de Naciones Unidas* (Managua, 1993).

Miranda, R. and W. Ratliff (1993) *The Civil War in Nicaragua: Inside the Sandinistas* (New Brunswick, New Jersey: Transaction Publishers).

Molieri, J. Jenkins (1986) *El Desafío Indígena en Nicaragua: El Caso de los Miskitos* (Mexico: Editorial Katún).

Montes, J. (1994) 'El Salvador – Combat Arms Update', *Jane's Intelligence Review*, Vol. VI, No. 7.

Montgomery, T.S. (1991) *'Fighting Guerillas: The United States and Low Intensity Warfare in El Salvador'*, Conference Paper No. 52, New York University (New York: New York University).

Moreno, D. (1994) *The Struggle for Peace in Central America* (Miami: University Press of Florida).

Munck, G.L. (1993) 'Beyond Electoralism in El Salvador: Conflict Resolution through Negotiated Conflict', *Third World Quarterly*, Vol. 14, No. 1.

Munck, G.L. and C. Kumar (1995) 'Civil Conflicts and Conditions for Successful International Intervention', *Review of International Studies*, May.

NCOORD *Newsletter* (various) – National Coordinating Office on Refugees and Displaced of Guatemala, Chicago, USA.

Newsweek (New York) (various).

O'Donnell, G. (1994) 'Delegative Democracy', in *Journal of Democracy*, Vol. 15, No. 1, January.

O'Donnell, G., P. Schmitter and L. Whitehead (eds.) (1986) *Transitions from Authoritarian Rule: Prospects for Democracy* (Baltimore: Johns Hopkins University Press).

Oglesby, Liz. (1991), *'Return and Reintegration of Guatemalan Refugees and Internally Displaced Populations: A Presentation of the Research of Myrna Mack'*, Congress of Latin America, Conference Paper No. 53, mimeo.

Opazo Bernales, A. and R. Fernández V. (1990) *Esquipulas II: una tarea pendiente* (San José: Editorial Universitaria Centroamericana).

Ortega, M. (1991) *Nicaraguan Repatriation to Mosquitia*, Hemispheric Migration Project, Center for Immigration Policy and Refugee Assistance, Georgetown University (1991).

Ortega Pinto, H.D. (1994) 'Análisis de los actores políticos y de las incompatibilidades básicas', *Estudios Internacionales*, Vol. 9.

Otsea, J. (1991) 'CIREFCA: at the crossroads', *Refugees*, No. 87, October (Geneva: United Nations High Commissioner for Refugees (UNHCR)).

Paige, J. (1993) 'Coffee and Power in El Salvador', *Latin American Research Review*, Vol. 28, No. 3.

Painter, J. (1987) *Guatemala: False Hope, False Freedom* (London: Latin America Bureau).

Pavlov, Y. (1994) *Soviet-Cuban Alliance* (Miami: Transaction Publishers).

PDH (Procurador de los Derechos Humanos) (1994) *Los Comités de Defensa Civil en Guatemala* (Guatemala: Procuraduría de los Derechos Humanos).

Peacekeeping and International Relations (Ottawa: Canadian Institute of Strategic Studies) (various).

Pelupessy, W. and J. Weeks (eds.) (1993) *Economic Maladjustment in Central America* (Basingstoke and London: Macmillan Press).

Poitevin, R. (1993) *Guatemala: la crisis de la democracia. Dudas y esperanzas en los golpes de estado de 1993*, Debate No. 21 (Guatemala: Facultad Latino-americana de Ciencias Sociales, FLACSO).

Policía Nacional (1986) *Memoria de la Policía Nacional*, mimeo (Guatemala).

Pritchard, D. (1988a) *Bitter Sweet: Salvadorean refugees in Nicaragua*, Unpublished MSc thesis, University College London.

Pritchard, D. (1988b) 'Return to the Atlantic Coast', *Refugees*, No. 59, December (Geneva: United Nations High Commissioner for Refugees (UNHCR)).

Pritchard, D. and K. Ambos (1987) 'From the Frying Pan into the Fire', *The Guardian*, 23 October 1987, p. 13.

Proceso (San Salvador) (various).

Procuraduría para la Defensa de los Derechos Humanos (1993) *Tercer Informe* (San Salvador, October).

Procuraduría para la Defensa de los Derechos Humanos (1994) *Anteproyecto de Ley de Seguridad Ciudadana* (San Salvador).

Programa Centroamericano: Servicios Legales, Derechos Humanos y Administración de Justicia (1994) *Estudio Diagnóstico de los Servicios Legales de El Salvador*, mimeo, November (San Salvador).

Przeworski, A. (1986) 'Some Problems in the Study of the Transition to Democracy', in Guillermo O'Donnell, P. Schmitter and L. Whitehead (eds.), *Transitions from Authoritarian Rule: Comparative Perspectives* (Baltimore: Johns Hopkins University Press).

República de El Salvador (1992a) *Constitución de la República* (San Salvador).

República de El Salvador (1992b) *Ley de la Procuraduría para la Defensa de los Derechos Humanos* (San Salvador, February).

República de Guatemala (1992) *Constitución Política de la República de Guatemala* (Guatemala, 1992)

República de Honduras (1976) *Ley Orgánica de la Fuerza de Seguridad Pública*, DL No. 369 (August, 1976).

Reyes, R. and J.K. Wilson (1992) *Ráfaga: The Life Story of of Nicaraguan Miskito Comandante* (Oklahoma: University of Oklahoma Press).

Ropp, S. (1992) 'Explaining the Long-Term Maintenance of a Military Regime: Panama before the US Invasion', *World Politics*, Vol. 44.

Rosada Granados, H. (1986) *Guatemala 1944-1985: táctica política y conducta electoral*, mimeo (Guatemala).

Rouquié, A. (1987) *The Military and the State in Latin America* (Berkeley: University of California Press).

Rouquié, A. (ed.) (1991) *Les Forces Politiques en Amérique Centrale* (Paris: Karthala).

Salamón, L. (1994a) *Democratización y Sociedad Civil en Honduras* (Tegucigalpa:

Centro de Documentación de Honduras, CEDOH).

Salamón, L. (1994b) *Policías y Militares en Honduras* (Tegucigalpa: Centro de Documentación de Honduras, CEDOH).

Salas, L. and J. Rico (1989a) *La Justicia Penal en Honduras* (San José: University of Florida/Editorial Universitaria Centroamericana).

Salas, L. and J. Rico (1989b) *La Justicia Penal en Guatemala* (San José: University of Florida/Editorial Universitaria Centroamericana).

Salas, L. and J. Rico (1993) *Administration of Justice in Latin America: A Primer on the Criminal Justice System* (Miami: Florida International University/Centro para la Administración de la Justicia, San José).

Sanford Commission (1989) *Pobreza, conflicto y esperanza: un momento crítico para Centroamérica: Informe de la Comisión Internacional para la Recuperación y el Desarrollo de Centroamérica* (Informe Sanford) (Madrid, 1989).

Sarti Castañeda, C.A. (1994) 'In Search of Human Security in Central America', *Regional Responsibilities and the United Nations System*, ACUNS Reports and Papers No. 1994-2 (Providence, Rhode Island: Academic Council on the UN System).

Schumpeter, J.A. (1976) *Capitalism, Socialism and Democracy* (London: Allen and Unwin).

Schwarz, B. (1991), *American Counter-Insurgency Doctrine and El Salvador* (Santa Monica: Rand Corporation).

Secretaría de Estado en el Despacho de Gobernación y Justicia (1992) *Anteproyecto de Reforma Constitucional*, mimeo (Tegucigalpa).

Solomon, J.A. (1994) *Institutional Violence: Civil Patrols in Guatemala* (Washington: Robert F. Kennedy Memorial Centre for Human Rights).

Spence, J. and G. Vickers (1994) *A Negotiated Revolution? A Two Year Progress Report on the Salvadorean Peace Accords* (Cambridge, Mass.: Hemisphere Initiatives).

Stahler-Sholk, R. (1990) 'Stabilization, Demobilization and the Popular Classes in Nicaragua, 1979-1988', *Latin American Research Review*, Vol. 25, No. 3.

Stahler-Sholk, R. (1994) 'El Salvador's Negotiated Transition: From Low-Intensity Conflict to Low-Intensity Democracy', *Journal of Interamerican Studies and World Affairs*, Vol. 36, No. 4.

Stanley, W. (1993) *Risking Failure: The Problems and Promise of the New Civilian Police Force in El Salvador* (Washington, DC: Hemisphere Initiatives/Washington Office on Latin America).

Stoll, D. (1993) *Between Two Armies in the Ixil Towns of Guatemala* (New York: Columbia University Press).

Thesing, J. (1993) 'Al rescate de la democracia en Guatemala. El golpe de Estado del presidente Serrano y sus consecuencias', *Temas y Documentos de Debate*, No. 45, May-June (Guatemala: Instituto Centroamericano de Estudios Políticos, INCEP).

Tico Times (San José) (various).

Tiempo (Tegucigalpa) (various).

Torres-Rivas, E. (1985) *Report on the Condition of Central American Refugees and*

Migrants, Center for Immigration Policy and Refugee Assistance, Georgetown University (Washington, DC: Georgetown University, Center for Immigration Policy and Refugee Assistance).

Torres Rivas, E. (1994) 'La gobernabilidad centroamericana en los noventa. Consideraciones sobre las posibilidades democráticas en la posguerra', *América Latina Hoy*, Revista de Ciencias Sociales, SEPLA, No. 8 (Madrid).

Touraine, A. (1992) 'Situación de la Democracia en América Latina', in Régine Steichen, *Democracia y Democratización en Centroamérica* (San José: Editorial de la Universidad de Costa Rica).

Tovar Siebentritt, G. (1994) 'From refugee to returnee', *National Jesuit News White Paper*, April/May.

Tribunal Electoral Supremo (1993) *Consulta Popular, Reformas Constitucionales, Exposición comparativa de las Reformas Constitucionales aprobadas por el Congreso de la República, con la Constitución vigente*, mimeo (Guatemala).

Tulchin, J. (ed.) (1992) *Is There a Transition to Democracy in El Salvador?* (Washington, DC: Lynne Rienner Publishers).

United Nations (1989) *Report of the Secretary-General S/20895* (11 October 1989) (New York: United Nations).

United Nations (1990) *The Blue Helmets: A Review of United Nations Peacekeeping* (New York: United Nations).

United Nations (1992a) *Report of Professor Tomuschat, E/CN.4/1992/5* (New York: United Nations).

United Nations (1992b) *Report of the Director of the Human Rights Division, S/24375* (12 August 1992) (New York: United Nations).

United Nations (1992c) *Report of the Special Expert for Guatemala, Mónica Pinto, E/CN 4/1992/5* (New York: United Nations)

United Nations (1993a) *Report of the Secretary-General on the United Nations Observer Mission in El Salvador S/26581* (14 October 1993) (New York: United Nations).

United Nations (1993b) *Sixth Report of the Director of the Human Rights Division, ONUSAL S/25521* (5 April 1993) (New York: United Nations).

United Nations (1994a) *Eleventh Report of the Secretary-General on the United Nations Observer Mission in El Salvador S/1994/1000* (26 August 1994) (New York: United Nations).

United Nations (1994b) *Twelfth Report of the Secretary-General on the United Nations Observer Mission in El Salvador S/1994/1212* (31 October 1994) (New York: United Nations).

United Nations (1994c) *Tenth Report of the Director of the Human Rights Division, ONUSAL* (6 May 1994) (New York: United Nations).

United Nations (1994d) *Eleventh report of the Director of the Human Rights Division of ONUSAL, S/1994/886* (28 July 1994) (New York: United Nations).

United Nations (1994e) *Report of the Secretary-General on the United Nations Mission in El Salvador S/1994/561* (11 May 1994) (New York: United Nations).

United Nations (1994f) *Informe del Experto Independiente, Profesor Pedro Nikken, sobre la evolución de la situación de los derechos humanos en El Salvador* (3 February 1994) (New York: United Nations).

United Nations (1994g) *Informe de la Experta Independiente, Sra. Mónica Pinto, sobre la situación de los derechos humanos en Guatemala E/CN.4/1994/10* (20 January 1994) (New York: United Nations).

United Nations (1994h) *Report of the Secretary-General: Establishment of a Human Rights Verification Mission in Guatemala* (18 August 1994) (new York: United Nations).

United Nations General Assembly (1994) *Report of the United National High Commissioner for Refugees, Questions relating to refugees, returnees and displaced persons and humanitarian questions A/49/534* (19 October 1994).

UNHCR (United Nations High Commissioner for Refugees) (1994) 'The Cartagena Declaration: A Decade of Progress', *Refugees*, No. 99 (Geneva: United Nations High Commissioner for Refugees, UNHCR).

United Nations Truth Commission (1993) *De la Locura a la Esperanza, La Guerra de 12 Años en El Salvador: Informe de la Comisión de la Verdad 1992-1993* (San Salvador: Naciones Unidas).

United States Department of State (various years) *State Department Country Reports: Guatemala* (Washington, DC: State Department).

United States General Accounting Office (GAO) (1993) *Foreign Assistance: Promoting Judicial Reform to Strengthen Democracies* (Washington DC, 1993).

UNO (Unión Nacional Opositora) (1993) *Declaración Política*, mimeo, 22 January (Managua).

URNG/Government of Guatemala (1995) *Acuerdo Sobre Identidad y Derechos de los Pueblos Indígenas*, mimeo (México, 24 March).

USAID (United States Agency for International Development) (1985), *Project Paper AID/LAC/P-830*, mimeo (Washington DC: USAID)

USAID (1991) *Estrategia de Asistencia Económica para Centroamérica, 1991 a 2000* (Washington, DC: USAID).

USAID, Centre for Development Information and Evaluation (1993) *Strengthening Democratic Institutions: The Case of Honduras* (Washington, DC: USAID).

USAID, Centre for Development Information and Evaluation (1994) *Weighing in on the Scales of Justice: Strategic Approaches for Donor-Supported Rule of Law Programmes* (Washington, DC: USAID).

Verner, J.G. (1984) 'The Independence of Supreme Courts in Latin America: A Review of the Literature', *Journal of Latin American Studies*, Vol. 16, No. 2.

Vickers, G. and J. Spence (1992) *Endgame: A Progress Report on Implementation of the Salvadorean Peace Accords*, Hemispheric Initiatives (Cambridge, Mass.: Hemisphere Initiatives).

Vilas, C. (ed.) (1993) *Democracia emergente en Centroamérica* (Mexico: Universidad Nacional Autónoma de México).

Walker, T.W. (ed.) (1991) *Revolution and Counterrevolution in Nicaragua* (Boulder and Oxford: Westview Press).

Walker, T.W. (1991) 'The Armed Forces', in Thomas W. Walker (ed.), *Revolu-*

tion and Counterrevolution in Nicaragua (Boulder and Oxford: Westview Press).

Walter, K. and P.J. Williams (1992a) 'The Military and Democracy in El Salvador', *Journal of Inter-American Studies*, Vol. 35, No. 1.

Walter, K. and P.J. Williams (1992b) *The Military Balance 1991/92* (London: International Institute for Strategic Studies).

Weaver, F. Stirton (1994) *Inside the Volcano: The History and Political Economy of Central America* (Boulder: Westview Press).

Weiss, T. (1993) 'New Challenges for UN Military Operations: Implementing an Agenda for Peace,' *The Washington Quarterly*, Vol. 16, No. 1, Winter.

Whitehead, L. (1983) 'Explaining Washington's Central America Policies', *Journal of Latin American Studies*, Vol. 15, No. 2.

Whitehead, L. (1987) *Central America: The Struggle for Peace and Development*, Warwick Open Studies Paper, No. 2 (Coventry: Warwick University)

Whitehead, L. (1988) 'Washington's Response to the "Arias Plan": A Provisional Assessment', in *Annales des Pays d'Amérique Centrale et des Caraïbes*, No. 7 (Centre Regional des Etudes de Amérique Centrale, CREALC, Université d'Aix-Marseille III).

Whitehead, L. (1991) 'The Imposition of Democracy', in Abraham Lowenthal (ed.), *Exporting Democracy: The United States and Latin America* (Baltimore: Johns Hopkins University Press).

Whitehead, L. (1992), 'Europe and the Central American Conflict: A Retrospective Assessment', *Oxford International Review*, Vol. III, No. 3.

Wilson, R. (1993a) 'Continued Counterinsurgency: Civilian Rule in Guatemala', in B. Gils, J. Rocamora and R. Wilson (eds.), *Low Intensity Democracy: Political Power in the New World Order* (London: Pluto Press).

Wilson, R. (1993b), 'Anchored Communities: Identity and History of the Maya-Q'eqchi' *Man*, Vol. 28, No. 1.

WOLA (Washington Office on Latin America) (1989) *The Administration of Injustice: Military Accountability in Guatemala* (Washington: WOLA).

Woodward, R. (1976) *Central America: A Nation Divided* (New York: Oxford University Press).

Woodward, R.L. (1993) *Rafael Carrera and the Emergence of the Republic of Guatemala, 1821-1871* (Athens, Georgia and London: University of Georgia Press).

Zarate, J.C. (1994) *Forging Democracy: A Comparative Study of the Effects of US Foreign Policy on Central American Democratisation* (New York and London: University Press of America).

Zartman, W. (1985) *Ripe for Resolution: Conflict and Intervention in Africa* (New York: Oxford University Press).

INDEX